Contemporary Italy

D0139671

Contemporary Italy

Economy, Society and Politics since 1945

Donald Sassoon

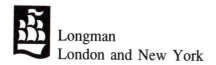

Longman
London and New York

Addison Wesley Longman Limited
Edinburgh Gate
Harlow, Essex CM20 2JE, England
and Associated Companies throughout the world.

Published in the United States of America
by Addison Wesley Longman Publishing, New York

© Addison Wesley Longman Limited 1986, 1997

All rights reserved; no part of this publication may be
reproduced, stored in a retrieval system, or transmitted
in any form or by any means, electronic, mechanical,
photocopying, recording or otherwise without either the
prior written permission of the Publishers or a licence
permitting restricted copying in the United Kingdom issued
by the Copyright Licensing Agency Ltd.,
90 Tottenham Court Road, London W1P 9HE.

First published 1986
Second Edition 1997

ISBN 0 582 21428–9

British Library Cataloguing-in-Publication Data

A catalogue record for this book is
available from the British Library

Set by 35 in 10/12pt Times
Produced through Longman Malaysia, PP

To
Philip Sassoon
may he live a long life in a better Italy

Contents

List of tables

List of abbreviations

AC	*Azione Cattolica*
ACLI	*Associazione Cristiana dei Lavoratori Italiani* (Association of Italian Christian Workers)
AN	*Alleanza Nazionale*
ARCI	*Associazione Ricreativa Culturale Italiana*
BOT	*Buoni del Tesoro* (Treasury bonds)
CA	Constituent Assembly
CAP	Common Agricultural Policy
CCD	*Centro Cristiano Democratico* (Christian Democratic Centre)
CGIL	*Confederazione Generale Italiana del Lavoro*
CISL	*Confederazione Italiana dei Sindacati dei Lavoratori*
CISNAL	*Confederazione Italiana Sindacati Nazionale dei Lavoratori*
CPSU	Communist Party of the Soviet Union
DC	*Democrazia Cristiana* (Christian Democratic Party)
EEC	European Economic Community
EGAM	Italian State Mining Company
EMS	European Monetary System
ENEL	*Ente Nazionale per l'Energia Electrica*
ENI	*Ente Nazionale Idrocarburi*
ERM	Exchange Rate Mechanism
ERP	European Recovery Programme
FIM	*Federazione Italiana Metallurgici* (Italian engineering union)
FIOM	*Federazione Impiegati Operai Metallurgici* (Engineering union)
IRI	*Istituto per la Ricostruzione Industriale*
ISTAT	*Istituto Centrale di Statistica* (Italian State Statistical Office)
MSI	*Movimento Sociale Italiano* (Italian Social Movement)
NAP	Nuclei Armati Proletari
NATO	North Atlantic Treaty Organization
OECD	Organization for Economic Cooperation and Development
OPEC	Organization of Petroleum Exporting Countries
PCI	*Partito Comunista Italiano*

PDS	*Partito Democratico della Sinistra* (Democratic Party of the Left)
PDUP	*Partito di Unità Proletaria* (Party of Proletarian Unity)
PLI	*Partito Liberale Italiano* (Liberal Party)
PPI	*Partito Popolare Italiano* (Italian People's Party)
PR	Proportional representation
PRI	*Partito Repubblicano Italiano*
PSI	*Partito Socialista Italiano*
PSDI	*Partito Social Democratico Italiano*
PSIUP	*Partito Socialista di Unità Proletaria*
PSU	*Partito Socialista Unificato* (Unified Socialist Party)
RAI	*Radiotelevisione Italiana*
RC	*Rifondazione Comunista* (Communist Refoundation)
SME	Small and medium-sized enterprise
STVP	*Südtiroler Volkspartei* (South Tyrol People's Party)
SVIMEZ	*Associazione per lo Sviluppo Industriale del Mezzogiorno* (Association for Southern Industrial Development)
UDI	*Unione Donne Italiane* (Union of Italian Women)
UIL	*Unione Italiana del Lavoro* (Union of Italian Labour)
UNRRA	United Nations Relief and Rehabilitation Administration

Preface to the Second Edition

This book is an introduction to one of the largest European democracies.

Italy was united relatively recently. It became a nation-state in 1861, but Rome became its capital only ten years later. As a 'geographical entity' (as Metternich called it) its history is more ancient and rich. Italy has given the world the poetry of Dante and the art of the Renaissance, the political theory of Machiavelli and the science of Galileo. It has produced the first international banking system, great explorers, famous composers.

Italy – under a constitutional monarchy after 1861 – gave the world also the first model of a modern authoritarian state, the fascist state. Since 1946 it has been a parliamentary republic. From 1946 to 1992–93 its politics was dominated a Christian democratic party (DC) which, although in power was opposed by a large and relatively successful communist party, always unable to come to power. I concluded the first edition – which appeared in 1986 – with these apparently pessimistic words: 'Thus with a governing party which no longer knows how to rule and an opposition which has never governed, and perhaps never will, Italy faces the future.'

Ten years later the governing party had not only ceased to govern but had disappeared altogether, leaving behind a trail of smaller parties dispersed across the political spectrum. Its allies, the socialists, the social democrats, the republicans and the liberals, had virtually disappeared by 1994. Before that had occurred, the opposition, that is the Italian Communist Party, had decided to metamorphose itself into a social democratic party, changed its name, its symbols and its entire organizational structure. A completely different party system began to emerge as new parties were formed or gained strength – such as the Northern League and *Forza Italia*, *Rifondazione Comunista* and *Alleanza Nazionale* – none of whom existed in their present form or name or importance prior to 1992.

There are many aspects of Italy which are widely admired outside: the glories of its culture, what is left of the natural beauty the country, its footballers, designers, car manufacturers. But the overall political picture is chaotic and confusing. The disintegration of the old political system, the rise and apparent fall of Berlusconi, the election of a government in which the post-communists play the leading role have added to the bewilderment. This is an area in which stereotypes abound to the frustration of Italianists everywhere who attempt, not always successfully, to explain that the land of sunny beaches, pizzas and songs is one of the leading economies of the world. This book seeks to provide the interested reader as well as students of Italian society with a text which gives not just the general picture, but also an understanding of the changes which have affected the country.

Italians are their own worst critics. They incessantly complain of their political leaders and of the corruption which has for so long and – alas – still plagues their country. This, however, cannot be the whole story. I have tried to explain and map out the changes which have affected the country in its economic structure, in its people, in its political system. A nation cannot be judged solely by those who rule it.

The result of this endeavour has been a book which is neither political science, nor sociology, neither history nor economics. It straddles these fields yet it cannot claim to give an image of the whole of Italian society, not even in the sense in which such a task can be contemplated. Space and my own limitations have prevented me from examining Italian culture, the changes which have occurred in its language and everyday life. Even when it comes to topics which are usually covered by books such as these I am only too aware of what I have left out, and rather than bore the reader with explanation and justification of what is not there, let me explain what is in it and why.

The book is divided into three parts: Economy, Society and Politics. Part One amounts to an economic history of Italy since 1945 and has a dual purpose: first of all it seeks to explain the transformation of the Italian economy from the point of view of the political system. I have tried to examine the economic effects of government policies and the way in which economics has been shaped by politics. In so doing I have tried to examine the constraints which have limited the terrain of successive Italian governments. The second purpose is simpler: to tell the history of Italy since 1945. I have chosen to do so 'through' economic history because I felt the narrative would somewhat alleviate the dryness of much economics and because it gave me the opportunity of emphasizing the extent to which political actors are not free to do as they choose. In the very first pages I explain how the most important political choices made by the first Italian governments, namely free trade within the American sphere of influence, were extremely compelling and virtually unavoidable. This, of course, does not mean that all political and economic choices are predetermined and that no criticism can ever be made of what was Italy's principal political party, the DC. It means, however, that the leading opposition, the Italian Communist Party (PCI) and its successor party, the *Partito Democratico della Sinistra* (PDS), has had gradually to realize how difficult it is to envisage major changes occurring in Italy or anywhere else on the basis of the nation-state and that, in the modern era, the requirements of the international market and of the international division of labour seriously limits the freedom of action of any national force. Thus any national force must become 'international', that is, it must seek to bear in mind constantly the international impact of national actions and the domestic impact of world events. This does not mean that I subscribe to the view that the international economy determines everything, because the international economy is also politically determined. It means, simply, that in the second half of the twentieth century it is no longer possible (assuming it has ever been possible) to consider separately economics and politics. Hence one-third of the book consists of five rather dense economic history chapters.

Part Two (Society) describes Italian society first in terms of social stratification: classes, income groups, occupation, etc., the changes which have taken place and the reasons behind the changes as well as the consequences. Then I examine Italian society in terms of social groups which cannot be reduced to classes. I have chosen women and youth (as opposed to, say, the old) for two reasons: the first is that both groups (but especially the former) have given rise to a social presence which cannot be ignored. Thus women are important because as women their entry into the labour market, their role as citizens and consumers, their position in the family, etc., have accelerated many of the changes which have occurred in Italian society. They are also important because feminist women have also challenged the existing conception of politics and have forced other political forces to react – and this holds true of communists and Christian Democrats as well as the Church and the trade unions. Also in Part Two I examine institutions which are not overtly political, but which do have political effects: trade unions, firms, the Church and the media. These very different 'institutions' are not strictly speaking political in the sense that their main business is something else; in the case of the trade union this is the defence of the working conditions of their members and of their standard of living, in the case of enterprise this can be profits, or product range, or size, etc.; in the case of the Church the maintenance and diffusion of its beliefs and values; in the case of the media, information and entertainment. All four, however, are in the business of organizing people: trade unionists, workers and managers, the audience and the faithful, and all have important political effects. For this reason I would not claim to have given an account of the complexities of trade-union negotiations, or of the production problem of modern firms, or of theology or of mass communications. In all cases I have tried to relate these institutions to what have been and still are the principal forms of organization of the Italian political system: parties.

Part Three (Politics) is the more conventional one: it explains the Italian Constitution, the role of parliament, elections and governments, the regional system and the political parties. This part comes last because I wanted to establish the general setting – historical, economic and social – within which the political system must operate. It does not mean that politics comes last because I have tried to let politics have a high profile throughout the book whether what is being discussed is Italy's export trade or the expansion of its universities.

The real protagonists of this book are in fact the political parties whose presence pervades the whole of Italian society in a way which is inconceivable in the UK or in the USA.

The post-war period begins with the political parties clearly in charge. They constituted the commanding forces of the Italian Resistance: the Committee of National Liberation was made up of a coalition of six parties. The partisan bands were organized on the basis of party affiliations. The trade-union movement was reorganized in 1944 on the basis of equal representation for the three leading parties:

Christian Democrats, communists and socialists. Pressure groups, civic organizations, the professions, etc., were directly connected to specific parties. The main
competition was between the PCI and the DC. The latter could rely on the formidable organization of the Roman Catholic Church and, through this, establish a presence in virtually all sectors of society. This forced the PCI to compete at the same
level. It was not possible to conceive of communist militancy in the traditional
way: a tightly led group of reliable and committed members. The PCI had to be a
mass party able to create and develop a whole range of organizations from sporting
associations to cultural clubs so as to penetrate into civil society at all levels and
challenge the DC.

It has been said that Italian political parties have 'colonized' Italian society. To
some extent that was true and may still be so. The mere act of joining a trade union
was always necessarily also a political act because the prospective member had also
decided whether to join the communist-socialist trade union, the *Confederazione
Generale Italiana del Lavoro* (CGIL) or the Catholic union, *Confederazione Italiana
dei Sindacati dei Lavoratori* (CISL) or the social-democrat/republican union, *Unione
Italiana del Lavoro* (UIL). The mere act of joining a sporting club was similarly
'political': which sporting club? The one run by the mainly communist *Associazione
Ricreativa Culturale Italiana* (ARCI) or the Catholic one or the less well-established
'third force' club? Recent events may have decreased the degree of party strength,
but not eliminated it.

The politicization of facets of civil life which in many countries would be outside politics also led to the politicization of economic life, particularly in the public
sector: state enterprises, banks, credit institutions, newspapers, were systematically
colonized by the government parties and in particular by the DC. This has not
changed. When Silvio Berlusconi entered politics he used his media empire, Fininvest, to create a political party. In the past parties colonized the economy. Berlusconi
did the reverse: he used the economy to colonize politics. The process may have
been different. The result was an excessive interconnection between political and
economic power.

It is, then, also because of this unusually high association between the political
level and the socio-economic one that it would have been difficult to write a book
on the Italian political system which did not emphasize economic and social factors.

This book has been written assuming no knowledge of Italy or of Italian politics
and history. Of course the reader who has some acquaintance with the history of
fascism or the development of Europe since the war will be at an advantage, as will
the reader who has some grounding in economics.

A general book such as this has had to rely massively on other people's research.
In many cases I have tried to give an idea of the kind of debates which surround
a particular issue by examining different interpretations.

Acknowledgements

My own acknowledgements and thanks must include first of all the scholars who have enabled me, through their writings, to come to some understanding of at least some of the issues concerning post-war Italy. Then I would like to renew my thanks to those who had helped me in the first edition and, first of all, to Bernard Crick who had the original idea for this book and encouraged me to write it, Leslie Cauldwell for the section on women, Philip Schlesinger for the section on the media, Bill Brierley and Paul Auerbach for that on the economy, Alice Lawson and Theresa Tennent of Westfield College Library, my old friend Beppe Vacca whose discussions on Italian politics and society have always been an immense reservoir of stimulating insights, Peppino Cotturri, Renato Mannheimer, Cesare Luporini (who, alas, is no longer with us), Carlo Donolo, Leonardo Paggi, Mario Telò and Ferdinando Targetti. I would also like to renew my thanks to Anne Showstack Sassoon who had read through the original manuscript and helped to improve it considerably.

For the new edition I would like to thank Jill Tilden, Derek Boothman and George Woodcock who have alerted me to a number of mistakes in the first edition, Renato Mannheimer, and the *Osservatorio Socio-Politico ISPO* which he directs, for providing me with useful survey data and precious advice. I thank Pia Locatelli for helping out so promptly and efficiently with various queries. I would also like to thank Giulio Sapelli, Director of the Feltrinelli Foundation for his help and friendship, Davide Bidussa, the Chief Librarian of the Feltrinelli Foundation for his courtesy. I also thank all the colleagues of the *Istituto per la Storia della Resistenza* and, in particular, Paolo Ferrari, for making my stay in Milan in September 1995 so enjoyable and for allowing me to use their facilities. I thank the British Council and *Centro Nazionale delle Ricerche* for funding this stay. I also thank Peter and Carola Sassoon for hospitality so generously provided during my sojourns in Milan. I am grateful to Joe and Doris Sassoon for sending me so regularly newspapers articles on relevant events and keeping me up to date with all things Italian.

I am also grateful to the following for permission to reproduce copyright material:

CENSIS for Table 7.5 taken from CENSIS Report 28 (1994); International Labour Office (ILO) for Table 3.1 taken from *Bulletin of Labour Statistics 1965*; ISTAT

(Istituto Nazionale Di Statistica) for Table 3.2; ©OECD for Table 2.1 taken from *National Accounts Statistics, 1950–1968*, Tables 5.1 and 5.2 taken from *Economic Outlook, Historical Statistics 1960–1989*; Oxford University Press for Table 3.4 taken from Podbielski, Giselle (1974) *Italy: Development and Crisis in the Postwar Economy*; Vittorio Valli for Table 4.6 taken from Valli, Vittorio (1979) *L'economia e la politica economica italiana, 1945–1979*; Verso for Table 4.3 taken from Parboni, Riccardo (1981) *The Dollar and Its Rivals*.

Whilst every effort has been made to trace the owners of the copyright material in a few cases this has proved impossible and I take this opportunity to offer my apologies to any copyright holders whose rights I may have unwittingly infringed.

Introduction

The country which emerged as Italy out of the process of political unification known as the *Risorgimento* was united only in name. Regional and economic divisions were only one aspect of the lack of unity of the country. Most of its inhabitants spoke not Italian – except in Tuscany and Rome – but their local dialect. Most of them were in fact 'outside' the political system altogether: they had not participated in the *Risorgimento* and remained barred from participation in political affairs even after the achievement of unity. The new Italian state, a constitutional monarchy, had in 1861 a very narrow electoral basis. Only 2 per cent of the adult population had the right to vote and, of these, less than 60 per cent did vote.

In the years that followed the suffrage was extended, but even by the 1909 elections only 8.3 per cent of the population was entitled to vote. The social bloc which constituted the Italian ruling class was internally as divided as the rest of the country. Northern industrialists and southern landlords did establish a compromise akin to the German alliance between landed and industrial interests (the 'rye and iron' alliance), but the terms of this compromise had to be constantly negotiated by the political representatives of these interests in the Italian parliament. By the beginning of the century the Prime Minister Giovanni Giolitti had, at least formally, a large parliamentary majority. The existing political parties, however, were loose coalitions with no strong membership and no definite programme. Italian governments had to construct their majorities on a day-to-day basis. Through patronage, corruption and wheeling and dealing, majorities were cobbled together in order to approve specific pieces of legislation. Each law required separate negotiations to achieve a majority. This system was known as *trasformismo*. Giolitti tried, sometimes successfully, to open up the parliamentary system to other groups, in particular to the socialists and the Catholics, but, on the whole, the basis of consent for the Liberal State remained narrow.

Until the First World War, then, parliament had an essential task: to provide the political terrain on which the different interests which constituted the Italian ruling class could negotiate and find their unity. This was possible because parliament, by and large, was relatively homogeneous: it represented the better-off fraction of the Italian population. This was due to the fact that the electorate was small, the socialists unwilling to bargain with the liberal establishment and the Catholics barred from taking an active part in politics by the Pope against whose wishes Italian unity had been achieved.

By 1913 quasi-universal manhood suffrage was introduced and the electorate grew to 23.2 per cent of the adult population. But the most important changes in Italian politics occurred as a result of the war. As in other countries, the war brought together masses of people, strengthened industrial concentrations, increased the numbers of wage workers, expanded urban centres (particularly Turin, Milan and Genoa) and gave the state wider economic functions and a more authoritarian political role. The war mobilized 5.5 million people, killed 600,000 and wounded 700,000. An entire region, the North-east (where most of the fighting occurred) was devastated. Inflation hit those on fixed incomes but enabled many sharecroppers to pay their debts and buy some land. Mass parties emerged: in 1914 the Socialist Party had 50,000 members, by 1921 it had 216,000. In 1919 for the first time in Italian history a Catholic party was created, the *Partito Popolare*, with 100,000 members. By 1920 it had 255,000 members. The trade unions had, before the war, less than 1 million members. After the war they had 4 million.

The elections of 1919 were fought under proportional representation. The Catholics of the *Partito Popolare* obtained 20.5 per cent of the vote, the Socialist Party 32.4 per cent. Half of parliament was now in the hands of mass parties who were outside the traditional system of *trasformismo*. Parliament could no longer provide the terrain for the unification of the ruling class. *Popolari* and socialists could not form a coalition: the former were anti-socialists, the latter anti-clerical. Workers occupied the large industrial plants of the North, revolutionary slogans backing the new Soviet republic appeared. Landless labourers voiced their discontent. The Liberal State was crumbling. It was no longer able to impose law and order. Its parliament could no longer be used as it had been in the pre-war period.

Fascism represented the extra-parliamentary solution to the Italian crisis. The old Liberal establishment, which acted as a sort of political representative of bourgeois and landed interests, could no longer utilize a deadlocked parliament. Extra-parliamentary violence was used increasingly, particularly by groups of the right. Mussolini, the leader of the National Fascist Party (the largest of these right-wing groups, with around thirty deputies in the Chamber) seemed to be willing to strike a bargain with the old establishment. It was at this stage, in October 1922, that the old Liberal establishment ceded power to Mussolini. It assumed that he would be a mere puppet, but it was wrong. Liberal Italy had played its last card, it would never rise again. However, the 'system' based on the systematic exclusion of the popular masses from politics had been rescued by changing the rules of the game: from now on Italy would be run by an authoritarian regime of a new type.

Having been granted political power – there was no real 'fascist revolution' despite what the fascists themselves claimed at the time – Mussolini proceeded to strengthen the authoritarian traits of the Liberal State by destroying its instruments – parliament and civil liberties – which had allowed the popular parties (socialists and Catholics) to emerge.

In allowing fascism to emerge and consolidate itself as a regime, the Italian bourgeoisie had demonstrated that it was unable, or unwilling, to develop its own mass party. The National Fascist Party was far from being a typical bourgeois party, but it performed many of its functions: it kept wages down by destroying the trade unions thus enabling Italian entrepreneurs to compete in foreign markets, it facilitated the rationalization of Italian capitalism through industrial concentration; in the 1930s it developed powerful instruments of economic intervention, such as the IRI (*Istituto per la Ricostruzione Industriale*) and saved the banking system from bankruptcy. The rise of fascism showed how weak the Italian Liberal State had been and how it had been unable to achieve the kind of popular consensus capitalism succeeded in obtaining in other countries.

Fascism, on the other hand, had been able to obtain at least the passive consent of large sections of the population. To do so it used a mixture of repression, indoctrination and bribery. At least until 1938 it had also been able to achieve a significant degree of popularity among the intellectuals. Fascism organized consent and used a veritable army of opinion-makers (teachers and broadcasters, clergy – after the Conciliation with the Church of Rome in 1929 – and journalists, technocrats and philosophers, artists and writers) to transform what was a fairly ghettoized intelligentsia into a force committed to fascism, the nation and the people. This commitment was not linked to the upholding of capitalist values. On the contrary, fascist propaganda insisted that it was trying to develop a social system which would be 'neither capitalist nor communist'. By 1938, as the alliance with Nazi Germany was established and Italy was being mercilessly dragged into a world war it was not equipped to fight, let alone win, the younger members of this intelligentsia turned against fascism. They did not, however, return to the ivory tower within which the Liberal State had confined them. They did not uphold the old liberal view that culture is above parties. They did not accept the view of the most distinguished of the anti-fascist philosophers, Benedetto Croce, who had written in his *Answer to the Manifesto of the Fascist Intellectuals*: 'Intellectuals as citizens exercise their rights and perform their duty when they join a party and serve it loyally. But as intellectuals they have one duty: to raise all men and all parties to a higher spiritual sphere by critical analysis and artistic creation . . . To mix up literature and politics, science and politics is an error . . .'

The intellectuals who had grown up with fascism and had accepted it before turning against it, remained committed to the slogan of 'going to the people'. During the Second World War, many of them even took up arms against fascism and joined in the Resistance. Even when this was over they did not return to the old liberal position: they remained politically committed to an extent unparalleled in the rest of Europe.

They fought with workers and peasants, with communists and Catholics. This heterogeneous coalition of anti-fascists was not held together – as in France or Yugoslavia – by charismatic figures such as De Gaulle or Tito. From its very inception the Resistance was organized by political parties: the Communist Party (PCI), the Socialist Party (PSI) and the Christian Democratic Party (DC). Much of the intelligentsia found its own niche in the Action Party. This had played a key role during the Resistance, but it disappeared soon after the war: intellectuals could not have their own political party.

When the war was over the only political structures which had survived were these political parties. The monarchy, discredited, was abolished by a popular referendum in 1946. The Fascist Party was banned. Yet no single party was strong enough to capture political power. This had to be jointly managed by the same coalition of parties which had organized the Resistance and fought against fascism: the DC, the PCI and the PSI. The PSI, the oldest of the three, soon revealed itself unable to obtain the mass following necessary for an independent role in the Italian political system. In the elections to the Constituent Assembly, in 1946, it had 20 per cent of the electorate. Its vote then fell drastically and, until its collapse in 1994, oscillated between 10 and 14 per cent. It could never call the tune but only choose which piper to follow: the PCI or the DC. At first it chose to ally itself with the PCI – the only socialist party in Western Europe to do so even during the Cold War. After 1956 it began to disengage itself from the communists. By the early 1960s it had joined the DC in coalition. With some interruptions it continued to be a subordinate ally of the DC in central government while sharing power in most 'red areas' with the PCI. Until 1992–94, when the post-war party system imploded, it enjoyed the peculiar benefit of being in an intermediate position between the DC and the PCI – able to extract concessions from the former with the threat of joining forces with the latter. Its long-term project was to supplant the PCI as the party of the Italian left. Alone of all socialist parties in Western Europe, it failed to do so perhaps because it never wanted to face the fact that the communist party it was in competition with was, as we shall see later, unique in the West.

When the PSI was a close ally of the PCI, that is, from the Second World War to about 1956, it modelled itself as closely as possible on the PCI. In foreign policy it was virtually indistinguishable from that of the communists: it defended the USSR, opposed the North Atlantic Treaty Organization (NATO) and rejected Marshall aid. Its own distancing from the PCI, after 1956, was not only due to domestic reasons such as the defeat suffered by the communist-socialist trade union confederation (CGIL) at the Fiat works in 1955 but mainly to the general crisis of the international communist movement: the de-Stalinization begun by the Communist Party of the Soviet Union (but soon interrupted) at its Twentieth Congress (1956) and the invasion of Hungary by Soviet troops. The PSI assumed that international communism had entered a phase of decline and that the PCI too would be part of this decline. The PSI began its rapprochement with the DC and, by 1963, had become part of the DC-led governing coalition.

Thereafter the PSI became more and more a junior version of the Italian Christian Democratic Party. It sought to compensate for the gradual loss of its working-class base by the uninhibited acquisition of a clientele system. This had become possible by its partnership in central government with the DC and in local government with either the DC or the PCI. From the mid-1970s the PSI became increasingly engulfed in a network of corruption which climaxed in 1992–93 resulting in its political death.

Yet the role of the PSI, though subordinate to the two larger parties, was not purely negative. The mere fact of being the PCI's sole ally at the outbreak of the Cold War, helped the leadership of the PCI to follow a relatively moderate course and to resist the temptation of sectarian and bitter opposition. When the PSI became the DC's main ally it enabled the more progressive factions of the DC to ensure that their party would not come under the control of right-wing factions which would transform it into a clerical party. The pendulum movements of the PSI were an important contributing factor to the maintenance of reasonable relations between governing party and opposition and the avoidance of extreme polarization.

The PCI had originated as a split from the PSI in Leghorn in 1921. There the Bordiga faction of the Socialist Party, unable to impose on the rest of the party the 'Twenty-one Conditions' which the Comintern had set for affiliation to the communist movement, seceded and formed the Communist Party of Italy, Section of the Third International. By the time it had emerged from the Second World War the party had undergone at least two transformations. In the first, the sectarian Bordiga leadership was removed in 1924 by Antonio Gramsci and Palmiro Togliatti with the decisive support of the Comintern. Soon afterwards the party was banned, Gramsci was jailed and Togliatti remained abroad in exile. During this period of clandestinity the party followed the vicissitudes of Comintern policies. In his prison cell Gramsci was laying the theoretical foundations for a new communist tradition sharply demarcated from the doctrine of Marxism-Leninism which Stalin's leadership was imposing on the rest of the communist movement. Togliatti, who had become the *de facto* leader of the PCI, had at first attempted to oppose Comintern policies, but in 1929 the Tenth Plenum of the Comintern imposed on all parties the new 'class against class' line which regarded a proletarian revolution to be imminent and all socialist and social-democratic parties to be the 'left-wing' of fascism. Togliatti obeyed adding, in reference to the intermediate political objectives he had been forced to drop, 'If the Comintern says that this is not correct, we shall refrain from posing these objectives. We shall think these things, but we shall not say them. We shall only say that the anti-fascist revolution shall be the proletarian revolution.'

During the 1930s the PCI was a small, marginal clandestine group of agitators and conspirators numbering a few thousands. Its messianic Stalinism enabled it to tolerate political persecutions and defeat. Its supporters assumed that, sooner or later, the day of the insurrection would come and, in Italy too, as in Russia, a socialist revolution would destroy capitalism. When the insurrection came, on 25 April 1945, it was a quite different affair from what had been imagined by the old generation of militants: it was the crowning achievement of the Resistance but it led to the establishment of a liberal-democratic system, not a socialist society.

The insurrection had been made possible by a number of factors: the successes of the Allied troops who had landed in Italy two years before, the collapse of the German war machine in the East and the Anglo-American landing in the West, and the broad basis of the Resistance itself which succeeded in uniting monarchists and republicans, socialists and communists, Catholics and anti-clericals. The PCI itself had undergone, in the course of the struggle, a further transformation: it had begun to shed the mentality and attitudes of a small sect of conspirators and to acquire the size and politics of a modern mass party. By the end of 1945 the PCI had nearly 2 million members. Togliatti had played the key role in this transformation. His authority among communist cadres was immense. He was helped in this by the fact that, as leader of the party, he could enjoy the benefit of the personality cult which had become an established feature of the communist movement. Undoubtedly the prestige of the USSR played a crucial part in this, but so did the fact that the PCI had been the leading force of the Resistance.

Togliatti took advantage of these factors to devise an alternative to the insurrectionist model which was still the framework within which much of the party was operating. Party membership was opened to all those who accepted its political programme: it was not necessary to accept the party's Marxist doctrine. The tripartite coalition with the PSI and the DC was assumed to provide an adequate form of government to oversee the transformation of Italy into a 'progressive democracy', a stage in the eventual transition to socialism. Gradualism and compromise were the order of the day. Togliatti and the PCI participated fully in the drafting of Italy's new Constitution. This based itself on the principles of liberalism but also recognized new 'social rights'; freedom of private enterprise was guaranteed but only 'as long as it did not conflict with social utility'.

The Cold War brought this compromise to an end. In 1947 the PCI and its socialist allies were expelled from the government. Italy was now clearly in the US sphere of influence. Togliatti had to follow the Soviet line once again, at least in foreign policy. At home the PCI continued to develop, with difficulty, the 'Italian road to socialism'. It sought to implant itself throughout Italian society using not only the traditional instruments of party and trade union, but also the cultural, recreational and sporting associations it had created. It organized its own intellectual cadres, its own press network, party schools, research institutes – in a word: its own 'society' – as the German Social Democratic Party had done at the turn of the century. This allowed the PCI to survive the worst years of the Cold War and, after the 1956, to develop further its own independent strategy.

The process was gradual and slow. At every turning-point in the history of the post-war international communist movement – China, Vietnam, Prague 1968, Afghanistan and Poland – the PCI increased its distance from Moscow. When the great turning-point of 1989 – the fall of the Berlin Wall – took place, the Party broke definitively with the communism and changed its name to that of 'Party of the Democratic Left'.

The DC was the newest party of the young Italian Republic, but from the very beginning it was the strongest. It enjoyed some unique advantages. In the first place, it was heir to the tradition of the Popular Party, the largely peasant-based Catholic party which had been created in 1919. In the second place, it could use the vast machine of Catholic societies and organizations which had been allowed to operate under fascism after the 1929 Concordat between Mussolini and the Church. These provided the DC with a useful network of leading cadres. Thirdly, the DC was able to rely on the support of the Church, from the Pope and the bishops to the village priests and including mass Catholic organizations such as *Azione Cattolica* (AC). Fourthly, the weakness of the old Liberal Party, the nearest equivalent to a clearly pro-capitalist party, meant that the DC soon became the obvious choice for industrialists seeking a friendly party. Once again the political weakness of Italian capitalism was evident: in the age of democracy it needed a party able to obtain the consent of the electorate, but there was no conservative party. It thus had to rely on a composite party: a coalition of traditional Catholics, young technocrats, populists and other disparate groups all united under the banner of Catholicism.

Finally, the DC was very soon able to become the only party on which the United States could rely to take Italy into the North Atlantic Alliance and to anchor it definitively in the Western camp.

These five factors were the base of the DC's success in becoming Italy's dominant party throughout the post-war period. The DC, however, realized early on that it could not depend on the Church for ever: it needed to develop its own political machine. This was done in a variety of ways. In the first place, the DC became the mirror-image of the PCI in the sense that it too developed a policy of 'presence' in all sectors of society through the creation of a variety of 'non-party' organizations linked more or less informally to the DC. Soon much of what is called 'civil society' was divided along party lines. Sport, culture, leisure time, pressure groups, and so on, became extensions of the main political parties.

In the second place, the DC could use its control over the state machinery and over public money to support specific social groups and interests. A network of clienteles was developed, particularly in the South. While the DC facilitated the growth of private industry, it was also able to alleviate some of the negative effects of economic growth by intervening directly to protect specific social and interest groups which were thus, in turn, dependent on the continuation of the DC in power.

Finally, the DC, because it was always in government and because it tended to be a party which actively encouraged the expansion of the public sector, had also at its disposal a vast array of jobs which it could offer to those who were politically reliable. Thus through professional and trade associations and a clientelist system of patronage, the DC developed a formidable machine thanks to which it could withstand the PCI and maintain its hold on the country.

However, all this was not enough to achieve a permanent electoral majority. Only in 1948 was the DC able to obtain more than half the parliamentary seats, but even then it decided to rule with other parties. It follows that the DC always had to rely on coalition partners: before 1962 the Liberal Party, the Republican Party and the Social Democratic Party; after 1962 the DC extended the coalition to include the PSI.

The strength of the DC in Italy was sufficient to ensure a remarkable continuity between 1945 and the victory of Silvio Berlusconi in 1994 all Italian governments had the DC at their centre. But this was not sufficient to guarantee government stability. The DC was itself a coalition of tendencies, factions and ideas. Negotiations and bargaining within the party had to be continuous. The politics of patronage and clientele entailed a proper share-out of political power according to the strength of the various factions. This constant process of bargaining could give rise to considerable internal dissent leading, at times, to government crises. These were followed by further bargaining for a new government with a new division of offices and power. This bargaining was far from being the prerogative of the DC. It also involved the other coalition partners. Thus each government was the result of a specific set of bargains struck within the coalition parties and among them. It follows that, though there was considerable agreement on the sort of coalition which emerged, there was constant strife over specific policies and appointments. Thus Italian governments have tended to be extremely short-lived.

This strife inside the government increased the power of the communist opposition. Though it never succeeded in breaking up the DC-led coalition system and in obtaining the support of some of the other parties, the opposition could intervene in the bargaining process by throwing its weight on one side or the other. Thus bargaining and compromise were the hallmark of the Italian system of government. It was a form of 'imperfect' consensus politics. 'Imperfect' because, unlike Austria, Holland and Belgium, the consensus always excluded the Communist Party while accepting its legitimacy as the main opposition party. Unlike the situation in the UK, there was no 'adversary system' whereby two more or less stable and disciplined parties face each other and alternate in government. On the surface of things the Italian system appeared to be markedly polarized, divided as it was between the DC and the PCI. In practice, however, all parties accepted the need for compromise.

The system functioned with a strong element of potential instability: had the PCI ever succeeded in ousting the DC from power it would have had to rule with a machinery of government largely created by the DC and would have had to face a system of clienteles (which included powerful interest groups, such as the banking system) unlikely to be supportive. Furthermore, agencies such as the secret services and the armed forces were accustomed to consider themselves 'at war' with communism and would probably have attempted to destabilize a regularly elected communist-led coalition government. Finally, the United States would have played a destabilizing role as long as it was convinced that a non-DC government in Italy would have caused an international shift in the balance of power in favour of the USSR. It was partly in order to prevent such a crisis situation that the PCI came to accept that Italy needed to remain within the North Atlantic Alliance and, until the early 1980s, envisaged that it could come to power only on the basis of an agreement with the DC: the so-called 'historic compromise'.

The PCI, however, was never entirely excluded from political power. In the first place, as I have already mentioned, the weakness of coalition governments and their internal dissension meant the support of the PCI was often required to pass legislation. Secondly, the PCI had always been in power in some key areas of central Italy. After 1970, the legislation which provided for regional devolution of power increased the extent to which the PCI could exercise some form of direct political control. Thirdly, the alliance with the PSI survived even the most bitter divisions within the left in at least two distinct settings: in some local government and in the largest of the three trade union confederations: the CGIL. As the PSI was in government most of the time between 1963 and 1993, the PCI had in the PSI a local government partner through which it could make its voice felt at executive level. Fourthly, in the 1970s PCI members were accepted in various state institutions, such as the board of Italian television or the national institute in charge of social security and pensions (the INPS). This enabled the party to develop some of the skills of political management which a permanent opposition would normally find difficult to achieve. Fifthly, because of the dominant position of communists in the CGIL the PCI was able to negotiate directly with government and employers. Thus the PCI was not in a pure opposition ghetto. Finally, its large size and the fact that it had always been able to attract intellectuals and professionals meant that there were very few institutions where it would have been difficult to find communist supporters or sympathizers. Even the top echelons of the armed forces had at least one communist sympathizer: General Nino Pasti who, after his retirement, was elected to parliament in 1976 in the communist list.

The existence of a permanent government party (the DC) and a permanent opposition (the PCI) suggests a considerable degree of what the Italian call *immobilismo*. It does not follow from this, however, that there was little change in the history of the first Italian republic. On the contrary, the transformations have been considerable.

During this period, the Italian economy was transformed beyond recognition. What was, in 1945, a prevalently agricultural country with some pockets of concentrated industrialization had become by the 1960s an industrial power. By the 1980s it was an established 'post-industrial' country which had caught up with the rest of Europe. In terms of purchasing power and standard of living, Italians had narrowed the gap with Germany and France, and closed that with the UK. The 'necessities' of the consumer society, such as remote-control colour television, multi-programme dishwashers, freezers, mobile telephones, laptop computers have been as available in Italy as in most other Western countries – and usually at the same time. In line with European countries, its agricultural population and its birth-rate decreased constantly. Church attendance dwindled, contraceptives came to be commonly used in spite of papal prohibition, couples lived together without being married. After 1970 divorce was legalized. Rapidly, Italians came to enjoy other 'benefits' of modernity such as legal abortions and pornographic material. The dominance of the DC, the strong presence of the Church and the puritanical tradition of the communist movement did not stop a lifestyle which was, by and large, an adaptation of many positive and negative aspects of modernization.

The market and the free enterprise system have played the major role in the diffusion of consumer goods in Italian society. But this has been only one aspect of its social transformation. As in the rest of Europe, the state intervened to keep costs of production lower than they would otherwise have been by taking into public ownership basic production inputs such as energy, and some of the infrastructure of the nation, such as transportation, and subsidizing them out of the public purse. Furthermore, the state also ensured that minimum standards of health, housing, education and old-age care and welfare were maintained. In other words, Italy too became a welfare state – though a hyper-bureaucratic and inefficient one. As in other European countries this was achieved and maintained on the assumption that there would be constant economic growth. This was the case in Italy for most of the 1950s and for well into the 1960s. Economic growth and the welfare state were the basis for that unwritten compromise between the dominant economic groups and the working classes which ensured a remarkable degree of social peace in most of Europe in the post-war period.

Problems began to appear in the 1960s and developed in the 1970s when economic growth slowed down, when the expansion of the tertiary sector associated with the welfare state was supported by a decreasing manufacturing sector, when the financial basis of public spending became narrower, causing inflationary tendencies. The public sector was less and less able to maintain a high level of employment and large areas of the private sector succumbed and had to be rescued by the state. In the 1980s attempts were made to control inflation by controlling public spending, containing wages and loosening the controls exercised on the private sector.

By the early 1990s, the wave of neo-liberalism which accompanied (and to some extent caused) the decline of socialist ideas and the collapse of communism had taken, in Italy, a particular form: northern taxpayers objected to the high level of state expenditure towards the South. Elsewhere the welfare state had been the target of those seeking to cut taxes. In Italy that target could only be the South, as the recipient of large sums aimed at development yet never able to resolve, once and for all, the so-called 'Southern Question'. This tax-payer revolt was led by a new party, the Northern League. This was the first serious challenge to the DC which did not originate from the Left. In 1992, The League was able to obtain the support of significant layers of Christian Democrat electorate in the North. This coincided with a major investigation into political corruption. By 1994 the PSI had disappeared and the DC had been reduced to 10–14 per cent. It was the end of the First Italian Republic.

The pattern I have just described (development of the welfare state, state intervention, crisis of the welfare state) occurred not just in Italy but virtually everywhere else in the developed West. Two points must then be made: in the first place Italian socio-economic development followed that of the rest of Europe in spite of the 'anomalous' nature of its political development, namely, the lack of an alternation of political parties in power and the dominance in Italy of two cultures, communist and political catholicism, which were not dominant in the rest of the West. In the second place, by the end of the twentieth century it is no longer possible to talk purely of 'national' development. International integration is such that – in Europe at least – countries face similar problems and similar solutions, though on the basis of their particular national political tradition.

International integration did not occur by accident. There are two fundamental ways in which Italy actively sought to be part of this process. In the first place, it became party to a supranational defence organization, NATO, which closely tied its foreign policy to that of the dominant superpower in the Western sphere of influence: the USA. In the second place, Italy was one of the original signatories of the Treaty of Rome which established the European Economic Community (EEC) and thus took a clear stand in favour of the creation of a specific European economic (and perhaps, eventually, political) entity. In both cases the treaties were signed after the *de facto* recognition that Italy was part of the West both politically and economically. This recognition was achieved in the immediate post-war period by the DC and their partners in government and was bitterly opposed by communists and socialists. Later the socialists accepted both NATO and the EEC. By the

1960s the PCI too had come to accept that participation in the institutions of the EEC had some potentially positive aspects. By the 1970s the PCI had become a supporter of the need for further economic integration and had recognized that this was an objective process which would have occurred even without the EEC. By 1976 the PCI had also accepted NATO. Thus thirty years after the end of the war all the main forces of the Italian political system shared the view that Italy's role in the world had two fundamental parameters: the NATO alliance and the EEC.

The chapters that follow will take the reader through Italian economic, social and political development. Due emphasis will be given to those aspects which are specific to Italy. What must not be forgotten is the international perspective. In our age the European nation-state is less and less able to control its economic destiny. Those who forget this, in politics as in political research, run the risk of dealing with the terminal stages of the twentieth century with the language and concepts of the nineteenth. These dangers are particularly present in what is, after all, a 'national' study. The temptation to remain enclosed in the narrow confines of national boundaries is particularly strong when dealing, as I do, with a country which, on the surface of things, has such marked peculiarities. I have tried to scratch this surface and in so doing bear in mind what an old German Jewish thinker (who has still a thing or two to teach us) wrote: 'If there were no difference between reality and appearance, there would be no need for science.'

Part one

The economy

Chapter 1

Economic reconstruction, 1945–1950

From the end of 1945 to 1950 there were in Italy five coalition governments, all led by Alcide De Gasperi, leader of the main party, the Christian Democratic Party (DC). The first three included the parties of the left, that is the PCI and the PSI as well as the minor parties of the centre. The fourth De Gasperi government (May 1947) signalled a turning-point in the history of Italian governments. As the Cold War broke out the left was expelled from the ruling coalition (as the communists were in France) and Italy was henceforth governed by the DC and its centrist allies until the early 1960s. The year 1947 was also a major turning-point in economic policy.

It is generally agreed that the kind of economic decisions taken by the various governments in this period were of momentous importance for the subsequent course of Italian history. The decisions to be taken centred essentially on two points:

1   The relation between the Italian economy and the international economy.
2   The relation between the Italian state and the economy.

The first decision regarded the extent to which the Italian economy should be inte-grated with the international economic system. In practice the room for manoeuvre in this field was very limited. With hindsight, Italy had no choice. The main eco-nomic constraint was the scarcity of raw materials: no oil, no iron, no coal. The country needed to import most of the primary products required for economic growth. To resort to protectionism in the conditions of the post-war economy would have entailed economic stagnation. There was an additional political constraint: Europe, and later the world, was being divided into two spheres of influence, the American and the Soviet. Italy was clearly in the American sphere and American pressures for free trade were extremely strong. Finally, there was an ideological element in favour of free trade. The revulsion against fascism as a political system spilled over into a rejection of fascist economic policy which included protectionism – widely regarded as its principal pillar.

The decision to 'choose' to open up the Italian economy to the international market is of importance for the following reasons: to open an economy means that one has to find appropriate trading partners, that means potential customers. Thus one has to gear one's production to their demands, and hence towards exporting the goods they will buy. Thus certain priorities must be established, certain industries must be favoured and certain economic interests will prevail at the expense of others. These choices will determine a particular class structure and the eventual incidence of a certain kind of labour, i.e. skilled or unskilled, male or female, southern or northern, etc. Besides, the choice of partners (again in the specific circumstances of the postwar period) was also 'forced' on Italy by the international situation.[1] The states of Eastern and Central Europe could not be Italy's trading partners because they had effectively contracted out of the international capitalist economy. Nor could these trading partners be those countries we now call of the Third World because their markets were then relatively small and dominated either by the USA (Latin America), or by the UK and France (Asia and Africa) or by all three (the Middle East). Hence Italy's trading partners could only be the countries of Western Europe and North America. It was thus not surprising that the decision to enter the world market entailed membership of the Atlantic Alliance and, later, of all the European economic organizations including the EEC. Of course, some countries thrived in this international economy without becoming either a member of NATO or of the EEC. But Italy could not opt for the neutral foreign policy which had protected Sweden from the ravages of the Second World War or which had been virtually imposed on Austria. Nor could Italy, devoid of an empire and common-wealth, stand relatively aloof from Europe as Britain believed it could do.

None of the political forces in government at the time (and those included, until 1947, the socialists and the communists) were opposed to an opening up of the Italian economy. There were differences on the extent of trade liberalization but none on the principle of free trade. Giving priority to exports, as was eventually done, was to accept that economic development would be determined by external circumstances (i.e. the demand for imports of Western Europe and North America). It also meant that certain sectors of the Italian economy, such as agriculture, would have to be sacrificed. To put it crudely, instead of making Fiat cars for the Euro-pean market (or eventually, washing machines or clothing) some of the resources available could have been directed towards making tractors for the agricultural sector. This could have expanded Italian food production which would have reduced Italy's need to import food. However, there were only two ways to revitalize the agricultural sector.[2] The first would have been to encourage the concentration of agricultural lands and their modernization along capitalist lines. This, however, would have caused the expulsion of considerable numbers of agricultural labourers from the countryside. In the conditions of 1945–50 this would have entailed a dram-atic increase in unemployment and would have been politically dangerous for the DC which relied on the consistent support of the peasantry. The other way, favoured by the left, would have been to ensure the creation of agricultural cooperatives helped by the state. This, however, would have considerably weakened the histor-ical alliance between northern industrial entrepreneurs and southern landlord inter-ests, and this too would have been politically dangerous for the DC. It is also not certain at all that the success of cooperatives in the North-East and the Centre of the country could have been replicated in the South whose rural traditions were markedly different.

It must be added that at no time did the left present a concrete alternative plan for the reconstruction of the Italian economy. This too must be seen as a contributing factor to their setbacks, namely, their expulsion from the ruling coalition in 1947 and their electoral defeat in 1948.

As we shall see later, Italy derived considerable benefit from export-led growth: both production and productivity increased, leading to the period of sustained growth known popularly as the 'economic miracle' of 1958–63. However, there were also serious negative factors. The examination of these leads us directly to a consideration of the so-called dualism of the Italian economy.

The concept of 'dualism' is used in different ways by various specialists of economic development. We shall use it in the sense in which it is normally understood in Italy, that is as synonymous with 'imbalance' or 'disequilibrium'. Historically, there are three kinds of dualism in Italy:[3]

1 *Regional dualism*, that is dualism between economically prosperous regions and those which are economically backward. In the Italian context this can be seen in terms of the gap between the industrial North and the agricultural South.
2 *Industrial dualism*, that is dualism between advanced, modern and highly productive sectors of industry and those which are not.
3 *Dualism in the labour market*, that is dualism between the labour force employed in relatively well-paid, stable jobs and that employed in badly paid, marginal and precarious occupations.

The evidence indicates that the opening up of the Italian economy increased rather than reduced all three kinds of dualism at least up until 1961 and probably (though here there is less agreement) until today. Export firms, overwhelmingly located in the North, came to use, increasingly, southern labour withdrawing it from agriculture thus exacerbating territorial dualism; they grew at a faster rate and had to adopt modern methods because they were competing in the international market (industrial dualism) and their workers were better paid and their jobs were more secure (dualism in the labour market).

Of course there are many countries which exhibit 'dualistic' features in their economic system. These features are difficult to quantify and comparative data in this field are notoriously unreliable. A study by Williamson attempted to quantify territorial dualism for a group of twenty-four countries in the period 1949–61.[4] Of the countries examined the one with the biggest regional variation was Brazil with an index of 0.700, while at the other end there was New Zealand with 0.063. The average was 0.299. Italy ranked sixth with 0.360, thus exhibiting a more marked dualism than India, Ireland and virtually all industrialized countries.

The opening up of the economy was not the only major problem facing the Italian political system. There was also the question of the relation between the state and the economy. In its crudest form the choice was perceived as being between a planned economy and a laissez-faire regime. In practice it was not so clear-cut. The PCI, for instance, was not in favour of a planned economy. That party and its leader, Palmiro Togliatti, were developing a political strategy which did not take

Soviet communism as its principal reference point. They took it for granted that Italy was not ripe for a socialist transformation partly because, as they were committed to the principle of a democratic transformation, they realized that there was not the necessary consensus, and partly because Italy's presence in the US sphere of influence made it impossible. Thus Togliatti, in August 1945, declared that even if the communists were in power on their own they would call on private enterprise for the task of reconstruction. He also added that – in existing circumstances – central planning was utopian; what was needed were, at most, 'elements of planning', i.e. limited state intervention in key sectors.[5] Only the left-wing faction of the PSI called for a national plan, but it encountered no support.

The true debate thus was not between 'central planners' and neo-liberals but rather between the latter and the supporters of what later would be called Keynesian macroeconomic intervention. At the time Keynes was virtually unknown in Italy. Most leading economists were neo-liberals whose belief in the beneficial spontaneous development of market forces was deeply rooted. Historically, the neo-liberals had been an important force in Italian economic culture, but the Italian State had always been interventionist. After 1945 economic liberalism gained considerable influence in economic affairs, though it never became dominant. What were the reasons for their relative success? In part this was a reaction against the *dirigisme* of the Fascist State which had set up a state-holding system and nationalized the banks. In the post-fascist climate the equation *liberty* = *liberalism* had strong currency even among left-wing intellectuals. Another reason was that neo-liberal were in virtual control of the economy. Though the communists and the socialists controlled (until 1947) the Ministries of Finance, Trade, Labour and Agriculture, the neo-liberals controlled the Treasury and, even more importantly, the Bank of Italy which, since the 1936 reform of the banking system, had become the key institution of the entire financial system.[6] In July 1947, after the expulsion of the left from the government, Luigi Einaudi, the foremost champion of economic liberalism, moved from the Bank of Italy to the Ministry of the Budget where he was able to pursue the deflationary policies he had been advocating. It is remarkable that – at the time – the strongest Italian political party, the DC, kept out of economic affairs preferring to allow the small Liberal Party and its political representatives, such as Luigi Einaudi, to dominate economic affairs. As De Gasperi explained to a communist minister who was urging him to adopt more radical policies:

> It is not our millions of voters who can give the State the thousands of millions and the economic power necessary for tackling the situation. Apart from our parties, there is in Italy a fourth party which may not have many supporters but which is capable of paralysing all our efforts by denying us loans, organizing a flight of capital and engineering price rises. Experience has convinced me that it is not possible to govern Italy today without inviting into the new government the representatives of this fourth party, the party of those who have money and economic power.[7]

Luigi Einaudi was the obvious political representative of the 'fourth party' inside the government. Other representatives of the 'party of money' could make their voice heard without requiring the mediation of an officially constituted political

party. The leading Italian industrialists were very clearly opposed to state intervention. Thus Angelo Costa, President of the Italian Employers' Confederation (the
Confindustria), explained that he thought that the adoption of interventionist policies for the location of industry along the UK model would be detrimental to the
Italian economy. He thought it would be preferable to 'move people' rather than
plants.[8] In other words, Costa was in favour of internal immigration rather than the
location of industry in the South. This clearly envisaged that the role of the South
in post-war reconstruction would have to be that of providing northern industries
with the necessary supply of cheap labour. Costa, however, accepted the need for
public works programmes in the South, but specified the conditions of acceptability
of these policies: wages in southern public-sector programmes would have to be
inferior to wages in the industrial northern sector in order not to compete for labour
with private industry. As we can see, the tenets of liberalism were here not adhered
to so closely. There is a clear vision of what the specific role of the state should
be: to intervene where private industry is reluctant to intervene and to do so on the
basis of a low-wages policy. A high-wage policy would have made Italian industry
less competitive on world markets and would have entailed a different approach to
the problem of post-war reconstruction. Thus a low-wage policy was not something
determined only by market forces but was to be, to use the word in its literal sense,
a *policy*, i.e. a conscious political decision which, in turn, determined a particular
range of political alliances which excluded the left.

It is true that there were technical obstacles to the adoption of a public works
programme directly conducted by the state (as opposed, say, to subsidies for industry): the inefficiency of administration and the lack of coordination between the
various state organs. Yet, when the political parties and the private sector were
united in favour of particular public works programmes, all obstacles vanished as
was the case when the Italian motorway system was developed towards the end
of the 1950s.

That low wages were a 'good thing' was also asserted, not surprisingly, by industrialists like Vittorio Valletta, the chairman of Fiat, the largest Italian private firm.
He explained that the main obstacle to the development of the Italian automobile
industry was the scarcity of raw materials. There were, however, three favourable
conditions: low wages, the possibility of importing American technology and the
possibility of withstanding foreign competition by concentrating on small cars. The
overall reduction of costs could be achieved by an expansion of the industrial scale
of production. Here we have in a nutshell a global understanding of the political
determinants of a specific pattern of economic growth: a government decision not
to engage in any activity which would push wages upward, the need to remain in
the American sphere of influence in order to have access to American know-how,
the necessity to develop as trading partners markets which would be interested in
small cars (i.e. Western Europe).[9]

The debate on state intervention had also an important role to play when the USA
launched its European Recovery Programme (ERP), better known as the Marshall
Plan. This programme presented Italian decision-makers with a new set of variables. The options were essentially two: to use American money to increase state

intervention in the economy by setting up infrastructures or to increase Bank of Italy reserves in order to maintain the stability of the currency and the equilibrium in the balance of payments. Here the left was in particular difficulty because both communists and socialists had rejected the principle of Marshall Aid and hence could not at the same time fight for a particular use of the programme. The neo-liberals in control of economic decision-making had already decided that the ERP money had to have a currency-stabilizing function. In so doing they did not have the support of ERP itself. Paradoxically enough the Marshall Aid administrators had a conception of the relation between the state and the economy which was not so different from that of some of the leaders of the PCI. The Americans who were working in the Marshall Aid programme were in fact deeply imbued with the spirit of the New Deal and had accepted much of Keynes' analysis. Their position and that of the United Nations Relief and Rehabilitation Administration (UNRRA) – the predecessor of ERP – was that Italy should adopt elements of planning to integrate the activities of the entrepreneurial classes with that of the state. Marshall Aid was supposed to be used for a rapid development of investments to ensure industrial growth, not, as the Italians by and large did, in order to increase reserves.

The PCI (and to some extent the small Republican Party led by Ugo La Malfa) wanted to direct the flow of public expenditure towards real investments. But Marshall Aid money was tied in with a set of political preconditions – to integrate Western Europe and North America in a web of political and economic relations of interdependence – which, for obvious international reasons, such as the start of the Cold War, could not be accepted by the Italian left. The link with Moscow prevented the Italian communists from intervening in a constructive manner, but such problems could not affect the ERP administrator for Italy, Paul Hoffman. In his report to the US Congress he maintained that deflation was unnecessary and that there was no need for the Italians to worry about the balance of payments problem that a Keynesian use of ERP might cause: this would be taken into account by an increase in aid. What the Italian government should do, suggested Hoffman, was to set up a plan in order to coordinate public intervention and the financing of public works programmes.[10] In fact the US authorities thought it strange that the Italian government which, through its state holding agency, *Istituto per la Ricostruzione Industriale* (IRI), virtually controlled the banking system and a significant propor-tion of industry, would not attempt some sort of planning aimed at reducing unem-ployment then at very high levels (19 per cent). The fact that there were differences between the US and the Italian governments on such an important question is sig-nificant. It puts in a different perspective the view held by many commentators, particularly on the left, which cast American-Italian relations as relations between master and servant and assumed that successive Italian governments were totally subservient to the *diktats* from Washington. In reality it would have been perfectly possible for Italian governments to be on good terms with Washington while fol-lowing a progressive economic policy as long as the communists were kept at a distance. Similarly invalidated are also the determinist arguments which held that once Italy had found itself in the Western sphere of influence it had no choice but to act in all economic matters as it did. The tendency to use the USA as a justification for a whole range of internal political decisions can be explained by the fact that this instrumental use of the special link with Washington was a strong factor in the legitimation of DC rule. Christian Democrats could always respond to criticisms by saying that: 'we do what we do because otherwise there would be no American help'. American-Italian relations were in fact more complex than they appeared at the time. Americans were ill-informed about Italy and were quite willing to be advised by political parties they assumed were reliable. In the climate of the Cold War, reliability and anti-communism went hand in hand provided the favoured partner could also establish some electoral popularity. The DC did fit the bill perfectly: it was anti-communist, it was popular, and not tainted by any direct association with fascism.

It does not follow that the DC could have been more audacious when it came to 'Keynesian planning'. After all, various forms of state intervention had been adopted in a number of European countries who were as anti-Soviet as Italy. In Britain the Labour government elected in 1945 embarked on a wide programme of national-izations and laid the foundation of the welfare state. Similar initiatives were adopted in the Scandinavian countries, in Belgium and in the Netherlands. In January 1946 the French government under Charles de Gaulle created the Commissariat General au Plan and, in 1947, the Monnet Plan was launched. France, Belgium and Holland also adopted a range of special taxes on private wealth and war profits.[11] But Italy seemed to have become the bastion of laissez-faire ideology. This had an effect on the amount of aid obtained. There was no planning structure within which an accurate estimate could be made of what Italy needed. Thus when it came to put in a bid for qualitative aid (i.e. in kind rather than in cash) Italy put forward its requests in a disorganized manner unlike the French special *Plan de modernisation et d'équipement*.[12]

Inside the DC, a technocratic left-wing, led by Ezio Vanoni and Amintore Fanfani, was advocating a version of indicative planning along the French model. They were supported by the small Republican Party, but they were all outflanked by the major-ity of the DC in alliance with the Confindustria, FIAT and leading industrialists like Gaetano Marzotto, a major textile producer, who, in 1946 to the question, 'Do you think that the state should indicate what quantity and kind of goods should be pro-duced?' answered 'This would be Russian Bolshevism!'[13]

But were the interventionists totally defeated? Did the Italian economy recover only on the basis of laissez-faire? We have already suggested that, strictly speak-ing, pure laissez-faire is an abstraction. In the conditions of the second half of the twentieth century, the state's decision not to intervene in order, for instance, to keep wages low, is a form of intervention. In the period 1945–50 as well as later, Italian economic decision-makers favoured economic growth based on low wages and sus-tained exports.

But were there also more direct forms of economic intervention? An examination of government policy shows that neo-liberal ideology, though influential, was not overwhelming and that the *dirigistes* were able to make some substantial gains. First and foremost there is the fact that the fundamental mechanisms of state inter-vention set up by the fascists were not eliminated. The important state holding company IRI was preserved. The holdings under IRI control were very diversified:

engineering, steel, electricity, telephones, the arms industry, etc. This had come about as a result of the crisis of 1929. The state had been forced to acquire greater control over the banking system and, in 1933, it created the IRI to administer the industrial holdings of three major banks which had been taken over. Italian banks had followed the German model in obtaining first a decisive influence and, eventually, a considerable portion of the shares of firms they were financing. Thus when the banks were taken over, the state also took over a diversified portion of Italian industry. By 1938 the IRI controlled 77 per cent of cast-iron production, 45 per cent of steel, 12 per cent of electricity and 82 per cent of shipyards. By 1942 it had 210,000 employees. Established as an emergency measure by the fascist authorities, the IRI became the main industrial group in Italy. Its survival was the major achievement of the interventionist 'party' against the neo-liberals. In the post-war period the IRI played a decisive part in the modernization of the steel industry. In the 1950s IRI had the central role in the public works programme which was one of the preconditions of the Italian economic miracle, but in the late 1940s its single, though important success was the steel industry.

The situation in 1945 was that one-third of the much-disrupted steel industry was still owned by the state through Finsider (an IRI company). In 1937 Oscar Sinigaglia, on behalf of Finsider, had prepared a Steel Plan aimed at expanding steel production in Italy and lowering steel prices by adopting a method of production based on the system of integral cycle (i.e. beginning from the raw material and not from scraps as had been the case hitherto in Italy). The plan had not been implemented because of the war and the opposition of private sector steel producers. After the war a modified version of the plan was put forward by Finsider. This was strongly opposed by the *Confindustria* and in particular by Giorgio Falck, then the leading private producer of steel in Italy.[14]

However, after the expulsion of the left from government and their electoral defeat in 1948, there were sufficient political guarantees for the private sector to tone down their opposition which was essentially a political one: not against state intervention as such but against an intervention in which the forces of the left would have had an important say. The Sinigaglia Plan was carried out partly thanks to ERP aid. Italian steel became internationally competitive. Even though production was at a standstill in 1945, by 1950 Finsider had reached pre-war levels (1 million tons) and when the Sinigaglia Plan was fulfilled in 1955 nearly 3 million tons were produced.[15] Steel production constituted one of the most important preconditions for the development of private engineering and private building programmes in the 1950s. The adoption of the Sinigaglia Plan showed that the IRI was able to carry out what no private steel company would or could have done: the introduction in Italy of modern methods of steel production. This modernized Italian industry enormously. This was done because, for the first time, steel was conceived of as an infrastructure which was to the immediate advantage of steel consumers and in particular to Fiat.[16] This also illustrates the general conception of the public sector held by the dominant political parties: that of supporting the development of the private sector. Before 1947 the left conceived of the public sector as having a leading role in development. Once the left had been defeated, the road had been opened for a conception of the public sector as subordinated to the requirements of the private one. Thus a *de facto* compromise had been reached between interventionists and neo-liberals: the former would look after the provision of adequate infrastructures, the latter would ensure that orthodox economic policies would be pursued.

The position of the neo-liberals was consolidated not because they fought against state intervention, but because they were able to impose their own conception of the 'correct' way of approaching the issue of inflation and of the balance of payments in the post-war period. It was probably on this terrain that the interconnection between the defeat of the left and economic policies can be best established.

The starting-point for this discussion must be, once again, the decision to 'open up' the Italian economy because this poses the question of the control of foreign exchange. Given that foreign currency was scarce and yet vitally necessary for paying for imported raw materials the government could have imposed strict exchange controls as, for instance, the British government did. To do so would have meant that entrepreneurs who wished to import raw materials, would have had to ask the government for foreign currency. The government would then have been in a position to use its control over foreign exchange to give priority to a particular economic sector. If this path had been chosen the government would have had, from the very beginning the leading role in the reconstruction of the Italian economy.

This interventionist position was not supported only by the left. Guido Carli, who eventually became Governor of the Bank of Italy and who is generally considered one of the great champions of 'orthodox' economic management, advocated exchange controls precisely because the government could then use foreign currency to buy those foreign goods which it considered necessary to the national economy.[17] Obviously the decision not to intervene would also have favoured some sectors at the expense of others. For instance it would have favoured exporters. They would be able to sell abroad and then enjoy freely the foreign currency gained. They could, for example, use it to speculate against the lira in what was called the 'parallel market', the *de facto* black market in currency. In March 1946 the government decided that exporters could keep for themselves 50 per cent of the foreign currency they had obtained and would have to exchange the rest in Italian currency at a rate fixed by the Central Bank. This compromise in economic policy reflected to some extent the political compromise between the DC and the left (at the time still in government). After the expulsion of communists and socialists from government the liberalization of the foreign exchange received a further boost: while the 50 per cent deposit system was maintained it was decided that the government would adapt its own rate of exchange to that of the 'parallel' black market every month. In practice this meant that the 'political' rate of exchange (i.e. that decided by the government) would follow that of the market – a clear acceptance of the principle that the state should follow the markets. This led to a constant devaluation of the lira because people preferred to hold dollars (see Table 1.1).

By 1949 the general economic situation had improved and the DC, following the electoral victory of 1948, was now solidly in control. Now the general direction of Italian economic development was clear. At this stage, and at this stage only, controls were imposed. The lira exchange rate was fixed at 625 lire per dollar and

Table 1.1 Devaluation of the lira, 1945–49

1945	1 dollar = 100 lire
1947	1 dollar = 350 lire
1949	1 dollar = 625 lire

remained there until August 1971 when the entire post-war system of fixed exchange rates collapsed with the American devaluation of the dollar.

But why had the value of the lira fallen continuously? The chief, but not the sole, reason was inflation. What one could have bought for 100 lire in 1938 would have required 858 lire in 1944, 2,060 lire in 1945, 2,884 in 1946 and 5,159 lire in 1947. Clearly, inflation was approaching the 'runaway' stage and was jeopardizing the Italian economy. Different strategies were put forward within the ruling coalition. One of the most contentious ones was the proposal to 'change the currency'. The motivation behind this proposal was that one of the liabilities inherited from the fascist administration was the considerable amount of paper currency in circulation.[18] Much of this had been accrued in the hands of individuals through black market dealings. This quantity of uncontrolled cash added considerable fuel to the inflationary process. The proposal coming from the left was that a new currency should be adopted (i.e. new banknotes) and the operation could be connected to a wealth tax. This would give the state a considerable amount of cash at its disposal which it could use for the financing of reconstruction.[19] Furthermore, this policy would have had the effect of a tax on war profits.[20] Far from being a revolutionary proposal, a change of currency had already been implemented in many European countries such as France, Belgium and the Netherlands.[21] However, this measure not only would have weakened the middle classes but would have also strengthened the interventionist position of the state and was thus opposed by the neo-liberals. Their delaying tactics were fairly successful, and the project was abandoned. Another anti-inflationary policy advocated by the left and in particular by the communist Finance Minister, Mauro Scoccimarro, who was worried about inflation, was the use of rationing and direct controls (as was being done in the UK under a Labour government). The neo-liberal Treasury Minister, Epicarmo Corbino advocated cuts in public spending instead. Unable to obtain what he wanted Corbino resigned in 1946 in what was regarded as a victory for the left. In reality Corbino was politically isolated: even the markets turned against him as the Treasury found itself unable to sell bonds.[22] But the left too was soon forced to abandon its ministerial positions and this permitted the government to resort to the policies advocated by the new Budget Minister, Luigi Einaudi (then Governor of the Bank of Italy and, in 1948, President of the Republic). The new policies consisted essentially of a drastic deflation achieved by a harsh credit squeeze. They did stop inflation, although some point out that inflation was on the decrease anyway.[23] The costs were not negligible. A credit squeeze was having a negative effect on investments, thus Italy was deprived of investments in those years when the political priority was post-war reconstruction. The Italian economy was substantially stagnant in the years

1947–50. It began to pick up only after 1950 and this was due essentially to external conditions: the Korean War had given rise to a general expansion of international demand and Italian exporters were able to benefit from this.

Of course the stagnation of 1947–50 was also due, in the final analysis, to international conditions. Priority had been given to anti-inflation policies because inflation was causing the constant depreciation of the Italian currency. The West, since the Bretton Woods Conference of 1944, had decided to establish a system of fixed exchange rates. If Italy, which had been admitted to the International Monetary Fund, wanted to partake of the benefits of the international economy it would have had to play by the rules and maintain the stability of its currency against the dollar.[24] It was thus necessary to deal with inflation in order to stabilize the lira and thus participate in the international economy.

The victory over inflation and the stabilization of the lira had also important political effects.[25] In the first place it undoubtedly helped the DC to achieve a major victory in the elections of 1948 because the containment of inflation ensured its growing popularity – especially among the middle classes. The DC was able to obtain this result without endangering the vast support it had among the rural classes, many of whom still relied on a quasi-subsistence agriculture and were not directly affected by the credit squeeze. Finally, the credit squeeze hit the bargaining strength of the trade unions. It was thus on the terrain of economic policy that the DC fought, in the post-war period, one of its major victorious battles: it emerged as the party of the middle classes without losing its rural connection. By incorporating the neo-liberal strategy in matters of economic policy it avoided the birth of a rival bourgeois party of the centre. Furthermore, it defeated the left not only by expelling it from government and clinching this expulsion with an clear electoral victory in 1948, but also by working successfully towards the break-up of the hitherto united trade-union movement in the same year. In so doing it established one of the conditions for the remarkable economic development in the 1950s: a low-wage economy.

Endnotes

1 Graziani 1971, pp. 22–3.
2 Silva and Targetti 1972, p. 18.
3 Valli 1979, p. 10.
4 Williamson 1968, p. 112. See also Valli 1979, pp. 11–12.
5 Palmiro Togliatti, speech to the Economic Conference of the PCI, Rome, 21–23 August 1945, extracts in Graziani 1971, pp. 111–13.
6 Castronovo 1975, p. 371.
7 Cited by Emilio Sereni, the minister in question, in his *Il Mezzogiorno all' opposizione*, Turin 1948, pp. 20–1.
8 Villari 1975, vol. two, pp. 486–7.
9 Graziani 1971, pp. 126–30.
10 Castronovo 1975, p. 384.
11 Castronovo 1975, p. 362.
12 Daneo 1975, p. 248.
13 Villari 1975, p. 519.
14 Villari 1975, p. 531.
15 Amoroso and Olsen 1978, p. 66.
16 Colajanni 1976, p. 15.
17 Carli 1946; now reprinted in Graziani 1971, pp. 113–15.
18 De Cecco 1972, pp. 162–3.
19 Gambino 1975, p. 111.
20 Silva and Targetti 1972, p. 17.
21 Castronovo 1975, p. 362.
22 Ricossa 1992, p. 42.
23 Silva and Targetti 1972, pp. 18–19.
24 Graziani 1971, p. 30.
25 Castronovo 1975, p. 382.

Chapter 2

The politics of development, 1950–1963

During the years 1950 to 1963 the European economies grew at a faster rate than ever before and Italy's grew faster than most, particularly between 1958 and 1963, a period which came to be known as 'the economic miracle'. It is not possible to understand the Italian political system unless one understands the economic and social transformation brought about by this development. It transformed Italy, hitherto a prevalently agrarian country, into a modern industrial state, yet it exacerbated the already incipient economic dualism. At the beginning of this period the Christian Democratic Party (DC) appeared solidly entrenched in power, dominating the centre of the political spectrum. The left, in disarray, had been marginalized, while the far right was equally excluded from all positions of power. By the end of the period the DC had completely recast its system of alliances. It had ditched the Liberal Party (*Partito Liberale Italiano* – PLI), committed itself to structural reforms and succeeded in wresting the Socialist Party (PSI) away from the communists. In 1950 the ideological supremacy of neo-liberal economists seemed unassailable. By the early 1960s Italy was about to embark on the biggest expansion of the public sector of the post-war period. In 1950 the trade unions were at the nadir of their power and influence. By 1963 the unions were poised to become one of the central forces of Italian society. In 1950 the socialists were the allies of the communists – the only country in Western Europe where this was the case. By 1963 the socialists were in government with the DC. Over the succeeding thirty years and until the end of the First Republic, the socialists would be – almost uninterruptedly – the allies of the Christian Democrats.

The 'economic miracle' did not resolve Italy's problems. What it did was to change the country sufficiently to force the political system to reconstitute itself on a new basis of consensus. To understand how this was done and the new range of problems this gave rise to, it will be necessary to examine in this chapter the kind of economic development which occurred and its fundamental features.

It should be stated at the outset that the essential characteristics of this period, namely the growth of the manufacturing sector, the integration of the country in the international economy and the development of rapid urbanization, were general features of all industrialized countries.[1] Italy had taken its part in the post-war cycle of economic expansion which had begun with the Korean War and ended in the first half of the 1960s with an exceptionally high rate of growth. The regional, industrial and labour market dualism described in Chapter 1 persisted and a new problem appeared: the massive development in private consumption (e.g. household goods) was not matched by a similar growth in collective goods and services such as education, housing, transport and health.

It would, of course, be interesting to speculate what sort of policies could have promoted economic growth, international integration and urbanization without increasing industrial and regional dualism. At the time, no political force presented a concrete economic alternative to the pattern which prevailed. This does not mean that this programme could not have existed, or that the kind of economic growth which actually occurred was somehow historically inevitable. For instance, Japan, a country with which it is not unreasonable to compare Italy, at least in the immediate post-war period, did not adopt, in spite of American pressures, free trade. It chose economic development under the direction of the state, on the basis of protectionism and of a deliberate compression of private consumption.[2] Japan invested heavily in the production of capital goods and infrastructures. The foundations were thus laid for a sustained growth which enabled the country to invade the world market from a position of strength. In so doing Japan built on its past: the war could be regarded as the interruption of an ongoing process. Its old project, the conquest of Asian markets, was fulfilled with a vengeance. First the old imperial powers – France and Britain – were virtually expelled from these markets; then Japan challenged the great industrial enterprises of Europe and North America in their home territory.

Those who seek to analyse Italian economic development purely in terms of economic decisions separately from political considerations can construct a credible alternative scenario of how the Italian economy might have developed. But economic decisions are never taken in isolation from political factors. It was not only the position of Italy in the US sphere of influence which 'forced' the internationalization of the Italian economy. Japan too was in the Western sphere, albeit in a different way. The Italian decision was determined by its specific geographical position which reduced the availability of export markets to the Mediterranean and Western Europe. Here again political factors intervened: Italy could not hope to enter the Middle Eastern markets – still the terrain of colonialism and semi-colonialism. In any case, these markets could hardly provide a terrain for serious export-led growth. Italy had to look to North-Western Europe. Its own industries had always considered the northern European sector as their natural outlet. Its history was interconnected with the development of West European capitalism in a way Japanese history was not. The presence of a strong left in Italy made it difficult to resort to the systematic squeeze on living standards which prevailed in Japan throughout the 1950s and part of the 1960s. The work ethic characteristic of Japanese development was not applicable to Italy. The Europeanization of the Italian economy was regarded by Alcide De Gasperi – Prime Minister until 1954 – as a factor guaranteeing the political reliability of Italy within the Western camp and the surest protection against communism.

Table 2.1 A comparison of economic growth, 1950–63

	Average growth rate (%)	
	1950–58	1958–63
Japan	7.3	11.1
West Germany	7.8	5.7
Italy	5.3	6.6
France	4.5	5.6
USA	3.0	4.2
UK	2.3	3.5

Source: © OECD, *National Accounts Statistics*, 1950–68. In column 1, 1953–58 for Japan and 1951–58 for Italy

Italy, however, shared with West Germany and Japan some specific advantages which might explain why the three countries that lost the war were able to overtake the others in terms of growth rates in this period. These three countries had a huge reserve of labour.[3] In Japan and Italy this 'reserve' was in the countryside while West Germany was the recipient of the steady stream of highly skilled economic and political refugees from the East Germany, and from the former German-speaking territories of Poland and Czechoslovakia. All three countries were the 'beneficiaries' of weak trade union movements. In Italy trade union weakness was due to its division along political and religious lines, to the use of anti-communism as a weapon in industrial relations (e.g. sacking communist shop stewards) and the use of internal migration as a mechanism militating in favour of low wages. Countries such as the UK were disadvantaged because they did not have a huge reserve of labour and were faced with a stronger trade union movement. Britain pursued a policy of full employment to maintain social peace. Its relatively low rate of growth was the result of attempts to avoid inflation and an adverse balance of payments. In France, where, unlike in Britain, high growth was achieved, the price exacted was inflation and a balance of payments crisis. This led to the devaluation of the French franc in 1958–59 and contributed to the de-stabilization of the Fourth Republic and the advent of Gaullism. Differences in growth rates are tabulated in Table 2.1. In the first period (1950–58), Italian growth rates were high, but not exceptionally so, particularly when compared with the second phase when even West Germany – which, unlike the other countries, had passed its peak – was overtaken.

Thus the period we are examining could be divided into two: 1950–57 were the years of preparation for economic expansion; 1958–63 were those of fast economic growth. Until 1958–59 the Italian economy followed the American cycle: when the US rate of growth of the national income increased (1955, 1959) that of Italy followed the general trend (as did Japan, West Germany and Western Europe in general). When the US rate decreased so did that of the other countries. However, after 1958–59 there was no close correlation between the US rate of growth and that of Italy: for instance, between 1959 and 1961 the rate slowed down in the USA

Table 2.2 Annual growth of hourly productivity, 1953–63 (%)

Food industry	4.6
Textiles	4.8
Engineering	8.6
Manufacturing	8.7
Chemical	10.8
Vehicle industry	10.9

but reached new peaks in Italy. This indicates that there was a phenomenon of emancipation of the Italian economy from the American one partly because Italian trading relations with other countries became relatively more important those with the USA, partly because internal factors (e.g. labour costs) became more important.[4]

We can now turn to a more detailed examination of the causes of the 'economic miracle' and the role of political decisions.[5]

The established view is that Italian economic growth was achieved largely thanks to foreign demand, in other words, that it was export-led. The increased competitiveness of Italian goods in the international market was achieved because Italian entrepreneurs faced lower labour costs than entrepreneurs in other countries, helped by the low value of the lira. In the period we are examining, international demand increased thanks to a combination of factors including American aid, American growth rates and their effect on international demand, technological progress, the cheap price of energy, especially oil, and the development of a mass market for consumption goods. These were factors which were, of course, common to all countries in the West. Italy happened to be favourably situated because, as I have indicated, it was able to control wages.[6]

Before returning to the question of wages, I will examine more closely the question of export-led Italian economic development. For this I shall rely on the views of Augusto Graziani, one of the most lucid exponent of this thesis.[7] As was pointed out in Chapter 1, if a country such as Italy wanted to be active in the international market it had to produce those goods richer countries would want. To do so it had to develop, virtually from scratch, the capabilities to compete internationally in the production of mass consumer goods, such as cars, light household goods and petrochemical products. The market for these industries was determined internationally. Home demand could not play a leading role, because a high home demand requires high domestic wages and wages in Italy were low. Thus Italy had to develop the economic structure of a rich nation by producing the kind of goods rich nations want, but without enjoying their living standards. This is precisely how the industrial dualism of the Italian economy was exacerbated: the gap between exporting firms and home-orientated firms grew. Productivity in the export sector was high (because they faced foreign competition) whereas it was low in the still relatively protected home sector. This is illustrated in Table 2.2.

The food industry was essentially home-orientated, the textile industry was at first home-orientated and only later joined the export sector, the rest were all export-orientated. Because profits were higher in the export sector self-financing was easier, that meant that firms operating in this sector could expand without any need for bank loans. The exporting sector needed to maintain a high productivity, hence its investments tended to be directed towards capital-intensive production and thus did not contribute as much as it could have to an increase in employment. It was the 'backward' private sector and the public sector which really helped to bring down the rate of unemployment. Between 1951 and 1963 employment grew by 100 per cent in the retailing sector, 84 per cent in the building sector, but by only 40 per cent in the manufacturing sector.

This explanation allows us to put into perspective the view that the poor wages of Italian workers were the essential fuel behind the 'economic miracle'. It is true that Italian wages were lower than those of many of its international competitors, but they were not uniformly low. Wages in the expanding sector were higher than those in the backward sector: another instance of dualism. This points to another interesting feature: a growing dualism in the price structure leading to the distortion in consumption mentioned at the beginning of this chapter. If we examine the internal composition of the aggregate level of prices we find that the prices of goods produced in the 'backward' sector tended to rise more rapidly than the home price of the goods produced in the export sector. This is essentially due to differences in productivity and efficiency. What were the consequences of this pricing dualism? Graziani points out that one major outcome was that some basic goods, such as meat, became relatively more expensive than non-basic goods such as television sets. Thus home demand for goods produced in the dynamic export sector increased at a relatively faster rate than the demand for goods in the home-orientated sector. This helps to explain a paradox that many visitors to Italy found difficult to understand: the average Italian had a diet which was poorer than that of most workers in other European countries but had the same sort of household goods: cars, transistor radios, vacuum cleaners, television sets, and so on. This distortion in prices coupled with the distortion in wages meant that Italian workers were demanding the same goods workers in richer countries were demanding, i.e. goods produced in the dynamic sector.

This thesis illustrates rather well the relative convergence of the Italian people towards the material standards prevailing elsewhere in the West – that is an essentially American pattern of private consumption. The consequences of this for the regional dualism which afflicted Italy can be immediately estimated: the North with its industries, its mass consumption and its efficient exporting sectors integrated in the world economy represented one pole of development; the other was the South which provided the North with the labour force and was dependent on non-private, i.e. state, forms of accumulation in order to achieve similar standards of living. This provides a framework for analysis which can be used to make connections between 'purely' economic factors and social and political ones. Graziani's export-led thesis, however, in spite of its undoubted appeal, should be partially modified for a number of reasons.

First of all – as we shall see – the export-led thesis cannot be sustained for the period 1950–57. The integration of the Italian economy in the international system took some time: there were still protectionist tariffs against a whole range of goods and this favoured the development of exporting industries, while there were lower barriers against the imports competing with the 'backward' sector. After 1957, with the entry of Italy into the EEC, foreign demand became of paramount importance. But before then it was home demand that led the way. The real boom in international demand occurred only after 1955, and it took some time before post-war investment became really productive. It also took some time before the weakness of the trade union movement had an effect on the relative level of wages, an effect which was enhanced by the constant growth of productivity. The view that exports were a major cause of the 'miracle' is valid mainly for the post-1957 period not for 1950–57.[8] In 1958 the value of Italian exports was 4.7 per cent of the total value of all exports of the top fourteen industrialized countries (same as in 1940). But by 1963 this had reached 7.3 per cent.[9]

Furthermore, the export-led thesis should take into account that the Italian balance of payments on current account (i.e. goods and services) would have registered a large deficit throughout the period 1953–57 had it not been for two items not related to the exporting capability of Italian firms: revenue from tourism and income from the money sent back to Italy by Italians working abroad. Without foreign tourists and Italian emigrants, in 1953–57 Italy would have suffered an average yearly deficit of over 373 million dollars instead 85 million dollars. The contribution of tourism and emigration was remarkable even in the years of the economic miracle. They turned what would have been an average deficit of 565 million dollars into an average yearly surplus of 258 million dollars.[10] It can thus be seen that, in spite of the remarkable growth of Italian industry, the economy as a whole derived considerable benefit from two 'industries', tourism and the export of labour, which are more typical of an underdeveloped country than of a modern advanced industrial economy. This illustrates one of the chief peculiarities of Italian development: it was based in considerable part on the underdeveloped features of the country. These features, far from constituting an obstacle to development, enabled Italian economic growth to take place in the form it actually did.

By far the most outstanding 'underdeveloped' feature which facilitated development was the lower level of wages. I previously pointed out that this was in part due to the large-scale unemployment existing in the 1950s – the agricultural reserve army of labour – and to the consequent weakness of the trade union movement. This situation had the same effect that an 'incomes policy' would have had. In fact it was only in the 1960s, when Italian wages in the North had reached European levels, that Italian decision-makers started discussing the possibility of introducing an incomes policy. Thus there was no sudden conversion to the principles of interventionism, but rather to the fact that an informal 'incomes policy' determined by indirect factors was in existence. Real wages were stagnant between 1950 and 1954 and between 1956 and 1961. Unemployment, at 7.8 per cent in 1950, had decreased only to 7.3 per cent by 1960, while the average unemployment in the rest of Europe was only 1.9 per cent, and this in spite of the emigration of 1.7 million Italians.[11]

Of course, low wages by themselves do not explain the competitiveness of Italian exports, let alone Italian economic growth. If that were the case we would not be able to explain why underdeveloped countries which can obviously rely on cheap labour have not been able to follow the Italian example. Of the many differences between Italy and underdeveloped countries in general, one of the most significant in the sphere of labour is the fact that the general cultural level of the southern Italian peasant, however low it may appear to some, is already structured by the ethics and the 'mentality' of the technological world. It is this 'cultural' aspect which permitted the transformation of the southern peasant into a high-productivity, assembly-line proletarian in a short period of time, whereas such a transformation is more complex in the majority of underdeveloped countries.[12] This cultural adaptability also means that the link between the towns and the countryside was not broken as it is frequently in underdeveloped countries. In the latter the modern sector is an island separated from the traditional sector. The industrial workers produced mainly for exports, received wages far higher than the income of those left behind and they spent it on imported goods. In Italy the link between city and countryside became a trading relation. The washing machines produced by a southerner working in the North could then be bought by his relatives who remained in the village thanks to the portion of the wages the same worker sent back.

The low-wage economy was largely due to the existence of a cheap supply of labour in the South. This supply did not have 'natural' causes; it was 'politically determined' by events such as the agrarian reform of 1950, which were in turn caused by the agrarian unrest of the late 1940s. The reform was promulgated in 1950 when the government distributed 40,000 hectares of land in Calabria. Later in the year land in all *latifundia* areas was redistributed. Another law established a fund for the rebirth of the South called the *Cassa per il Mezzogiorno*. This reform was criticized on many counts: it covered only uncultivated land in the latifundia areas and the compensation paid to the expropriated landlord was too generous. As Allum has written: 'it was a political operation to transform a part of the rural proletariat of the agro-towns into peasant proprietors which it hoped would turn them into defenders of the status quo. At the same time, it provided the machinery for their control; the land agencies were to exercise the new kind of patronage.'[13]

The Cassa did not develop the industrial potential of the South. What it did was to release potential labour from the rural sector by intervening in favour of what it defined as 'viable' farms. The Cassa expanded the market for northern industry by increasing southern incomes through public works programmes and laid the basis for a state clientele system to the advantage of the leading party of government, the DC.[14] In the first five years (1950–55) the Cassa established rural infrastructures, developed land reclamation projects, and subsidized the agrarian reform. This was of benefit to agriculture. The subsequent five years paved the way for a change in policy which finally resulted in the 1960s policy of attempting to industrialize the South.[15] However, throughout the 1950s, it was assumed that it was neither possible nor desirable to do this.

The ideological reason behind this view was the conviction that land-owning peasants would be more conservative than workers. It was thus preferable, from a Christian Democratic point of view, to keep them on the land and out of factories where, inevitably, they would have come under the influence of communist trade unionists. If this had really been implemented *in toto*, northern industry would have been forced to subsidize inefficient farming while being deprived of a potential labour force. The government had to perform a delicate balancing act: after all, the agrarian reform was conceived as a consensus-seeking operation. Thus the government protected only existing capitalist farms and those created by expropriated landlords and enterprising farmers. Poor peasants, left on too small a parcel of land, contributed to the acceleration of the Italian economy in the period 1958–63 by massive internal migration. Thus government policy protected a section of the southern population and more or less forced the rest to seek a life away from the land. The strategy of public works programmes controlled by the Cassa and other state agencies was meant to consolidate the infrastructures, strengthen the agricultural sector and develop tourism. This was the economic basis for a new coalition of interests in the South. State intervention could be accepted by the North because it developed a market in the South for northern produce without increasing the competitiveness of southern industry. It obtained the favour of southern interests because it helped to expand the building industry and developed a vast network of small peasant properties.

When internal migration soared, the extensive public works programme which had been undertaken on the basis of previous population levels was cut down. Furthermore, the population which did not emigrate to the North moved to the coast where there was more work: tourism, retail and a small manufacturing sector. The state thus saw its main task as one of creating the infrastructure for private industry. It did not yet act in the South as an entrepreneur, but it helped the development of many small firms. In 1961, 60 per cent of those employed in southern industries worked in firms employing fewer than ten people. This network of small enterprises which grew in the South was closely linked to public spending and was hence indebted to local and national political interests.[16] Government action in the South was of greater help to the North. The funds spent on the infrastructure, for instance motorways, helped northern industries both directly because the North produced the materials used, and indirectly because it gave impetus to the demand for manufactured products such as cars. Furthermore, the employment of southern labour in the public works, because of the precarious nature of employment in the building and construction industries, left the South in a marginalized and exposed position. Those who had left their land to work in one of the Cassa projects could not return to it when the project was terminated: they had to move further north. Finally, the public spending programme helped to sustain domestic demand for the products of northern industries.[17]

Thus this form of state intervention in the South, like all the previous ones in the preceding century was subordinated to the interests of the leading industrial economic groups. Both the agrarian reform and the Cassa's public works programme contributed to the end of the *latifundia* system and to development of small-scale peasantry and, hence, to new opportunities for leaving the countryside.[18]

The aggregate effects of state intervention led to a continuous decline in the importance of agricultural production. Even though productivity in agriculture increased by 44 per cent between 1951 and 1967 its proportion of the national income dropped constantly: from 20–21 per cent in 1951 to 13–14 per cent in 1967. This

Table 2.3 Public investments, 1950–61 (in thousand million lire)

	1950–51	1960–61	Growth 1950/51 to 1960–61	
			absolute	%
Agriculture	242	487	245	101.2
Housing	306	1,008	702	229.4
Transport and communications	278	848	570	205.0
Other sectors	790	1,610	820	103.8
Stocks	173	316	143	144.8
Total	1,789	4,269	2,480	138.6

was accompanied by an unprecedented emigration of agricultural workers: 2.5 million between 1951 and 1967. By 1963 Italy was self-sufficient only in three major agricultural products: rice, fruit and vegetables and wine. She produced less grain, meat, milk and sugar than France and West Germany.[19] The decline of agriculture and its cost in terms of balance of payments were thus the negative counterpart of the low wages policy of the government.

So far I have done nothing more than to establish the role played by the state in the determination of a low-wage system which enabled Italian entrepreneurs to enjoy a competitive advantage with respect to their foreign competitors. Nevertheless, low wages were not the only element in the growth of exports which, in turn were not the only cause of Italian economic development.

The other causes can be established by disaggregating national income statistics.[20] The figures show that between 1951 and 1961 national income grew by 78.3 per cent while consumption grew by only 59.8 per cent. Thus the growth in consumption cannot account for the growth in national income. There must be other factors, namely public spending, exports and gross investments. I have already stated that exports began to play an important role only after 1957–58. As for investments, which grew considerably (138.6 per cent) between 1951 and 1961, we must bear in mind that private, profit-seeking investments were the result of a growth in demand not their cause.

What is it, then, that caused a growth in demand? Apart from foreign demand (which led to exports) we are left with public spending and state investments. As public spending, such as spending on education, health, armed forces, police, did not grow any higher than the national income, the central role must have been that of public investment. Let us examine the figures given in Table 2.3, taking each sector in turn.

Agriculture

Investments in agriculture were state investments or state-induced investments directed towards modernization.

Housing

Investment in this sector was in part due to the need to replenish the housing stock damaged by the war, in part to urbanization. Yet nearly 40 per cent of investment in housing received state subsidies and the financial regulation of housing was such that the state was in virtual control of it. The expansion of the building programme was particularly marked in the period 1950–58 (before the export boom began).[21] Though most housing was built by the private sector, the determinant element was the Housing Plan promulgated by the government in 1949. The effect of public housing policy was to encourage private investment in housing. Much of this was of a speculative nature. It also created a strong link verging on corruption between local authorities and real estate entrepreneurs. Housing plans were not integrated with public transportation. This meant that land distant from the inner city was not developed, thus forcing up the demand for houses as near as possible to the centre of towns and causing overcrowding.[22] Unlike in the UK and the USA there was no major move towards suburban housing. In the UK suburbs developed in part because of an efficient commuting system based on public transport. In the USA, where public transport was often non-existent, the geography of cities and their specific layout permitted the widespread use of private cars. Neither condition applied to Italy. There was no move towards extensive public housing – as there had been in the UK under conservative governments. State intervention in housing enabled the private sector to prosper, but was not coupled with public intervention directed towards improving the negative consequences of these policies.

Transport and communications

This sector includes roads, air transport, railways, radio and television, telephones and the merchant navy which were all state owned or part owned. Here again public investments led the way and interventions such as the motorway programme gave a major impetus to the private sector.

Thus the 'economic miracle' – contrary to received opinion – was in large part due to the state itself, acting not in competition with private enterprise but as a major element in its growth. Neo-liberals were influential among the monetary authorities and in the Bank of Italy, but for essentially political reasons the DC could not behave like a traditional pro-capitalist laissez-faire political party. In order to promote capitalism, it had to use what were in fact 'Italian-style' Keynesian interventionist policies. No commitment to a particular economic school was required, only the necessity to establish and maintain a solid popular consensus. This involved mediating between the private sector and large sectors of the population. Anti-communism and religious piety could not be the only cement for the new political and economic power bloc the DC was forming in Italy. It was necessary to provide jobs in every village and town. Italian state intervention did not follow a 'plan' along the French model of indicative planning. The Italian state intervened massively, but without a plan. Public intervention was conceived as an instrument of social control, as a way of preventing the growth of the Italian Communist Party, as a way of entrenching the electoral supremacy of the DC and as a way of providing private enterprise with favourable conditions for growth. In the formation of this new political power bloc the use of the state was essential.

Even though there was no real plan, the concept of planning as such began to make headway. Even in the early 1950s there was a recognition that the private sector could not 'spontaneously' resolve the dualism between North and South. It was in this context that the left-wing of the DC succeeded in preparing in 1954 the so-called Vanoni Plan (from the name of the Minister under whose auspices the plan was prepared, Ezio Vanoni). This established three general objectives for the next ten years:[23]

1   The creation of 4 million new jobs in the non-agricultural sector.
2   The narrowing if not the outright elimination of the income differential between North and South.
3   Equilibrium in the balance of payments.

In order to reach these objectives the economy would have had to grow at least at 5 per cent a year. In fact the economy grew at a rate slightly higher than this while the balance of payments was in equilibrium after 1958. However, non-agricultural employment grew by only 2.6 million units and the gap between North and South was as wide as ever: southern per capita income as a percentage of average per capita income was 62.7 per cent in 1951. In 1963 the gap was virtually unchanged: 62 per cent.

More effective than any attempt at indicative planning was the rather *ad hoc* method of public intervention which came to prevail. This was achieved through the *Istituto per la Ricostruzione Industriale* (IRI) and the *Ente Nazionale Idrocarburi* (ENI) – the state hydrocarbon company set up in 1953 which provided many of the infrastructures required for industrial growth. Further incentives were provided by the abolition of most protective tariffs in 1957 when Italy became one of the founding members of the European Economic Community (EEC). In order to eliminate the gap between North and South something more than the good intentions of the Vanoni Plan would have been necessary. What was required was that the rate of growth of southern incomes be twice those of the North (i.e. 8 per cent against 4 per cent). In order to achieve this, total investment in the South would have had to be twice as large as investment in the North.[24] Only a command economy could have accomplished this. To achieve the ambitious objectives of the Vanoni Plan, a quite different political framework would have been required. In the circumstances the Vanoni Plan remained a dead letter. The state, however, already controlled much of the 'commanding heights' of the economy through the expanding system of state holdings. In 1952 the IRI was in control of the three 'banks of national interests' and hence of the banking system. Furthermore, it controlled 60 per cent of cast iron and iron mineral production, 60 per cent of armaments and munitions, 25 per cent of precision engineering, 25 per cent of electricity, 60 per cent of the telephone system and the *Radiotelevisione Italiana* (RAI) (then still the only radio broadcasting system, television was introduced later under the RAI).

By 1955 the IRI had 187,000 employees as well as a vast number of shareholdings in private firms from chemicals to paper and printing, from building to motorways and hotels.[25]

By 1962 the IRI was the second industrial group in Europe, second only to the Royal-Dutch-Shell Petroleum Company.[26] At first the expansion of the group followed the principles of intervening to bail out private firms from bankruptcy. It was the creation of the ENI in 1953 which forced IRI to adopt a more dynamic posture.

The motivations for the establishment of ENI differed markedly from those behind the setting up of the IRI. The IRI had been conceived by the fascist state as a temporary 'rescue' operation, while the ENI was created in order to give the state the exclusive rights over the extraction of methane gas in the Po Valley. The opposition of private enterprise was very strong, since this was the first time the state had attempted to acquire full control over a natural resource. The form of this intervention was a company entirely owned by the state. *Ente Nazionale Idrocarburi* was led by an imaginative and dynamic man, Enrico Mattei, a former Resistance partisan and a member of the DC. Mattei had been able to use his connections within the left wing of the DC to protect the ENI, but thanks to the considerable political and economic resources at his disposal he was able to become relatively autonomous from the state. With the birth of ENI, the Italian state-holding form of public intervention became an authentic *system* of state participation in industry, the so-called 'parastate' system. Its expansion coincided with the period of rapid growth of the Italian economy. In 1959 one-fifth of all investments came from the parastate sector. By 1962 it accounted for one-fourth of all investments and for one-third by 1964.[27] The *Ente Nazionale Idrocarburi* expanded horizontally, particularly in those sectors of the economy which were controlled by only one or two private firms who were, therefore, less able to monopolize the market. Hence ENI also fulfilled the function of anti-trust legislation.[28]

The political autonomy of the IRI and the ENI from Parliament was well-established. However, they worked in close connection with the DC, exploiting its factional struggle. Furthermore, because they provided considerable employment and commanded enormous resources, they also provided a terrain for the expansion of party clienteles and the share-out of jobs and positions both within the parties of the governing coalition (the parties of the Centre until 1963) and within the factions of the DC. Thus the guarantee of the permanence of the system of state participation was increasingly connected with the permanence of the DC at the centre of the political system.

There was little cooperation or organic connection between the ENI and the IRI, and neither of them became the vanguard of Italian industrial growth. However, Italy derived considerable benefits from them. Thanks to ENI's attempt to by-pass the oil cartel of the seven largest international oil companies, Italy was able to negotiate direct deals with oil-producing countries and thus obtain access to sources of cheap oil, one of the fundamental conditions for European economic growth. Moreover, the ENI and the IRI reorganized the port of Genoa, strengthened the industrialization of the triangle Venice-Mestre-Porto Marghera, one of the centres of the petrochemical industry and a DC stronghold, improved steel production on the north-western Tirreno coast and developed the petro-chemical industry in Sicily.[29] All this, however, was done in a haphazard way and without any clear national plan for economic development. The achievement of the ENI and the IRI was that they succeeded in establishing those industrial infrastructures (cheap steel, cheap petrochemicals, a motorway system, cheap energy) which allowed rapid Italian economic growth. As the President of the Banca Commerciale (one of the big three banks) Raffaele Mattioli wrote in 1962: 'One of the most remarkable achievements of IRI was this: . . . IRI, without expropriation or nationalizations saved the whole of free enterprise. Practically without noticing it, IRI, while consolidating itself and expanding activities under permanent state control, protected and ensured the effective and long-term survival of private enterprise.'[30]

Thus the public sector, instead of competing against private monopolies and/ or adopting a strategy in favour of collective needs, ensured the expansion of the private sector.[31] The other economic instruments at the disposal of the state, such as monetary policy and fiscal policy were not used to favour of economic growth.

Monetary policy formally depended on the Treasury, but it was in practice under the control of the Bank of Italy which not only was independent from the state but was also run by anti-interventionists. After the deflation of 1947 which contributed to the end of the post-war inflationary spiral and which helped to ensure a regime of low wages, the Bank of Italy continued its restrictive policy until 1955. Between 1955 and 1963 monetary policy was less restrictive. This, in fact, did not matter very much: a restrictive monetary policy seeks to influence interest rates on the assumption that high interest rates will contain demand and thus help to reduce inflation and/or benefit the balance of payments. This depends, however, on the centrality of interest rates and hence of bank lending as the fuel with which to activate economic growth. By the mid-1950s, however, the level of profitability was so high in the private sector that much of new investment was due to the reinvestment of existing profits. In other words firms did not need to borrow because they were able to use their own profit. Thus monetary policy neither helped nor was an obstacle to economic growth.[32]

Fiscal policy proved to be an unreliable instrument mainly because direct taxation, not being very progressive, has little automatic anti-inflationary effects (progressive taxation has a built-in anti-inflationary bias because as incomes are pushed up by inflation a greater proportion of wages and salaries are taxed. This reduces the proportion of disposable income, hence reduces the growth of private consumption and so of demand). This disadvantage could have been partially removed by a prompt intervention of the fiscal authorities, but the fact that the burden of taxation in Italy took the form of indirect taxation reduced the clout of fiscal policies. This also meant that profits and incomes from self-employment were not hit as much as they could have, not least because there was widespread evasion. Again this was not a 'natural' factor. It is, rather, a conscious decision of the authorities. The tax-evaders were (and are) the professional bourgeoisie, the self-employed – whether dentists or plumbers – small and medium-sized entrepreneurs and others who constituted the social and electoral base of the DC.[33] It was thus essentially for political reasons that monetary rather than fiscal policy was the main instrument of economic policy of Italian governments. It should be added that most European countries favoured monetary controls, particularly Belgium and West Germany, while the UK stood out alone for relying heavily on fiscal manipulation. Other countries adopted some elements of planning either by sponsoring investments (France) or some forms of incomes policy (Sweden, the Netherlands).[34]

I have so far illustrated the state's contribution to economic growth and sought to account for the kind of intervention and 'non-intervention' that paved the way for the 'economic miracle'. At least until 1960 there was very little opposition to the government by the trade unions. The left, excluded from power and increasingly divided, could do very little. The trade unions were divided too and had to face the ever-growing influx of non-unionized labour from the countryside and a level of unemployment which constituted a formidable obstacle to militant trade unionism. But what of private enterprise? While from the technical and economic point of view it was able to modernize itself and to become more efficient and more productive, the same cannot be said for its politics. Its fundamental outlook was profoundly anti-trade union, an understandable policy but also a shortsighted one for it should have realized that Italian trade unions would eventually be able to reassert themselves, particularly as the era of massive unemployment was coming to an end and the southern reserve of labour was being reduced. The only long-term trade union policy private industry adopted was that of trying to deepen the divisions within the labour movement: it sought to strengthen the Catholic trade union (the CISL) and the social-democratic one (the UIL) against the CGIL (socialist and communist) by sacking communist shop stewards and trade unionists or shifting them to the most demanding jobs or to self-enclosed sections of the plants.

The short-sightedness of Italian entrepreneurs also manifested itself in their policies with respect to the parastate sector: they opposed ideologically any extension of the state in the economy. I have already mentioned in Chapter 1 the Sinigaglia Plan on steel which encountered the outright opposition of the employers' association, the *Confindustria*, and of the steel tycoon Giorgio Falck. Such opposition grew as Enrico Mattei, the chairman of ENI, decided to expand horizontally into territory dominated by the giant Montecatini: petrochemicals, plastic and synthetic rubber. The *Confindustria* even allied itself with the seven giant oil companies, the 'Seven Sisters', against ENI when this moved into oil.[35] Yet, as we have seen, the growth of the state sector was to the economic advantage of private enterprises or, at least, of some of them. By the end of this period of exceptional growth the Italian economy was dominated by giant private firms: Edison in electricity, Fiat in cars, Olivetti in typewriters and office machines, Pirelli in rubber products, Snia Viscosa in textiles, Montecatini in chemicals.

The process of economic concentration which accompanied this growth also took the form of transforming many small and medium-sized firms into real dependencies of the large firms. This was the case particularly in the car industry dominated by Fiat. In fact any study on political power in Italy must give a major place to Fiat, which in this period became a vast empire whose economic decisions would influence politics as well as economics. In the first place, Fiat increased production by 400 per cent between 1950 and 1961; it was an authentic monopolist as it controlled 90 per cent of car sales in Italy (no single car manufacturing company in the world had such a formidable base in its home market). Productivity at Fiat increased by 126 per cent between 1950 and 1960.[36] These figures still do not give us an idea of the political power wielded by Fiat. It has been calculated that by 1963 20 per cent of investments in sectors other than the car-manufacturing one were directly due to Fiat. Not only small and medium-sized firms were affected but also large ones: ENI, the steel industry, chemicals. Every 1,000 lire produced by Fiat generated an increment of production of nearly 2,000 lire in the economy as a whole and an increase in exports of 210 lire.[37] As the car industry expanded it created greater demand for motorways, for oil, plastics, rubber, steel. In a sense it could be said that Fiat 'planned' the Italian economy. Furthermore, Japanese cars were successfully kept out of Italy until the 1980s.

Finally, profits between 1953 and 1960 increased by 45 per cent in the car industry and by 54 per cent in the chemical industry which thus established themselves as the leading sectors because the average growth of profit for that period was 28 per cent. But it must not be thought that the development of the Italian economy was a great victory for private capitalism alone. Landed property and real estate companies grew in unison with private industrial capital and became ever more intertwined with it.

Profits grew so rapidly in that period that not all entrepreneurs reinvested them in industry. Many sought to use them for speculative reasons in the land and housing market. This was also true of self-employed professionals who had a considerable amount of cash at their disposal thanks to widespread tax evasion. Urbanization led to an ever-expanding demand for housing in urban centres. I have already explained that, unlike the UK and the USA, urban centres were the most sought-after place of residence. This means that housing decreased in value in proportion to its distance from the centre. As cities expanded the value of the agricultural land immediately surrounding it became more expensive because it was in the front line of future housing investment. As it is sold by farmers and bought by real estate speculators it provoked 'ripple' effects in both directions: it forced up land and house values all the way to the centre of the city as well as towards the outlying agricultural land. Thus the layout of the city reflected the class structures: in the centre, the rich, the professional bourgeoisie and senior bureaucrats, then, in successive concentric circles, those employed in the tertiary sector of the economy, white-collar workers, then factories and factory workers living in public housing in the outskirts and then, finally, the agricultural areas and the farmers.[38] Of course this is the general pattern: rent control legislation ensured that there were still pockets of low-income families living in the centre of cities, but there was certainly no room for the masses of agricultural workers looking for jobs in industry.

Private investment in housing with state and local subsidies as well as tax concessions contributed to the asymmetrical development of luxury housing as opposed to low-income groups. This is understandable in the absence of a determined effort by central government for a more balanced approach to housing: to build a luxury house in the centre of town created proportionately more profits than building homes for industrial workers. Thus the years of the 'economic miracle' if they were good years for industrialists were golden years for real estate entrepreneurs. I mentioned that profits between 1953 and 1960 in the car and petrochemical industries increased by about 50 per cent, but average rents in the whole of the country increased by 100 per cent and in northern urban areas they increased by 300 per cent. This occurred in a period when retail food prices increased by 33 per cent and wholesale prices by 13 per cent.[39] Wages in the non-agricultural sector, on the other hand, increased by only 23 per cent between 1955 and 1960.[40] This was the economic balance sheet of the relation of forces in Italian society as the 'economic miracle' was drawing to a close.

Endnotes

1 For a general analysis of Italian economic growth which gives due weight to a variety of factors including agriculture see Sapelli 1994a.
2 De Cecco 1971.
3 Salvati 1973.
4 D'Antonio 1973, pp. 12–14.
5 For an overview in a truly comparative framework of the entire post-war experience see Sapelli 1995b.
6 Castronovo 1975, p. 408.
7 Graziani et al. 1969; see also Graziani 1969; and his introduction in Graziani 1971. The export-led model is based on the pioneering work of Kindleberger 1964. The best application of the export-led model to Italy available in English is Stern 1967.
8 Salvati 1977, p. 103.
9 Castronovo 1975, p. 407.
10 My figures on the basis of the discussion and the figures in D'Antonio 1973, p. 202.
11 Castronovo 1975, p. 407.
12 De Cecco 1971, p. 982.
13 Allum 1972, pp. 118–19.
14 D'Antonio 1973, p. 236.
15 Ibid., p. 238.
16 Graziani 1971, pp. 55–7.
17 Fabiani 1977, p. 158.

18 D'Antonio 1977, pp. 49–50.
19 Coda-Nunziante and De Nigris 1970, pp. 200–5, also in Graziani 1972, pp. 174–7.
20 The following remarks and discussion on the composition of investments are based on a memorandum by G. Ackley published for the first time in Graziani 1972, pp. 156–65. Salvati 1977, p. 104 makes the same point.
21 Castronovo 1975, p. 404.
22 See Graziani 1972, p. 20.
23 Valli 1979, p. 110.
24 Napoleoni in Graziani 1972, p. 201.
25 Castronovo 1975, p. 422.
26 Ibid., p. 425.
27 Colajanni 1976, pp. 17–8.
28 Castronovo 1975, p. 422.
29 Ibid., p. 426.
30 Quoted in Villari 1975, vol. 2, p. 672.
31 Castronovo 1975, p. 480.
32 D'Antonio 1977, p. 44.
33 Ibid., p. 46.
34 Aldcroft 1978, p. 190.
35 Castronovo 1975, p. 421.
36 Figures in Castronovo 1975, pp. 429–30.
37 Ibid., p. 431.
38 Silva and Targetti 1972, p. 24.
39 Figures in Castronovo 1975, pp. 419–20.
40 Source: ILO 1965.

Chapter 3

From 'miracle' to crisis, 1963–1969

The crisis of the system of alliances based on the centrist coalition led by the Christian Democratic Party (DC) began not after the end of the 'economic miracle', but in the middle of it. Towards the end of the 1950s the DC increasingly sought to reach an understanding with the Socialist Party (PSI) whose pact of unity with the Communist Party (PCI) had been rescinded following the events of 1956 (de-Stalinization and the Soviet invasion of Hungary). In February 1960, fearing a new coalition based on a pact between the PSI and the DC, the Liberal Party (PLI) forced a government crisis with the avowed intention of sabotaging the negotiations and strengthening the right wing of the DC. In April of that year, Fernando Tambroni formed a government entirely made up of Christian Democrats. In the Chamber of Deputies that government was able to obtain a majority only thanks to the support of the Monarchist Party and of the neo-fascists. Throughout Italy there was a strong popular reaction led by communists and socialists. The police reacted and fired on the crowd in several cities. The Tambroni government fell thus demonstrating the impossibility of reorganizing the alliance system of the DC on the basis of support from the far right. Thus there could now be only one alternative to centrist coalitions: the 'opening to the left,' i.e. a DC-PSI coalition. These were the main steps towards the 'centre-left' government:

1 22 July 1960: Amintore Fanfani (DC) formed his third government with the parliamentary support of republicans and social democrats. At the last minute the PSI abstained.
2 March 1961: the PSI approved the general policy of the 'opening to the left'.
3 January 1962: the DC approved the general policy of the 'opening to the left'.
4 February 1962: Amintore Fanfani formed his fourth government with the abstention of the PSI.
5 21 September 1962: the Chamber of Deputies approved the nationalization of electricity, the price demanded by the PSI to form a centre-left government with the DC.

6 Following an increase in communist votes at the elections of April 1963,
   the right wing of the DC launched a counter-offensive to prevent Fanfani
   and Aldo Moro (the leading proponents of the centre-left) reaching
   agreement with the PSI.
7 Giovanni Leone (DC) led a transitional government made up of Christian
   Democrats only (Summer 1963).
8 October 1963: the PSI approved the formation of centre-left government.
9 4 December 1963: the new centre-left government coalition was launched
   with Aldo Moro as Prime Minister and Pietro Nenni, leader of the PSI,
   as his deputy. The left wing of the PSI, hostile to the alliance with the
   centre, formed a new party, the Socialist Party of Proletarian Unity
   (PSIUP).

Thus it took more than three years to establish the new centre-left government.
The dates show that the initial impulse for this realignment cannot be traced to
the end of the 'economic miracle'. Nevertheless, there is no doubt that one of the
causes of the move away from the centrist coalition which dominated Italy since
1947 was the revitalization of the trade union movement in 1960. The more progressive tendencies of the DC realized that it was necessary to take on board some
of the demands of the trade unions and to do so in a way that would divide the PSI
from the PCI. The incorporation of the socialists in the sphere of government as
junior partners in a coalition in which two minor parties would also be present (the
Republican Party and the Social Democratic Party) meant that the DC was prepared
to share some of the power it had accumulated with others, if, by doing so, it could
be guaranteed the continuation of its position of centrality in the political arena.
The isolation of the communists was one of the aims of the formation of the new
coalition, but as the 'economic miracle' was coming to an end it became increasingly clear that the process of economic development had left open a number of
problems whose resolution entailed the expansion of the social basis of government
and a commitment to social reforms.

That the existence of unresolved problems was an acknowledged fact can be
seen by looking at the literature of the period. In their book *Ideas for Economic
Planning* two of the leading proponents of the centre-left coalition, the economists
Giorgio Fuà and Paolo Sylos-Labini pinpointed the problems with great accuracy.[1]
They recognized that one of the achievements of economic development in the
1950–63 period was the diminution of unemployment. Nevertheless, they pointed
out, structural distortions continued to pervade all fields of economic activity, from
agriculture to employment, from consumption to the differential in incomes between the various regions of the country, from the retail sector to industry. The data
confirm the existence and persistence of this gap, whether we look at incomes,
production or productivity. Besides these well-known structural problems there
also was a new predicament, namely inflation: in 1960 it was 2.7 per cent, in 1961
2.8 per cent, in 1962, 5.1 per cent and in 1963 7.6 per cent. Furthermore, even
though total productivity in manufacturing industry grew at a rapid pace for the first
time since the war such growth was inferior to the growth of total wages (i.e. basic

Table 3.1 A comparison of unemployment rates in Italy, the UK and West Germany, 1955–64 (%)

Year	West Germany	UK	Italy
1955	5.1	1.1	7.6
1956	4.0	1.2	9.4
1957	3.4	1.5	8.2
1958	3.5	2.0	6.6
1959	2.4	2.2	5.6
1960	1.2	1.6	4.2
1961	0.8	1.5	3.5
1962	0.7	2.0	3.1
1963	0.8	2.4	2.5
1964	0.7	1.7	2.7

Source: *Bulletin of Labour Statistics 1965*, International Labour Office, Geneva

wages plus any addition to the pay packet due to productivity bonuses, overtime, etc.).[2] What this means is that the link between productivity and wages had been broken. Until then wages grew at a lower rate than productivity enabling the subsequent growth of profits to finance the improvements in plants and machinery and hence productivity. The only way to increase both wages and productivity is through technological innovation. For the Italian economy, open to the world as it was and is, this is an expensive strategy: technologically Italy was and has remained, relatively speaking, backward. Know-how had to be imported; innovations come from outside and have to be paid for, deepening Italy's dependence on international constraints.[3]

Thus the crisis which underlined the political realignment to the left had not only structural aspects but also contingent ones: a crisis of profitability which led to the end of the self-financing of enterprises. The revival of working-class militancy had led to a profit squeeze. In 1962 the trade unions had sufficiently recovered their strength (partly due to the full employment conditions achieved in the North) to obtain the first large-scale wage rises since the post-war period: while the average annual increase in wage rates was around 4.4 per cent in the 1954–61 period, it jumped to 10.7 per cent in 1962 and to 14.7 per cent the following year.

Let us now examine the elements which brought the 'economic miracle' to an end in greater detail. It has been suggested that one of the causes of the end of the 'miracle' was the fact that Italy had reached a situation of full employment. Yet in 1963 Italy still had 2.5 per cent unemployment and if we compare Italian developments with West Germany and the UK we can see that it had still a relatively high level of spare labour (see Table 3.1). What these figures do not show and cannot show are changes in 'disguised' unemployment, i.e. that the decrease in unemployment is due not to the growth of employment but to the lowering of the participation of the population in the labour force (e.g. women abandoning the labour force) or due to the increase in emigration facilitated by the free market of labour established by the EEC. In other words, the increase in wages was not due to full

Table 3.2 Trade union militancy and wages, 1960–71

Year	Yearly percentage increase in real wages	Yearly percentage increase in money wages	Million of hours lost in strikes
1960	5.4	10.8	46.3
1961	5.9	11.1	79.1
1962	6.9	16.4	181.7
1963	11.1	21.6	91.2
1964	7.1	11.9	104.7
1965	4.1	5.5	55.9
1966	4.9	6.9	115.8
1967	5.1	10.6	68.5
1968	5.9	8.7	83.9
1969	5.4	10.1	302.6
1970	14.1	16.9	146.2
1971	9.1	15.1	103.6

Source: ISTAT

employment per se, but to the fact that emigration deprived the Italian North of a proportion of the reserve male labour force.[4]

Furthermore, there was a downturn in Italian agriculture and contraction in employment in sectors such as clothing and shoe manufacturing. This meant that employment decreased in sectors employing marginalized and casual labour while employment increased in the 'modern' sectors which were better organized from a trade union point of view. It is this pattern in the labour market which caused the upturn in wages.[5] We can also look at it from another point of view: as women left the labour force, families depended increasingly on a single breadwinner, usually male, and this stimulated the militancy of the male labour force. 'Full employment' had been reached but only in the North, among the male labour force and in the advanced sectors of the economy. Table 3.2 shows the effects of this renewal of trade union militancy on wages. As we can see there were two wage explosions in this period, 1969 and 1970, both due to the trade union militancy of the preceding year.

The effect of the strikes of 1962 was to diminish the effectiveness of one of the conditions which had made Italian enterprises competitive: low wages. Hitherto Italian enterprises had been able to increase production through an increase in employment, now there was essentially only one avenue open (apart from causing a slow-down in wage increases in a tightening labour market): the expansion of production through an expansion in productivity. Wages in 1962 and 1963 had for the first time outstripped productivity: the answer of Italian capitalism in the successive years would be to try to increase productivity without increasing employment. What the period 1963–69 showed was that it was no longer possible to solve the problems of the Italian economy thanks to the passivity of the labour movement.

Italy had entered the EEC with some evident structural handicaps: constant emigration, scarcity of primary products, particularly sources of energy, low productivity in agriculture and backward technology. This was compensated by the ability of Italian entrepreneurs to contain costs thanks to the low level of technological innovation necessary to produce household electrical goods and other Italian exports, and thanks to low wages.[6] This, however, left Italy dangerously exposed to foreign competition from Third World countries (which could compete on the terrain of low technology and cheap labour), and from the advanced countries, such as Japan and West Germany, which were able to establish a close link between exporting ability and technological progress.[7] Italy resorted to a dual strategy – deflation and state intervention.

While the new ruling centre-left coalition was planning a systematic intervention in the economy, the Bank of Italy was continuing its traditional deflationary line in direct continuity with the Einaudi policies of 1947. In September 1963, less than two months before the official entry of the PSI into the governing coalition, the Bank of Italy imposed a harsh credit squeeze. Its effects were immediate. Firms found it more difficult to borrow from the banks. Investment decreased by 8.6 per cent in 1964 and by 7.5 per cent in 1965.[8] Demand decreased and a depression ensued with consequent negative effects on employment which fell by 2.5 per cent by 1965 (by 4 per cent in the industrial sector alone).[9] There was a slow-down in internal migration and a decrease in the share of gross national product going to wages. As usual, those firms which were hit the most were those orientated towards the home market, while firms orientated towards exports such as chemicals and engineering were hit the least.[10] Those who favoured the credit squeeze as a way of tackling inflation assumed that inflation was principally due to wage rises and, as the wage rise of 1962–63 seemed to have been a once and for all affair, they assumed that the inflation spiral was a short-term phenomenon which could be contained by a drastic if painful credit squeeze. Others believed that inflation and the accompanying balance of payments deficit were due to structural imbalances in the Italian economy and the lack of planning. Among the latter we find the chief supporters and proponents of the centre-left.

From the point of view of the authorities the credit squeeze had had the merit of slowing down inflation, readjusting the balance of payments and, more importantly, dampening down the militancy of the trade unions which renewed the labour contracts of 1966 with remarkable acquiescence. Nevertheless, it had become accepted in government circles that it was necessary to initiate some form of planning. Readers will recollect that the Vanoni Plan of 1954 (see Chapter 2) had remained a dead letter; however, planning as a concept had not been abandoned and even before the formal launching of the centre-left, the Budget Minister, Giuseppe Pella, appointed in March 1961 a commission chaired by G.U. Papi which included both entrepreneurs and trade unionists. This was the beginning of a long saga of attempted planning which I shall summarize.

The Papi Commission was based on the concept of indicative planning which involved the projection of future public spending and state intervention so that entrepreneurs could tailor their plans in accordance with expected government policy. By August 1962 the framework established for the Papi Commission was abandoned as inadequate for the kind of intervention the economy required. The new

Budget Minister, the republican Ugo La Malfa, in a famous 'Note' appended to his main report identified three structural imbalances in the Italian economy: between agriculture and industry, between North and South and between public and private consumption. To resolve these imbalances the following framework was suggested:[11]

1 To cut down funds given to projects which did not expand productive capacity (e.g. public housing).
2 To increase forced saving through taxation.
3 To plan the quantity and the direction of both private and public investment.
4 To obtain the cooperation of the trade-union movement for a policy of wage restraint in exchange for an improvement in social services (a proposal which would have required, presumably, a modification of item 1).

This was the first time a leading government spokesman discussed the structural problems of the Italian economy and proposed ways of eliminating them. The domination of liberal economists seemed to have come to an end. La Malfa appointed three commissions: one to deal with tax reforms, one to deal with monopolies and the third was to become the foremost planning body to be chaired by Pasquale Saraceno, a Catholic economist deeply committed to planning. The following may give the reader an idea of the saga of Italian planning in the 1960s.

The Saraceno Commission met throughout 1963 and included among its members experts, industrialists and trade unionists. By January 1964 the report was ready and the new Budget Minister, the socialist Antonio Giolitti, accepted it in June 1964. The plan, now called the Giolitti Plan could not be approved in Parliament because, by then, there had been a change in government. Finally, the new government (still a centre-left coalition) appointed a new Budget Minister, Giovanni Pieraccini, who accepted the plan in 1966. This plan, now the Pieraccini Plan, was approved by Parliament in July *1967* though the plan was intended for the five years from 1966 to 1970. The Pieraccini Plan went beyond the framework established by La Malfa: it dealt not only with the 'three structural imbalances' but also with the question of 'social investments' (e.g. health and education). The aims of the Pieraccini Plan were the following:

1 Full employment. This would entail an increase in the non-agricultural labour force of 1.4 million.
2 The increase in the rate of growth of agricultural production and the narrowing of the gap between farm and non-farm incomes.
3 The reduction of regional imbalance through the creation of a proportionately greater number of industrial jobs in the South than in the North.
4 A new pattern of employment which would favour the satisfaction of collective needs over private ones.

In order to achieve this it would have been necessary to obtain an annual increase in incomes of 5 per cent while maintaining price stability, balance of payment equilibrium and free trade. The plan had not been conceived as a self-contained piece of legislation. It was the equivalent of a new economic deal, an attempt to reverse the direction of economic affairs by obtaining the consensus of those strata that had not significantly benefited from the 'economic miracle'. It signified, in other words, a fundamental change in economic conception symbolized by the debate over the interpretation of Article 81 of the Constitution. This article established that any bill entailing new expenditure must indicate how the money was to be raised. Until 1961 the ruling interpretation was the liberal one, namely, that there could be no deficit spending, in other words the government could not borrow in order to cover the proposed expenditure except in the short term (i.e. until 'real money' would be raised from, say, taxation). The liberal economist and politician Luigi Einaudi had asked for the insertion of Article 81 in the Constitution specifically in order to ensure that politicians would not seek popularity and votes through the use of public expenditure.[12] In 1961 this was challenged by the Keynesian-interventionist front led by La Malfa. The new interpretation asserted that a balanced budget could be obtained through deficit spending provided this sought to stimulate the use of unused national resources, thus increasing the wealth of the nation and, indirectly, the Treasury.[13]

Savers, however, were deserting the national money market and were beginning to send their cash abroad. So while the state needed to borrow considerable sums, savers exported their money. What was needed was a new system to channel funds into banks and direct them towards both public and private investments. The state, now committed to planning, could have created a new institution which would have supervised the financial intermediaries (banks and financial institutions). No such institution was created. Instead the defeated neo-liberals inside the Bank of Italy were able to ensure that the control of the financial system would remain in the hands of the Bank of Italy.[14] Thus the planning debate of the early 1960s was resolved with a political compromise and, although the planners seemed to emerge as the victors, the neo-liberals kept a right of veto through their control of the financial system. The effects of the compromise were, as we have seen, the apparent contradiction between the policies of a centre-left government, which sought to intervene in a reforming direction and the credit squeeze of 1963 imposed by the Bank of Italy. Short-term policy remained under the control of the conservative elements (the anti-interventionist neo-liberals), the long term was left to the reformists: the 'future' not the present was to be planned by the interventionists. Unable to establish any link between the present and the future, between short-term crisis management and long-term economic restructuring, the Centre-Left government was never able to implement its proposed reforms except for the nationalization of electricity. But even this reform resulted in an unexpected compromise between reformists and anti-planners: generous cash payments for the shares hitherto held by the electricity companies.[15]

The vast amount of cash thus generated provided the impetus for a spate of mergers and takeovers. The creation of the new state electricity company (ENEL) brought the telephone system under state ownership. Then ENEL began to diversify outside the electricity sector and to behave as other state holding company: it acquired shareholdings in Olivetti and in Montedison (itself a result of the 1966 merger between the chemical giant Montecatini and the former electricity giant Edison). The formation of ENEL gave added impetus to the expansion of the state-holding system, gave rise to a new generation of state entrepreneurs whose names would dominate Italian industry in the 1960s and 1970s: Giuseppe Petrilli, Pietro Sette and Eugenio Cefis. At the same time the DC extended its control over the state sector partly because its base in agriculture was decreasing and partly because control over a sector of industry could help the party to satisfy the employment aspirations of migrant workers from the South.[16] Thus a reform which would have had to play a leading role in the restructuring of the Italian economic system, played a far more decisive role in the expansion of the power of the DC.

The interconnection between political power and economic intervention was just as visible in the domain of state intervention in agriculture. The first agricultural plan, or 'Green Plan' was promulgated in June 1961. Its aims were to consolidate efficient farms and to raise both productivity and employment on the land – an unlikely event in the conditions of the time.[17] The funds which the state was ready to provide were very large. Nevertheless, small farmers were unable to make ends meet and still found it preferable to leave their lands and go to the cities to find employment. Thus the first Green Plan did not achieve its formal objectives: what it did was to enable some southern farmers to survive and thus contain the flood of emigration. In any case the solution of the 'Southern Question' should not have been seen purely in terms of agriculture, but only in terms of the correct relation between agriculture and industry. Two possible strategies were discussed in the early 1960s:

1   Agriculture as the foundation of economic development.
2   Agriculture to be subordinated to export-orientated firms.

The second strategy – which assumed that international demand would go on expanding – was eventually adopted. Agricultural productivity would grow not because of structural intervention in agriculture, but simply because internal emigration would continue towards export-orientated firms. Public expenditure would ensure the location of industry in the strongest areas while agriculture would be helped only where it was already efficient (as in the first Green Plan).

As we noted in the preceding chapters the agrarian reform of 1950 had resulted in the development of small private holdings. The reform and subsequent funding had also enabled the old agrarian classes to transform themselves into capitalist farmers. They managed to retain a modicum of competitiveness within the EEC even though they were unable to meet national needs. What happened in the 1960s is that international factors became even more important for agriculture. The development of the Common Agricultural Policy (CAP) had a decisive impact in Italy. The CAP's pricing policy were applied throughout the Common Market in a homogeneous manner, but its effects were very differentiated: it affected farms of varying sizes in different ways.[18] The CAP did not help Italy because, unlike in France and West Germany, Italian agriculture was polarized between many small farms and a few very large farms. Small farmers could not apply large-scale economies and enjoy the advantages of CAP pricing policies. Furthermore, the CAP pricing policy favoured crops which could be found in northern and western Europe rather than in Mediterranean Europe. While northern Italian export-orientated industry derived considerable benefits from the EEC, no equivalent benefits were available for agriculture either in terms of modernization or improvements of agricultural incomes. Furthermore, Italy had to contribute to the agricultural funds and hence to the support of the French and Dutch farm prices where agriculture was and is more efficient than in Italy. The expansion of the EEC regional budget which would devote funds to the poorer areas of Europe was opposed by West Germany and France. Moreover, in the 1970s, there was increased competition for this fund because of the enlargement of the EEC to other countries with marked regional problems: the UK, Ireland and Denmark.[19] In fact it would be difficult to conceive of a free-trade policy which would not cause an expansion of strong areas and contraction of weak areas.

As a result of these policies thousands of small farms disappeared while the larger farms increased their size by a total of 800,000 hectares. In 1950 the agrarian reform had distributed 700,000 hectares, taking them away from the landlord.[20] Ten to twenty years later these were won back by landlords now transformed into capitalist farmers.

The subordination of agricultural development to industrial development was no longer the unintended effect of the laissez-faire policies of the 1950s. It had now become the overt strategy of the interventionism of the 1960s. This entailed a novel approach towards the South: industrialization. The new industrial policy for the South had two political motivations:[21]

1   To enable local entrepreneurs to become fully-fledged industrialists instead of remaining artisans or farmers.
2   To attract northern investment.

This new strategy was based on a system of incentives which established in the South favoured areas of development for major public works. These, located in Bari, Brindisi, Cagliari, Salerno and Taranto, drained off aid from other areas, thus creating a new dualism between development and underdevelopment within the South. These large public projects were very often the creation of state enterprises. The IRI established, through its Italsider company, giant steelworks near Taranto. The ENI set up large oil refineries in Sicily. These large-scale technologically advanced plants had no connection with the rest of the southern economy. They were a sort of enclave with little or no contact with small local firms. They established, on the contrary, a direct connection with the North. Their economic isolation from the rest of the southern economy earned them the appellation of 'cathedrals in the desert'. Furthermore, these firms were able to obtain considerable funds from the state in the form of subsidies, low-interest or interest-free loans as well as direct grants as a part of invested capital (in some areas as high as 20 per cent).[22]

Given such financial benefits, large private firms were quick to reach an entente with those who controlled public spending and regional aid to the South. Thus the growth of state-dependent southern social strata which established clientelist relations

Table 3.3 Employment in the South, 1951–70

	1951		1961		1970	
	000s	%	000s	%	000s	%
Agriculture	2,774.3	51.9	2,203.5	39.4	1,615.0	29.0
Industry (inc. building and construction)	1,210.3	22.6	1,601.1	29.0	1,795.1	32.3
Tertiary	983.8	18.4	1,282.2	23.0	1,542.7	27.7
Public employees	378.7	7.1	482.2	8.6	611.4	11.0
Total	5,347.1	100	5,588	100	5,564.2	100
	100					

Source: D'Antonio (1973), p. 256

with the governing groups went hand in hand with the partial industrialization of the South. The clientele system was not a remnant of an underdeveloped society. On the contrary, it fed on and grew with state intervention in the South. The *Cassa per il Mezzogiorno* began to finance basic large-scale enterprises, both private and public: electricity, steel, gas, chemical, paper – all industries which are fairly capital intensive and which contribute little to employment.[23]

Investment in the South did little to mop up unemployment. This problem was tackled through the expansion of the bureaucracy and of the public purse. By the beginning of the 1970s, 30.4 per cent of all salaries and wages in the South were due to employment in the public administration sector, while the Italian average was 20 per cent. Conversely, while in Italy as a whole industrial wages and salaries were 47 per cent of all incomes, in the South this was only 33 per cent.[24] Clearly the chief source of employment in the South was, increasingly, the central and 'local' state, as is illustrated in Table 3.3.

The massive decrease in employment in agriculture was partly due to the change in emphasis in the direction of state intervention in the agricultural sector. This became clearer with the second Green Plan (1966): small farmers were to be neglected and public intervention was increasingly directed towards electrification and irrigation projects which, in practice, favoured existing entrepreneurs in rural areas rather than the marginal farmer.[25]

Another channel had to be found for small farmers. The funds which had been withdrawn from the agricultural budget reappeared in new forms, such as invalidity pensions, which increased at a phenomenal rate in the mid-1960s; it is easy to understand why. Unlike old-age pensions, invalidity pensions depend on 'subjective' factors such as a certificate from a compliant doctor employed by the pension fund controlled by the small farmers and funded by the state. By 1974 the pension funds paid invalidity pensions to nearly 1.5 million small farmers against 625,000 for old-age pensions.[26] That invalidity pensions were used for political reasons is evident: while in the northern province of Mantova in 1973 there were only 53 invalidity pensions for every 100 old-age pensions given to small farmers, in the southern provinces of Enna, Benevento, Campobasso and Frosinone (to mention but a few) the ratio was 10,000 disability pensions for every 100 old-age pensions.[27] Between 1970 and 1975 public expenditure on all pensions trebled and amounted to more than 10 per cent of GDP. By 1975 there were 12.6 million pensioners of which 5 million were in receipt of disablement pensions.[28]

The relative failure of industrialization in the South and the diminution of employment on the land thus brought about a considerable expansion of the 'protected sector' in the southern economy: a sector where the state played the leading role through direct use of public spending (pensions), through tax concessions for the location of industry, through direct state investment (IRI and ENI) and through the expansion of the bureaucracy. The centre-left coalition decision to resolve the 'Southern Question' quickly became the political cover for an operation which sought to protect the South from the worst consequences of the end of the 'economic miracle'. The growth in public expenditure was increasingly seen as proof of the lack of 'industrial vocation' of the South. There were demands that intervention in the South should stop and that the state should concentrate on the North.

Yet all the efforts of the state did little to protect the South. The recession of 1964–65 (engineered by the credit squeeze of 1963) meant that there was little northern investment in the South in spite of state aid, of low wages and weak trade unions. There was instead a flight of northern capital to the EEC. Industrial concentration in the North meant that it obtained a proportionately larger share of public funding for works programmes than the South. In 1965, the *Cassa per il Mezzogiorno* expanded its financing only after the North had been given guarantees of similar state funding. The drop in national demand meant that northern industry attempted to expand its trade with the South, thus weakening those southern industries which already existed and whose conditions of existence depended on local demand.[29] The income gap between North and South was still large in 1967 although, when compared with 1950, it was narrowing: if in 1950 southern per capita income was 40 per cent of northern per capita income, by 1967 this had become 48 per cent.[30]

Northern industry did not react to the decrease in profitability through an increase in investment in the South, exporting capital. At home the crisis of profitability was resolved not through capital investment but by the reorganization of the work process: more overtime and a speed-up in assembly lines. This was the basic strategy adopted to resolve the crisis.[31] It depended on the possibility of 'squeezing' the existing labour force. This strategy depended, in turn, on the fact that the trade union militancy of 1962 had been short-lived and that the reserve of labour available was still considerable.

The fact that even state investment in the South was capital intensive meant that internal migration continued even though there was comparatively little increase in employment in the North.[32] This can only mean that existing employed labour in the North was being displaced by fresh recruits.

The chief type of labour to be displaced was female labour. According to official figures female employment decreased by 1.1 million units between 1959 and 1967. Female labour was expelled from agriculture because of the general shrinkage of employment in agriculture. It was expelled from industry because of the competition from migrant male labour. Male labour in agriculture did not decrease at the same rate because the effects of state intervention and of EEC policies (the Mansholt Plan) was to favour the expansion of capitalist farms which determined a growth in the number of day labourers. The proletarianization of the rural labour force thus followed the pattern of employment in industry: a preponderance of male labour. Furthermore, the crisis in the textile industry, a traditionally large employer of female labour, accelerated this tendency. It should be added that Italy was the only industrialized country in Europe to exhibit the dual feature of growing industrialization and a decrease in female employment. Massimo Paci, author of the pioneering study on the structure of the labour market in Italy in the 1960s, explains that internal migration did not raise overall activity rates (i.e. the proportion of the employed labour force to the total population) precisely because of this substitution effect.[33] Furthermore, he shows that migration also contributed to the lowering of activity rates in the South: often male workers left behind their families – women, children and the old. Many of them, deprived of their most productive workers, could no longer fend for themselves. They became increasingly dependent on remittances from the North and state aid. Even when the entire family moved to the North the situation did not improve from the point of view of female participation in the labour market. There were limited opportunities in non-agricultural jobs due to the lack of technical training for women, the inadequacy of social services such as child care and the shrinking of handicraft activities and of the textile industries. There was also an aversion to working outside the home both on the part of women themselves and of their male family members.[34]

Behind the expulsion of the female labour force from production there were not only factors of an 'objective' economic nature and ideological elements ensuring the continuing subordination of women, there were also political decisions. Given the considerable increase in public spending and the outright creation of semi-fictitious employment by the state, one could have expected that some resources be diverted to the creation of more employment opportunities for women through a network of child care centres and training programmes. Yet this occurred much later. At this stage one can do little more than speculate as to the political reasons behind this inadequate response. Could it be that the ruling coalition feared that a rapid entry of female labour into production would further disrupt the foundation of the family (already profoundly modified by industrialization and emigration) thus generating social pressures difficult to control? Or that the tensions provoked by higher male unemployment would have had greater social and political consequences? In other European countries female employment was on the increase throughout the 1960s. Italy was the main exception to this rule.

The specificity of the Italian case is probably due to the concurrence of ideological, social and political factors which did not exist to the same extent in comparable countries such as France. But it was not only female labour which was excluded, the same fate was suffered by male labour over 45 years of age and below 25. The changes in the structure of activity rate per age and sex can be seen from the figures in Table 3.4.

Table 3.4 Labour participation rates by age group and sex in 1960 and 1970

Age group	Male		Female	
	1960	**1970**	**1960**	**1970**
14–19	67.3	38.4	45.3	28.9
20–24	78.3	69.4	48.3	43.3
25–29	96.2	93.9	36.2	33.2
30–34	98.1	98.2	34.4	27.7
35–39	97.6	98.2	34.3	29.9
40–44	96.7	97.3	33.5	30.8
45–49	96.0	95.0	31.9	29.2
50–54	92.8	90.7	30.5	25.9
55–59	86.5	81.1	24.2	18.3
60–64	60.5	48.2	17.9	10.6
65+	30.0	12.9	8.5	2.6
Total	81.2	73.1	31.7	24.8

Source: Podbielski (1974), p. 127, ISTAT figures.

While the decrease in female participation in the labour force was partially counteracted by the rise in male incomes, the decrease in employment opportunities for young people took two forms: one 'private', that is, the continued permanence of young people in their parents' home (giving rise to problems associated with the so-called 'generation gap') and one 'public', that is, the growth in educational opportunities. There is in fact a close relationship between the increase of public spending in general and the decrease of the population employed in productive activity and there is an even closer connection between the decrease in youth employment opportunities and public spending in education. Schools can be conceived as places that can contain labour which would otherwise be unemployed. Later the universities too become a 'parking place' for otherwise unemployed youth.

The concurrence of an expansion in the public sector with a general tendency towards capital-intensive investment determined a remarkable growth of the tertiary sector.[35] It should be added that this also determined a considerable expansion of the so-called 'rentier' sector, i.e. people living off real estate rental. This development was partly caused by the lack of a sustained public housing programme (virtually abandoned after 1963) and by the growth of highly paid professionals, civil servants and managers. The high incomes acquired by these strata enabled them to invest money in real estate and/or spend it on luxury housing and second homes.[36]

Thus the changes brought about by the end of the 'economic miracle', the capital-intensive strategy adopted by entrepreneurial groups, and by the growth of the public sector and of state intervention, were considerable. But their effects were to be even more far-reaching than what has been suggested so far. Much of the 'economic miracle' was based on the growth of small firms, often set up by former workers and artisans. These were now in considerable difficulties. In spite of government subsidies the crisis of 1964–66 took its toll. In fact the crisis would have been even more dramatic than this had the rest of the world economy been in a recession, but international demand was still strong enough to sustain Italian exports. Furthermore, the increase in wages due to the trade union struggles of 1962 meant that the home market was not as depressed as it would otherwise have been.[37]

The spate of mergers which followed increased the concentration of Italian industry. Between 1966 and 1967, 29 private firms owned directly or indirectly 34 per cent of all shares; the top 100 firms (out of 60,000 firms in manufacturing industry) controlled 40 per cent of all exports.[38] As Castronovo points out, Italian industry began to look like an iceberg: at the top there were three large public enterprises (ENI, IRI, ENEL) and five or six private firms – Fiat, Pirelli, Snia Viscosa (textiles), Italcementi (cement) and Falck and Finsider (steel); at the bottom there were 72,000 small and medium-sized firms employing between 11 and 500 workers.[39]

How did Italy emerge from the crisis of 1964–66? The economy picked up again but thanks to productivity gains rather than new plants. Productivity was achieved through the speeding up of the work process, the reorganization of existing plants and 'rationalization' through mergers. The profits thus generated were, on the whole, exported rather than reinvested at home. Public spending, as in other advanced countries, continued to grow. It was not financed by direct taxation, but through an increase in employers' and employees' contributions and other forms of indirect taxation. Thus the burden fell disproportionately on low-income groups (employers' social security contributions are, *de facto*, a tax on employment as well as a cost which – in that period – found its way into price increases). After the once-and-for-all increase of 1962, wage increases were roughly matched with productivity until 1969. This temporary wage truce had the same function as an incomes policy. Instead of using direct means to control incomes, as the Labour government did in Britain (1966) the Italian government, though raising the threat of a statutory incomes policy, preferred to use familiar indirect means – deflation and internal migration. But these techniques of control of industrial relations were less effective at a time when trade union confidence had been bolstered by militancy and full employment. By 1969, when the short-lived recovery was coming to an end, deflationary policies were difficult to pursue. To succeed they would have needed to be implemented over a long period of time and be even more severe than in 1963. The very high level of industrial conflict which occurred in the 'hot autumn' of 1969 meant that the labour movement had become too strong to be defeated with traditional methods.

The 'hot autumn' was the most acute social conflict since 1947. There were 302 million hours of strikes in 1969 and again 146 million in the following year (see Table 3.2). The causes of the conflicts were varied and here we cannot do more than list them:

1   The speed-up of the assembly lines and the intensification of the work process had brought about a worsening in working conditions. In this context it is significant that the demands of the trade unions were not purely about wages: the most popular slogans and demands were all concerned with non-monetary issues such as the quality of life at work.

2   A general dissatisfaction with the quality of life outside the factories
contributed to the strength, unity and politicization of working-class
demands. The congestion in urban centres due to urbanization and the
waves of migration had reached crisis conditions. There were considerable
pressures on public services, health, education and housing.[40]

3   The state seemed unable to resolve any of these problems, in spite of the
many promises made by the politicians of the centre-left coalition. The
growth in spending in the public sector was badly administered and took
the form of subsidies, extension of bureaucracy and payment to clientele
groups. At the same time there was little public investment in social
services and housing.

4   Economic policy seemed to be indecisive: the saga of attempts at
planning showed that the divisions within the ruling parties prevented a
clear and dynamic approach. Financial and economic policy was further
paralysed by the existence of four decision-making centres: the Ministries
of Finance, Treasury, Budget and the Bank of Italy.[41]

5   There was a profound dissatisfaction with the entrepreneurial classes,
much admired during the years of the 'miracle' and now increasingly
considered greedy and devoid of a sense of national responsibility. The
paradox of a country which exported both labour and capital played a
role in the lack of popularity of entrepreneurs.

6   There were changes in the composition of the labour force.[42]

As we mentioned there were fewer women and fewer workers over the age
of 45. The labour force was becoming increasingly made up of workers between
the ages of 25 and 45. It was also more homogeneous than before as older skills
became supplanted by new methods of production. This younger, male working
class included, however, an important proportion of people who had left their land
five, ten and in some cases fifteen years before. They had expected to be among
the beneficiaries of the 'economic miracle'. Instead they had seen their working
conditions deteriorating, and few improvements in housing, health and the education of their children. With the decrease in female employment these male workers
were supposed to be the sole breadwinners. They had been employed in factories
long enough to have lost their initial fear 'to make trouble', but they had not
been employed so long as to be able to remember the repression in the factories
which had occurred in the period 1949–55. As we shall see in the next chapter,
their militancy took not only government and employers by surprise but also the
organized labour movement, from the trade unions to the PCI and the PSI. This
'new' working class was more open to questions of equality and social justice; they
fought against differentials and for a better deal.[43] They were, of course, at the
bottom of the pile; they had the worst jobs, the longest hours, the least satisfactory
housing conditions. If they had been the only ones to strike then the movement
of 1969 would not have had such major political repercussions. It would have
been a movement of the 'wretched of the earth', of marginalized workers. Instead
it was able to march united with the bulk of the working class and create a situation

of semi-permanent labour conflict which transformed the Italian labour movement from a subordinate element of the Italian political system into one of its chief actors. In this situation deflation was no longer a feasible option. The working-class movement, particularly the engineering workers, had acquired a novel self-confidence which rendered a massive 'guided' depression impossible. Those in power resorted instead to price inflation as a means of lowering the real costs of labour. This strategy was facilitated by the inflationary spiral which hit the Western economies after 1972 and by the end of the international system of fixed exchange rates (devaluation of the dollar in August 1971).[44] But this, as they say, is another story which belongs to the next chapter.

Endnotes

1 Fuà and Sylos-Labini 1963.
2 Silva and Targetti 1972, p. 17.
3 De Cecco 1971, p. 983.
4 Valli 1979, p. 72.
5 Ibid., p. 73.
6 Castronovo 1981, p. 417.
7 Onida 1977, p. 70.
8 Valli 1979, p. 123.
9 Castronovo 1981, p. 461.
10 Graziani 1971, p. 71.
11 Castronovo 1981, p. 456–7.
12 Falzone, Palermo and Cosentino 1976, pp. 231–2.
13 Amato 1976, p. 132.
14 Ibid., p. 135.
15 Forte 1966, extracts in Graziani 1971, pp. 209–10.
16 Castronovo 1981, p. 463.
17 Amato 1976, p. 41.
18 Fabiani 1977, p. 165.
19 Castronovo 1981, pp. 498–9.
20 Fabiani 1977, p. 166.
21 Castronovo 1981, p. 446.
22 D'Antonio 1973, pp. 238–9.
23 Valli 1979, p. 107.
24 D'Antonio 1973, p. 239.
25 Amato 1976, p. 52.
26 Ibid., p. 60.
27 See Amato 1976, p. 71. See also Castellino 1976.

28 Reviglio 1977, p. 117. In the UK, a country with a population comparable to Italy the sum of all those in receipt of invalidity and disablement benefits as well as those in receipt of war pensions in 1975 was – at that time – just over 1 million – see Department of Health and Social Security 1975.
29 Graziani 1971, pp. 73–1.
30 Saraceno 1972, p. 261.
31 This is the thesis which informs Michele Salvati's Il sistema economico italiano: analisi di una crisi, see Salvati 1975.
32 Employment in southern industries as a proportion of total employment in industry actually decreased between 1961 and 1971, see D'Antonio 1973, p. 238.
33 Paci 1973.
34 Podbielski 1974, p. 126.
35 Vainicher 1977, p. 57.
36 Garavini 1974, pp. 68–9.
37 Graziani 1971, pp. 71–2.
38 Castronovo 1981, p. 461.
39 Ibid., p. 465.
40 Graziani 1971, pp. 74–5.
41 Castronovo 1981, p. 468.
42 Ibid., p. 475.
43 Ibid., p. 476.
44 D'Antonio 1977, pp. 57–8.

Chapter 4

From the 'hot autumn' to interdependence, 1969–1985

The 'hot autumn' of 1969 is an historic date in the development of post-war Italian society. Its significance – even if only its economic effects are considered – cannot be underestimated. Any periodization would single out 1963–69 as the phase in which, at one and the same time, the crisis of the 'model' of economic development which had led to the 'economic miracle' became manifest (1963) and irreversible (1969).

The economic importance of 1969 can be highlighted by simply listing the following data.[1]

1   Increases in wages before 1969 were matched by increases in productivity. After 1969 wages increased at a rate higher than the cost of living index and higher than productivity.
2   In the 1960s hourly wages increased at a rate which matched the increases in other countries of the Organization for Economic Cooperation and Development (OECD): 10 per cent in Italy, 9 per cent in OECD. After 1969, and throughout the 1970s, hourly rates in Italy increased yearly by 20–25 per cent, double the average of the OECD countries.
3   Inflation rates in the 1960s in Italy were in line with the rest of the OECD, but after 1973–74 Italian rates were, on average, twice those of the OECD countries. They remained higher than the average even after 1985.
4   Between 1969 and 1970 labour costs increased by 16 per cent.
5   In manufacturing industry money wages rose by 9.1 per cent in 1969 and by 23.4 per cent in 1970. Real wages, of course, rose by much less because of the increase in the cost of living index.
6   The share of the national income going to wage-earners went up from 56.7 to 59 per cent. In industry it went up from 60.7 to 64.1 per cent.

What does this tell us? First of all, that in terms of productivity and inflation rates Italy no longer followed the general pattern of OECD countries. Secondly, that such 'deviation' from the pattern of the other advanced capitalist countries brought the average purchasing power of Italian workers on a level with those countries. The result was to destroy the main comparative advantage of Italian entrepreneurs: low wages. Having lost this advantage Italy remained a special case, but one with new characteristics.

The 'hot autumn', however, was not only about wages. It occurred at a time when the whole of Italian society seemed to be in upheaval. The student movement had become a major political phenomenon and, although it never reached the peaks of France in May 1968, it lasted far longer, shaping, directly or indirectly, the crisis of Italian society. It was the source of disparate but related phenomena: terrorism, the birth of a host of small left-wing parties, the women's movement, dissent within the Church and the radicalization of large number of intellectuals. Furthermore, as we shall see in subsequent chapters, 1969 also caused profound changes in the organization of the labour movement, in the trade unions and in the political parties.

The 1969 movement also brought about a situation in which wage increases could no longer be reversed by the kind of 'capitalist counter-offensive' which had been a hallmark of the 1960s, analysed in the previous chapter. In 'qualitative' terms this mean the following:[2]

1   A greater working-class control over the use of the labour force in factories. After 1969 it would be far more difficult for entrepreneurs to increase productivity by increasing the speed of the assembly lines or by reorganizing the labour process.
2   Workers themselves were able to acquire a greater degree of control inside the factories which made them more independent both from the trade union hierarchy and from the employers. Changes had to be negotiated at shop-floor level.[3]
3   Entrepreneurs could no longer use marginal or casual labour for the lowest and less skilled jobs inside the factories to the same extent as before. This was partly due to the decrease in female employment; it was also due to the fact that workers had obtained a uniformity of contracts and wage levels which did not exist before.
4   The strength of the labour movement was such that the government had to pass a new law in 1970, known as the Workers' Charter (*Statuto dei Lavoratori*) which strengthened considerably the bargaining power of the workers and made illegal a number of anti-trade union practices.
5   It was now far more difficult to sack workers, both because of the strength of the movement and because of new legislation.
6   There was a shortening of the working week and overtime was abolished in a number of large firms.

Entrepreneurs were ill-equipped to face this challenge. The strategy they had adopted in the 1960s backfired: they had reduced the volume of productive investments and increased productivity by squeezing the labour force. Now they were left with a rebellious labour force and obsolete plants. They could not hope for an expansion of international demand. Approaching on the horizon were the years of worldwide inflation, dollar crisis, energy crisis and low growth. The Italian economy entered this period of crisis with a political system which had relied for its stability on a constant economic growth. There was a void of ideas and, in this void, the first instinct of the financial authorities was to try, once more, to use their traditional instrument: deflation.

The increase in labour costs due to wage rises had caused an increase in prices. Unlike 1962–63 when the small firms operating on the home market had been the first to increase prices, this time it was the export-orientated sector which passed on the increase in wages to their customers at home and abroad. This could now be done because inflation was also hitting the other industrialized countries and the increase in prices did not entail a decrease in the competitiveness of Italian firms. However, the balance of payments was in deficit not only because of an adverse balance of trade but mainly because of a sustained flight of capital. In itself this was nothing new: after the nationalization of electricity there had been a constant export of capital. But in 1969 this had reached massive proportions partly because of high interest rates abroad and partly because of a widespread desire to avoid taxation. Thus the deflationary policy of the authorities was also intended to raise Italian interest rates and entice savers to keep their money in the country. The credit squeeze of 1969 was not very effective. Aggregate demand for consumption goods fell a little, but there was no increase in investment and this meant that the long-term problem of re-equipping Italian industry was not tackled. Once more short-term objectives of monetary stability prevailed over longer-term ones of industrial regeneration.

At this stage it will be useful to explain briefly the kind of economic theory which inspired the Bank of Italy, the leading monetary authority.[4] Its central assumption was that entrepreneurs wished to maintain stable profit margins and, whenever costs increased they would attempt to transfer this rise on to prices. This strategy was likely to encounter internal and external obstacles. Internally, that is to say on the home market, competition from other firms made it more difficult for any single firm – at least in the short run – to increase prices. Abroad the possibility of price increases was limited by the behaviour of other firms whose own labour costs had not increased as much as Italian labour costs. Thus for the Bank of Italy Italian prices were relatively inflexible because of the degree of international integration of the Italian economy.

But there were other ways of preserving existing profit levels: by increasing productivity. The same amount of labour would produce more at similar prices. Internally it would be possible to increase sales because the increase in wages would bring about an increase in demand. Externally, a productivity increase would enable the country to keep up with or even undercut foreign competition. The problem with increasing productivity – if one could no longer discipline the labour force – was that it was necessary to increase investment. This could be done either by financing out of profits, or by borrowing from the banks. The former was made more difficult by the lower profit rate. By borrowing, costs would be increased by interest rates. Thus the Bank of Italy held the view that increases in wages brought two kinds of pressure on the economy: an inflationary pressure because they stimulated an increase in prices, and a movement towards a recession because they caused a decrease in investment. It followed that wage increases were a 'bad thing'. In the course of the 1970s the Bank of Italy had finally reached the conclusion that mone-tary intervention (credit squeeze, deflation, etc.) could only reduce aggregate demand but not encourage investment.

There was another option open: an incomes policy. Although this was no doubt the preferred option it was impossible to apply. There can only be two kinds of incomes policy – voluntary or statutory. A voluntary incomes policy was not on the cards. The trade unions were unwilling to accept it unless it were part of a major package of internal reforms which would have entailed a great increase in public spending. A statutory policy required a docile labour force which was hardly the case in Italy in the 1970s. Thus there remained a single option to be pursued in order to enable firms to maintain their levels of profitability: internal inflation and devaluation.

Domestic inflation usually redistributes profits to the advantage of the larger and more efficient firms, but does not necessarily alter the overall level of profits. To ensure that inflation would not have negative repercussions on foreign trade it was then necessary to devalue the lira so that the external prices of Italian goods remained competitive. The problem with constant devaluation was that it had im-portant inflationary effects. This was so because once exporters asssumed that the government would always bail them out by devaluing they would not resist price rises, knowing that every upward movement in prices will be followed by a match-ing decrease in the foreign exchange value of the currency. Moreover, a devalu-ation of the lira, while making Italian exports relatively cheaper, made imports more expensive thus stoking up further inflation rate.[5] Price control experiments were repeated on and off throughout this period with fairly disappointing results.

The strategy of inflation-devaluation also failed because in 1973 the energy crisis exploded when the Organization of Petroleum Exporting Countries (OPEC) was able to impose a massive increase in oil prices.

The main difficulties experienced by the Italian economy in this period were due to the fact that it had lost its main competitive advantage, namely low wages, and that it had become totally interdependent with the international economic system. The post-war decision to open the Italian economy to the outside world had de-pended for its success on international competitiveness which in turn depended on low labour costs. By the early 1970s Italy was fully integrated into an international economic system but could no longer rely on low wages. The option of reintrodu-cing protectionism was never seriously considered by Italian political parties, whether of the government or of the opposition. The main argument against protectionism was that, in essence, it was too late: international constraints were by then too great. Protectionism would have severely damaged the most efficient sectors of the economy and caused a deterioration of living standards.

Of course it could be argued that the level of international integration did not have to reach such massive proportions. Economic development did not have to be based so strongly on exports. The home market could have played a more important role. Agriculture did not have to be left to fend for itself with the result that Italy became a food importer. Italy could have played a more important role in EEC agricultural policy instead of trailing behind the French and the Germans, and could

Table 4.1 International trade, 1958–74

	Imports as % of GNP	Exports as % of GNP	Imports + exports as % of GNP
1958	11.6	10.6	22.2
1970	18.0	17.2	35.2
1974	29.8	23.7	53.5

Table 4.2 International trade, a comparison (imports + exports as % of GNP in 1974)

UK	60.5
Italy	53.5
France	42.1
W. Germany	41.0
Japan	30.5
USA	14.2

Source: Peggio (1976), pp. 38–40

have made a more significant attempt to modernize its administration and restructure its agriculture instead of using such a small proportion of the 'Guidance Fund' of the EEC agricultural policy (which meant that Italy used a lower percentage of this fund than any other EEC country).[6] That the level of international integration of the Italian economy increased remarkably in the period to the mid-1970s can be seen from Tables 4.1 and 4.2.

In order to sustain such high level of participation in international trade, an economy which is so integrated must possess some special advantages. From a geographical point of view Italy could be a link between the markets of northern Europe and those of the Mediterranean. Yet its geographical position also meant that it faced competition from both the Mediterranean south (olive oil, wine and citrus fruits) and from the rest of Europe (manufactured goods).[7] Besides, Italy suffered from a number of structural handicaps, the main one being the lack of natural resources in relation to its population. The UK has oil, gas and coal. Norway has oil. France and West Germany have coal and fertile soil. The Netherlands has gas and fertile soil.[8] Italy has no oil, no gas, no coal. Agriculture need to be concentrated in a relatively small area as vast streches of land are difficult to cultivate (e.g. mountain areas), or lack proper irrigation.

These structural handicaps, whether due to natural and objective factors or to past governmental mistakes, could perhaps have been partially compensated by foreign investment. Italy could offer investors the industrial structure of an advanced country, a skilled labour force and wages still relatively lower than those of most advanced countries. In fact in the 1970s there was a much greater intervention of multinational companies than had occurred in the previous decade. But this intervention took the form of acquiring existing firms, of using state subsidies and low wage labour without resulting in any considerable investment in advanced technology.[9] On the contrary, it could be argued that such intervention made it more difficult for Italy to develop new technologies. Research and development was carried out abroad, in the USA, in West Germany and in Japan. Production requiring low technology inputs was diverted to Italy. The growth of multinational companies tended to accelerate the international division of labour and production was diversified following the logic of using factors of production at the lowest costs at world level. Thus Italy's position in the international division of labour constantly deteriorated.

This process was further accelerated by what was probably the most significant, if temporary, change in the conditions of international trade which occurred in the 1970s: the shift in the terms of trade towards the producers of primary products and, in particular, towards the oil exporting countries. This meant that industrial countries now had to export much more in order to acquire those primary products they needed for economic growth. Hence a number of Italian industrial and agricultural products faced greater competition on world markets (as well as on the home market). Italy had to export more and more. An obvious strategy (adopted, for instance by France) was to produce products with a high technological content, but Italian industry was not equipped for this.[10]

How did other countries react? The USA devalued the dollar in 1971 and 1973. It decreased its commitment to finance other countries' development and this meant that military spending too was decreased in South-East Asia. By 1973 the US balance of trade was no longer in deficit and the USA became competitive again in many sectors. This encouraged foreign investments, particularly from West Germany and Japan.[11]

West Germany became the leading motor of the European economy: its export trade accounted, by the mid-1970s, for one-third of all EEC exports. Similarly, in Asia, Japan became the pillar of a new Far Eastern industrial development which included the network of the 'newly industrialized countries' of South Korea, Singapore, Taiwan, Hong Kong as well as the Philippines and Thailand.

Thus the devaluation of the dollar had profound effects on the international economy: the strong (Japan and West Germany) grew stronger, and the weak (Italy and the UK) grew weaker. The USA which had a high rate of inflation before the OPEC price rise dealt with it by squeezing incomes while reflating the economy, thus accelerating inflation in the USA and in the rest of the world. Inflation in the USA had the effect of depreciating the value of the dollar with respect to other leading currencies, and low interest rates in the USA meant that there was a massive out-flow of capital from the USA to Europe and Japan.[12] The presence of this enormous monetary mass which constituted the Eurodollar market contributed to the inflationary spiral in Europe which was – with the significant exception of West Germany – higher than in the USA.

The devaluation strategy was adopted in 1973 as Italian inflation rates reached a comparatively high level (see Table 4.3). This was also the year of the first massive increase in oil prices. The devaluation of the lira proceeded constantly throughout this period against all other currencies, as can be seen in Table 4.4

Table 4.3 Rates of consumer price increases in six major industrialized countries, 1970–81 (%)

	1970	1971	1972	1973	1973	1974	1975	1981
USA	5.9	4.3	3.3	6.2	11.0	9.2	5.8	11.0
Japan	6.3	6.3	4.8	11.8	22.7	12.2	9.3	3.9
France	5.2	5.5	5.9	7.3	13.6	11.8	9.6	13.9
W. Germany	3.7	5.3	5.5	6.9	7.0	6.9	4.6	6.5
Italy	4.9	4.8	5.7	10.8	19.1	17.2	16.7	18.7
UK	6.4	9.4	7.1	9.1	15.9	24.2	16.8	11.4

Source: For 1970–80, IMF and Parboni (1981) p. 79: for 1981, *Financial Times*, 14 November 1981

Table 4.4 Foreign exchange rates, 1972–85

Currency	1972	1973	1975	1977	1979	1981	1983	1985
US Dollar	583	602	652	882	848	1202	1638	2081
Swiss Franc	152	191	252	368	476	658	751	749
Sterling	1460	1478	1447	1540	1627	2316	2402	2365
French Franc	115	134	152	179	188	211	198	207
Deutsche Mark	183	227	265	380	422	534	605	634
Yen	1.94	2.16	2.20	3.30	4.07	5.52	6.92	8.11

Source: Bank of Italy, 1972–78; *Financial Times*, 1981; *La Repubblica*, 25 November 1983; *Financial Times*, 20 March 1985

which indicates the amount of Italian lire needed to purchase one unit of foreign currency.

The 1973 fluctuation of the lira had differentiated effects on the Italian economy. Firms depending on imports for their production suffered while exporters did relatively well. There was, however, a huge increase in public spending which helped the recovery. This lasted only until 1974, the year in which Italian inflation rates became the highest in the West. Since then Italian inflation has remained at a relatively high level.

After 1973 the problem arose of eliminating the ever-growing deficit in the balance of payments. International loans, and particularly West German loans were used frequently, but the Bank of Italy deflated by squeezing credit. As usual, this restrained large firms less than the small and medium-sized firms. This new credit squeeze stopped the recovery dead in its tracks and initiated one of the most serious economic crises of the post-war period.[13]

Let us now take a look at the gradual slowing down of the Italian economy and at the kind of reorganization which occurred in the 1970s.

The average rate of growth of the national income dropped from 6.56 per cent in the period 1959–63 to 5.96 per cent in the years 1964–70 and to 3.36 per cent in 1970–74. The average yearly rate of growth of industrial production dropped from

9.07 per cent in the period 1959–63 to 6.20 per cent in 1964–70 and to 3.38 per cent in 1970–74. Finally, the ratio of investment to income, that is, the amount of lire one needs to invest in order to obtain one lira increase in income, went up from 3.76 in 1959–63 and 3.50 in 1963–70 to 6.32 in 1970–74.[14] Clearly it was necessary to re-equip Italian industry. One of the chief problems, however, was that this re-equipment required a major restructuring. The industries which had been the keystones of the 'economic miracle' were successful not only because of the skills of Italian entrepreneurs, but because they were based on low wages and a low level of technological content, as was the case with typical Italian exports such as textiles, clothing, shoes, furniture and household goods. Italy has thus been able to adapt itself to the spaces left open in the international economy. In so doing, however, it would, in all probability, face the competition of newly industrialized countries of the Third World which have low wages, and would find it more difficult to produce those goods where a high technological content is necessary. For goods with average technological content, such as machine tools, cars, oil-related products, rubber and metal goods, only in two cases (cars and oil-related products) was there adequate technical progress. For goods with high technological inputs, such as electronics, aircraft, scientific and precision instruments, computers, high-quality chemicals and microprocessors, only plastics and chemical goods kept up with international competition and were adequately catered for. Italy's dependence on foreign technology became manifest: in 1972 it imported 152,000 million lire worth of patents but exported only 27,000 million.[15]

Such restructuring around high technology would have required state intervention of a different calibre: efficient and ruthless. But by the 1970s the state sector had become a political instrument in the hands of the Christian Democratic Party (DC), its economic functions were subordinated to the policies of enabling the survival of that party and the kind of economic structures which had grown with it. The path of high technology was never seriously considered. There remained, apparently, one avenue: the attempt to circumvent the gains achieved by the working class in 1969–70 by reorganizing the system of production in such a way as to maintain the production of traditional goods while resisting Third World competition. To put it in a simpler way: to produce low cost clothing and shoes with a competitive edge against the products of Hong Kong and Taiwan it was necessary to compete on quality and fashion.

To achieve this production was decentralized by shifting it from large industrial groups to an array of small firms and cottage industry. Employment in this sector assumed various forms: domestic labour, underemployment, juvenile and even child labour, casual and part-time labour and even prison labour. The pressures towards this decentralization of production and the creation of a second, 'hidden' or 'black' economy were essentially two:

1   Escape from trade union constraints: labour payments in the 'black economy' did not have to correspond to wage rates offered in the 'open' sector. Health and safety regulations could be easily circumvented and there are fewer or no strikes.

2   Escape from the full burden of taxes, by avoiding paying employers' and employees' contributions which are the highest in Europe.[16]

Thus an increasing proportion of the labour force began to work in conditions which are reminiscent of the low-wage economy typical of the 1950s. This situation was all the more easily accepted because the wages generated in the 'black' economy were usually added on to those in the 'open' sector. It was often the case that while the male worker continued his employment in the 'open' sector the other members of the family were employed in the 'hidden' sector. Thus the family income increased considerably while individual wages could remain relatively low. There is also the growth of the so-called *doppiolavoro* (second job): the reduction of overtime enabled many workers to take a second job where they did not pay any taxes or contributions.

It is difficult to estimate the size of the 'black economy'. The state statistical office (*Istituto Centrale di Statistica* or ISTAT) estimated that the number of people who were employed in 1980, even though they were not officially registered as such, was between 1 million and 3.5 million. To these should be added all second 'unofficial' jobs. It is difficult to assess how far this problem is specific to Italy. It has been pointed out that Italy used little foreign labour until the mid-1980s and that, in a sense, the 'black economy' is the Italian version of immigrant labour. In the late 1970s the proportion of foreign labour in EEC countries was around 7 per cent and in West Germany and France the proportion is of 10 per cent.[17] Of the 6 million foreign workers employed in EEC countries only 1.5 million came from other EEC countries. The importance of foreign labour is not only that it can be exploited more easily, but that it is far more flexible and mobile. When it is no longer usable it can simply be got rid of. Resident labour is better protected and nowhere more so than in Italy (in the 'open' sector, of course): equal pay, daily hours worked, lower retirement age, greater difficulties in laying off workers, etc. OECD statistics show that the rate of withdrawal from the labour market was lower in Italy (particularly after 1974) than in the USA, Sweden, France and the UK.[18]

The effects of the decentralization of production towards the hidden sector permitted Italy to achieve a growth rate which, though inferior to that of the 'economic miracle', was higher than that of most of the industrially advanced countries of the OECD. In 1980 Gross Domestic Product (GDP) increased by 4 per cent against −0.2 per cent in the USA, 1.4 per cent in France, −1.4 per cent in the UK, 1.9 per cent in West Germany. Only Japan (+4.2 per cent), Portugal (+4.7 per cent) and Finland (+4.9 per cent) did better.[19] This was in no small part due to the fact that between 1973 and 1979 the sectors of the economy which expanded were, with the exception of the chemical industry, sectors where there was a strong presence of 'black labour' such as leather, shoes, clothing and furniture.[20]

Once more the South did not derive any particular benefit from this development. The small and medium-sized firms of the 'hidden' sector were located, on the whole, in the Centre and in the North. The larger firms, both public and private, had decreased the rate of growth of their investments partly because of the financial crisis they were undergoing, partly because of the heavy losses encountered by some (e.g. steel due to world overproduction and Japanese competition). This serious crisis meant that they were not likely to invest more in the South and that state resources which could have been used otherwise had to be directed towards enabling existing firms to pay their debts or reorganize existing plants.[21]

The problems of the South were further multiplied by the failure to restructure agriculture. As a result Italian food imports from the rest of the EEC increased at a steady rate (sixteen times since 1957), while agricultural exports since then increased by only three or four times).[22] In 1972 the EEC established some directives for the modernization of agriculture and the training of agricultural producers. Marginal farmers no longer obtained funds to modernize their farms but to enable them to sell their land. Thus the public bodies which had been instituted in order to help smallholders had now to get rid of them. One way of doing this was for the Ministry of Agriculture to transfer some of its former functions to the regional authorities which had been instituted in 1970. But the ministry resisted this proposal for political reasons: the ministry wanted to continue to give subsidies to those organizations and associations with which it had been connected for years and with which it had established a dense clientele network often based on personal relationships. From the point of view of the ministry what mattered was the danger that any transfer of funds would decrease its powers of patronage. The result of this essential internal struggle between centre and periphery was a compromise: the regions obtained some resources and the ministry kept all powers of guidance and coordination and, more importantly, control of the funds to be used as compensation to the marginal farmers for the sale of their lands.[23]

The absolute priority always given to political matters over economic ones reflected not only the deepening Italian crisis but also the internal crisis of the DC. Economic decision-making acquired more and more the characteristics of warring feuds. The very concept of planning lost the reformist significance it had had, at least formally, under the centre-left governments of the 1960s. Now public investments in the state sector, rather than responding to an industrial strategy, reflected the interests of the public entrepreneurs themselves who used them as joint ventures with politicians of the governing parties. Having created the state-holding sector as relatively autonomous from parliamentary control, the DC now found that it had created authentic centres of power with which it had to negotiate. These centres of power used the economic resources at their disposal for political ends. For instance when, in the 1970s, the state mining company (EGAM) acquired shipbuilding shares it did so not because it needed to diversify into shipping but because it wanted to get hold of the newspapers belonging to the shipping owners.[24]

Thus the interconnection between the leading groups of the public sector and the ruling political bloc became closer. The political power of the public corporations was not established by law but relied on the connection established with particular factions within the DC. With the expansion of the state, the political cadres of the DC increasingly occupied economic positions in banks, credit institutions and, of course, economic institutions such as the *Cassa per il Mezzogiorno* and public corporations. This process is of course not unique to Italy: there is everywhere a constant intertwining between business and politics. The difference is that in some countries, such as the USA, it is business that 'colonizes' politics and not the other way round.[25]

How did the entrepreneurial world counteract this tendency? At the ideological level the employers' association, *Confindustria*, stressed the need for an efficient modern state based on the principles of managerial and technical efficiency which would appeal to the new middle classes against the paternalism of the DC.

Big business criticism of the DC centred on the following points:

1. Private enterprise was being squeezed by a spendthrift government, by high wages and by excessive trade union power.
2. Public spending was inefficient and simply transferred resources through the banks to the state. The consequent enlargement of economic activity did not generate profits and/or new investment.
3. Employers' contributions to social costs were too high.
4. The index-linked scale of wages squeezed profits.

An examination of the complaints levelled by private enterprise anywhere in Europe or North America would show that there was nothing specifically Italian about these grievances. However, in most other countries public spending was identified with the left. In Italy it was identified with the DC, and – until the collapse of this party – there were no alternative to the right of the DC, at least not within the established constitutional system. Gianni Agnelli, the President of Fiat, and the most lucid representative of big business, encapsulated the problem facing Italian entrepreneurs when he explained that the agreement established between private enterprise and the DC could work as long as each kept to its side of the pact: the exercise of political power to the DC and economic growth to private enterprise. However the DC, in order to exercise political power had to maintain mass support, and had to organize public spending accordingly. The consequence of this was that, according to Agnelli, private enterprise had to begin to involve itself directly in politics.[26] The analysis focuses on only one aspect of the problem, but it was not far off the mark. The strategy, however, in the conditions of the time, was unrealistic because it assumed that the political problem of establishing a mass consensus could be better achieved by a clearly capitalist party (which, at the time, could only have been a somewhat 'regenerated' DC). This party would still need to use public spending in order to achieve the massive investment that a regeneration of Italian industry required. There would have to be a time-lag during which the social groups currently protected would be left to fend for themselves. This would either destabilize the political system from the right or bring to the fore the only alternative to the DC within the constitutional system: the Italian Communist Party (PCI).

To foreclose both options, the DC attempted to incorporate the PCI in its own system of government. This was the strategy adopted during 1976–79 when the PCI was offered (and accepted) a subordinate role in political decision-making – the DC version of the Historic Compromise. The strategy was unsuccessful because the Communists pulled out before they became too deeply enmeshed in the DC system.

The political and economic strategy of private enterprise in the 1970s was also unrealistic because its analysis assumed that there is an organic contradiction between the 'healthy' forces of private enterprise and the economic activity of the state sector.[27] Apart from the fact that the *Confindustria* itself had, by the mid-1960s, been converted to the concept of planning and that Agnelli himself, on the morrow of the 'hot autumn', had recognized the central importance of trade union involvement in economic decision-making, it is simply not true that the state sector had operated against the interests of private business. The crisis of accumulation which hit Italy in the 1970s was also due to the fact that private capital was invested abroad where returns would be higher, or invested at home in non-productive use such as real estate. State subsidies and public works programmes were often directed towards the creation of energy inputs and primary products which supported the production cycles of big business. Furthermore, private firms and high income groups enjoyed a *de facto* low tax burden because of massive tax evasion and the widespread possibility of tax avoidance.

It is true that the 'restructuring' of larger private firms by decentralizing production towards small firms thus expanding the 'hidden' sector marked the development of market conditions outside state control (really 'free' enterprise). But the growth thus generated could be achieved precisely because of the much criticized inefficiency and lack of authority of the Italian state. This free market restructuring, coupled with the expansion of public spending, further exacerbated the distortions of the labour market. The level of activity rate (defined as the percentage of the population in the labour force) was lower in Italy than in most other advanced countries, as was the case in the 1960s as well. The same can be said about the participation rate of women in the labour force: it was still exceptionally low, although it is difficult to assess the extent to which the expansion of the 'black' economy entailed an increase in female employment. Furthermore, if we examine the distribution of labour in the Centre-North and in the South we can note a continuing disequilibrium.

Between 1973 and 1976 (see Table 4.5) the economy of the South and that of the North exhibited the following similar traits: a decrease in employment in agriculture; a small decrease in employment in the building industry and in public works; an increase in employment in the tertiary sector and a fairly stable level of unemployment. The two most striking differences were first that, after the tertiary sector, agriculture was still the largest employment sector in the South while industry was the largest in the North and, secondly, unemployment in the South was roughly twice as large as unemployment in the North.

Another important difference between North and South was the variance of participation rates. Those employed as a percentage of the potential labour force were, in 1975, 31.5 per cent in the South and 38.9 per cent in the North. The equivalent statistics for West Germany in 1974 was 42.2 per cent, for France 39.9 per cent and for the UK 42.9 per cent.[28] Thus participation rates in the north of Italy did not show a significant variance with those of industrialized countries. It is the southern statistics which modify the Italian total and which show, once more, the historical failure to unify Italy.

Table 4.5 Distribution of employment in the South and North, 1972–76

Year	Labour force (000)	Agriculture %	Industry %	Building and public works %	Tertiary %	Unemployed %
The South						
1972	6,127	28.13	15.84	12.17	38.55	5.28
1973	6,140	27.42	16.27	11.77	39.33	5.19
1974	6,157	26.52	16.87	11.61	40.53	4.45
1975	6,192	25.19	16.98	11.51	41.24	5.05
1976	6,336	25.15	16.88	11.11	41.57	5.27
The North						
1972	13,835	11.36	33.42	11.36	44.61	2.69
1973	13,934	10.80	33.61	7.63	45.43	2.50
1974	14,118	10.46	33.85	7.45	46.19	2.02
1975	14,205	9.88	33.51	7.29	46.90	2.40
1976	14,305	9.33	33.33	7.09	47.45	2.78

Source: SVIMEZ 1976 Report on the South

With the constant shrinking of the agricultural sector the traditional reserve army of labour which was at the disposal of the Italian economy had virtually disappeared.[29] It is in this period that there was for the first time in modern Italian history an entry of foreign workers, particularly from Ethiopia, Somalia, Libya, Egypt and the Philippines. These, however, essentially found employment as domestic workers and on the periphery of the 'black' economy. A new important component of the reserve army was urban-based youth which was exercising increasing pressures on the labour market. Thus a greater number of young people were in fact encouraged to stay on at school and to enter the universities which by then were operating an open-door policy. The consequence of this process was to increase the percentage of young qualified unemployed. According to official figures in 1978 there were in Italy 1.5 million unemployed. Of these about half were looking for their first job. Unemployment in the South was 9.9 per cent while in the North it was 6 per cent. Male unemployment was 4.7 per cent while female unemployment was 12.6 per cent. Of those between the ages of 14 and 19, 31 per cent, and of those between 20 and 29, 14 per cent, were unemployed.

The rate of unemployment for those leaving school at 18 (13.9 per cent) was higher than the unemployment rate of those who had left at 14 (9.3 per cent) or before (4.3 per cent). This is, of course, a vicious circle: those with higher qualifications want jobs in the 'open' economy where they are better paid and more secure. But employment in this sector is either stagnant or is given to those with some work experience, often gained in the hidden economy. There is thus a transfer from the 'black' economy to the 'open' one. Younger entrants in the labour market cannot accede directly to the 'open' sector and their qualifications make them reluctant to enter the 'black' sector.[30]

Table 4.6 Ratio between incomes in the province of Modena
(skilled industrial worker = 100)

	1971	1974	1977	1978
Skilled worker	100	100	100	100
Agricultural worker	72	72	94	100
Primary school teacher	158	152	116	116
Dustman	149	136	145	153
Junior doctor (hospital)	608	457	280	245
Consultant (hospital)	1,093	781	481	409

Source: Valli 1979, p. 154

Obviously the constant growth of the supply of graduate labour has had the partial effect of containing the levels of salaries among white-collar workers and, in general, throughout the 1970s, of decreasing income differentials between salaried workers and wage-earners. The push towards equality, however, has been chiefly determined by the operation of the *scala mobile*, the indexation of wages. According to the formal model of wage indexation there is an automatic mechanism whereby earnings increase in such a way as to match the rate of inflation. In practice, this occurs only in part because of the way in which the mechanism works and because the increase in pay occurs only after the increase in price. When this mechanism was instituted in 1952 it had the effect of maintaining and, in some cases, widening the differentials. The egalitarian policies of the trade unions forced a revision of this mechanism in 1975 when it was established that incomes would be increased by a fixed and equal amount of money. This had the result of lowering differentials the greater the inflation rate. For instance, suppose Martini earns 10,000 lire a month and Rossi earns 20,000 lire, and suppose each percentage point of price rise determines an increase of 2,000 lire. If inflation is at 10 per cent there will be a 20,000 lire increase across the board. The relative position after adjustments will be that Martini earns 30,000 lire and Rossi earns 40,000 lire. The differential in real terms is smaller: before the rise Rossi earned twice as much as Martini, after the rise, only one-third more. The overall narrowing of differentials can be seen in these figures on income distribution in the province of Modena (see Table 4.6).

The trend towards equality was, however, counterbalanced by an increase in differentials within certain categories of workers. In certain cases, firms would increase the payment of fringe benefits to senior executives in order to maintain or extend existing privileged positions. Thus in 1978 at Fiat the effect of the *scala mobile* and the wage bargaining round which had been centred on the principle of 'equal increase for all' would have produced a differential between basic and maximum wages of 100:143. To compensate for this loss on the part of the better-paid executive, Fiat increased their salaries so as to establish a differential of 100:247.[31] However, with the exception of senior executives it would be true to say that in the entire sector which is subject to international competition (virtually the whole of private manufacturing industry and some state enterprises) the differentials narrowed considerably. In sectors not export-orientated, such as banking and insurance and national monopolies such as electricity, large differentials were main-tained. Among local government employees there were abnormal and unjustified differentials even between workers doing exactly the same jobs. A parliamentary investigative commission established soon after the 1975 agreement revealed that an employee of a northern region would be paid by the regional government an average of 5.1 million lire a year, in central Italy 5.4, in southern Italy 5.7 and in Sicily and Sardinia 5.9.[32] Another study by Accornero and Carmignani revealed that the average income of a regional employee was inversely proportional to the average income in the region as a whole: the higher the income per regional em-ployee the poorer the region.[33] More striking was the fact that a porter employed in a private manufacturing firm did earn between 4 and 7 million lire a year (1976 figures), if employed by a regional government the same person could earn anything between 2.7 million and 8.4 million lire, but porters in the Italian Chamber of Deputies could muster a yearly income of between 8.5 and 17 million lire.[34]

These differentials were a divisive element favouring the growth of corporative unions which negotiated outside the framework of agreements established by the leading three trade union confederations. In some sectors they constituted *de facto* clienteles with special links with factions of the political parties of the ruling coalition. But the differentials were also a reaction against the tendency towards equality which was often seen as excessive – especially by those of the losing side.

The tendency towards equality through the indexation of wages was also con-sidered a major factor towards the increase in Italian labour costs. The rate of growth of these were higher than any other European country with the exception of the UK (but absolute labour costs in both these countries were, if anything, lower than those in West Germany, France, the Netherlands, Denmark and Belgium). We are talking, obviously, of labour costs measured in national currencies. The devalu-ation of the lira has been such that if we were to convert all measurements of labour costs into say, dollars, the Italian rate of increase would be slightly below average.[35]

The argument about the cost of labour dominated Italian debates on economic policies at least since the beginning of the 1970s. The government's three-year plan for 1979–81 (the Pandolfi Plan) isolated the cost of labour and the ever-increasing growth of public spending as the key problems facing the Italian economy and as the central internal causes (the major external cause being the high cost of energy) diverse phenomena such as the constant depreciation of the lira, the decrease in competitiveness, stop-go policies and many others.[36]

The document was silent on other possible factors which might have contributed to the depreciation of the lira and the high level of inflation such as high interest rates and capital flight.[37] It was thus not surprising that it indicated three conditions for the achievement of high rates of growth, an increase in employment and the development of the South. The plan's objectives were:

1   To reduce the proportion of public spending of the GDP.
2   A freeze of the rate of increase of real wages.
3   An increase in the mobility of labour.[38]

To refuse to adopt this strategy was tantamount to 'giving up staying in Europe'.[39] It was in order to 'stay in Europe' that the Italian government, against the advice of the majority of economic experts, decided to join the system of exchange rates known as the European Monetary System.

In 1983 the socialist leader, Bettino Craxi, became Prime Minister. The economic programme he adopted was intended to lower inflation rates and bring Italy to the levels of its foreign competitors. During 1984 Italy's inflation decreased from 15 per cent to 10.6 per cent, Italian exports to the USA increased by a record 46 per cent and the Italian economy as a whole grew by 2.8 per cent instead of the 2 per cent which had been forecast. The gap between Italy and its competitors, however, was not bridged. In the top seven industrialized countries the rate of growth was 5 per cent rather than the forecast 3.3: the USA grew by 7 per cent (rather than 4.5), France and West Germany by 1 per cent over the forecast, Japan by 1.5 over the forecast. All countries increased their exports to the USA thanks to its record balance of payments deficit and the strength of the dollar which made all other countries' products relatively cheap. As for the decrease in the rate of inflation, the Craxi government's major success, this was in line with the general trend in the industrialized countries. In absolute terms, however, Italian inflation rates were still over twice as high as the average of the OECD countries. As for unemployment, this was 10.3 per cent in 1984, second, among the top seven, only to the UK.[40] This confirms the view that the Italian economy had become far more dependent on the international economic cycle, and particularly on the US cycle, than on the decisions of the government.

Over the following years the separation of the Italian economy from the political system became more pronounced. The advent of a new international economic agenda dominated by the revival of neo-liberalism and deregulation was the most important feature of this separation which affected most European countries. In Italy, however, this would be far more serious as the political system imploded and gave rise of an unprecedented political crisis. We shall deal with this crisis in Chapter 15, while the next chapter will examine the vicissitude of the Italian economy from the mid-1980s to the mid-1990s.

Endnotes

1 Baratta et al. 1978, p. 4. See also figures in Castronovo 1975, p. 476.
2 Castronovo 1975, p. 477.
3 Garavini 1974, p. 29.
4 This analysis of the economic assumptions of the Bank of Italy relies on Graziani and Meloni 1980, pp. 59–80.
5 Valli 1980, p. 89.
6 Amato 1976, p. 55.
7 Onida 1977, p. 75.
8 Ibid., p. 73.
9 Peggio 1976, p. 51.
10 Colajanni 1976, p. 12.
11 Onida 1977, pp. 70–71.
12 Parboni 1981, pp. 79–80.
13 Valli 1979, p. 135.
14 Figures in Colajanni 1976, p. 8.
15 Castronovo 1975, p. 482.
16 Garavini 1974, p. 60.
17 Cantelli 1980, p. 51.
18 Ibid., p. 88.
19 National Accounts of OECD in the *Financial Times*, 7 December 1981.
20 See figures in Cantelli 1980, p. 81.

21 Valli 1980, pp. 99–100.
22 Fabiani 1977, p. 167.
23 Amato 1976, pp. 62–4.
24 Ibid., p. 101.
25 Garavini 1977, p. 28.
26 Colajanni 1976, p. 46.
27 That there is such a contrast is the thesis asserted in a best-selling book by two leading Italian journalists: E. Scalfari and G. Turani *Razza padrona. Storia della borghesia di stato*, 1974.
28 Valli 1980, p. 105.
29 Fabiani 1980, p. 3.
30 For this analysis see Valli 1980, pp. 151–2.
31 Trentin 1980, p. 3, interview by B. Ugolini. The figures are official Fiat figures.
32 Figures in Baratta et al. 1978, p. 109.
33 Accornero and Carmignani 1978a, pp. 122–5.
34 See figures in Baratta et al. 1978, p. 109.
35 See figures in Filosa and Visco 1980, p. 108.
36 'Piano 1979–81. Una proposta per lo sviluppo una scelta per l'Europa', in Nardozzi 1980, p. 28.
37 See Valli's critique of the Pandolfi Plan in Valli 1979, pp. 140–4.
38 'Piano 1979–81. Una proposta . . .', in Nardozzi 1980, pp. 39–40.
39 Ibid., p. 23.
40 Data in *La Repubblica* 3 January 1985, p. 2, in Visco 1985, p. 1 and in Barclays Bank 1984.

Chapter 5

From boom to crisis, 1985–1996

The years 1985–87 were a period of euphoria and consumption. Italian GNP became larger – or so it was claimed – than that of the UK. This event was called the *sorpasso* (overtaking) and filled Italians with much-needed national pride. Italy was now the fifth economic power in the world, after the USA, Japan, West Germany and France. The figure had been arrived at thanks to some creative accounting which attributed perhaps excessive weight to the officially unrecorded contribution of the hidden economy. Nevertheless, there was no denying that significant progress had been made.

As can be seen from Tables 5.1 and 5.2, Italy remained, throughout the 1980s a relatively high inflation and high unemployment country. However, inflation had fallen from a peak of 21.2 per cent in 1980 to 5.8 per cent in 1986, although it was still at this level in 1995, well above that of Italy's main competitors. Unemployment, though still high, was probably less than it appeared because those employed in the hidden economy were not officially counted. Its growth rates, however, were consistently higher than the OECD average. A consumption boom ensued. Much credit was given to the socialist leader Bettino Craxi who had been prime minister for a near-unprecedented five years. What was the origin of this success?

Given the high degree of interdependence of the Italian economy the obvious general explanation is that Italy benefited of the general world and European recovery and of the fall in the relative price of oil (1986) – a sort of 'counter-shock' compounded by the fall of the dollar. There were also distinctively Italian factors. Some have argued that among the most important causes of the recovery one should include the termination of the *scala mobile*, the indexing of wages (see the section on the trade unions in Chapter 8), a greater flexibility on the part of trade unions and fewer strikes (1986 saw the lowest recorded number of strikes). Moderation in wages were due in part to trade unions weakness, in turn caused by the increase in unemployment, in part to the government pledge to ease income tax.[1] Membership of the European Monetary System (EMS) fixed the exchange rate of the lira and, though this did not automatically lead to lower inflation, was used to justify stringent monetary policies and imposed a discipline on employers. Unable to rely on further depreciation of the lira, employers were now more reluctant to grant wage increases. Under a fixed exchange rate regime, the more open the economy, the more

Table 5.1 Unemployment and inflation in fourteen European countries, 1960–89 (%)

	Unemployment		Inflation	
	1974–79	**1979–89**	**1973–79**	**1980–89**
OECD-Europe	5.1	9.1	11.9	7.4
Austria	1.8	3.3	6.3	3.8
Belgium	5.7	11.1	8.4	4.8
Denmark	6.0	8.0	10.8	6.9
France	4.5	9.0	10.7	7.3
Finland	4.4	4.9	12.8	7.3
Germany	3.5	6.8	4.7	2.9
Greece	1.9	6.6	16.1	19.4
Holland	4.9	9.8	7.2	2.8
Italy	6.6	9.9	16.1	11.1
Norway	1.8	2.8	8.7	8.3
Portugal	6.0	7.3	23.7	17.5
Spain	5.3	17.5	18.3	10.2
Sweden	1.9	2.5	9.8	7.9
UK	4.2	9.5	15.6	7.4

Source: © OECD, *Economic Outlook, Historical Statistics 1960–1989*, Paris 1991, p. 43. Holland: my calculation on OECD data. Inflation rates calculated on consumer price indices; Turkey and Iceland excluded from OECD-Europe inflation average. Data on unemployment for 1974–79 in Austria and Denmark calculated on the basis of figures in Angus Maddison, *Dynamic Forces in Capitalist Development*, Oxford 1991, p. 263

Table 5.2 GDP growth in fourteen European countries, 1973–89 (% average annual rate)

	1973–79	**1979–89**
OECD-Europe	2.6	2.3
Austria	2.9	2.0
Belgium	2.2	2.0
Denmark	1.9	1.8
France	2.8	2.1
Finland	2.3	3.7
Germany	2.3	1.8
Greece	3.7	1.8
Holland	2.7	1.5
Italy	3.7	2.5
Norway	4.9	2.8
Portugal	2.9	2.8
Sapin	2.2	2.7
Sweden	1.8	2.0
UK	1.5	2.3

Source: © OECD, *Economic Outlook, Historical Statistics 1960–1989*, Paris 1991

the export-orientated sectors were subjected to something akin to an incomes policy because they could not increase prices without penalty. This discipline, however, did not work in sectors sheltered from foreign competition such as the public
sector, most private services and the construction industry. As a result inflation in
the sheltered sector was 139.1 per cent in 1982–90 while in the sector exposed to
foreign competition it was only 79.1 per cent. Employment in the exposed sector
dropped by 14.7 per cent while it actually increased by 19.1 per cent in the sheltered sector.[2] Nevertheless, the discipline had some beneficial effects. It has been
estimated that inflation would have been 3–4 per cent higher if the lira had been
allowed to float.[3] The lower inflation and the more stable international economic
environment led to a more optimistic climate. This encouraged Italian entrepreneurs
to seize the opportunity provided by the world recovery. Large-scale entrepreneurs
were able to raise capital through new issues engineering a stock exchange boom
interrupted by the crash of October 1987. As we have seen in the preceding chapters,
finance-raising had always been a major problem for Italian firms. Raising cash by
selling new shares was difficult. Firms were always forced to finance themselves
out of profits or by borrowing. But now it looked as if – finally – small investors
were beginning to trust the stock exchange. Nevertheless, this remained grossly
underdeveloped in Italy. It could not account for the economic upturn. The paucity
of shareholders meant that Italian capitalism remained underdeveloped. Capitalist
property was either in the hands of individuals, for instance Silvio Berlusconi's
Fininvest, or a family, for instance the Agnellis' Fiat or the state (ENI, IRI, etc.).
Medium-term capital to industry was provided by a secretive, semi-public investment bank, Mediobanca, founded in 1946 by the largest three state-owned banks.
Led, directly or indirectly by the same man since its foundation, Enrico Cuccia,
Mediobanca protected large industry from the interference of the state and of the
political parties.[4] In so doing, however, considerable economic power continued to
be concentrated in a few hands.

Much of the credit for the recovery – I hesitate to use the term of 'second economic miracle' peddled, somewhat over-enthusiastically, by sections of the media
– must go to what was in effect the backbone of the Italian economy, namely the
small and medium-sized enterprises (SME) of the 'Third Italy', that is, those employing between eleven and 500 workers. This term was coined by Bagnasco, to
denote the areas of North-East and Central Italy where industry is prevalently small
craft-based firms as opposed to the 'Second Italy' of the South and the 'First Italy'
dominated by large firms in the industrial triangle of Genoa, Turin and Milan in the
North-West.[5] In industry (excluding construction) 37.4 per cent of workers were
employed in firms with fewer than fifty employees while firms with more than 500
employees accounted for 29.4 per cent of the total (1991 figures).[6]

As previous chapters have established, there was nothing new in the prominent
role of the SMEs. Far from decreasing under the onslaught of large firms, they
prospered in the 1980s even more than in the 1970s while the number of workers
employed in large firms decreased by 800,000.[7]

The two trends were interlinked. Many of the tasks performed by the large firms
were subcontracted to smaller firms enjoying lower labour costs. In fact the SMEs

should be roughly divided into two sub-sectors. The first was a *de facto* satellite of large firms. It made component parts for them and was completely dependent on their business cycle. If Fiat faced problems, its satellite firms would suffer tenfold. The second sub-sector was involved in relatively independent activities, although in many instances they too depended on larger firms subcontracting work to local artisans – as is the case in the Tuscan leather goods industry.[8] Located in the 'Third Italy' (mainly the regions of Marche, Emilia, Tuscany and the Veneto) it used advanced techniques to produce traditional goods Italy was so skilful at exporting: leather goods, jewellery, shoes, clothing, textiles in Prato, metal goods in Suzzara (Lombardy), ceramic tiles in Sassuolo near Reggio Emilia, pasta, ham and cheese in Parma and Piacenza. There were few SMEs in the South: 18.7 per cent of the total (1991) while one-third of Italians reside in the South.[9] This highly flexible sub-sector enjoyed the support of the local authorities, whether the Christian Democrats in the Veneto or the Communists in Emilia and Tuscany. It was thanks to this relatively traditional industry (enhanced by the growing reputation of Italian design) that Italy managed to keep its share of exports up – nearly 40 per cent of firms with fewer than 50 employees depend mainly on foreign markets –[10] while the productivity of Fiat was lagging behind that of its European competitors.[11] It should not be thought that the SMEs were under-sized. They operated close to the optimum level for the kind of production they were involved in.[12]

The SMEs could adjust rapidly to changes in demand. They had low organizational costs. During a recession they could fold down at low cost only to spring up again later, also at low cost. The local ethos was not one of cut-throat competition between rival firms but, on the contrary, one of close inter-firm cooperation. The entrepreneurs operating in this sector had to be multi-skilled and therefore equally flexible. They could easily evade taxation. Entrepreneurs lamented that they paid the highest employers' contributions in Europe: in 1989 it corresponded to 67 per cent of employees' net income against 27 per cent in Germany and 14 per cent in the UK.[13] But they preferred to ignore the fact that evasion of national insurance contributions by small and medium-sized enterprises was estimated to be around 70 per cent.[14] Indeed, to escape Value Added Tax (VAT) they had an incentive in being as small as possible, contracting out jobs whenever they could.[15] The origins of many of the industrial districts where the SMEs prevailed lay in the rural system of sharecropping which forced the family to develop managerial skills such as purchasing, book-keeping, and the cost-benefit analysis of new investments. They built on locally pre-existing design and craft skills and good technical schools.[16]

This is not to say that the 'Third Italy' presents, as some have believed, a simple model which can be easily copied. It was obviously not sufficient to be small or to have some easily identifiable entrepreneurial skills. There had to be a proper mix of many factors of which one of the crucial ones was the relation between entrepreneurs and the workforce. We take as an example a comparative study of the textile industry in Biella (Piedmont) and in Prato, near Florence.[17] The Biella area – a world leader in the clothing industry – consists of 83 small towns and villages with a population of 200,000. Of the 5,000 firms operating in the area, 3,000 operated exclusively in the wool clothing business employing 35,000 workers and exporting a third of their products to Germany, Japan, France and the USA. In the 1970s Biella faced a major recession caused by the increasing competition from the new industrialized countries of Asia. During the succeeding restructuring, all firms with more than 500 workers disappeared while smaller firms emerged each specializing in a particular phase of the production cycle.[18] This structural change-over had been negotiated between employers and the trade unions, both united in a 'pact for development' aimed at saving local industry.[19]

The Prato textile industry had much in common with that of Biella – even their distant origins in the fifteenth century. The relatively large textile mills which had been a characteristic of Prato faced, after the Second World War, a major crisis. Many of the firms folded, selling or renting the machines to their now redundant workers. What emerged was the so-called 'Prato Model' whose chief characteristic was a division of labour based on a cottage industry with each phase of the production process handed out to individual workers and their families by intermediaries. At first, in the 1950s, Prato specialized in woollen goods of low quality: cheap blankets, uniforms, etc. Later, in the 1960s and 1970s, production was redirected towards better quality clothing. Such adjustments could not prevent the crisis of the 1980s, which led to a reduction in the number of firms operating, from 15,000 firms in 1981 to 10,000 in 1995, a trend clearly divergent from that of Biella. Most observers attribute the crisis in Prato not only to competition from Asia but to the lack of cooperation among local firms. At a time of crisis, the intermediaries who distributed the work to be undertaken (corresponding to the different phases of production) among the different productive units played the one against the others in an effort to keep costs down. What enabled Biella to prosper more than Prato was greater cooperation and social consensus. In Prato, there was a rich community life and a 'pro-enterprise' communist culture (17 per cent of communist party members were small entrepreneurs or artisans), but large firms had a greater economic influence, and there was a deep politico-cultural conflict between the large firms, whose owners were overwhelmingly Christian Democrats and the surrounding 'red' sub-culture. The SME model appeared to work better in Biella than in Prato because of the peculiarities of its local culture. Yet – one should add – things worked far better in Prato than in most other provinces. Italian opinion-makers, influenced by mythical foreign models, have regularly lamented the lack of an entrepreneurial mentality in Italy, pointing out that the two dominant sub-cultures of the country, the communist and the Catholic, have an anti-entrepreneurial or even an anti-capitalist spirit. Yet, when all is said and done, Italian enterprises thrive in the regions where these two sub-cultures are strongest. For example, between 1955 and 1984 the municipality of Modena (one of the strongholds of Italian communists) enabled 584 firms to be established on land it had especially purchased for local economic developments. It then helped these small firms and many others by setting up, in 1980, the CITER (*Centro Informazione Tessile Emilia-Romagna*) which provided information to artisans and small entrepreneurs in the clothing industry on market trends, types of yarn available, current prices, technology obtainable and fashion trend – the sort of information which was previously available only to medium and large firms.[20]

Even though the central state has helped Italian industry far more than in Germany, France or Britain it is widely seen as absent or inefficient or as little more than a machine which gathers votes in exchange for subsidies. But local government is often able to work in close cooperation with local enterprise. The banking system, which is made up of a myriad of small local banks, works, in this instance, in favour of the SMEs. Small banks take decisions and allocate loans on the basis of their knowledge of the local industrial districts and on their direct knowledge of the entrepreneurs.

But can the SMEs enable Italy to meet the challenges of the twenty-first century? The prognosis cannot be optimistic. To take the last point first: it seems inevitable that, as the European single market becomes established, there will be a thorough rationalization of the banking sector. This means that large banks will take over small banks and impose a homogeneous system. This will contain banking costs and will help large firms who prefer to deal with banks of comparable size. But flexibility and local knowledge will be lost as distant head offices will impose a uniform system. There are no institutional investors – as there are in Japan and Germany – which would enable the Italian SMEs to cope with the gradual restructuring which is necessary.[21]

How long can Italy withstand the competition of non-European countries in clothing, leather goods, shoes, which, with wood, furniture, agricultural and industrial machines constitute 40 per cent of Italian exports?[22] Too much of Italy's exports was concentrated in these fields. Italy was still the major world exporter of clothing but it was closely followed by South Korea, Taiwan, China and Hong Kong.[23] How can it restructure itself towards the new science-based industries when the gulf with its north-western European partners and when small firms are less able than large firms to take on board technological innovation? The trend is not favourable as Italy is actually losing ground even in the advanced sectors in which it had a foothold, such as photographic equipment and office machines. As the import of high technology are bound to increase so will Italy's deficit in this sector.[24] Italy's export in high technology goods such as computers, precision instruments, chemicals and pharmaceuticals was – in the early 1990s – only 5.9 per cent of the total against an EEC average of 9.7 per cent, in France the proportion was 12.4 per cent and in the UK 15.5 per cent.[25] Once, Italian offices were full of Olivetti typewriters; now they are full of computers assembled in Asia. Italians work on software produced in the USA while Olivetti struggles to survive. The 'Third' Italy may have, so far, saved the other two but it is not really a model that can be exported or that can survive indefinitely into the future. In the conclusion to her survey of Italian economic history, Vera Zamagni remarked sadly that Italy, though now an advanced country, had never been a model for others, unlike Britain as the first industrial nation, Germany and its 'mixed' banks, France with its efficient public sector bureaucracy, the USA with its multinationals and Japan with its joint government and industry long-term planning system. Italy, Zamagni remarked, simply imitated and still imitates what has been done elsewhere.[26]

An economic structure based on small firms is not conducive to adequate research and development. Spending in this field, vital in the twenty-first century, was far too low in Italy. In 1990 public aid in this area was around 3–5 per cent compared to 10–11 per cent in France and 18 per cent in Germany.[27]

Italy may boast that it is the fifth economic power in the world but it has the infrastructures of a poor country, ahead of Ireland, Spain, Portugal and Greece but well behind all other European Union countries.[28] The ports are insufficient and badly organized. The rail system is probably the worst in Western Europe. The telecommunication network does not work properly. The water supply is defective. The postal system is so unreliable that Italians do not trust it to deliver their cheques and go to the bank for most of their payments. A letter takes twice as long in Italy as it does in France, Germany or Britain even though the Italian postal system employs 200,000 people. Of the 168 European regions (1990 EEC) classified in terms of their infrastructures (transport, communications, energy and education) the top three are Hamburg, Paris and Bremen with a classification index number of, respectively, 318, 235 and 233 (the higher the number the better the infrastructure). Italy's 'best for infrastructure' region, Liguria, is thirteenth with 161, Lombardy is thirty-seventh with 125. Eleven Italian regions including prosperous ones like the Valle d'Aosta, the Trentino, the Marche and Umbria, are classified in the bottom 62. Basilicata, infrastructurally the most deprived, is 145th with an index of 34.[29]

The further south we proceed, the more deficient are the transport, education, communications and energy systems. The classification of Italy's 95 provinces in terms of infrastructure show that the top 50 are all north of Naples and the bottom 20 are all south of Rome.[30]

The much-vaunted *sorpasso* turned out to be a remarkable missed opportunity. Unlike France, Italy had failed to take advantage of the international economic expansion of the 1980s and its international competitiveness declined at the end of the 1980s.[31] As had been the case during the previous 'economic miracle' the gains from recovery were frittered away in an unparalleled consumption boom. While many Italians swaggered around in designer clothes (or their imitations) and travelled abroad in unprecedented numbers, the old contrast between public squalor and private affluence emerged in full. The educational system was in disarray. The universities remained unreformed and organized on behalf of a professorial mafia and not of increasingly disenchanted students. The justice system in particular was in a state of near-total paralysis. The proliferation of permits required led to their being widely ignored. Litigation often ensued, leading to thousands of court cases. Bureaucratic complexities, the restrictive practices of judges, lawyers and magistrates and administrative inertia led to legal delays of Dickensian proportions. Rather than wait for permits with the attendant risk that they not be granted, people simply went ahead with illegal building or home improvements, left their taxes unpaid, their television licence unrenewed, their fines outstanding until an inevitable amnesty wiped the slate clean and everything could start again.[32]

Italian entrepreneurs who had tolerated the inefficiencies of the Italian state machine by supporting successive DC-led governments were increasingly dissatisfied. With the development of the single market and the growing importance of the European dimension they saw these ineptitudes of the bureaucratic machine not as a fact of life or something which could be ignored but as a real obstacle to their expansion.[33] For many small industrialists, however, administrative chaos provided a powerful incentive to circumvent altogether the state by evading taxation and hiring workers outside the normal labour market thus allowing them to compete against their colleagues in other countries which found this sort of endeavour more difficult to pursue.

The situation in the South was as disastrous as ever. It is true that standards of living had improved, that the income gap between North and South had been closed and that wages were the same. However, the system of state-sponsored large-scale industry had proved to be unviable while small-scale industry developed only in some areas. The old network of southern small firms were wiped out by the technologically superior organization of the northern ones. The industrial restructuring of the first half of the 1980s had been led mainly by the Centre-North and had been consolidated in the second half by cheaper oil prices (the 'oil countershock') and stable prices.[34] The level of investment in the South remained as low as ever. The South produced only 10 per cent of Italian exports.[35] Unemployment remained very high, increasing throughout the 1980s at a faster rate than in the North, especially among the young. By the early 1990s the unemployment rate in South was around 20 per cent while that of the Centre-North was 6–7 per cent. Production per capita in the South was half that of the Centre-North while consumption was two-thirds.[36] In the mid-1980s, 20 per cent of the southern population was still employed in agriculture (in 1945 it had been 50 per cent), but the lowering of tariffs meant that Italian agriculture was less protected while being penalized by European Union policies which still favoured German and French farmers at the expense of those of the Mediterranean member countries. Sixteen per cent were employed in industry, only 3 per cent more than in 1951 while those employed in house building and services had doubled. As illustrated in Chapter 3, the South has far more than its fair share of pensions for disabled people, thanks to the complicity of local doctors who certify them and politicians who encourage them; yet this is seen as the outcome of the lack of a benefits for the unemployed and the fact that, as fewer people have been employed in a pensionable job, fewer qualify for a 'proper' pension.

The politicians' traditional method of simply throwing money at the problem had not succeeded in eliminating the North-South gap. If standards of living had improved it was mainly due to the flow of money from the central government not to a revival of enterprise. As long as there was significant growth in the economy, southerners could expect the cascade of money to continue. By 1992 – when the Ministry for the South and the *Cassa per il mezzogiorno* was abolished – the population of the South received 35 per cent of public expenditure (in line with its population), but it contributed only 18–22 per cent towards tax revenues. In the 1990s, however, the ever-recurrent call for controlling public expenditure, now between 50 and 60 per cent of GNP (not particularly out of line, it should be said, with many other European countries) and a more stringent fiscal mechanism led northerners to turn against further handouts to the South and to support the first explicitly anti-southern party to have emerged in post-war Italy.[37] Much of this antagonism is, empirically, unjustified. As suggested in previous chapters, the 'backwardness' of the South turned in favour of the North. The vast emigration from the

South was of far greater benefit to the northern economy than to that of the South. Emigration had traditionally forced the young, male and, presumably, the more actively minded population out of the South. What was left was a society of old people and women whose education provided few if any incentives for productive work and a marked gender imbalance.[38] Today, even though those between the age of 20 and 25 are 40 per cent of the southern population, the South has proportionately fewer universities and fewer university teachers, many of its students have to go to the northern universities, while those who remain tend to seek degrees in law rather than those in technology-based courses, reflecting the demands of the main employers: the public sector. As a result 90–95 per cent of research and development takes place in the North.[39]

The *Cassa per il mezzogiorno* may not have been successful but it was not the 'bottomless pit', the vast drain on public expenditure which most Italians believe it was: a rough calculation of all expenditure of the Cassa in the period 1951–81 showed that this consisted of 0.85 per cent of national income – less, for instance, than the cost of the Steel Plan in 1948 which was 3 per cent of national income.[40]

The criticisms of state intervention in the South should be put in perspective. Its objective was to provide the South with much needed infrastructures on the assumption that the private sector would create employment. The private sector, in spite of incentives, was unable to generate any kind of internal industrial take-off. In so far as there were any industries in the South, these were due to the intervention of the state. The claim that, had the state done nothing or little, the South would have been the beneficiary of adequate private investment is unsustainable. Nor was Italy (North or South) a beneficiary of foreign direct investments. The productivity achieved by Italian industry in the late 1980s provided an opportunity for investing in the South. Instead, the new wealth was absorbed by public spending, higher wages by those employed and found its way into private consumption.[41] While in other countries poverty is clustered among groups such as single mothers or pensioners, in Italy it is concentrated in the South: 26 per cent of its population are poor while only 9 per cent of the population of the Centre and the North could be so described (the poor are defined as those whose income was less than half the average income).[42] Official government figures (ISTAT 1991) tell a similar story: 6.1 per cent of all Italian families are poor, divided between 4.2 per cent in the South, 0.6 per cent in the Centre and 1.2 per cent in the North.[43]

It may be thought that this dire situation would have had profound repercussion on social peace. On the contrary, the South remained the bedrock of electoral support for the governing coalition. The Christian Democratic Party and its main ally, the Italian Socialist Party, lost votes in the North, especially in 1992 to the Northern Leagues. The DC and the PSI were saved by their growing southern electorate – until the final collapse of the First Republic. How can this be explained?

In spite of the growing re-discovery of the market and the neo-liberal rhetoric which was developing in Italy in the 1980s – an effect of the seductive power of Thatcherist and Reaganian simplicities – Italian politicians did not (until 1992) make the slightest forays onto the dangerous terrain of 'reaganomics'. In the 1980s the 'buzz-word' was 'decisionism'; it was not about neo-liberalism. The assumption was that Italy's economic problems would be fixed if only a stable and strong executive could be formed. Economics took a back seat while an endless and ultimately unproductive debate on institutional reforms took place.

In the meantime it was vital to keep the electorate happy by ensuring that private consumption could go on expanding by market means if possible or by state activity if necessary. In the 1970s exporters could be kept happy thanks to repeated devaluation while wages were allowed to expand, checked only by inflation. When this had to stop a new mechanism was introduced to enable Italian consumption growth to continue. The public debt was increased at a rapid rate through the repeated sale of state bonds or BOTs (*Buoni del Tesoro*). This offered their holders a high rate of interests and enabled the state to finance economic expansion and, more to the point, to avoid retrenching the public sector which was the main lifeline of the South.

The mechanism could be thus slightly caricatured: the vast savings Italians were able to accumulate through non-payment of taxes would have been channelled abroad had the lira continued to depreciate. To obtain the revenue lost from its own reluctant taxpayers, the Italian state 'bribed' them by offering them not only a stronger lira (anchored to the EMS) but also a high rate of interest on the BOTs and tax exemptions (in any case BOTs can be held anonymously). Thus those who were able to avoid taxes gained twice: in the first place, because they did not pay taxes, and secondly, because the state had provided them with a risk-free and profitable outlet for their savings. What of those wage-earners whose income was taxed at source? Those who were employed in the public sector saw their wages and salaries increase regularly at a faster rate than wages in the private sector against the trend of the rest of Europe.[44] Those who were employed by large-scale private industry were the main losers, though they benefited indirectly because the high spending levels enabled a consumption boom to keep private industry in business.

The main drawback to this expansion was that each year the state had to pay back to BOT-holders more interest. This led to an enormous increase in the public debt. The outcome of this perverse mechanism – induced by the desperate need of the leading political parties to remain in power – was alarming. While Italian industry was losing competitiveness on foreign markets turning the 1980s in the only period of post-war Italian history in which the country did not grow significantly more rapidly than the rest of Europe, consumption expansion fuelled imports leading, in 1991, to a major foreign trade deficit. This led to even higher rates of interests and higher state deficit in an effort to entice Italian savers to keep their holdings in BOTs. By the early 1990s some 20 per cent of state revenue was directed towards interest repayment. At the same time, high interest rates further squeeze production investment while increasing consumption because savers obtain high untaxed earning from their BOTs.[45]

As I write, Italy is still trying to come to grips with the consequences of those years. It was not easy to find a remedy because 80 per cent of the Italian population actually experienced an increase in living standards in the late 1980s. Calls for austerity fell on deaf ears. In the early 1990s economists pointed out that it was necessary to reduce consumption in favour of investment and to reduce domestic demand in favour of exports so as to reduce the balance of payments current account deficits.[46] As the political system was crumbling it was more difficult than usual to get politicians to campaign on what would, unavoidably, be unpopular policies. The weakness of Italian governments was directly related to the corresponding strength of the political parties in parliament. However, the parliament which resulted from the 1992 elections was quite exceptional. This will be examined in the conclusion (Chapter 15) when we deal with the crisis of the First Republic. Here it will be sufficient to point out that the electoral results had been a major disappointment for the traditional ruling parties (the DC and the PSI) even though the performance of the former communists (now the Party of the Democratic Left) had been dismal. In the North the separatist Northern Leagues had made inroads into the traditional DC electorate. A few months before the election the investigation of Milan magistrates had begun to reveal the extent of corruption and to examine the involvement of politicians in the complex system of kickbacks which became known as *Tangentopoli*. As a result, the government (July 1992 to May 1993), though presided by Giuliano Amato, a socialist close to Bettino Craxi, had an unusual autonomy from the political parties. As nearly one-third of members of parliament – almost all belonging to the parties supporting the government – were notified by the magistrates that they were being investigated for corruption, the Amato government could proceed to deliver in the summer of 1992 one of the most substantial austerity packages in Italian history.[47]

The Amato government increased charges on health users, cut the growth of public expenditure on health and national insurance, increasing the contributions to be paid by employees and employers, sold part of the public housing stock, terminated many of the terms favourable to the trade unions in the public sector.[48] Salaries in the public sector were capped. A series of easily collectable taxes on house ownership, bank deposits and on the self-employed were introduced. Public expenditure was contained and a privatization programme was launched while many existing constraints on competition were removed.[49] On 31 July 1992 Amato reached a landmark agreement with the trade unions further reducing the indexing of wages. This had been long considered the most formidable obstacle to reducing Italy's inflation. By then, however, a new 'main obstacle' had been discovered. The real culprit, it turned out, was the considerable imbalance in public finances. In 1981 the public debt had been 61 per cent of GNP; in 1991 it had reached 101 per cent of GNP. Financing expenditure by selling BOTs and paying higher wages to public sector employees was not a cost-free operation. The markets did not think that the indexation deal was particularly significant, even though the government and the press had hailed the new agreement as a major breakthrough.[50] After all, inflation had decreased throughout the OECD. The lira continued to be sold throughout the summer. A run on the currency is often a self-fulfilling prophecy. To maintain the exchange rate it would have been necessary to increase interest rates, but, if these had been increased, the government would have had even more problems with adjusting its finances because it would have had to pay more to borrow money.[51] The Bank of Italy threw half the country's foreign reserve in the defence of the lira but to no avail. On the 13 September 1992 the Amato government withdrew the currency from the Exchange Rate Mechanism (ERM). The lira was, once again, free to find its own level and collapsed by 14 per cent against most European currencies (but not, significantly, against the peseta and sterling – also victims of the exchange rate crisis of 'black' September). The fall of the lira, as it turned out, was beneficial to the economy, at least in the short run, as Italy regained some of its lost competitiveness and succeeded, by 1993 to eliminate its balance of payments deficit. In fairness it should be added that even before the expulsion from the ERM, Italy's competitiveness had begun to improve, thanks to an increase in productivity (due to unemployment), greater innovation and a lowering of costs (due to weaker unions and state concessions on employers' contribution).[52] The political costs, however, were significant. Traditionally, Italy had been one of the staunchest supporters of European integration as opinion polls repeatedly confirmed. Membership of the ERM, as we have seen, had also an economic dimension because it established a discipline which had permitted the country to escape the devaluation-inflation vicious circle. Italians had welcomed the Maastricht Treaty including its social protocol and the principle of setting out criteria of economic convergence. In 1990 the Italian government, in agreement with the trade unions, had led the country into the so-called 'narrow' band of the ERM (2.5 per cent currency fluctuation instead of 6 per cent). After September 1992 Italy seemed, once again, to be going its own way. Yet, from a different perspective, the policies of the Amato government appeared to indicate that, at last, Italy had joined the new neo-liberal consensus which had prevailed throughout most of Europe in the 1980s. What had prevented Italy from following the new Zeitgeist was the fact that the ruling parties behaved *de facto* like social-democratic parties in the sense that they were deeply committed, for electoral reasons, to pursuing a policy of high public spending. The crisis of these parties enabled a relatively autonomous government to do what Italy should have done all along. However this 'neo-liberal' turn, it was pointed out, occurred without any great ideological fracas *à la* Thatcher.[53] What Amato and his supporters were saying was that, finally, 'the party was over'. Italians had been extravagant long enough; now they had to pay. The time for austerity had come. What is often forgotten is that one of the key components of Thatcherism had been a diminution of *direct* taxation which had resulted in a redistribution of the burden of taxation from the poor to the rich resulting in a 'Yuppy' boom at roughly the same time as that of Italy. Secondly, the Thatcher years in the UK had been characterized by a confrontation with the trade unions who were systematically excluded from decision-making. This did not occur in Italy under Amato or any of the two successive 'technocratic' governments led first by Carlo Azeglio Ciampi, former Governor of the Bank of Italy, and then – after the interval of the Berlusconi government – by Lamberto Dini, former Director General of the Bank of Italy. The only bid to by-pass the unions was that attempted by the Berlusconi government of 1994. It resulted in total failure.

The Dini government of technocrats of 1995 continued in the steps of the Amato and Ciampi governments: prudent austerity in agreement with the unions, gradual privatization leading to the remarkable reduction of the extent of IRI stateholding and a strengthening of Italy's position abroad after the collapse of the lira. These policies were continued by the first post-war government in which the left (i.e. the PDS) had the dominant weight: the Olive Tree Alliance led by Romano Prodi. By November 1996 the lira had re-entered the ERM at 990 lire to the Deutsche Mark (it had sunk to below 1,200 under Berlusconi), and heroic efforts were made to meet the Maastricht criteria for monetary union.

The third major neo-liberal plank was deregulation. It is true that Italy's regulatory system was particularly pronounced in large-scale industry: the Statuto dei Lavoratori had enshrined in law trade union rights which had been sapped elsewhere while indexation had created a highly inflexible wage regulation system. There was also considerable regulation of the housing market while small shopkeepers were subjected to fiscal controls unparalleled elsewhere in Europe. However, the backbone of the Italian economy, the small and medium-sized firms, could escape such controls with greater ease than elsewhere.

The fourth great plank of neo-liberalism was privatization. During the 1980s there were no significant privatizations in Italy. While the UK was privatizing companies employing 400,000 employees in 1979–85, during a similar period (1980–86) privatized Italian companies employed 50,000 workers. What decision-makers were particularly concerned about was how to make the ENI and IRI profitable or, at least, less of a burden on the state, rather than how to sell them. In fact, not the government but the IRI and ENI themselves were in effect in charge of the privatization programme, keeping the revenues from companies sold to the private sector.[54] Some privatization did occur, for instance the IRI-owned car manufacturer Alfa Romeo was 'privatized' in the sense that it was sold to Fiat, hardly an increase in competition – quite the reverse. Some antitrust legislation was started in 1990 but only under European Union pressure.[55] In November 1996, the PDS-dominated Prodi government announced that, by 1998, IRI would be divested of all its holdings in banking, foodstuff, retail, motorway, shipping, steel and telecommunications keeping only the RAI, some high technology and defence (Finmeccanica) and the airline Alitalia. The public sector giant created by Mussolini would be cut down to size by the successors of the Italian Communist Party.

Neo-liberal ideology did not hold sway in Italy as it did in Anglo-Saxon countries. Italy conformed to the continental European pattern in which economic policies followed a deregulatory path on a pragmatic and not an ideological basis. The main peculiarity of Italy's path was that the limited neo-liberal turn required the actual dismantling of the basic party political structures rather than a shift within these parties, as had been the case with Felipe González in Spain or François Mitterrand in France or, for that matter, Thatcher's conservatives.

The Italian 'turn' against the state should be seen in the context of a well-established distrust of it. Even Italian entrepreneurs, traditionally beholden to the existing political structure, were disengaging themselves from government partly because the growing internationalization of the economy made this attachment less relevant and partly because they were increasingly reluctant to pay the kickbacks necessary to obtain special favours.[56]

The state was seen as the chief culprit for Italy's economic woes. It was said that the private sector had taken the brunt of the restructuring of the 1980s. It had lost

employment, had become leaner, more efficient, productivity had increased, inflation decreased. Meanwhile, as we have seen, the ruling political parties continued
to increase employment and salaries in the state sector leading to an increase
in prices in non-manufacturing higher than the increase in manufacturing. The
inescapable conclusion was that inflationary pressures originated mainly in the
public sector.[57]

Economic development had thus created an environment in which the principal
ingredients of the political crisis of the 1990s could thrive. The most important was
the notion that the Italian state – as represented by the old ruling coalitions – had
become an obstacle to economic prosperity: it was unable to achieve the proper
integration of the country into Europe, unfit to resolve the 'Southern Question',
inept in providing the required infrastructures. As long as there was enough growth
in the economy to provide for the continued protection of Italy's large public sector, such dissent could be held at bay. When it became counterproductive, the ruling
coalition lost even the important support of the principal economic operators.

Endnotes

1 Alberto Bertoni, 'Disinflation and the Financial Structure of Firms' in *Review of Economic Conditions in Italy*, Banca di Roma, no. 2, July–December 1994, pp. 142–4.
2 Brunetta and Tronti 1993, pp. 154–5.
3 Ferraguto 1992, p. 35.
4 Castronovo 1995, p. 525.
5 Bagnasco 1977.
6 Zuliani 1994, p. 71.
7 Castronovo 1995, pp. 500–1.
8 Bianchini 1991, p. 338.
9 Zuliani 1994, p. 71.
10 Ibid., p. 77.
11 Castronovo 1995, p. 508.
12 Zuliani 1994, p. 73.
13 Micossi and Pai 1994, p. 48.
14 Vicari 1993, pp. 258–9
15 Regini 1995, p. 7.
16 Bianchini 1991, p. 338.
17 This example rests on a case study by Richard M. Locke, see Locke 1995.
18 Locke 1995, pp. 45–46.
19 Locke 1995, p. 47.
20 For these and other details see Brusco and Righi 1989.
21 Onida 1993, p. 68.
22 Paganetto et al. 1993, p. 103.
23 Ibid., p. 105.
24 Tajoli 1992, pp. 192–3.
25 Paganetto et al. 1993, p. 104.
26 Zamagni 1993, pp. 485–6.
27 Onida 1993, p. 67.
28 Alò and Rosa 1990, pp. 10–12 and 23.
29 Data in Alò and Rosa 1990, pp. 27–9.
30 Ibid.
31 Brunetta and Tronti 1993, p. 153.
32 Vicari 1993, p. 264.
33 Castronovo 1995, p. 542.
34 D'Antonio et al. 1993, p. 191.
35 Zamagni 1993, p. 474 and D'Antonio et al. 1993, p. 182.
36 D'Antonio et al. 1993, pp. 179–80 and Bruni and Micossi 1992, p. 263.
37 Castronovo 1995, pp. 536–9.
38 Zamagni 1993, p. 475.
39 Paganetto et al. 1993, p. 122.
40 De Meo 1988, pp. 156, 160–1, see also his calculation on the effects of internal migration to the North on pp. 162–3.
41 D'Antonio et al. 1993, p. 192.
42 Sarpellon 1992. Of course, as in most other countries immigrants and old age pensioners account for a disproportionate percentage of the poor.
43 Paci 1993, p. 272.
44 Treu 1991, p. 308 and Micossi and Pai, 1994, p. 41.
45 Baldassari 1993, pp. 80–2.
46 For instance, Baldassari and Modigliani 1993, pp. 4–5.
47 Castronovo 1995, p. 546.

48 Regonini 1993, p. 372.
49 Brunetta and Tronti, 1993, pp. 158–9.
50 Vaciago 1993, p. 24.
51 Ibid., p. 25.
52 Paganetto et al. 1993, pp. 101–2.
53 Regonini 1993, p. 387.

54 Bianchi, Cassese and Vincent della Sala 1988, pp. 87–9.
55 Regonini 1993, pp. 361–8.
56 Cazzola 1992, p. 154.
57 Bruni and Micossi 1992, pp. 258, 261.

Part two

Society

Chapter 6

Classes and migrant workers

The debate on social classes

Part One of this book was devoted to an overview of Italian economic development and attempted to offer a historical perspective of its integration in the world economy, its rapid industrialization and its consequences: prosperity and crises, growth and unequal development. It is already apparent, even without examining any further data, that the most significant change – historically speaking – was the shift from agriculture to industry. Not only is this not peculiar to Italy but it is, in a sense, a tautology: any process of industrialization involves a shift of population from the countryside. We are not, however, dealing simply with two sectors of the economy: industrial and agricultural production. There is also a third sector, populated overwhelmingly by intermediate groups usually labelled the 'middle classes'. These 'middle' groups can also be found in the manufacturing sector, for instance artisans or white-collar workers and in the rural economy, for instance independent small farmers.

It is thus immediately apparent that when we talk about the classification of the population we can use essentially two criteria: distribution in terms of broad occupational definitions, for example manufacturing, agriculture and services, or stratification in terms of social class, for example upper class, middle class and working class. One can of course use other criteria, for example income levels. This would be important if we wanted to know whether Italy was becoming a more equal society in terms of income while an analysis of the distribution of purchasing power would indicate whether Italy was becoming a richer society.

Here we want to concentrate on the stratification of the population in terms of social classes and then examine briefly the distribution in terms of occupational sectors and conclude with a brief examination of emigration and the new immigrant 'underclass'. The reason for insisting on social classes is that they are politically important. In spite of the rise of social 'subjects' which cut across classes (e.g. women) political parties tended to define their strategy and their demands in terms of specific classes. For example the Italian Communist Party defined the working class as the main protagonist of progressive social change, as the class whose aspirations it sought to defend and promote, though it always recognized that the working class needed to establish alliances with other classes and, in particular with the 'middle strata'. If, however, an analysis were to establish that the middle strata were being constantly 'proletarianized', then the whole concept of class alliances would become more problematic. Let us take another example. The Christian Democratic Party was said to rely on a mechanism of consensus in which the middle strata played the central and crucial role. If that was so, then it would have been in the interest of this party to maintain the strength and expansion of this sector, or, alternatively, to adopt a different political strategy. It is thus not surprising that one of the most important attempts to analyse social classes in Italy, that of Paolo Sylos Labini, caused much controversy.[1] With the end of both the PCI and the DC in 1989–93, class analysis lost its importance. The main parties of what we must continue to call, for lack of a better word, the 'second' republic, appealed to an undifferentiated population – at least in class terms. Other new appeals privileged other dimensions, particularly the regional one. The move away from class politics was made easier in Italy than elsewhere – for instance the UK – because, even during the First Republic, it was apparent that classes were not a strong indicator of party preferences. Neither of the two main parties – the PCI and the DC – had ever conceded to the other the representation of either the working classes or the middle classes.

Sylos Labini had borrowed his central concepts from the classics of political economy, the works of Adam Smith and David Ricardo, who had divided the population in terms of the origin of their incomes: incomes from profit (capitalists), from rent (landlords) and from wages (workers), but they were also perfectly aware that an important section of the population derived its income from its independent activity (artisans and farmers). Sylos Labini thus proposed the following classifications:

1 *The ruling class, or bourgeoisie.* This included both capitalists and large landlords as well as the managers of enterprises and leading professionals.
2 *The middle classes.* This was further subdivided into three categories: the *relatively independent petty bourgeoisie* (farmers and sharecroppers, artisans, shopkeepers and small business people, small professional people); the *salaried petty bourgeoisie* (white-collar workers and teachers, technicians, etc.); special categories (members of the clergy and the military).
3 The *working class.* This included the industrial working class, agricultural labourers, manual workers employed in services and transportation, domestic servants, shop assistants, construction workers, etc.

Sylos Labini's work dealt with a considerable time-span – from 1881 to 1971 – and was based principally but not exclusively on census reports. We shall deal only with the post-war period (see Table 6.1).

It is, however, of interest to state briefly Sylos Labini's conclusions from the broader 1881–1971 study:[2]

1 The most important result was that, between 1881 and 1971, the salaried middle class expanded massively from 2 per cent in 1881 to 17.1 per cent

Table 6.1 Distribution of population by social class, 1951–71

	1951 (%)	1961 (%)	1971 (%)
Bourgeoisie	1.9	2.0	2.6
Middle classes	56.9	53.4	49.6
1 salaried	9.8	13.1	17.1
2 independent	44.4	37.2	29.1
3 special category	2.7	3.1	3.4
Working class	41.2	44.6	47.8

Source: Sylos Labini (1974), p. 156

in 1971, while the independent petty bourgeoisie declined from 41 per cent in 1881 to 29.1 per cent in 1971.

2   The relative weight of the whole of the middle classes with respect to the working class changed little: in 1881 the middle classes were 45.9 per cent, in 1971 they accounted for 49.6 per cent, in 1881 the working classes were 52.2 per cent, in 1971 they were 47.8 per cent.

3   The top bourgeoisie remained fairly stable: 1.9 per cent in 1881 and 2.6 in 1971.

In fact the most significant changes were those since 1951. In that year, the middle classes were at the peak of their growth. The salaried petty bourgeoisie increased in absolute percentage points more in the twenty years between 1951 and 1971 than in the previous seventy years. The relatively independent petty bourgeoisie, which had increased during the fascist period to 47.1 per cent decreased rapidly between 1951 and 1971. The most interesting changes were those which occurred within the classes and subclasses. The relative stability of the bourgeoisie disguised the fall in the number of landlords and the rise of entrepreneurs and managers.

The decrease in the percentage of the relatively independent petty bourgeoisie was due exclusively to the contraction in the numbers of farmers (from 30.3 per cent in 1951 to 12.1 per cent in 1971), those of shopkeepers and artisans increased. The decline in the agricultural working class is very evident between 1951 and 1971 (from 11.8 per cent to 6.2 per cent), but this was not a new phenomenon: it was 35.6 per cent in 1881 and declined ever since. The industrial working class (including building workers) moved from 18.7 per cent in 1901 to 22.9 per cent in 1951. This was hardly a spectacular increase. The period of real growth was between 1951 and 1971 when it grew rapidly to 33 per cent. These figures simply confirm the massive shift from the countryside to the town.

As we stated earlier, Sylos Labini's figures and interpretation became the object of debates and controversies. We will take a brief look at these before proceeding to examine in a more detailed manner the changes which have occurred within each category.

The first problem surrounding the statistical analysis of social classes is that concerning the validity of the data themselves. Antonio Chiesi pointed out that the

Table 6.2 Census versus Sylos Labini (1961) social class data

	Census data (%)	Sylos Labini data (%)	% difference
Bourgeoisie	2.1	2.0	−0.1
Middle class	45.2	53.4	+8.2
Working class	52.7	44.6	−8.1

Source: Ridolfi (1975), p. 74

main sources of statistics (ISTAT, DOXA, Bank of Italy) were all open to serious criticism.[3] Others, such as Paolo Ammassari lamented that the study of social classes in Italy began in a serious way only in 1968. Until then, instead of being in the hands of sociologists, as apparently it should be, such study was in those of historians suspicious of 'positivist' approaches because of their Crocean or Gramscian-Marxist formation.[4] Sylos Labini himself did not always make his own statistical sources clear. For most years he used the census data, but as these were not yet available for 1971, he used instead the Yearbook of Labour Statistics 1972 and constructed his 1961 tables also on the basis of the Yearbook.[5] Had he used the census of 1961 for the 1961 statistics, he would have obtained a different set. The differences were considerable, as Luca Ridolfi demonstrated (see Table 6.2). The data are different but the categories and the construction of these categories, i.e. their definitions, are identical. The result is that the census data 'produce' a significantly larger working class – an extra 1.4 million workers – and a significantly smaller middle class – a loss of 1.8 million – than it would appear from Sylos Labini's calculations.

The other problem with Sylos Labini's class analysis was a familiar one: the question of demarcation lines. A doctor could be in the bourgeoisie if he/she was a famous practitioner with a wealthy clientele, or a 'relatively independent petty bourgeois' if he/she was a modest country doctor, or a 'salaried middle class' if employed in a hospital. Furthermore, there was the problem of 'mixed' status, for example a factory worker with a plot of land.

Broad categories, such as those used so far, disguise quite different social conditions: the relatively independent petty bourgeois could be an affluent jeweller in the centre of Rome or Milan or someone with a stall selling cheap jewellery in a local market. These considerations led to more studies which further differentiated within classes establishing new categories.

Carlo Trigilia used a concept of bourgeoisie identical to that of Sylos Labini, but his middle classes were divided into white collar and independent middle class. This was the same as Sylos Labini, but excluded independent 'precarious' or 'casual' activity, which Trigilia included instead in the 'casual' proletariat. He then identified a class called the 'central' proletariat which included all workers, urban and rural, working in firms employing more than ten people. Finally, there was the 'marginal proletariat' in turn divided into a 'peripheral' proletariat (workers in firms employing less than ten workers), and a 'casual' proletariat which included small farmers and other casual independent workers and labourers.[6]

Table 6.3 Economically active population per social class (%)

	1951			1961			1971		
	Italy	North	South	Italy	North	South	Italy	North	South
Bourgeoisie	**2.1**	**2.2**	**1.9**	**2.2**	**2.4**	**1.9**	**3.2**	**3.3**	**2.6**
Independent middle class	**37.0**	**37.2**	**37.0**	**26.1**	**26.3**	**25.9**	**17.4**	**18.1**	**19.1**
Agriculture	28.5	28.7	28.2	18.2	17.4	19.8	9.5	8.0	12.9
Industry	4.0	3.8	4.5	3.8	3.9	3.8	3.9	4.6	2.4
Tertiary	4.5	4.7	4.3	4.1	5.0	2.3	5.0	5.5	3.8
White collar	**10.7**	**11.9**	**7.8**	**13.9**	**15.7**	**10.3**	**21.5**	**23.3**	**17.8**
Private Sector	4.2	5.3	2.0	7.3	9.1	3.6	11.9	14.3	6.8
Public Sector	6.5	6.6	5.8	6.6	6.6	6.7	9.6	9.0	11.0
Central proletariat	**17.0**	**21.9**	**7.6**	**21.5**	**27.0**	**10.1**	**25.1**	**30.6**	**12.8**
Marginal proletariat	**33.2**	**26.8**	**45.7**	**36.3**	**28.6**	**51.8**	**31.8**	**24.7**	**47.7**
Peripheral	4.6	3.9	6.2	7.1	8.9	3.4	7.7	9.2	4.2
Casual	28.6	22.9	39.5	29.2	19.7	48.4	25.1	15.5	43.5
Agricultural	11.8	6.3	22.4	9.4	3.2	21.8	5.8	1.6	15.5
Industrial	10.7	10.4	11.2	12.0	9.4	17.3	9.7	6.3	17.3
(of which in construction)	4.9	4.2	6.4	7.4	5.2	11.6	5.4	3.4	10.0
Tertiary	6.1	6.2	5.9	7.8	7.1	9.3	9.6	7.6	10.7
Total	100	100	100	100	100	100	100	100	100

Source: Trigilia 1976, p. 262

This subdivision would probably, on further investigation, give rise to as many problems as Sylos Labini's version. It offered, however, a more detailed picture. The main findings are shown in Table 6.3. A careful study of this shows that:

1 The bourgeoisie expanded more in the North than in the South.
2 There was a very large decrease of the independent middle class in both North and South, but in agriculture this class decreased more in the North than in the South; in industry it increased in the North and decreased in the South and in the tertiary sector it increased more in the North than in the South.
3 The number of white-collar workers more than doubled, but the increase in the South was greater than the increase in the North. This was mainly due to the expansion of white-collar jobs in the public sector in the South. However, the main impetus behind the increase in white-collar jobs overall was due to the private sector.

4 The central proletariat increased far more in the North than in the South.
5 Overall, the marginal proletariat did not change significantly between 1951 and 1971.

However, the 'peripheral' proletariat increased considerably in the North while it actually decreased in the South (this consisted of workers in firms employing less than ten people). The 'casual' proletariat decreased in the North and increased in the South. The southern increase in the casual proletariat was entirely due to the increase of the casual workers in the tertiary and industrial sectors because there was actually a decrease in casual workers in agriculture.

I think it is now possible to go beyond the simple statement that the chief characteristic of Italian development had been the shift from agriculture to industry. The pattern of transformation of social classes had quite specific contours in northern Italy and contrasted sharply with the South. The largest single class in the North was the 'central' proletariat (30.6 per cent in 1971) while the largest single class in the South was the 'casual' proletariat (43.5 per cent in 1971). The 'surplus' population in the South, expelled from agriculture, did not find an outlet in industrial enterprises in the South and was thus in part 'exported' towards capitalist enterprises abroad or in the North. Those who stayed were absorbed in the tertiary sector of the independent middle class, in the white-collar private sector, in the casual tertiary sector and in the casual construction industry. Otherwise unemployable southern labour found jobs in the 'politically protected' sectors enhanced by DC-led political patronage.

In the North industry absorbed southern labour, expelled female and older male labour. In the 1960s it restructured itself through an increase in productivity and a further expulsion of labour. This excess labour in the North found a place in the expansion of white-collar jobs in the private sector, but also in the decentralization of industry towards smaller units of production (the 'home' of the peripheral proletariat). As we saw in the previous chapters, there was a considerable expansion of small firms, often *de facto* satellites of larger ones, achieved by subcontracting to small 'family' firms, often women working at home.

The changes in social classes were not determined by the economy alone but also by politics. Government policies shaped the pattern of reciprocal exchange between North and South.

The policy of southern industrialization was directed towards capital-intensive large-scale production (see Chapters 3 and 4) with little impact on southern employment. Nevertheless, it was sufficient to expand purchasing power (further enlarged by the increase in state jobs) and hence the market. This market attracted the products of northern industry. Traditional southern industry, often small-scale and inefficient, could not compete, particularly as it faced an increase in labour costs (wages, etc.). Small firms were forced out of business and their excess labour emigrated to the North, abroad, or found a home in marginal urban employment, particularly in the construction industry and in the tertiary sector.[7]

The consequence of this rather complex process of political and economic development was a growing internal differentiation of southern society both in the

Table 6.4 Employment by sector, 1971–94

	1971 (%)	1981 (%)	1994 (%)
Agriculture	17.2	11.2	7.8
Industry	44.4	39.8	32.7
Others	38.9	49.0	59.5

Source: For 1971 and 1981, Grussu (1984), p. 36 on the basis of census data and ISTAT figures 1994 and 1995

geographical and in the occupational sense. The inland areas of the regions of Molise, Basilicata and Calabria were clearly backward areas, devastated by emigration. Employment was concentrated in an under-capitalized and poor agricultural sector or in local government jobs. There was hardly any industrial proletariat. In the coastal areas of Sicily, Sardinia, Abruzzi, Campania and Apulia there was large-scale industrial developments or peripheral industry dependent on them. As Trigilia pointed out, 90 per cent of state funds towards southern industry between 1961 and 1971 went to these coastal area.[8] Between 1971 and 1994 the percentage of those employed in both industry and agriculture in Italy decreased and the tertiary sector grew to include well over half the active population (see Table 6.4).

Even among those employed in industry the shift in these twenty-odd years has been away from blue-collar workers (see Table 6.5). Thus the numerical importance of the working class was in diminution. Italy had become a 'post-industrial' society like other advanced Western countries. The 'services' columns in Table 6.5 include a range of services which are mostly associated with the public administration of 'caring' services, that is with the welfare state (though it includes private domestic services and entertainment). Here too Italy 'fits in' with the trend of most of the advanced countries while Spain, Portugal and Greece belong to a group of latecomers. By the 1990s a greater proportion of the Italian population was employed in the 'community' services than in manufacturing as was the case everywhere except Germany. A considerable proportion of this 'post-industrial' sector was the direct result of the development of the welfare state. The state had thus become a major actor in the structuring of social classes.

The remarkable shrinking of the traditional working class can be exemplified by examining employment in the iron and steel industry, the backbone of the industrial world. Here too Italy generally conformed to the prevailing trend. However, the Italian decrease was far less significant than elsewhere because successive governments, for political reasons, protected the steel industry which was largely in state hands.

As can be seen, if the discussion on social classes had remained concentrated on the three broad classes or on the size of manufacturing, all one would have been able to note was that Italy had followed the general pattern of more 'advanced' countries. We would have been able to use the figures to substantiate the hypothesis that economic development follows the same pattern and the same logic everywhere: from the countryside to the towns. But the key difference between Italy and the

Table 6.5 Economically active population in manufacturing and social services (%)

	Manufacturing				Community, social & personal services			
	1960–61	1970–71	1980–81	1992–93	1960–61	1970–71	1980–81	1992–93
Austria	29.8	31.5	30.4	26.6	14.1	16.0	19.6	23.4
Belgium	34.6	32.1	21.9	17.7	21.4	20.6	26.4	32.9
Denmark	28.5	25.9	17.2	19.9	22.2	24.2	32.0	35.0
Finland	21.5	24.7	24.8	18.8	14.8	18.1	24.7	31.8
France	27.0	25.8	22.3	18.9	20.1	20.1	25.4	27.8
Germany	36.5	37.6	32.7	28.2	18.8	19.0	n/a	26.5
Greece	13.4	17.2	18.7	18.8	12.1	10.8	15.0	18.9
Holland	29.9	24.0	18.8	16.6	23.5	21.1	28.6	32.7
Italy	26.6	31.1	22.3	19.8	13.5	17.4	19.3	24.9
Norway	25.5	26.7	20.2	14.3	18.4	20.2	30.4	37.2
Portugal	23.3	21.7	24.1	23.7	14.6	14.3	19.2	24.1
Spain	17.7	25.4	24.4	19.0	14.1	15.7	16.0	20.0
Sweden	34.2	28.3	24.0	16.8	19.9	26.1	34.0	37.1
UK	34.8	32.4	20.6	18.9	24.3	27.3	23.7	25.5

Sources: ILO, *Yearbook of Labour Statistics 1945–89, Retrospective Edition on Population Censuses*, ILO, Geneva 1990, ILO, *Yearbook of Labour Statistics 1991, 1992*, and *1994*. For the 1980–81 figure for Germany, see OECD *Historical Statistics*, cit.: Column 1960–1: Spain 1950; France 1962; *Column 1970–1*: France 1968; *Column 1980–1*: France 1982; *Column 1990–1*: France 1989; Denmark and Italy 1990; figure for Germany refers to West Germany. *Community, Social and Personal Services* corresponds to Division 9 of the Service sector. It includes domestic services, public administration, social and health services, education, entertainment and excludes all financial and business services

Table 6.6 Workers in the iron and steel industry, 1973–90

	1973	1990	% change
Belgium	52,512	20,019	−61.88
France	107,872	24,678	−77.12
Germany	171,688	86,688	−49.51
Italy	72,795	42,359	−41.81
UK	139,601	32,799	−76.51

Source: Table constructed on the basis of figures in Eurostat, *Iron and Steel. Yearly Statistics 1992*, Luxembourg 1992, pp. 6 and 12

other European countries is the centrality in Italy of the 'Southern Question' and the more important role of the state in the economy.

All Italian governments since Unification have had to grapple with the Southern Question and their actions have tended to shape economic and social development. Thus – as Picchieri has pointed out – the contraction of the peasant class slowed down precisely when it was felt to be needed for political stabilization by the fascist authorities in the 1930s and by the DC in the 1950s.[9] Contrary to all 'laws' upheld by economic determinists, the number of small shopkeepers not only did not decrease but even increased, and this was largely due to the intervention of the political authorities.[10] Only in the early 1990s did the number of shopkeepers begin to fall and, even then, by small amounts so that in 1994 Italy still had 1.6 million shops.[11] The resistance of small shopkeepers fed on the lasting ambition of many workers, particularly those whose memories of an independent occupation was recent – i.e. workers from the countryside – to set up shop on their own, 'to be their own bosses'. This constituted such a powerful group that their opposition to the June 1995 referendum seeking to abolish Sunday working and rigid opening and closing times was sufficient to convince a majority of the electorate to back them in defeating it.

The overall expansion of the middle classes outside the rural sector (the middle classes as a whole, including the peasantry, as we have seen actually contracts) was also due, according to Sylos Labini, to the fact that the 'big bourgeoisie', being numerically small and needing allies, tended to facilitate the expansion of these groups.[12] Though this could not be a *conscious* objective of the top social class – there is no mechanism enabling a class to act in a conscious political way – it suggests that the sole aim of the DC was not the political protection of various middle strata groups.[13] Christian Democratic economic policy was also directed to help and protect large private firms through fiscal and monetary means, through public investments in key sectors such as steel and motorways.[14]

'Protected' middle-class incomes in the years of the 'economic miracle' constituted the necessary home market for those household goods which the export-orientated private firms made. A home market sustained only by working-class incomes would have entailed higher labour costs, thus wiping out the competitive advantages of Italian industry. Middle-class incomes which did not depend on the private manufacturing sector were highly functional to the 'economic miracle'.

Alessandro Pizzorno, who pointed this out, also noted that evidence of the political strength of the Italian middle classes was provided by the remarkable fact that virtually all government crises in the 1950s were caused by either one or the other of the three small parties who were usually in government with the DC: the Social Democrats, the Liberals and the Republicans – all parties whose electorate was predominantly middle class.[15]

Once again it is necessary to remind the reader that the middle classes did not expand as such. What expanded, apart from the shopkeepers (and in this case the numbers are not significant), were the white-collar sectors. But these expanded all over Europe. The distinctive trait of the Italian situation was that the working class was still expanding – as was typical of latecomers. The overall contraction of the independent middle classes in the 1950s and 1960s would have been even higher if shopkeepers had decreased (as they should, at least according to received opinion), if the middle class had not been protected and if the government had not expanded white-collar jobs in the public sector. Finally, one should note an important and influential section of the middle classes: the professions. Entry to these

Table 6.7 Class structure, 1974–89

	1974	1989
Big bourgeoisie	1.3	4.1
White collars	20.2	32.4
Urban petty bourgeoisie	16.4	19.3
Rural petty bourgeoisie	10.1	5.0
Working class	45.9	35.4
Rural workers	6.1	3.8

Source: Paci 1991

are rigorously controlled by the professionals themselves through competitions, registration and examinations, even for professions like journalism. These controls make it easy to estimate their numbers. In 1991 there were over 1.1 million professionals such as doctors, vets, lawyers, accountants, architects and freelance nurses.[16] Italy has remained a country with a larger than necessary population of lawyers and doctors. As for freelance nurses, they tend to be nurses with regular employment who are able to 'moonlight', helped by the widespread habit of doctors of prescribing medicine to be administered by injection rather than the less costly oral method.

Some would argue against concentrating excessively on the middle classes because what was peculiar about post-war Italian economic and social development was the expansion of the working class.[17] One should add that such an expansion continued throughout the 1960s while the participation rate of the population in the labour force dropped from 43.3 per cent in 1960 to 35.9 per cent in 1972 (the biggest drop in the OECD countries). In fact the expansion of the industrial sector in terms of the labour force employed in it was second only to Japan. The working class decline occurred much later.

Massimo Paci, in a recent attempt to follow Sylos Labini in the difficult task of representing the Italian class structure (see Table 6.7), emphasized the growth of the 'big bourgeoisie' of white-collar workers against the decline of the working class and of all rural groups.

These figures show a consistent upward occupational mobility. Again, far from being a purely Italian phenomenon, this is in line with the experience of other European countries.[18] Thus, increasingly, more and more Italians began to classify themselves as 'middle class' though many would also use the ambiguous word *lavoratori* to describe themselves. A *lavoratore* is a 'working person', though the term can also be employed to denote a member of the working class, thus communist rhetoric could continue to appeal to the *lavoratori* without giving rise to the same images of factory workers that the English term 'workers' or 'working class' would suggest.

In the light of developments of the 1980s and 1990s more weight should be given to the divide between those employed by the state who benefit from an effective job protection system and those in the private sector. The 'class' of state employees expanded from 3,548,000, or 17.3 per cent of the employed labour force in 1981, to 18.7 per cent in 1991.[19] Meanwhile the gradual abolition of the *scala mobile* led to a widening of the differentials in those employed in the private sector.[20]

In the course of the 1980s traditional class analysis gave way to new ways of classifying the Italians. Consumption styles, life styles, values and attitudes, such as 'pro-modern' or 'traditional', became frequently used in the media in the course of fashionable attempts to find a sociological way of depicting the country. These attempts, regardless of their analytical value, showed how difficult it had become to encapsulate an increasingly complex social structure in a traditional way. This complexity was further exacerbated by the changing pattern of emigration. The constant transfer of people from the agricultural sector to the industrial sector was always accompanied by a strong emigration. In other words, the expansion of manufacturing could not mop up all 'surplus' labour from the countryside. Here we get nearer to one of the central particularities of Italian economic development. Italy was the only one of the advanced industrial countries that sustained a rapid economic development while exporting labour instead of importing it, as was done by virtually all of Italy's main competitors in Europe.

Labour migration

Until the 1970s, emigration had been a virtually uninterrupted phenomenon throughout the history of modern Italy except for the 1930s. Between 1861 and 1973, 26 million Italians left Italy and – up to 1965 – about 6 million returned. Initially (1876–1910), emigration was from the Veneto region towards the American continent, mainly Argentina and Brazil (about 1.5 million) and from the South to the United States (6 million).[21] In the same period there was also some emigration to the coal-mining regions of Europe, Belgium, France, Germany and the United Kingdom. After 1922 the USA stopped immigration from Italy, but in spite of that and in spite of obstacles on the part of the fascist authorities, emigration continued throughout the 1920s: 2.5 million left mainly to France and Argentina.[22]

The post-war period saw a massive emigration. Between 1946 and 1975, 7.25 million people left Italy, but net migration (i.e. the difference between emigration and returned emigrants) was around 3 million. Initially (1946–54), there was a certain balance between emigration towards other European countries and that directed towards other continents, but after 1955 Italian emigration was essentially European; its main destination was Switzerland, France (up to 1958) and West Germany.[23] This emigration was essentially male, on short contract, working on assembly lines, construction and in services such as catering and cleaning.

The export of labour continued thus until 1973. In that year for the first time in the history of modern Italy more Italians returned home than left Italy: between 1973 and 1978 the 'balance of labour' showed a gain of nearly 68,000 people.[24] The return of Italian emigrants was mainly due to the international economic crisis which hit construction and manufacturing, particularly assembly-line work in the car sector. This led countries such as West Germany to 'unload' some of its redundant labour force, foreign workers being the first to be sacked.

The advantage gained from importing labour by economies such as that of West Germany was remarkable. In the years of its economic miracle, Germany imported cheap labour when needed. At the outset of recessions, it was able to dispense with such labour. But what of Italian industry? During its period of fast economic growth it was also able to import labour, but it was imported – so to speak – internally from the South. Internal Italian migration acquired, from the very beginning, a form of permanent 'immigration'.[25] The workers who left the countryside for the northern industrial triangle of Milan-Turin-Genoa had equal citizenship rights. They could not be politically discriminated against or isolated by language barriers or fear of being expelled. Furthermore, Switzerland or West Germany had saved all the expense of educating the imported workers. As many came when young and able-bodied and without their families, they saved the host state expenses associated with schooling, pensions, health services, etc. In other words, foreign workers were putting into the economy far more than they were getting out of it in terms of social services.[26] But in Italy the southern 'immigrants' were there with their families, their needs, their possibility of influencing political organizations and trade unions and, in 1969, they were in the forefront of the events leading to the 'hot autumn'. This is when the central importance of the Southern Question made itself manifest in the North: Italy's reserve army of labour had fed the 'economic miracle' and when this came to an end the tensions remained, grew and exploded. A few years later Italy stopped being an exporter of labour.

In the mid-1970s, for the first time in its history, Italy began to import foreign labour. Since then the inflow of migrants has been considerably greater than the outflow. As Italy had no history of immigration, border controls were and are lax and migration mainly illegal, the data available are not very reliable. Nevertheless, it has been estimated that there were 186,000 foreign workers in the country in 1975, 350,000 in 1980, and 896,000 in 1991.[27] Other estimates – such as ISTAT – put the 1989 figure at 1.15 million immigrants. Of those foreign workers legally resident on 31 December 1990, i.e. 635,000, nearly 78,000 came from Morocco, 41,000 from Tunisia, 34,000 from the Philippines, and 29,800 Yugoslavia. What did this new immigrants do? Those – mainly women – from the Philippines and the Horn of Africa (i.e. Ethiopia and Somalia) were prevalently domestic servants or 'family collaborators' as the accepted euphemism would have it. Many of the others – in spite of their relatively high qualifications – worked in the fields as casual labourers doing the menial jobs Italians were no longer willing to perform, such as picking tomatoes when the crop was ready. The remainders appeared to be cleaners or travelling salesmen plying their trade in tourist centres. Unlike immigrants in other European countries, very few of them worked in factories or in the public sector.[28]

Italy had finally acquired its own 'underclass'. Racist incidents were reported with increasing frequency and controversial legislation was adopted to deal with the issues these brought forth. Law 943 (1986) established the principle of equality of rights between home workers and extra-EEC immigrants as well as an amnesty for illegal immigrants in accordance with the ILO Convention of 1975 which Italy had signed but not upheld.

Racism escalated leading to the brutal murder of Jerry Masslo, an African, in August 1989. There followed anti-racist demonstrations in October 1989.[29] Most political parties, the mass media and the trade unions adopted a policy of anti-racism with the allegedly 'liberal' Italian Republican Party and – less pronouncedly – the far-right MSI departing somewhat from this consensus and, while refraining from adopting the racist language of Le Pen's National Front in France, advocating more draconian controls.[30] Nevertheless, the MSI did not vote against the 1986 law on immigration.[31] Further legislation (the Martelli Law of 1990) was passed to tighten regulations, in part as a response to pressure from the European members of the Schengen agreement (abolishing border controls) who viewed with alarm the laxity of Italian immigration controls. In the 1990s the general benevolent attitude of the political establishment class began to change. The forced and brutal repatriation of 21,000 illegal Albanians ordered by a socialist minister took place without provoking an uproar.

Controlling the entry of immigrants present great difficulties in Italy. A long seaboard difficult to police, the relative proximity of the Albanian and North African coastline, the lack of experience in establishing such controls, the enormous and economically vital influx of tourists who must not be put off by excessive bureaucratic control, makes Italy particularly vulnerable. The widespread pattern of casual labour and the mentality associated with the black economy with its avoidance of controls compound the problem.

With the fall of the First Republic other issues held the attention of public opinion, but by 1995 an anti-immigration consensus had emerged: the Dini government passed a law, with the support of the former communists of the PDS, aimed at repatriating all new illegal immigrants involved in criminal activities (in line with the legislation of most other European countries). As a further amnesty had to be promulgated to avoid mass deportation, the Northern League, finding the new law too soft, voted against it. Immigration was well on the way to becoming a major issue in Italian politics.

This new 'underclass' is still far from the proportion of that of other European countries (not to speak of that of the USA). Nevertheless, it further complicates the social profile of Italian society in line with developments in the rest of Europe. The casualization of the labour force, the North–South divide, the gap between public and private sectors, the growth of immigration, the complex pattern of regional employment makes traditional class analysis of less relevance than twenty years ago.

Endnotes

1 Sylos Labini 1974. For other contributions see: Calza Bini 1973, Maitan 1975, Braghin, Mingione and Trivellaro 1974.
2 Sylos Labini 1974, pp. 27–34 and 156.
3 Chiesi 1975, pp. 214–15.
4 Ammassari 1977, p. 16.

5 This was only made clear in a letter sent by Sylos Labini to the journal *Quaderni Piacentini*, no. 60–1, p. 129.
6 Trigilia 1976, pp. 260–1.
7 Ibid., pp. 278–9.
8 Ibid., p. 279.

9 Picchieri n.d., p. 97.
10 Sylos Labini 1974, pp. 29–30 and Barbano 1979, p. 189.
11 ISTAT 1995, p. 236.
12 Sylos Labini 1974, p. 85.
13 Cassano 1979, p. 19.
14 Sylos Labini 1975, pp. 174–5.
15 Pizzorno 1974, p. 336.
16 Paci 1993, p. 82.
17 Ammassari 1977, p. 66.
18 Paci 1993, p. 64.
19 Ibid., p. 91.
20 Ibid., p. 147.
21 Isenburg 1980, p. 336.

22 Ibid., p. 341.
23 De Rosa 1992, p. 174 and Birindelli 1976, p. 180.
24 Calvaruso 1980, p. 34 and De Rosa 1992, p. 174.
25 Trentin 1977, p. xxxix.
26 Trentin 1977, p. xl, see also Castles and Kosack 1973, pp. 244ff.
27 Calvaruso 1980, p. 35 and Veugelers 1994, pp. 34–5.
28 Martiniello 1991, p. 80.
29 Bonifazi and Gesano 1994, p. 273.
30 Bonifazi and Gesano 1994, p. 274.
31 Veugelers 1994, pp. 38–43.

Chapter 7

Women, families, feminism, youth

Women and families

If we can talk of women as 'social subjects' it is largely because of the development of an Italian women's movement which arose, as in most West European
countries, in the 1970s. One should really speak of a 'rebirth' or 'second wave' if
it were not for the fact that – in Italy – the first wave of feminism which originated
at the turn of the century did not possess the presence or the strength of that in
Anglo-Saxon countries.

Modern Italian feminism drew its principal ideological inspiration from the American women's movement, that is from the country with the most developed system
of sectional politics or 'pressure-group' politics and the least developed system of
class-orientated politics in any of the advanced industrial countries. This 'borrowing' was inevitable. The Italian political tradition did not offer much to women. In
the marketplace of ideologies there was a version of Catholicism which did offer
a role to women, but a subordinate one (the role of the homemaker and of the
mother), there was a version of Marxism, which, in spite of the enrichments brought
about by thinkers such as Antonio Labriola, Antonio Gramsci and the communist
leader, Palmiro Togliatti, was still concerned essentially with the forging of alliances between social classes as organized by specific political parties.

Another major influence on the formation of Italian feminism was the student
movement of 1968. This expressed a critique of authority and of accepted forms
of organization and behaviour while reproducing – within itself – the subordination
of women.[1] Thus those radical women who were attracted to the politics of the
students' movement perceived fairly early on that there was a marked contradiction between the aspiration of the movement in general and its patriarchal form of
organization.

Politics and ideology tell only part of the story. There were also structural preconditions behind the women's movement such as an increase in female education,
which made women more competitive with men in a number of occupations, and
a decrease in the birth-rate, which meant that women were anchored to domestic
chores for a shorter period of time.[2] The main reason behind the rise of Italian

feminism must be found in the increased complexity of women's roles in society and their relation to it. Initially, the family was at the centre of women's struggle, though it was no longer the main institution within which women could find their place in society. More women were entering the labour market. This entry was, however, occurring at a rate that was much lower than that of other Western countries (see Chapter 3). In fact, female employment even fell during the 'economic miracle' as women were substituted by young male migrant workers from the South. This did not take place through the deliberate sacking of women workers, but by taking advantage of their high turnover in the labour market, i.e. the fact that their initial entry into it was a temporary one (i.e. it is interrupted by pregnancy and child-rearing).[3] The rise in the standard of living facilitated their being kept out of the labour market. The wages earned by male workers increased and this maintained and reinforced the division of labour between the male breadwinner and the female homemaker. When the 'miracle' was over, women began to return to the labour force, but they tended, on the whole, to take jobs in the so-called 'hidden economy' of casual labour and small family firms (cottage industry, subcontracted labour, sweat-shops, etc.).

By 1980 the participation of women in employment was not substantially different from that in other countries as shown in Table 7.1.

These processes led to the growing complexity of women's roles. The role which was assigned to them was that of the caring and loving of the good wife and good mother. However, extra income was needed; this required women to enter the workforce making it more difficult to fulfil their assigned family role. This tension was felt by virtually all working women. The necessity for women to work was further accelerated by some of the changes in the family in Italy in the post-war period. The most visible quantitative aspect of this was the decrease in the size of the family itself, from 3.9 persons in 1951 to 3.2 in 1976 and 2.8 in 1991 (3.1 in the South) the concurrent decrease in the average number of income-earners in the family (from 2.3 in 1900 to 1.7 in 1951 to 1.5 in 1961 to 1.2 in 1971 to 1.1 in 1976).[4] This meant that instead of two or three workers in a family, there were only one or two. In the 1960s and 1970s children increasingly left the family home when they could work. Census data shows that there was a sharp decrease in the number of 'extended' families (defined as being made up of a married couple, their children and other relatives) while there was a growth in the number of households made up of one person only, childless couples and those whose children have left the home.[5]

In 1971 households made up of five or more members were nearly twice that of one-person households. Between 1971 and 1981 one-person households increased by 5 per cent (from 12.9 to 17.9 per cent of all households). Households made up of six or more persons went down from 9.7 to 5.4 per cent of all households. In the North one-person households were twice as many as large households.

As the extended family declined – though far less in the South than in the North – there was a parallel growth of the welfare state. This, albeit very partially, began to provide a range of services previously offered by the family, e.g. care of children and old people. The services of the welfare state, however, were available only if

Table 7.1 Women's employment, 1960–81, in selected countries

	Female population as % of the total active population			Female working class as % of the industrial working class		
	1960–61	**1970–71**	**1981–82**	**1960–61**	**1970–71**	**1980–81**
Austria	40.4	38.4	40.4	20.9	19.4	16.9
Belgium	26.5	29.6	36.4	15.7	16.1	13.7
Denmark	30.8	36.6	44.2	17.1	15.1	16.9
Spain	18.2	19.6	24.8	n/a	13.3	11.8
Finland	39.4 ,	42.1	46.6	23.1	23.4	22.3
France	34.6	34.9	40.9	33.3	15.6	16.2
Germany	. 37.1	34.9	38.5	19.7	17.6	n/a
Greece	32.8	28.0	27.1	17.5	14.6	16.8
Italy	24.9	27.4	34.4	17.3	17.5	20.6
Holland	22.3	25.9	32.3	8.9	7.3	6.6
Norway	22.8	27.6	41.4	11.0	11.3	15.0
Portugal	17.7	25.2	35.3	17.6	23.1	22.7
Sweden	29.8	38.1	45.0	14.6	16.6	14.5
UK	32.4	36.5	38.9	18.2	18.4	16.1

Source: My elaboration on data in ILO, *Yearbook of Labour Statistics. Retrospective Edition on Population Census, 1945–1989*, ILO, Geneva 1990. The figures for France are, respectively, for 1962, 1968 and are estimated for 1982; for Germany the figures in the 1980–1 columns are for 1982. My definition of the 'working class' corresponds to ILO occupational groups 7, 8 and 9, and includes all production and related workers, transport equipment operators and labourers. It excludes all white-collar occupations, all service workers such as caretakers, cleaners and waiters, all agriculture, farming, and fishing, all the unemployed and self-employed

there was an individual who was prepared to engage in the necessary bureaucratic practices needed to obtain these services, whether bringing the children to a nursery or filling in forms. The fact that more women went out to work has weakened the traditional family and hence also one of the conditions that enabled the Italian welfare state to be less efficient than elsewhere. The function of unpaid 'agent' of the welfare state was seen as natural to women: it was an extension of their role of 'loving and caring homemakers'. At the same time, women were also expected to compensate where public services failed. Finally, the extension of the consumer society and the constant and dramatic decrease in the self-sufficiency of the household (compare a peasant family with an urban family which must purchase virtually everything it needs) added on another task for women: the purchase of private services.[6] To sum up, women worked before they had children, then they left work to look after their children, then they often returned to work. Throughout, they functioned as 'agents' of the welfare state within the family (purchaser of public services) and 'agents' of the consumption sector of the economy within the family (purchaser of private services), while compensating for the deficiencies of the welfare state. They often had to work in whatever peripheral, casual or marginal jobs were available if the man's wages could not provide for the family needs. They also had to fulfil their traditional roles of procreators and homemakers (household chores, cooking, etc.). Compared to this, the life of the man was a rather simple one: work, leisure and sleep. The arrival of children has for women a far greater impact than it has for men whose use of time changes little. There is, of course, some positive correlation between female labour participation and some welfare state infrastructures. As is to be expected female participation is greater in the North and in the Centre than in the South.[7] While Piedmont spends 20,142 lire per inhabitant on nursery places, Sicily spends only 5,102; while the red regions of Emilia and Tuscany spend, respectively, 32,281 and 19,492 lire the region of Campania (whose main city is Naples) spends only 3,428 per person (1988 data).[8]

The complex life-cycle of women was thus characterized by three phases: (1) pre-child-bearing employment; (2) housework when children are under the age of six; and (3) both housework and extra-domestic paid employment when children started school.[9] This also meant that women entered the labour market in the knowledge that there would be an interruption (phase 2) and that, when they re-entered it, they would face the specific conditions of phase 3. The prospect of an uninterrupted career was thus seldom available to women. Furthermore, paid employment during the long phase 3 had to be adapted to the requirements of their domestic commitments. Thus women tended to 'prefer' jobs such as nursing (which can be done at night), cleaning offices early in the morning, school teaching, etc. These are also jobs which are, in a sense, an extension of the traditional 'caring and loving' role of women.[10] More recently, this pattern has become even more complex. Forty per cent of the women with children under five worked, usually in full-time jobs, helped by relatives, home helps and a fairly widespread system of child care centres.

Women's employment tended to be concentrated in the services sector, but they also acted as substitute land workers as male labour left the countryside for the towns. In 1951 out of 100 people working in agriculture 24.6 were women, but by 1976 31.6 were women. The female labour force in industry (as a percentage of the male) dropped from 21.9 per cent to 20.1 per cent between 1951 and 1976, while in the tertiary sector it increased from 29.9 per cent (1951) to 36.7 per cent (1976).[11] Between 1977 and 1982 the female labour force in the tertiary sector increased by 23 per cent and more in the South (+32 per cent) than in the Centre-North (+18 per cent) while the male labour force increased in the tertiary sector by only 11 per cent.[12] These figures do not reflect the extent to which women were concentrated in the service sector, because many of those working 'in industry' were in fact working in the service sector of industry. Until the late 1970s this sector was, in general, low paid, less trade unionized and technologically less advanced.[13] Italian women appear to be less involved in part-time work than many other European Union countries (see Table 7.2). Needless to say the statistics are likely to underestimate the presence of women in the casual sector (where part-time work predominates) because this is where the so-called 'black economy' predominates.

Studies of women's employment in various categories of the service sector found that they tended to be concentrated in the lower-paid or less secure jobs.[14] Nevertheless, a significant improvement did take place. While in 1953 there were only

Table 7.2 Women and part-time work, 1992–93

	A: Part-time employment as a proportion of total employment	B: Women share in part-time employment	C: Percentage of women employed in part-time work in the European Union, 1993
Austria	9.1	89.1	
Belgium	12.4	89.7	25.0
Denmark	22.5	75.8	40.1
Finland	7.9	64.3	
France	12.7	83.7	23.8
Germany	14.1	91.0	30.7
Greece	4.8	61.3	8.0
Holland	32.8	75.0	60.1
Ireland	n/a	n/a	16.5
Italy	5.9	68.5	10.9
Luxembourg	6.9	88.5	16.4
Norway	26.9	80.1	
Portugal	7.2	67.4	10.0
Spain	5.9	76.8	11.9
Sweden	24.3	82.3	
UK	23.5	85.2	43.6

Sources: For A and B: Department of Employment cited in the *Financial Times*, 29 September 1994, p. 8, 1992 figures. For C: Eurostat, *Unemployed Women in the EC. Statistical Facts*, Brussels and Luxembourg 1993, pp. 18–19

2.6 per cent of women in the top civil service grades, by 1975 this had gone up to 12.8 per cent. Overall female employment in the civil service jumped between 1953 and 1975 from 10.4 to 31.9 per cent; this, however, has occurred concurrently with a lowering in the prestige of civil service occupations.[15] It has been found, in fact, that women, unlike men, were attracted to civil service jobs not because of status but because of the security of tenure some of them might be able to enjoy – a pension, the hours of work and welfare schemes as well as the formal criterion of 'equality of opportunity'.[16]

The growth of female employment in the 1980s coincided with the increase in female education. It is thus not surprising to find out that a higher proportion of the better educated women were in employment than those who left school early.[17] This explains why women increased their presence in the better paid professional jobs, even though they were still at the bottom of the career ladder. Whether this represents mainly the lagged effect of past discrimination or the continuing existence of prejudice is not yet clear.

The census data on professional employment reveal the systematically subordinate position of women even in this sector.[18] Though women are nearly half the members of what the census calls the 'liberal, technical and scientific professions', they have the lowest position. In education the proportion of women is inversely related to the prestige and income of the job: an overwhelming majority (90 per

Table 7.3 Women studying in universities, 1960–75 (% of total student population)

	1960	**1975**
Austria	31.8	34.4
Belgium	19.1	33.3
Denmark	32.0	39.0
Finland	52.8	49.0
France	38.2	n/a
Germany	27.4	32.1
Italy	38.0	46.2[a]
Holland	18.2	26.3
Norway	22.1[b]	41.2
Sweden	37.5[c]	44.2
UK[d]	23.9	32.8
Scotland	27.2	37.5

Notes: a: 1970; b: 1955; c: 1959; d: England and Wales only. 1975 data for Finland exclude Provisional Teachers' Colleges
Source: P. Flora (ed.), *State, Economy and Society in Western Europe 1815–1975. A Data Handbook*, vol. 1

cent) of elementary school teachers are women, a preponderance of middle and high-school teachers (62 per cent) and a minority of university teachers (31 per cent, usually in untenured positions).[19] Over half the health professionals are women, but they are overwhelmingly in the majority among technicians and nurses. A minority are doctors (23 per cent) and only a few senior surgeons.[20] Progress has not been insignificant: in 1961 only 5 per cent of doctors were women.[21] The data for 1991 reveal that women are only 16.4 per cent of entrepreneurs and senior executives, 35.4 per cent of 'highly specialized intellectual professionals' but only 5 per cent of executives.[22] Women tend to concentrate in certain specialities: women doctors tend to specialize in paediatrics, maternity, mental illness, hygiene and prevention – all less remunerative than surgery. Women lawyers are attracted to family law not company law. Women entrepreneurs tend to be concentrated in the clothing industry not in machine tools.[23] It should be said that – at least in so far as middle- and upper-income groups are concerned – Italian women do not fare worse than their counterparts in other European countries and that they have reached parity where university education is concerned, as shown in Table 7.3.

In middle-class families the parity achieved in the education of women can be explained by the commitment to equality in education of the parents who can afford to educate all their children irrespective of gender. Among the self-employed, how-ever, there is a greater proportion of female offsprings who are educated. This is, presumably, designed to compensate the girls because the family firm will go to the boy.[24]

The central institution which defines women's general role in society, the family, became increasingly unstable – though to a lesser extent than in other Western countries. The concept of 'the crisis of the family' is now common currency in sociological literature and it has become increasingly difficult to talk of the 'typical' family (say, a gainfully employed husband, a housewife and a couple of children). Some data can be used to confirm the thesis of the crisis of the family, though a more accurate definition is that of crisis of the *traditional* family. In Italy there was a decline in the number of marriages from 7.1 per thousand inhabitants in 1950–52 to 5.9 per thousand in 1978. However, this collapse was entirely due to the years 1972–78, and marriages actually went up until the early 1970s, though, by 1989 there were 5.4 weddings per 1,000 inhabitants (in line with other European countries) against 7.8 per 1,000 in 1960. Divorces went up until 1988, they declined afterwards.[25] On the whole, Italy has a low rate of divorce: its propensity to divorce shows a rate of 10 per cent like Spain against 31 per cent in France and 40 per cent in the UK.[26] On balance, one can say that the Italian family turned out to be remarkably resilient, having survived the impact of the sexual revolution, the entry of women in the labour market and the collapse of fertility rates. In fact, given the crisis of political parties and of the welfare state, one could even say that the family has turned out to be the principal form of self-help organization.[27]

There was an increase in 'common law' marriages, in people living on their own and in the number of young people living with their parents. The last feature is very specific to Italy (and Spain). Common law marriages in other European countries occur overwhelmingly among young people prior to the decision to have children. In Italy not only are there far fewer common law marriages than elsewhere, but they tend to occur among middle-aged people who have separated or divorced from their previous partners.[28] There has also been an increase in births out of wedlock: from 2.4 per cent of all births in 1961 to 3.6 per cent in 1978 and 7 per cent in 1992.[29] This is comparable to the Greek, Spanish and Swiss rate but contrast sharply with rates in France (25 per cent) and Denmark (45 per cent). As usual the differences between North and South Italy are very pronounced: in the North, families are smaller, the number of divorces and legal separations are three times that of the South, there are more couples living together and more children born out of wedlock. In other words, the North, for better or worse, is more in line with the rest of Western Europe. The stereotypical large Italian family (mum, dad and at least four children) is now a small minority of all families: 3.5 per cent against 14.4 in 1961. There were, correspondingly more and more households made up of a single member, twice the number in 1981 than in 1961.[30]

Two aspects of family life distinguish Italy from most other European countries: the drop in fertility rates and the protracted period young people live at home with their parents.

Italy, like other southern European countries, used to be a high fertility country. In the 1980s a dramatic turn took place. By 1991 Italy had a lower fertility rate than France and Sweden. Italian fertility dropped well below the replacement rate. This is defined as that rate of fertility required to maintain existing population size, i.e. 2.05 children per woman. By 1991 not a single Italian region had managed to sustain even this rate. The most fecund women were in Sicily (1.71) and Campania (1.7T), the lowest in Liguria 0.98.[31] On average, though, there is little variation in the size of the family: the average spreads from 2.5 members in Piedmont to 3.3

in Campania. Should this trend continue for the next thirty years 40–45 per cent of Italians would be over 60 years old and there would be more Italians over 80 years old than under 20.[32] It is unlikely that either government pressures or Catholic anti-contraceptive propaganda will make Italian women return to the high fertility rates of the past. The most obvious solution to this demographic crisis would be an increase in immigration or a technological revolution which increased productivity by leaps and bound. This is, of course, a Europe-wide problem, though it is more marked in Italy. In the years 1985–90 the average European fertility rate was 1.68 children per woman. The following countries were below this average: Spain (1.6), Belgium (1.57), Holland (1.55), Denmark (1.47), Germany (1.40) with Italy at the bottom of the league with 1.27.[33] In 1994 more Italians died than were born; the population grew a little only because of immigration.

The drop in fertility rate was accompanied by a considerable lengthening of the period the young stay at home with their parents. Young Italians – like young Spaniards – stay with their families far longer than their cohorts in other European countries. A survey indicates that a staggering 80 per cent of those aged between 15 and 29 live with their parents, this includes nearly half the males aged 29 and 25 per cent of the females.[34] This is unprecedented in Europe, except in Spain. Youth unemployment which is particularly pronounced in both Italy (32 per cent of the 15 to 24 age group) and Spain must be a major contributory factor. A chronic housing crisis must be another. Yet it is often the case that many of the stay-at-home young men and women have a job. This must mean that some of the young have succeeded in acquiring and maintaining a *modus vivendi* with their parents in spite of the so-called generation gap.[35]

Many diverse factors seem to be at work here. In the long-term this may well provide the inter-generational solidarity which will compensate for the inevitable demographic and pension crisis which will result from the drop in fertility rates and the lengthening of life expectancy (about which more below). Many objective factors are at work in keeping the young with their families. We have mentioned youth unemployment and the housing crisis. We should add the fact that many first occupations are of a casual and temporary nature. First jobs are used by the young as a stepping-stone to better things. Thus adolescence is lengthened as the not-so-young are still deciding at the ripe age of 29 what they will do when they really grow up. Marriages are delayed contributing to the lowering of the birth rate. While – at least outside Italy – the prevailing stereotype is that Italian women marry young and produce numerous children, the actual statistics tell quite a different story: the index of fertility for women under the age of 20 is, in Italy, 6.4 while in Norway it is 16.7, in the UK it is 32.9 and in the USA it is an astonishing 59.4.[36] The phenomenon of young welfare-dependent single mothers which so exercises policy-makers in the UK and the USA simply does not exist in Italy.

Further 'encouragement' for the young stay-at-home is provided by the fact that the proportion of 15 year-olds who leave school to start work has been continuously decreasing while the proportion of student/workers has been increasing. There are no grants or loan systems to enable the young to support themselves at university or to chose to go to a university outside their home town. What they can do instead is to stay at home, do odd jobs and take their time to complete their degrees. Entry into universities is easy. The only requirement is the successful completion of high school. There is no marked incentive to go to the 'best' universities (as would be the case in the USA or the UK) because there is no entrenched and obvious picking order of excellence – though it is generally accepted that universities in northern and central Italy are better equipped than those of the South. It is possible to stay on at university for very many years: failed exams can be taken again and again and one can delay taking them for years. Registration fees are very low. Besides it is difficult for young people to find a home and extended mortgages are difficult to obtain.[37]

This surprising co-existence under the same roof of different generations might appear to be the harbinger of major social conflicts, but so far there is no trace of this. Is traditional familism the main explanatory key? Perhaps, but much points to the development of a new kind of 'modern' familism. Before the 1960s the traditional life-cycle was one whereby someone moved fairly rapidly from childhood to adulthood. The period of childhood was characterized by schooling. When this finished there began the period of work which lasted until old age. Marriage occurred fairly early on.

In the 1960s there was a lengthening of the period of 'youth' and of the time spent with one's own family. At that time there was a real 'generation gap' which fascinated sociologists throughout the industrial world. This was as pronounced in Italy as elsewhere.[38] The traditional functions of the family, that is, the protection of its members against the 'big wide world' and the control over their life-styles, could not be carried out in the same way when the family was no longer dealing with children but with young adults. The family acquired a new function: the economic defence of its members. Young people stayed with their families because they needed to. As they did not leave to form other families they proceeded to challenge the very institution of the family, to develop an anti-familial ideology, a different cultural ethic, particularly a new sexual ethic. Add to this the impact of urbanization and migration, the consequent disruption of traditional patterns, the influence of foreign models of behaviour, particularly American, and we have the development of new forms of age-based solidarity. This solidarity was different from the traditional one based on the family as well as from the more modern one based on the place of work (e.g. trade unions and professional organizations). It was this particular set of circumstances which gave rise to a specific condition: 'youth' and the accompanying formation of a specific youth market based on cultural forms such as music and clothing. This market could exist for two reasons: young people had income of their own thanks to their participation, though limited and casual, in the labour market and they received some money from their parents. Parents were able to give this money because the standard of living of the average family had increased, and were willing to do so because money helped to resolve, at least temporarily, the increasingly strained parents–child relationship.

By the 1980s and 1990s the new generation of parents, having been brought up in a more prosperous and permissive age and but still under the influence of the Italian familist tradition, were able to coexist with their grown-up children while accepting their life-styles. Nevertheless, having children had become more costly, emotionally as well as financially, than in the past. They were less likely to go to work at an early age and help with the family budget, less likely to leave home and support themselves. Parents were thus investing considerable resources in their children at a time when the burden of the household was increasingly difficult to bear due to the near-disappearance of the traditional housewife. The decision to have fewer children was not the result of an anti-family mentality but of the desire of many couples to devote substantial emotional and financial assets to their off-springs. Had the reduction in fertility been the result of anti-familism we should expect to see a considerable increase in childless households. In fact there are relatively few such couples in Italy. It appears that residual familism enables the Italian family to cope better than elsewhere. Italian children are likely to grow up without siblings and with both parents at work, but they are probably surrounded by grandparents, and even great grandparents (in the early 1990s there were 2.8 million children under the age of 5 and 1.9 million people over the age of 80).[39] Thus the drop in fertility is likely to be the result of the rational choice of Italian women to have, when possible, only one child.

The one-child family enabled women to experience childbirth, yet to be able to hold on to a job and cope with the prospect of this child not leaving home until he or, less often, she, was over 30 years old. Women, however, increasingly found that they were having to look after their elderly parents for an extensive period, sometimes even longer than they looked after their child.[40] In the long-run this might turn out to have some beneficial effects. It is possible, after all, that the lengthy coexistence between the parents, child and grandparents, might cement the development of an inter-generational solidarity which is rapidly disappearing elsewhere. This might compensate for the inevitable problem which the conjunction of a lengthening of the life expectancy with the drop in fertility rates will bring about: the formation of a large class of pensioners.

In the 1960s Italians could expect to live, on average, until they were 65. As men retired at 60 (women at 55) they would not expect to draw their pensions for many years. By the mid-1990s life expectancy had reached 75, in line with European average. At the beginning of the century there were 5.67 children (0–14 years of age) per person over the age of 65. By the end of the 1980s there were 1.29 children for every over-65. By 1992 there were as many children as people over 65.[41] As in most continental countries, Italian pensions are financed with the contributions of those currently working. It is therefore difficult to shift to a system, like that in use in the UK, where those working pay a contribution which is invested in funds and which, eventually will be used to pay for their pensions. To reform it all at once would be difficult because it would be like asking those now working to pay for the old and also for themselves when they retire. When there are more children than old people, this system can work because the young generations provide the future fiscal basis for adequate pensions as the cost of maintaining the pensioners is distributed among more than one person. This is no longer the case. There will be fewer taxpayers in the future, a smaller percentage of people will be employed, and the old will live longer. This coincides with the crisis of the welfare system and the decreasing willingness on the part of taxpayers to finance it. More-over, the welfare state, which had been devised with a young population in mind, turned out to be more favourable to the old (who received generous pensions) than to the young (who faced unemployment and lower pensions for themselves in the future).[42] The Italian benefit system is more favourable to pensioners than to children. OECD figures (1988) revealed that Italy spends 3.8 times more public money on the old than on children, against 3.16 in Germany, 2.34 in Sweden and 2.13 in the UK.[43] Compared to other countries, the Italian pension system is generous: families whose principal income derived from a pension were under-represented among the poor (1990 figures).[44] In 1993 over 21 million pensions were received in 1993 (some people have more than one pension), 22 per cent more than in 1980.[45] There are now more pensioners than employed people. This constitutes a formidable lobby which politicians who want to win elections will ignore at their peril. It is a lobby which will be far more articulate than in the past: better educated, healthier and with high expectations. After all, the West Europeans who will reach pensionable age in the first 10–20 years of the twenty-first century may turn out to have been an outstandingly privileged group: they would have received a good education, benefitted from sexual freedom without AIDS-related penalties, enjoyed full employment, an expanding welfare system, a growing economy and no wars.

Feminism

Though, as stated earlier, the new Italian feminism originated in the 1960s, women's entry into politics started earlier. Under fascism, the state sought to organize the subordination of women around their central role of 'devoted spouse and exemplary mother', using organizations such as the *fasci femminili* (not very successfully) and finding ideological reinforcement in the papal encyclical *Casti connubi* (1931) which was the fullest statement by Pope Pius XI on woman as wife and mother.[46]

During the Resistance, some politicized women formed the *Gruppi di difesa della donna* (1943) which became the *Unione Donne Italiane* (UDI). The UDI included communist, socialist, Liberal and Action Party (a radical republican party) women, but no Christian Democratic (DC) women. Thus, the first political organization of women in liberated Italy owed its existence to the main political parties and especially to communist women.[47] There was no independent organization of women. The campaign for the extension of the suffrage to women was a muted affair, mainly because all the political parties agreed; those of the left supported female suffrage for ideological reasons, the DC supported it because they would benefit the most.[48]

The two leading parties – the DC and the PCI – had immediately perceived the importance of women's support. The PCI had no base among women as such. Its natural base, the organized working class, was essentially male because there were few women in occupations organized by the trade unions. The PCI had thus to rely on the UDI, but this was not a successful organization. In spite of its claim of being

Table 7.4 The representation of women in politics, 1975–c.90

Country	Percentage of women elected in Lower Chamber, 1975	Percentage of women elected as deputies			
		Year	In lower Chamber	In main party of the left	In main party of the right
Austria	7.6	1990	21.9	SPÖ: 26.3	ÖVP: 11.7
Belgium	6.6	1990	9.0	Soc: 10.0	CVP: 14.0
Denmark	15.6	1990	33.0	Soc Dem: 34.8	Cons: 23.3
Finland	23.0	1991	38.5		
France	1.6	1988	5.7	PS: 6.3	RPR: 6.9
Germany	5.6	1990	20.5	SPD: 27.2	CDU: 13.8
Greece	2.0	1990	5.3	PASOK: 4.8	ND: 5.3
Holland	9.3	1989	27.3	PvdA: 32.7	CD: 18.5
Italy	3.8	1992	8.0	PDS: 20.6	DC: 4.8
Norway	15.5	1989	36.0	Labour: 50.8	Cons: 29.7
Portugal	8.0	1991	7.6		
Spain	n/a	1989	13.4	PSOE: 18.3	PP: 9.3
Sweden	21.4	1988	38.1	Soc Dem: 40.0	Mod: 27.0
UK	4.2	1991	6.8	Labour: 10.4	Cons: 4.6

Source: Snyder 1992 and Lovenduski and Norris 1993. Source for 1975 data, Paoletti 1991

independent from the PCI until the late 1970s, it was basically a communist front organization. Its membership dropped from its high point in 1950 of 1 million to 200,000 in 1960.[49] The PCI had always had a smaller proportion of women members than the DC, roughly 25 per cent against roughly 36 per cent, but it certainly did more to promote the advancement of women in the party than the DC. In 1972 there were 7.2 per cent of women in leadership positions in the PCI against 2.3 per cent in the DC. By 1976 the gap had grown (13.1 per cent in the PCI against 2.0 per cent in the DC).[50] In the Chamber of Deputies elected in 1983 19.9 per cent of PCI deputies were women (38 out of 198) against 2.6 per cent for the DC (6 out of 255) and 1 out of 73 for the Socialist Party (PSI). The total number of women corresponded to 7.9 per cent of all deputies – more than twice those in the British House of Commons. How women fare in elections throughout Europe is depicted in Table 7.4. In 1987, 80 women were elected to the 630 members of the Italian Chamber of Deputies including 44 who had been on the PCI's electoral list. The party had urged its disciplined supporters to vote for them thus contributing decisively to this advance.[51]

In 1992 only 52 women were elected to Chamber (including 22 for the Democratic Party of the Left, the former Communist Party). This drop was due to a modification in the electoral system which had reduced from four to one the number of preference votes electors could use to select candidates from within their party's list; this favoured the better known politicians who were overwhelmingly male.[52] Others have argued that the main reason was the drop in the vote of the most feminist party, the PDS.[53]

In 1994, 96 women were elected, more than ever before and half under the banner of the left. What determined this massive increase (over 1992)? The elections had been fought under a new system in which one-quarter of all deputies (155) would be elected by proportional representation of party lists and the remaining 475 on the basis of first-past-the-post in individual constituencies. In the constituencies women obtained only 10 per cent of the available seats (i.e. 44 seats), but they did extremely well in the much smaller party list section where 52 women (nearly one-third of the total) were elected. Why? Because the new legislation established that each party list had to alternate men and women.[54] Since then the Constitutional Court ruled this particular piece of the legislation unconstitutional on the grounds that it discriminates against men. The consequence was that the number of women elected in the 1996 Chamber of Deputies went down to 67, nearly half the total elected in the list of the PDS, confirming its position as the party which, by far, offered women the best opportunity for being elected.

The first Italian woman to be elected to a senior political position was the communist leader Nilde Jotti when she became President of the Chamber of Deputies – constitutionally the third highest office of state – in 1979. She remained in charge until 1992. By then further progress had been made by other parties. Irene Pivetti, a member of the Northern League, became President of the Chamber in 1994. Susanna Agnelli became Foreign Secretary in Lamberto Dini's 'technocratic government' of 1995–96.

In spite of its inability or unwillingness to promote women, the DC always had the largest number of female cadres. It was greatly helped by an organization of the Church, *Azione Cattolica* (AC). This organization was based on the parish and not on the party. It was thus not 'party-political', which presented a distinct advantage. AC was open to members of both sexes, but women always prevailed: in 1946 AC had 151,000 men and 370,000 women, by 1969 it had 183,000 men and 459,000 women.[55] This corresponded to the fact that women have been and are more regular churchgoers than men while the overall number of regular churchgoers has been constantly declining.

Though the DC obtained its initial support among women thanks to the Church and organizations such as AC, it could not organize them politically while holding the view that women should stay at home following the contradictory exhortation of Pope Pius XII's call to women to get out of 'the trenches of home and family' in order to defend the home and the family.[56]

The DC was always conscious of the strategic importance of the family. Thus when a divorce bill was successfully introduced in parliament in 1970 it voted against it and proceeded to organize a referendum for its repeal, the first referendum since 1946. It threw all its strength and resources into the battle on divorce. The attempt to repeal the law failed: only 40 per cent supported the DC. Many women – including many DC women – voted against it. The referendum on divorce was one of the most important defeats of the DC in the post-war period. For the first time it could not count on some of its 'collateral' organizations (as pro-DC institutions are called): AC refused to support the DC on divorce, the Catholic trade union movement, the CISL, refused to give any indication to its members on how to vote, the pressure group of socialist-Catholics 'Christians for Socialism' as well as the Association of Italian Christian Workers (ACLI) upheld the principle of the non-interference of the Church in state matters.[57] The theme of autonomy from political parties, which had been one of the central aspects of the women's movement, had an effect on the PCI's women's organizations: the UDI went beyond the cautious line adopted by the PCI (which tried to block the referendum before fighting it) and embraced the demands of the feminists.

The decisive role of women in defeating the referendum to abrogate the divorce law was confirmed by surveys. Italian electoral results are given for every single polling station, which makes it easier to verify the behaviour of relatively small, homogeneous segments of the electorate. Thus the result of a polling station in the northern town of Ivrea (54 per cent of its electors voted in favour of divorce) could not be defined as other than startling when we consider that the bulk of the voters in that particular polling station was made up of nuns from the local convent. Research in maternity hospital polling stations in three Italian towns revealed clear pro-divorce majorities: 80.7 per cent (Bologna), 71.2 per cent (Turin) and 84.2 per cent (Florence).[58] Using the same maternity hospitals and comparing voting in general elections, Marina Weber established that in the period 1968–76 there was a shift to the left on the part of women of child-bearing age which was more pronounced than the shift to the left for Italy as a whole: 'In all three centres the PCI obtained a gradual increase in its share of the vote and one which was higher than that achieved nationally. The DC vote declined in all three centres by a greater amount than its national performance.'[59]

Even women who were members of the DC were, to some extent, influenced by a feminist orientation. They were not only responding to the birth of an ideology, but also to some of the changes which were occurring in Italian society. The very existence of consumerism led many women to enter the labour market and caused a conflict between aspirations and their designated role in the traditional family.[60] DC women tended to be more 'conservative' on political questions, but they were in favour of some sort of compromise between the roles of housewife and wage-earner. Many may be against divorce and abortion, but they demand legal equality between men and women and more educational facilities for women.[61] This is consistent with the outlook of the DC; it would be quite wrong to assume that this is an 'anti-woman' party. Christian Democrats, precisely because they enjoyed the support of many women, were more sensitive to women's issues than was generally acknowledged. The DC, though traditionalist on matters of sexual behaviour, family life, abortion and divorce, had passed a law in 1950 giving protection to working mothers, established compulsory and paid leave for pregnant women two months before and three months after birth and ratified the 1954 ILO Convention on Equal Pay earlier than any other European government.[62]

As a result of women's pressures, the DC and the PCI joined forces to pass a reform of family law (1975) which changed some of the more anachronistic aspects of Italian legislation: the concept of adultery as a criminal offence was abolished, legal separation could be obtained when the marriage had broken down and no longer, as used to be the case, only when one of the two parties was 'guilty', children born out of wedlock were given the same rights as 'legitimate' children. In 1977 a law was passed against sexual discrimination.[63] In 1978, against strong DC opposition, a law legalizing abortion was passed by the Italian parliament and the attempt to reverse it with another referendum was clearly defeated with a majority of 67.9 per cent.

The PCI hesitated before throwing its full weight behind the abortion campaign (as they had done during the previous divorce campaign). The communists had seriously over-estimated the traditionalism of Italian women and the power of the Church. Though they had declared in 1972, that 'the woman question' had become one of the central questions of the nation', they were convinced that they would lose the abortion referendum.[64] The resulting legislation – at least on paper – was one of the most progressive in Europe in terms of the principle of the woman's right to choose.

The women's movement was not simply confined to legal changes. It presented itself as a major challenge to the organization of politics and the dominance of political parties. It arose when the country moved to the left (1968) but sought from the very beginning to demarcate itself from old conceptions of left politics. It criticized in particular the PCI, which had revealed itself unable to tackle the 'woman question' in a decisive manner.

The original form of organization of the women's movement was the small consciousness-raising group within which women could rediscover themselves and could found a new concept of femininity. The slogans which were at the centre of women's struggles emphasized the desire to reappropriate a world which had been colonized by men: *Donna è bello* ('Womanhood is beautiful') – clearly imported from the USA and derived from the black power slogan: 'Black is beautiful' – and *L'utero è mio e lo gestisco io* ('I am in charge of my own uterus') which emphasized control.[65]

Twenty-five years or so have elapsed since the birth of the new Italian feminism. There is little doubt that it scored some remarkable successes both in the domain of ideas and in the institutional field. Nevertheless, it too, like virtually every other political organization in Italy, from the political parties to the trade unions, has been in crisis for a number of years. Feminism's preferred institution, the small consciousness-raising group, was not sufficient terrain for an institutional struggle. Modern feminism criticized parties and legislative assemblies, yet at the same time it accepted the fact that desired legal changes require the intervention of these institutions. The forms of organization of the women's movement do not permit it to have direct access to sources of power and institutional change. In this situation it can only act as a pressure group and thus subordinate itself to the mediation of institutions such as political parties. Another problem, related to this and present also in a number of other industrial countries, is that the forms of organization of the women's movement make it difficult to establish a positive relation with other movements. In other words, the question of 'alliance' is not only a problem for other parties and organizations such as trade unions, but it is also a problem for the women's movement itself. As Maria Luisa Boccia wrote: 'No social subject transforms its aspirations into a political project . . . unless it is able to have a positive relation with other subjects and other movements.'[66]

Over the last ten years, intellectual feminism has appeared to be increasingly detached from the everyday preoccupations of the majority of women seeking a less male-dominated society and has not been able to lead campaigns of the importance of the battles for divorce and abortion rights. Most of the feminist best-selling books are still translations from American (or French) authors. The ever-growing number of TV chat-shows are dominated by male gurus and 'experts' with the addition of women who appear to have been selected for their looks. 'Serious' weekly news magazines, such as *L'Espresso* and *Panorama* are regularly illustrated with photographs of half-naked women. Surveys show that the virtual demise of the DC has not led to a shift of women to the left: more women than men support Berlusconi's Forza Italia and, even more decisively, the traditional Catholic groups which formed the *Centro Cristiano Democratico* (CCD).[67]

Youth

The existence of a 'youth question' is as controversial as the existence of a 'woman question'. The debate usually centres on whether the internal differentiations within the age-group 14–24 are so considerable as to render any attempt to subsume all its members under the general category of youth quite meaningless. There are, however, numerous elements which also indicate that even the differentiations can have a meaning only if we acknowledge that at some time during the post-war period there emerged – not only in Italy but in the whole of the industrial world and in many urban centres of the 'Third World' – a category of people which exhibits specific economic, political and cultural characteristics and which have in common the fact of 'being young'.

We have already noted that in Italy the participation rate of the population, that is, the ratio of the labour force to the population, has fallen more rapidly than in most other industrialized countries. This reflects the fact that new jobs are not being created in proportion to the growth of the population. Potential entrants in the labour force therefore find it more difficult to find a job. If, in 1960 the participation rate of males between 20 and 24 years old was 78 per cent (48 per cent for females), by 1973 it had fallen to 66 per cent (43 per cent for females).[68] Thus an increasing number of young people had to delay their entry into the labour force and thus 'choose' to remain in education or to be unemployed. The demand for education had thus an 'objective' basis, but it could also arise because there was an effective expansion of the 'supply' of education. The authorities had assumed that the rapid economic growth of the late 1950s and early 1960s would continue and various official reports (e.g. the SVIMEZ report of 1961) had stressed that more highly qualified people were needed and that education had to expand accordingly.[69] As we know, the rapid growth of the period of the 'economic miracle' had come to an end around 1963, yet education, particularly university education, expanded throughout the 1960s (as in the rest of Europe and North America). Thus the educational sector became increasingly a 'parking area' (as it was called in Italy) for otherwise unemployed young people, and at the same time it constituted a terrain where employment could be provided for otherwise unemployed graduates (teachers and researchers).[70]

The expansion of education not only increased the numbers of educated young people but also changed qualitatively the nature of education in Italy. At the end of the fascist period Italian universities were essentially elite institutions and not, as they subsequently became, the focus for the aspirations of millions of young people. The function of the universities under fascism and under the liberal regime which preceded it was the ideological and cultural reproduction of a narrow ruling class. An elite of students was taught by an elite of teachers.

With the birth of the Italian republic the pressures for mass education multiplied. All main political parties were in favour of it. The PCI maintained that it was necessary to expand education at all levels, not only because this was necessary in a democratic society, but also because it was one of the main means of bridging the technological gap which existed between Italy and its main international competitors.[71] The DC and the PSI, particularly in the years of the centre-left, expanded education not only because they expected a concomitant expansion of the productive system, or because it would keep the number of young unemployed down, but also in order to meet the expectations of their own supporters and of the population at large. In any case the expansion of the state and its economic and welfare institutions did require the production of greater numbers of graduates.

Given the inability of the labour market to absorb the increasing number of graduates the qualifications of the average unemployed person grew. The main reason behind graduate unemployment was the fact that while education expanded the share of graduates taken up by industry began to fall after 1961. In that year Italian industry took up 16.9 per cent of graduates. By 1964 this fell to 4.4 per cent, then it went up again to 12.5 per cent in 1969 only to fall to 5.7 per cent in 1976.[72] In 1980 there were 1.25 million unemployed aged between 15 and 29 and of these 40 per cent had a degree or a higher diploma. By 1993 the official unemployment rate for this age group was 23 per cent, one of the highest in Europe.[73]

What does unemployed youth do? In the North there is an abundance of casual labour and few stable jobs. Young people there tend to accept casual labour because it is clearly seen as a stop-gap measure and they assume that, sooner or later, they will obtain a 'decent' job. Many of them continue to study while working because university attendance is not compulsory. In the South, where the rate of youth unemployment is very high, casual labour is highly exploitative and is not seen as 'temporary' at all. Southern youth fear that once they accept this kind of work it will become permanent. Consequently, it is sought only by those with no qualifications. The others are on the constant look-out for safe and secure work, and this is usually a public sector job.[74] The private sector provides employment opportunities mainly in the North. Once again the state had to intervene to compensate for the incapacity of the private sector to provide adequate employment opportunities in southern Italy.

Italy shares with 'latecomer' countries such as Spain and Greece a particularly high rate of graduate unemployment. Youth unemployment is much higher than in

Table 7.5 Youth unemployment

	1981	1991	1993
North-West	13.6	11.7	14.6
North-East	15.4	9.5	11.8
Centre	22.8	23.5	22.2
South	30.5	42.2	38.0
Total	21.3	24.1	23.0

Source: CENSIS 1994, p. 259

most other European countries, and much higher in southern Italy than in the rest of the country, as Table 7.5 shows.

So far we have established that the young particularly have been exposed to the problem of unemployment. This does not prove the existence of a 'youth question'. What we want to do now is to relate the question of the labour market to the question of the expansion of education. We noted the relation between the lengthening of the period of study and the growth of youth unemployment and that the expansion of Italian universities was essentially an expansion in terms of number of students admitted. As the actual structures of the universities are not adequate for the number of students registered it is practically impossible for all students to attend classes regularly, consult with their teachers, use the library, etc. In practice, less than 20 per cent of university students actually attend courses. Because of the ease of access to university (the school-leaving diploma enables a student to register at any Italian university of his/her choosing), Italian students are *de facto* part-time students who study on their own and use the university building only during examinations. The paucity of student grants or of cheap student loans means that students are even less economically independent than their American or British counterparts. They are forced by economic necessity either to rely on their families for a long period of time (Italian degrees take four to five years, but on a part-time basis it would obviously take even longer), or to have some form of temporary employment, or both. The kind of temporary jobs students find tend to be the sort of casual, marginal and 'black economy' jobs that other young people find. Thus there is a trend towards the homogenization of most young people at a lower 'subproletarian' level.[75] The transformation of universities into part-time institutes, and the ease of access to them occurred as a result of the students' struggles of the late 1960s (one of the main student demands was for 'open access' against the traditional elitism of the universities). This coincided with the decentralization of Italian large firms and the development of small firms as *de facto* extensions of the former. Thus the new labour market for youth was formed at the same time as there was an objective necessity for young people to find temporary jobs.

There is little doubt that Italian universities are not constructed in the interests of the students. How else can the extraordinary crowding of universities, the bureaucratic rigmaroles students must tackle, the sudden and unexplained cancellation of lectures, the lack of resources dedicated to libraries be explained, together with the absence of a system to deal with students' academic progress, their financial or emotional problems, the quality of their life. It is not always easy for Italian students to find where lectures are held. Their teachers do not know their names. It is perfectly possible to obtain a degree without ever attending a single class or writing an single essay. All that is necessary is to pass oral exams. The dates for these exams can be changed by teachers quite arbitrarily. Marks (out of 30) are given on the spur of the moment, at the end of an exam which is hardly ever longer than half hour. Student accommodation is virtually non-existent: in 1992 there were only 1,249 places for the 180,000 registered at the University of Rome, 'La Sapienza', and 420 places for the 80,000 students registered at the University of Naples.[76] The system is extremely inefficient. Many students graduate many years after their entry. Of the students registered in 1988 only 32.2 per cent graduated in 1993.[77]

The formation of a 'youth condition' in the 1960s took at first essentially cultural forms.[78] These united young people not only across regional divides, but also across countries. This was made possible by technological and media developments, the production of cheap records, cheap clothes, radio and television broadcasting of new music and new modes of speech.

The influence of the USA in youth culture cannot be underestimated. The USA exports to the rest of the world, particularly the urban-based world not only the technical infrastructure for the construction of a youth culture, but also the main cultural forms themselves, not to mention the sociological language with which to decode and understand them. During the 1960s in Italy more than anywhere else in Europe, American youth culture (music, clothes, etc.,) was integrated into a highly politicized form of protest. This remarkable politicization, more deep-rooted and longer lasting than the only other comparable phenomenon in the rest of Europe, the French events of May 1968, concerned essentially the student population. Why did Italian students become politicized in the years 1969–77? Why more in Italy than elsewhere? And which forms did this new politics take?

There is no satisfactory answer to the first question although there have been many useful suggestions. So far we have only established the causes and the existence of a cultural and sociological youth condition, but not why it should give rise to a political movement. One possible avenue for research would be to investigate one essential aspect of the student condition: of all youth only students (now a majority of the age group) actually have a structure within which to organize: the education system.[79] Young workers in large car plants can also do so, but not as young people (note, however, that the workers' revolt of 1969 was spearheaded by young workers). Another avenue for research would investigate the specificity of the history of Italian intellectuals in their relation with the state. Here we can only lay down the fundamental parameters.[80]

The fascist regime had successfully broken the critical independence which intellectuals had maintained *vis-à-vis* the Liberal State. Under fascism, intellectuals could no longer maintain their position of being a separate group 'above politics'. They became essential to the fascist attempt to organize consent from above. The Fascist State intervened in cultural affairs; this led to the politicization of intellectuals, it gave them a role and a political commitment. Their numbers expanded through the expansion of radio, the cinema and other forms of popular culture. When the war broke out many of these intellectuals, far from becoming disillusioned with politics, transferred their allegiance to the left, and fought in the Resistance in the ranks of the socialist and communist parties and the small Action Party. After the war most of these young intellectuals did not return to a pre-fascist 'liberal' concept of intellectuals as being above politics. They joined political parties and maintained a high level of political participation.

By 1968 there was thus in Italy already a strong tradition of political activity among intellectuals. Until then students had followed more or less in the footsteps of their elders, that is, by joining political parties, although there was a diminution of political participation in the years of the 'economic miracle'. The years of the centre-left revitalized political debates, but the developing 'generation gap' meant that the politicization of young people could not go through the main channels: the established political parties and the Church. They found themselves in a mass society which the much-heralded reformism of the centre-left had failed to reform and to modernize. They were faced with a strong and well-established labour movement within which they could not find a specific role. They were faced, too, with a new sexual ethic coming from the country that their own political establishment was presenting as the model of the good society, the USA, while Italy appeared to remain under the influence of the clergy.

The anti-authoritarianism characteristics of the young generation found a political outlet in the student movement which was against all forms of leadership and authoritarianism, at first within the universities against the excessive powers of the senior professors, then against the political parties (particularly those of the left) and the trade unions which were accused of excessive bureaucracy. The essential themes of the student revolt were those common to leftist students in other countries: the Third World, the war in Vietnam, the democratization of the universities. Many of the most active students were not 'new' to politics. They had been active in the ranks of the Young Communist Federation or in various Catholic groups. The movement as such represented many things: the formation of new radical elites, the struggle for the modernization of university structures and also new youth demands culturally incompatible with authoritarian or technocratic models of development.[81] Here, too, a comparative analysis with other industrial countries would show the similarities. What is peculiar to Italy is that the birth of the student movement occurred at the same time as both the Church and the PCI, the two principal centres of political ideology, were in crisis. The PCI was, in the 1960s, rethinking its relations with the Soviet bloc, with Europe and the Third World, as well as with the centre-left's attempt to modernize Italian society. The Church, too, faced with the challenge of modernity – that is, the economic boom, urbanization, mass schooling, the media, consumerism, Americanism, etc. – was changing course. With Pope John XXIII (1958–63), the Church had dropped its strident anti-communism and had begun to re-examine its relations with the Third World. Until then, the organizations of young Catholics were politically very much like all Catholic organizations: they were instruments of the Church whose aim was to pressurize the DC to maintain its line of intransigent anti-communism.[82] After Pope John this changed and Third Worldism entered the organizations of young Catholics, also inspired by progressive Latin American priests such as Camillo Torres and Helder Camara.

On the whole, the student movement was decentralized. Many students, however, faced with what to them seemed the excessively moderate line of the PCI, attempted to rediscover the 'lost' heritage of the labour movement by forming Leninist groups. This was not simply a return to the past. It was an attempt on the part of the students to form a direct relation with the labour movement without going through the established organizations of that movement – the PCI and the trade unions. Thus even when students were forming revolutionary organizations that were even more centralized than the PCI, they were rejecting one of the fundamental aspects of the Italian political system: the organization of society by the political parties.

The student events of 1968 forced both the PCI and the DC to react. Although the initial reaction of the PCI was hostile to the student movement and although one of its main leaders, Giorgio Amendola, asserted that it was necessary to fight on two fronts, i.e. against the government and against the students, the then party leader, Luigi Longo, was much more flexible.[83] Longo recognized that it was also the PCI's fault if there was such a wide gulf between the party and the students, that the party had become too sectarian and too bureaucratic and that the importance and political autonomy of the student movement had to be recognized. From the left of the party the self-criticism was even more pronounced: Rossana Rossanda, one of the leaders of the *Manifesto* group within the PCI (expelled in 1969) declared that the PCI had been mistaken not to accept that there could be a mass movement outside its control.[84] The entire strategy of the PCI was based on the assumption that the only sources of legitimate power in Italy were political parties. The growth of the youth question and of the student movement, like the growth of a feminist movement, forced them to adopt a different approach.

The reaction of the DC was different. Though hostility prevailed, attempts were made to understand what the student movement represented. The fact that the movement's main target was so often the PCI meant that the DC could hope that its overall effect would be, if not a general weakening of the PCI, at least a temporary setback. Of its leaders, however, Aldo Moro, who ten years later was kidnapped and then killed by young terrorists of the Red Brigades group, tried to go beyond an attitude of mere condemnation. In a speech in November 1968 he suggested that the revolt of the young was no mere anarchy, but represented a set of political demands which had to be answered by all Italian political parties, that it was a revolt against old ideas and an old system of power.[85] The line which eventually prevailed was to accept some of the general demands of the student movement such as making access to the universities easier without proceeding to a general reform. Masses of students entered the universities, causing a rapid growth of disciplines considered to be 'relevant' to the interests of the students, such as sociology and political science. By the 1970s the universities had acquired the economic characteristic of being a temporary refuge from unemployment.

It was evident that graduates expected to find jobs commensurate with their qualifications. These expectations could not be fulfilled and this caused much resentment.

University studies had been considered by many to be the way out from manual labour and from monotonous and repetitive work. Distaste for manual and routine work was one of the causes of the growth in student numbers. This was an attitude which was not particular to students alone, but applied to an increasing proportion of the younger generation as well. The old Catholic and communist rhetoric of work as a noble activity had little appeal to the new generations. Work was now seen as a sad necessity and it is perhaps because of this that often the young were readier to accept temporary or 'demeaning' work than their parents. Being a worker in a factory was no longer seen as a situation in which one could be inserted in a network of solidarity with one's peers. In rejecting the traditional conception of work the young were also rejecting the work their parents were engaged in, but often the parents themselves devalued their own work by insisting with their children that a good education would enable them to change their life-style and live differently.[86]

By the mid-1970s many small revolutionary organizations that had emerged from the youth movement entered into a crisis. Organizations such as *Avanguardia Operaia* (The Workers' Vanguard), *Potere Operaio* (Workers' Power) and *Lotta Continua* (The Struggle Goes On) had not been able to establish a significant presence in the labour movement, even though three of them had managed to produce daily newspapers and to establish some sort of influence, not only among young students but also among some young workers in large plants such as Fiat. The crisis of these organizations was in good part due to the fact that they had tried to subvert the system by using traditional instruments, political parties. *Avanguardia Operaia* and the Party of Proletarian Unity (PDUP), a left-wing party originating from the *Manifesto* group of ex-PCI members, merged and established themselves as the critical conscience of the PCI, slightly to the left of it. *Potere Operaio* decided to become a clandestine organization in order to prepare for armed struggle, but in so doing it lost many of its supporters, some of whom turned to established politics, particularly to the PCI. *Lotta Continua* turned itself into a daily newspaper which, eventually, suspended publication.

By the second half of the 1970s a clear majority of the young were voting for the parties of the left (54 per cent against 46 per cent of those over 25 years old), contributing to the successes of the PCI in the local elections of 1975 and the general election of 1976.[87] Many had become involved in the struggle to defend the divorce law in Italy and had begun to campaign in favour of abortion. This led them away from 'revolutionary' politics in the traditional sense towards single-issue campaigns more along the lines of the American experience, leading to an upsurge in campaigns for civil liberties: to reform the Italian prison system, to fight for a more humane treatment of psychiatric patients, to liberalize drugs, etc. Yet even these seemed destined to follow the party logic of the Italian political system: the campaigns were increasingly dominated by a new and small political party, the Radical Party.

By the late 1970s there was a general deterioration in the condition of youth. In the course of the 1970s Italy became a European centre for the sale of hard drugs, and heroin consumption reached an alarming level. The presence of chronic violence, the development of criminality among youth, drugs and a general political disaffection with the system provided the opportunity not only for the development of connections with the mafia (through the drug market) but also for the transformation of *Autonomia* into a recruiting terrain for terrorist groups such as the Red Brigades.

By the mid-1990s it is was generally accepted that the majority of young people were either not interested in politics or were to the right of those who had been young in the 1960s. They were more likely to vote for the parties of the right than for those of the left – a change which had begun to manifest itself in the mid-1980s.[88] By 1994, the right-wing *Alleanza Nazionale* had become, proportionately speaking, the most popular party among the young. Older radicals lamented the growing conformity of young people. Youth, now seemingly at peace with their families, was no longer rebellious, no longer a 'political subject' which could be harnessed to the agenda of the left.

Endnotes

1 Filippini 1978, p. 170.
2 Alberoni 1979, vol. 1, p. 263.
3 Cutrufelli 1980, p. 33.
4 Mancina 1981, pp. 16–17 and ISTAT 1995, p. 72.
5 Saraceno 1979, p. 837.
6 Ibid., pp. 846–8.
7 Paci 1993, p. 111.
8 Ibid., p. 486.
9 Balbo 1978, p. 4.
10 Ibid., pp. 4–5.
11 Data in Accornero and Carmignani 1978b, p. 52.
12 Data in Gasbarrone 1984, p. 30.
13 Bianchi 1979, p. 158.
14 Occhionero 1976, p. 129.
15 Ibid., pp. 139–40, 149.
16 Ibid., p. 150.
17 Abburrà 1992, p. 25.
18 See also Altieri 1992, p. 74.
19 Paci 1993, p. 113.
20 Ibid., p. 86.
21 Abburrà 1992, p. 32.
22 CENSIS 1994, pp. 233–5.
23 Paci 1993, pp. 86–7.
24 Ibid., p. 385.
25 ISTAT 1995.
26 Pinnelli 1992, p. 403.
27 The best treatment of this theme is Turnaturi 1991.
28 Barbagli 1994 in Ginsborg 1994, pp. 291–2.
29 Data in *Rapporto sulla popolazione in*

Italia, Istiuto dell'Enciclopedia italiana, Rome 1980, quoted in Mancina 1981, pp. 17–19 and Barbagli 1994, p. 292.
30 Golini and Misiti 1992, p. 170.
31 Ibid., p. 167.
32 Ibid., p. 166.
33 Sgritta 1993, p. 16.
34 Cavalli 1993, p. 37.
35 Ibid., p. 38.
36 ISTAT 1995, p. 588.
37 Cavalli 1993, pp. 36–7.
38 Fedele 1975.
39 Golini 1994b, p. 60.
40 Palomba and Menniti 1994 in Golini 1994b, p. 80.
41 Sgritta 1993, p. 17.
42 Ibid., p. 24.
43 Ibid., p. 23.
44 Ibid., p. 27.
45 ISTAT 1995, p. 131.
46 De Grand 1976, p. 956.
47 Mafai 1979, pp. 50–1.
48 Ibid., pp. 60–1.
49 Balbo 1976, p. 88.
50 Data in Weber 1981, pp. 193–6.
51 Guadagnini 1993, p. 190.
52 For a fuller analysis see Guadagnini, op. cit., pp. 186–8.
53 See Ceccanti 1993, p. 34.
54 The lists are regionally based ones, so small parties gaining only one seat in each 'region' will usually return the male

candidate who tops the list. This explain why women did not gain half the list seats.

55 Weber 1981, pp. 189–90.
56 Menapace 1974, p. 54.
57 Caldwell 1978, pp. 89–93.
58 Weber 1981, p. 198.
59 Ibid., p. 129.
60 Menapace 1974, p. 63.
61 Ibid., pp. 58–60.
62 Beccalli 1994, p. 91.
63 Mancina 1981, p. 10.
64 Berlinguer 1975, p. 410.
65 Rossi 1978, esp. pp. 23–42.
66 Boccia 1980, p. 23.
67 See survey of 13 September 1995, ISPO/ Nielsen.
68 Data in Fedele 1975.
69 Bassi and Pilati 1978, p. 77.
70 Ibid., p. 79.
71 Vacca 1977, p. 170.
72 Figures in Accornero and Carmignani 1978c, p. 186.

73 CENSIS 1994, p. 259.
74 Carmignani 1980, p. 14.
75 Bassi and Pilati 1978, pp. 68–73.
76 Simone 1992, p. 1073.
77 CENSIS 1994, p. 190.
78 This is the period when Italian sociologists begin to examine youth as a cultural subsystem, see: Ardigó 1966, Livolsi 1976 and Alberoni 1970.
79 Cecchi 1975, p. 42.
80 On the relation between fascism and intellectuals, see Mangoni 1974, lsnenghi 1979 and Turi 1980.
81 Melucci 1978, p. 16.
82 Rodano 1978, pp. 196–7.
83 See Amendola 1968 and Longo 1968.
84 See Rossanda 1968.
85 Moro 1979, p. 223.
86 Accornero 1978, pp. 218–23.
87 Bassi and Pilati 1978, p. 8.
88 Mattei, Niemi and Powell 1990, p. 337 and Giovannini 1988, p. 506.

Chapter 8

Instruments of political mobilization

Throughout the so-called 'First Republic' the most important instruments of political mobilization in Italy have been, undoubtedly, the political parties. The profound dislike for politicians which coexists with an astonishing interest for their personalities, tactics and pronouncements, has not stopped Italians from developing a higher level of party activism than in most other West European countries. Consider the USA where parties tend to be mere electoral machines, 'not the centres of passion . . . they are part-time organizations . . . parties do not appear to stand for anything very meaningful. Perhaps their most outstanding characteristic is their lack of ideology'.[1]

The specific role of political parties will be examined in Part Three ('Politics'). In this chapter I want to examine instead the impact in Italy of instruments of political mobilization other than political parties.

The central importance of parties has meant that Italy has never been a 'growth area' for their traditional competitors: pressure groups. Where these existed they were either quickly absorbed by parties or became parties themselves (such as the Radical Party). I have chosen to focus on the interrelations between four specific 'instruments of political mobilization' and political parties: the trade unions, business, the Church and the media. Quite clearly the primary function of these four 'instruments' are not political but, respectively, the defence and improvement of the conditions of their members, business profitability, religion and information (including, in the private media, the sale of advertising as well as information). In the pursuit of these aims all four deal with politics and depend – to some extent – on some form of consensus and legitimacy. This is not necessarily, or not always, political, but it always has political effects. In all four cases there is, in the postwar period, a fairly close identification between each of these forces and political parties, but in the 1960s and 1970s there was a growing autonomy which contributed to the apparent crisis of Italian political parties and hence of the political system itself. The kind of 'political mobilization' each of these four forces achieved is specific to its traditional role: trade unions organize at the point of production and mobilize workers through meetings, strikes and demonstrations, their strength depending on the degree of consensus achieved. The Church mobilizes the faithful through specific religious rituals and a range of activities in the home and the community. Industry and business organize economic activity, influence the shape of the market and the pattern of consumption, organize entrepreneurs and negotiate with the political system. The media contribute to the structuring of an increased proportion of leisure time, give shape to information, filter and condition political messages.

Trade unions

The reconstruction of the Italian trade union movement began in the course of the Second World War. From its very inception the new *Confederazione Generale Italiana del Lavoro* (CGIL) was a creature of the three leading anti-fascist parties: the Socialist Party (PSI), the Communist Party (PCI) and the Christian Democrats (DC). In June 1944 representatives of these parties signed the so-called 'Pact of Rome' which was the basis of the reconstituted CGIL. Formally the CGIL declared itself to be 'independent of all political parties' and at the same time to be an expression of the common will of the three main parties.[2]

Traditionally, European trade unions have had two purposes: an economic one seeking to improve the wages and the working conditions of their members, and a wider political function. This is often achieved either by connecting the trade union to a party of the left (socialist or communist party), or by acting as the collective representative of the working class and, in this guise, negotiating with or putting pressure on the government of the day. Though not all unions are committed to socialism, in virtually all other European countries the principal trade union has a socialist orientation.

In the post-war period, Italy shared with Belgium, France and a few other countries the peculiarity of having a divided and highly 'political' trade union movement connected to more than one party. The socialist and communist presence was by far the most weighty in the new unified CGIL, but they could not afford to dominate it for fear of driving out the Catholic minority. That being the case, it was established that, irrespective of the internal relation of forces, each of the three components of the union would have equal representation on the Executive Committee and each would be represented by a joint general secretary. Thus from the very beginning the actual structure of the union reflected the ruling post-war coalition (i.e. DC, PCI, PSI). This also meant that the CGIL was not in any sense an opposition force. Its leading personnel overlapped with the leadership of the three governing parties and could hardly challenge them.

Given the Catholic presence the CGIL could not be classified as a socialist trade union. Nevertheless, it had an ideology: anti-fascism. This 'glued' together its three components in the same way as it held together the DC, the PCI and the PSI in the governments of 1945–47. As long as anti-fascism was the major issue in the political life of the country both government and trade union could be united. But what of the 'economic' function of trade unions? For the DC component of the CGIL the trade unions were expected to control any pressures which could endanger the possibility of economic reconstruction. This meant controlling wages. The CGIL accepted a wage truce and convinced its working-class supporters to enhance productivity without immediate monetary rewards – as the French communist-dominated CGT did in the same period for the same reasons.

For the left, particularly the PCI – already dominant within the organized working class – a period of social peace was also necessary. The PCI had ruled out a socialist insurrection. Palmiro Togliatti was developing a conception of the transition to socialism in an advanced capitalist country which precluded any resort to insurrectionary tactics. The PCI favoured a period of social peace for two other reasons. In the first place, in order to implant itself in the Italian social system the PCI could not rely simply on the support of the working class. It needed to develop a system of alliances which would include the emergent middle classes. In order to obtain at least the passive consent of these groups it was necessary to guarantee some stability in their economic position. This meant emphasizing the struggle against inflation, while at the same time improving the prospect of employment. In this context a wages struggle could not be given priority. Secondly, an improvement in the political position of the working class required a strongly interventionist state which would be committed to a policy of structural reforms. These reforms would reduce and perhaps eliminate the power of financial and industrial monopolies which, in the analysis of the PCI, constituted the terrain upon which fascism had emerged.

Given the policies and strategies of the two essential components of both CGIL and government (the socialists were unable – at that early stage – to demarcate themselves clearly from the communists), it is not surprising if the trade unions behaved in 1944–48 as if they had signed a form of social contract with the ruling coalition. However, it was not just a question of political strategy. The fact of the matter is the CGIL was not only unwilling but also unable to lead a strong wages campaign, because the working class was weak. Its weakness was part and parcel of the general weakness of the Italian economy, the widespread misery and poverty, the homelessness, the extent of unemployment. At first one fundamental concession was extracted: the labour market was 'blocked', making it virtually impossible for entrepreneurs to make anyone redundant. However, when the ban on dismissals was abandoned in 1946 in exchange for the promise of maintaining existing employment levels, the CGIL lost some of its control of the labour market. Nevertheless, it succeeded in obtaining price controls and an agreement on the indexation of wages in 1946 (in exchange for a seven-month wage truce). By the winter of 1947 price controls could not be sustained and the indexation of wages never really protected the workers against inflation.[3] Nevertheless the very fact that the working-class parties shared in governmental power for the first time in the history of united Italy gave great psychological strength to factory workers and their trade union representatives, even though this was not translated into wages militancy.

The unity of the trade union movement depended on the unity of the anti-fascist coalition. The unity of the latter depended on the international situation and the extent to which the Western Allies and the Soviet Union could find a *modus vivendi* in the post-war period. The Cold War destroyed this possibility and with it all the attempts in Europe to maintain coalition governments with communist participation.[4] As the post-fascist trade union movement had been created in Italy on the basis of a strong party political unity, the break-up of the tripartite coalition in May 1947 led inevitably to the break-up of the CGIL. Thus party politics had an immediate effect on trade union politics. Two years after the right wing of the PSI formed the Social Democratic Party (1947), their trade union supporters left the CGIL and formed their own trade union which, in 1950, took the name of *Unione italiana del lavoro* (UIL).

In 1948 the DC-aligned Catholics left the CGIL, establishing at first the so-called 'Free CGIL' which, a couple of years later, took the name of *Confederazione Italiana dei Sindacati dei Lavoratori* (CISL).

The break-up of the trade-union movement further aggravated the already weak position of organized labour. Throughout the 1950s hardly any gains were made. The influx of workers from the South had the effect of transforming the labour market into a highly flexible mechanism outside the control of the trade unions. Militant workers could be easily sacked, and the general threat of redundancy dampened the prospects of an economic struggle.[5] From an organizational point of view the structure of trade unions at the local level was weak and as a result the main form of bargaining was highly centralized.

Entrepreneurs had no interest in encouraging plant-level bargaining for this could only strengthen the trade union at the shop-floor level.[6] The most important workers' organization within the factories were the 'internal commissions'. These were not, strictly speaking, trade union organizations. They were elected by all workers whether or not they belonged to a union. The internal commissions did not negotiate wages, but only some aspects of labour conditions. They could not rely on any backing external to the factories. In practice they were ineffective and at the mercy of the employers.

Elections to the internal commissions merely reflected national elections as the three trade union federations tried to get their own members elected to the commissions. Thus, even at the local level the organization of workers reflected party political divisions.[7] When in 1954 the CGIL lost control of the internal commissions at Fiat (which passed on to the DC-aligned CISL) this was a major defeat for the PCI.

Alessandro Pizzorno has described the 1950s as being dominated by a sort of social pact between the state and the entrepreneurs.[8] The entrepreneurs agreed to drop protectionism and accepted international competition. In exchange (and in order to keep wages low) the state would ensure 'social order'. This was done by repressing the CGIL and expanding public spending. Thus the state intervened to help private capital to increase productivity more rapidly than wages. From the point of view of the workers this had the same effect as an incomes policy: real wages hardly increased between 1948 and 1954. The CGIL was still able to organize workers on the basis of an ideological commitment towards a 'better tomorrow', on the basis of future gains rather than concrete results, but the Catholic CISL was able to offer the workers something more concrete: not a vague future, but the real prospect of the 'economic miracle'. The assumption on which the CISL was working was that the period of constant growth would last for a whole historical period and that the unions would benefit from it. Their model was that of 'American' trade unionism: unions would accept that the economy should remain the prerogative of the private sector and seek in exchange a growing share of the cake.

The CISL tried to break with the Italian tradition of highly centralized collective agreements in favour of decentralized bargaining. Until 1955 the CGIL fought tooth and nail against this approach, arguing that it would endanger the unity and the organization of the workers. As a leader of the CGIL, Luciano Lama, has admitted, it was the competition from the CISL and principally the defeat at Fiat in 1955 that forced the CGIL to review its position.[9]

The repression of the CGIL was facilitated by the fact that, thanks to the DC, in the post-war period there was no serious attempt to establish a new legal framework for industrial relations. If that had been done – given the prevailing anti-fascist climate – the unions would have obtained considerable advantages. The effect of not intervening was to keep on the statute books all the anti-strike regulations which were contained in the penal code established during fascism by Alfredo Rocco.[10] These were, of course, incompatible with the new Constitution, but as Italy did not have a Constitutional Court until the mid-1950s, they were not challenged. Thus offences such as 'to instigate class hatred', 'to organize a general strike', 'to hold a seditious demonstration', 'to insult the forces of law and order or the government' were all upheld.

In fact legislation restricting trade unions was further extended by Mario Scelba, the DC Minister for the Interior: in July 1947 it was decided that any assembly of workers within the factory gates required prior police permission. Later Scelba described the CGIL general strike after the attempt on Togliatti's life (1948) as an 'insurrectionist act' and proceeded – again with the help of the judiciary – to arrest and try hundreds of trade unionists.[11]

By 1960 the pattern of labour relations began to undergo a profound change. In structural terms the main causes were the growth of the working class in quantitative terms (see Chapter 6), its territorial concentration, the absorption of unemployment either directly or through emigration. This set the scene for the changes of the 1960s. At the international level the harshest years of the Cold War were over. International coexistence made the staunch anti-communism of the 1950s look outdated. The end of the post-war boom and of the Italian economic miracle which led to the birth in Italy of the centre-left coalition and the massive expansion of the public sector meant that the state took it upon itself not only to reform the economic system but also to become an economic power in its own right: it was no longer content to leave the economy to private capital. The trade unions felt stronger and the success of the wage offensive of the early 1960s made further economic development on the basis of low wages less likely.

The growing legitimation of trade unions depended only in part on the changing structure of the labour market. It was also the result of changes occurring in the political balance of power. The CISL and the UIL, who enjoyed privileged access to government because 'their' parties were in power, had been putting pressures on them to reform industrial relations. In the late 1950s and even more so in the early

1960s the state, through the *Istituto per la Ricostruzione Industriale* (IRI) and the *Ente Nazionale Idrocarburi* (ENI), began to use the public sector as an instrument for a more conciliatory pattern of negotiations with the trade unions.[12] By 1960–62 the state sector in practice negotiated also on behalf of the private sector because the kind of industrial relations system which developed in the IRI–ENI system could not be opposed by the increasingly divided employers' association, the *Confindustria*. Until then access of the trade unions to the political level had to be mediated through political parties. The unions could mobilize their own rank and file only on the basis of party alliances, union leaders owed their positions to parties and their styles of leadership, strategies and appeals were systematically borrowed from political parties.[13] Yet access to politics was limited because the CGIL parties (socialists and communists) were not in government and the CISL and the UIL could only work through those factions within the government parties which represented them. With the entry of the PSI into the government (the centre-left coalition) the status of the CGIL changed. The CISL was considerably strengthened because the left-wing factions of the DC – who had been strongly in favour of a centre-left coalition – had defeated the DC right.

The trade unions were able to use their strength not only to impose better wage levels in the early 1960s but also to begin to distance themselves from the political parties. This took place because the new centre-left coalition, by giving a role to the three trade union confederations, favoured direct negotiations with entrepreneurs and unions. The unions were promised social reforms and business was promised modernization. A system of triangular or tripartite consultation between government, employers and unions began to develop in Italy as in other European countries.[14]

The development of trade union involvement in politics brought about profound changes in the trade unions' perception of their role. Traditionally, the CISL had not been particularly interested in institutional and political reform, which it considered best left to the political parties, i.e. to the DC.[15] Moreover, it thought that the centre-left coalition could modernize the Italian economy without altering the institutional framework. As it became involved in political consultations, the CISL had to begin to re-examine its own tradition and to recognize the limitations of 'non-political' trade unionism. The third and smallest confederation, the UIL, had been a fairly marginal force until the centre-left coalition. The UIL welcomed the new coalition because it assumed that the break-up of the alliance between the PSI and the PCI would have repercussions in the trade union field, i.e. that the socialists would leave the CGIL and join them. This would have established a perfect 'fit' between the three trade union centres and the three leading political parties. It would also have facilitated the reunification of the PSI and the Social Democrats. However, by 1964, the CGIL socialists – who were, anyway, closer to the PCI than most of their comrades – renegotiated their positions within the CGIL with the communists and obtain more power for themselves.

The tensions within the CGIL between communists and socialists were sufficient to convince the CGIL to become increasingly independent from the PCI. All unions now relied less on political parties.

In the course of the 1960s Italian unions came to a better understanding of the weakness of governments in modern complex societies. They saw that political power did not have a centre, but was diffuse throughout political and civil society. This gave them an incentive to penetrate as much as possible into the various apparatuses of the state and at all levels. In so doing they modelled themselves on the DC system of power: establishing a presence in social and political life. Thus at the same time as they were distancing themselves from political parties the three trade union confederations were also developing some of the attributes of political parties.

In 1968–69 a third phase opened up in industrial relations. One of its main features was a new type of labour conflict: a high level of militancy, an active involvement of non-unionized workers, a dislike of bureaucracy expressed in rank-and-file slogans such as 'we are the union' and 'the work contract is just a piece of paper'.[16] They refused to accept any connection between an increase in wages and an increase in productivity: 'more money, less work'. Some of the conflicts escalated in violence: the police killed two agricultural labourers at Avola in November 1968, and two more trade unionist demonstrators at Battipaglia in the following year. Later that year a policeman was killed in Milan, and on 12 December 1969 a bomb in a Milan bank killed sixteen people. At first anarchists were suspected, then fascists; the trials dragged on for over a decade while political violence escalated. This did not prevent the growth of trade union power in Italy. The decade after 1968 was characterized by a high level of sustained militancy and by an increase in workers' control over the conditions of work. If we compare 1968–78 with 1960–68 we note that in the earlier period wage differentials between skilled and unskilled workers had tended to increase, while in the second decade wage bargaining was directed towards reducing differentials. The ethics of equality pervaded labour relations and found a practical outlet in the new agreement with the Confindustria of 1975 over the indexation of wages. Furthermore, after 1968 collective bargaining was further decentralized towards firm – and plant-level bargaining.

The unrest of 1968 would not have occurred with that level of intensity if the Italian unions had been stronger. A strong and well-entrenched union movement would have exercised a measure of restraint and control, partly in order to protect vested interests, partly in order not to jeopardize the existing power relations. A weak trade union movement had little interest in controlling rank-and-file unrest and, by definition, little strength with which to control it.

The new factory council system developed particularly, though not exclusively, where trade unions were weak. The growth of authentic grass-roots organizations (the factory councils) and of the factory delegates elected by the councils (i.e. by all workers in a factory) posed a problem for all unions. The unions could have tried to repress the councils by withholding any protection at the national level. Alternatively, they could have accepted the coexistence of two levels of organizations within the factory: a factory council open to all workers, and alongside it the formal trade union organization. The third alternative, the one eventually adopted, was to declare that the factory council was the organ of the trade union movement at the factory level. This had several effects, the most important of which was to unite the still nationally divided trade union movement at the shop-floor level through the factory council. Perhaps one should not overstress this rank-and-file unity. It was only too obvious that the workers would choose delegates among the most active members of the trade unions and that the delegates' committee would still approximately reflect the relations of forces within the trade-union movement. What the system did, however, was to involve all workers in the trade unions through the councils. This obviated the weakness of having a generally low level of formal membership and increased the credibility of the three confederations. Later, union leadership was reasserted when the three confederations established the principle that the delegates of the factory councils had to be members of the union.[17] Thus what had begun as a rank-and-file challenge to the trade unions became the basis for increased cooperation between the CGIL, UIL and CISL. Furthermore, the growth of the factory councils enabled the unions to penetrate into hitherto non-unionized firms.

There is yet another aspect of the 1968–69 struggles which must be mentioned because it has a bearing on the relation between unions and political parties. In the course of these struggles groups to the left of the PCI were able to have a remarkable effect on working-class struggles.[18] In some cases these were made up, at least in part, of 'new', i.e. migrant, workers in the large factories of the North where the unions were weak. In many cases workers responded positively to the students' unrest and adopted similar forms of struggle such as the meeting open to all (interpreted by some as a rebirth of the Soviets) as the central decision-making structure within the plant. The leftist groups were far more successful in Italy than in the UK or West Germany, or even France where – May 1968 notwithstanding – they had very little impact. This was partly due to the weakness of the unions themselves, partly to the crisis of the PCI in the 1960s, and also to the fact that the socialist language of the students, whether mediated by libertarian concepts or by orthodox 'Marxist-Leninist' ones, was not foreign to Italian workers. By 1968 various aspects of Marxist culture were so embedded in Italy that students propounding socialist and communist slogans at factory gates were given far more attention than their comrades in the rest of Western Europe, not to speak of North America where workingclass culture is generally hostile to socialist ideas. However, any leftist notion that the factory council could be used in an anti-parliamentary function as the nucleus of future 'workers' soviets' met the strong and successful opposition of the CGIL.[19]

The struggles of 1968–69 also resulted in the adoption by parliament in 1970 of the *Statuto dei Lavoratori* (the Workers' Charter) which enshrined many rights which had been achieved in the course of the struggles, including the legal recognition of the factory councils. It made 'anti-trade-union' behaviour on the part of the employer an offence. It allowed paid time off from work for factory council delegates and the right to have an assembly of workers on the factory premises during working hours. It made it difficult to make workers redundant. One of the reasons why this legislation was passed was that the political establishment recognized that it was necessary to strengthen the trade union leadership against its grass roots.[20]

The political role of the trade unions developed as they negotiated directly with the government. Political parties seemed to become less important and resented the growth of trade union power. However, a system of permanent negotiations between unions and governments could not develop, first because the trade union movement did not achieve the goal of reunification, then because governments were never able to produce concrete economic programmes and, finally, because the trade unions were not able to become the centre of a new powerful social bloc which included the new social movements.

Let us examine each of these three elements. First, the debate on trade union unification could only develop on the basis of the autonomy of each confederation from the political parties. By 1969 the CGIL had accepted this required the adoption of the principle of 'incompatibility' between holding a union post and office in a political party. The three confederations accepted this principle but disagreed on the extent to which it should be applied: did it apply only to the overlap in membership between the executive committees of the parties and those of the trade unions? Did it also imply that trade union officials should not be elected to parliament? Should the principle be extended to all levels? Extension to all levels would mean that the secretary of a trade union branch would not be able to be elected to the executive committee of his party cell or branch.[21]

A compromise was reached. In 1972 the three confederations decided to proceed towards a full merger by March 1973. What blocked it was the collapse of the centre-left government and the election of the right-wing DC leader Giovanni Leone as President of the Republic (with the help of neo-fascist votes) in spite of the combined opposition of the PCI and the PSI.[22] Once more dissension within political parties affected the unity of the trade union movement. The CGIL leader, Luciano Lama, suggested that in order to maintain the momentum towards unity, the trade unions should join in a 'federal pact' while maintaining their separate identities. This solution, initially seen as temporary became permanent.

The government of national unity of 1976–79 gave added impetus to unification, but its break-up signalled the ever-increasing difficulty of trade union unity. After 1980 the unions faced a long period of uninterrupted decline. All hopes of unification vanished in 1984 when – as we shall see – the dispute over the wages indexation system divided the communist trade unionists from all the others.

Secondly, the lack of concrete government programmes became far more marked in the 1980s. Italian governments lived day to day, simply responding to a variety of pressures from interest groups. The Socialist Party, under Bettino Craxi who had become Prime Minister (1983–87), had turned decisively against the PCI and even the unity between socialists and communists within the CGIL appeared precarious. Trade unions were forced to behave like pressure groups. Each union tried to apply pressure on a 'friendly' party or on a faction within a party in order to defend the gains of the past in a period of high unemployment. In this situation to maintain a united front became increasingly difficult.

Thirdly, trade union difficulty in organizing and leading a vast social movement was due to both structural and ideological reasons.[23] Structural factors included the growth of sections of the Italian population which were outside the traditional reach of trade unions, such as the tertiary sector, white-collar workers in industry, small firms (while the number of those employed in large firms decreased), the unemployed, old-age pensioners. To these structural factors we should add:

1 the existence of the 'new' youth movement of 1977 known as the Autonomi which involved not only students but also young workers, many of whom sympathized with terrorism;
2 the growth of organizations of unemployed opposed to organized labour (in Naples there have even been attacks on trade union offices);
3 the growth of the 'autonomous' unions, i.e. unions outside the 'Big Three';
4 the growing disaffection of white-collar workers with the trade unions' policy of reducing differentials;
5 the growth of different forms of work: part-time, overtime, two jobs and seasonal and casual work.

To these difficulties was added the fact that the unions found it increasingly hard to maintain their legitimacy among ordinary workers. There was a widening gap between union activists and the rest of the working class. The limitations of existing trade union democracy were openly recognized even by prestigious communist leaders such as Giorgio Amendola (never a supporter of the factory council system) in a controversial article.[24]

On many traditional trade union matters such as safety regulations and working conditions the factory council system worked reasonably well and strengthened the trade union movement. However, it was also necessary to deal with economic and social life outside the factory gates by intervening in the formulation of economic policies at the regional or national level. This required the possession of a degree of expertise and knowledge the activists might have but not the mass of workers. Thus the gap between the two increased.[25] The factory council system worked effectively only within the factory. Outside it, workers' support was obtained not on the basis of their concrete understanding of the issues but on an ideological support for the trade union leadership. The way in which the unions approached bargaining was by putting on the table short-term economic demands, such as wages and working conditions, alongside as more general ones, often giving in on the short-term demands in exchange for vague and ill-specified long-term promises.[26] They were thus bargaining away the basis of their concrete support (short-term economic gains) in exchange for items of a political package which could not be delivered and on which working-class commitment was imprecise and ambiguous.

There is another reason for the growing crisis of trade union legitimacy: traditional bargaining on wages and working conditions involved those affected by them, i.e. all or most factory workers. But issues concerned with local planning affected all the inhabitants of a particular area and implied that some form of popular participation was required outside the confines of the factory gates. This was not – and perhaps could not have been – achieved by the trade unions. It was tried by political parties on the basis of devolved power at the regional, city and neighbourhood level, but this often became little more than a reproduction of the traditional parliamentary relations between government and opposition.

As unemployment rose throughout the industrialized world the strength of the trade unions decreased. The ability of large firms, such as Fiat, to reduce its workforce was a blow to trade union control over the labour market. Nevertheless, deflationary public spending cuts did not enjoy in Italy's political establishment the degree of political support it had in the UK under the Thatcher government. Instead the Italian ruling coalition, under pressure from employers' organizations, tried to intervene by reducing labour costs (modifying wage indexation) and raising indirect taxes. The unions found themselves fighting an increasingly defensive battle precisely in a period in which their own credibility on the shop floor was under challenge. The effective end of trade union unity occurred in February 1984 when the socialist Prime Minister, Bettino Craxi, issued a decree revising unilaterally the wages indexation system, reducing the amount of protection it offered against price rises by between 10 and 20 per cent. The CISL and the UIL, but not the CGIL, accepted the reduction. The split was compounded by the fact that the minority socialist faction of the CGIL had been willing to accept the government's offer.

The CISL accepted the reduction of wages indexation for political reasons: by breaking with the CGIL in a period when trade unions were weak and under attack, the CISL could appear a reasonable and realistic trade union with which the government could negotiate. The government did not have many resources for a deal, but it could give the CISL that legitimacy which trade unions – throughout Europe – were finding more difficult to obtain. With the CGIL 'out in the cold' and the UIL too small, the CISL hoped to become the main protagonist of future negotiations with the government.

The CGIL could not have accepted Craxi's proposals without a major *quid pro quo*. Its activists within the rank and file, mainly communists, could not accept an agreement which decreased their purchasing power and further isolated their own political party. The CGIL was in no position to alienate itself from its rank and file and there was a prompt response from the PCI and the CGIL: on 24 March 1984 a massive demonstration of around one million people converged on Rome to back up the parliamentary tactics of the PCI aimed at ensuring that the government decree would not become law within the statutory 60 days. The PCI was successful, but the government promptly introduced another, more limited, decree. The PCI called for a referendum to repeal the new measure. This was held in June 1985 and resulted in a blow for the PCI and for the communist majority in the CGIL.

The crisis of the trade union movement affected the CGIL perhaps more deeply than the other union federations. In the first place the future of the CGIL was tied to the fact that it could not rely on a favourable government being elected in the near future. Most European trade unions have or have had 'their party' in power and/or stand a reasonable chance to see it in power again. The CGIL was never in this position. Insofar as it was concerned the Italian political system was 'blocked' and the PCI was unlikely to govern.

By the time First Republic collapsed, the unions were able to regain some position of influence. The unpopularity of all political parties enabled them to appear as one of the few remaining functioning institutions of civil society. They were helped in this by the fact that redundant workers and pensioners can, if they go on paying reduced dues, remain members of the unions. As both these groups expanded, the unions found that they could were still sufficiently representative to be regularly consulted by governments (see Chapter 5). The Amato and Ciampi governments (1992–94) were forced by their political weakness to seek union consent for the deflationary policies pursued. This partly explains why there has been no development of the ferocious anti-unionism which has prevailed in the UK. There were still recognized as the chief interlocutor of the government, as was clearly the case when the Ciampi government negotiated with them the virtual abolition of indexation (23 July 1993). The Berlusconi government of 1994 – the first government coalition with no links to any of the unions – tried to ignore the unions and paid the price by having to face, in December 1994, the largest trade union demonstration in Italian history, which defeated its plans of pension reforms. The succeeding government of Lamberto Dini eschewed the confrontational tactics of Berlusconi and successfully negotiated with the unions. The election of the left-of-centre Prodi government in 1996 has ensured that the trade unions will continue to be consulted and to exercise some influence.

Unions, however, will not be able to avoid facing the problems common to the movement in other countries: the process of de-industrialization compels them to compensate by recruiting in the public sector. Where privatizations occur, the unions will lose strength. Where they do not, union demands will appear to clash with the ever more reluctant taxpayers and the accepted need to cut public spending. The polemic against the state which escalated in the wake of the Tangentopoli scandals, further weakened the unions which were seen, rightly so, as the last great defender of the state as the regulator of the economy and the dispenser of welfare.

Italian unions made the same mistakes as their counterparts in other European countries. They never seriously attempted to develop a framework for the regulation of industrial conflict. They always tried, understandably enough, to keep open their freedom of action even though, in so doing, they also kept open the freedom of action of their capitalist opponents. When neo-liberalism swept throughout Europe, affecting even Italy, the unions found themselves in difficulties.[27] When most trade unionists were employed in the private manufacturing sector, a strike caused far more damage to the employers (and perhaps the strikers themselves) than to anyone else. This was not the case in the public sector and in the tertiary; as this sector expanded it became clear to the three confederations that some form of regulation was necessary. They sought to negotiate this with the government but attempted to exclude the new, small autonomous trade unions. These were particularly active among groups of workers ready to use their power to obtain concessions regardless of the consequences, such as air traffic controllers and train drivers.[28]

It was difficult in these circumstances to expect the public to support strikes when, quite clearly, strikes were directed against them. Even the PCI dissociated itself from strikes in the public sectors which caused aggravations to ordinary citizens. On 23 April 1990, an unusual headline appeared in the front page of the communist paper *L'Unità* significantly calling for 'the right to travel'.[29] In an attempt to placate public opinion, in January 1988 the confederations virtually drafted their own legislation regulating public sector strikes. This was passed in parliament only in 1990 but many thought it was too lax. Finally, the age structure of the unions is getting dangerously lopsided towards the older age-groups – a side-effect of the large youth unemployment and the presence of many pensioners in the unions. The new parties of the centre-right appear to be hostile to the very concept of trade unionism (unlike the DC during the second half of the First Republic), while those of the centre-left seek to distance themselves from the unions.

How and whether unionism will survive in the next century are not questions which are confined to Italy.

Private enterprise

In Chapter 1 we pointed out that, in the absence of any strong alternative or opposition, the doctrine of economic liberalism prevailed and influenced the chief economic decisions of the first post-war governments. This was one of the rare moments of Italian history since the *Risorgimento* when the entrepreneurial class could feel that it shared in political power, perhaps even that it was at the centre of it. Guido Carli, for many years the Governor of the Bank of Italy and then President of the Confindustria (the Employers' Federation) complained that the Italian state had always been the state of the petty bourgeoisie, never that of the so-called 'productive' classes: 'The State has never been the representative of the interests of the capitalists or of the workers. The ideals and the culture of the Italian State have been those of the petty bourgeoisie.'[30] Similarly, industrialists have frequently complained that there is no industrial culture in Italy.[31] The leaders of the DC were close to the Church and the countryside; in so far as they had a political philosophy it was the social doctrine of the Church. The anti-fascist political right was against any form of state involvement akin to the New Deal or Keynesianism. The fascists had sought to control capitalism. The left thought that Italian capitalism was backward and deprived of any internal capacity for growth. When the PCI–PSI trade union federation, the CGIL, put forward in 1949 a 'Labour Plan' which was essentially Keynesian, it encountered the indifference of the PCI. Even the *Confindustria* chose to subordinate itself to the DC and to Catholic values, assuming that the Church would work in favour of social control over Italy's recalcitrant working class. Only some politicians close to the leader of the Republican Party, Ugo La Malfa and the President of the powerful (state) bank, the Banca Commerciale, Raffaele Mattioli, propounded some version of reformist capitalism. This ideology, commonly referred to as *Terza Forza* or Third Force, was never dominant, except perhaps very briefly during the 1960s.[32]

As we have explained, this anti-industrial bias was no disadvantage. The Italian state removed as many obstacles as it could from the industrialists' path and added some strong incentives. In any case, an entrepreneurial culture was thriving precisely in those areas which were under the political hegemony of allegedly anti-entrepreneurial forces: Catholic Veneto and communist Emilia Romagna. Capitalists have been unusually revered in post-war Italy. During the late 1950s, the period of greatest expansion of Italian industry, there was a group of outstanding captains of industry, names such as Valletta (Fiat) Pirelli, Olivetti, Cenzato (Montecatini

– chemical industry) and many others. Though, in the 1970s, industrialists were unpopular they came back into fashion, so to speak, in the 1980s. Carlo De Benedetti (Olivetti), Raoul Gardini (Montedison), the Benetton family, Silvio Berlusconi, Gianni Agnelli were treated by the Italian press like film stars or members of the British Royal Family: where they ate, what they thought, the books they read and what they wore became the subject of endless fascination. A magazine even bought the picture of Gianni Agnelli sunbathing in the nude (the Chairman of Fiat was nearly 70 years old at the time). When Tangentopoli hit the headlines, their popularity decreased somewhat. Some of those who had been accused or suspected of corrupting politicians were hounded and some, notably Raoul Gardini, committed suicide. It should be said, though, that much of the opprobrium was directed towards those who had received bribes – politicians and civil servants – rather than those who handed them out. The fact is that Italian capitalism has always been directed by well-known and visible personalities who were often the leading shareholders, rather than the faceless managers of multinationals acting on behalf of equally faceless shareholders such as pensions funds. Moreover, Italian large-scale capitalism consisted of relatively few firms. In the 1950s the dominant force had been Fiat. It always worked closely with the political authorities and was able to influence the economic strategy of the DC and hence of the government. The Italian state helped Fiat by providing the infrastructure for the development of a large market for cars by building motorways, keeping the price of petrol low, and running down public transport. Fiat had a privileged relation with the DC and particularly with its 'modernizing' wing led by Amintore Fanfani. It took bold initiatives abroad, the most important of which was the development of a large Fiat plant in Togliattigrad in the USSR.[33] Fiat maintained its distance from those large private companies such as the electrical and chemical industries, which were leading a campaign against Fanfani and which fought tooth and nail against the emergence in the early 1960s of a centre-left government.[34] Fiat had been able to project an image of progressive, i.e. 'American' capitalism, by distancing itself from the rest of the *Confindustria* which it considered too right-wing. Yet within its plants Fiat maintained a repressive regime against the trade unions, particularly the CGIL. Militant workers were isolated or expelled. In 1971 it was discovered that in the 1950s Fiat had collected thousands of files on its workers. This had been done with the help of the police, the *carabinieri* and the Italian secret service. The information thus collected was used to sack workers or intimidate them in a determined attempt to weaken the CGIL and strengthen the Catholic trade union, CISL.[35] However, apart from the stick there was also the carrot in the shape of higher-than-average wages and some company-based benefits.[36]

With the advent of the centre-left coalition in 1963, Fiat began to take some interest in the affairs of the *Confindustria*. As the Fiat-DC reformist line was being developed there emerged a rough division of labour between these two centres of power. The DC would split the left by allying itself with the PSI, adopt a policy of structural reforms and modernize the Italian economy. Fiat would attempt to rally the bulk of private enterprise around this strategy. The then Fiat President, Valletta, tried, not always successfully, to wrest the *Confindustria* from the conservative

Catholics who were opposed to the centre-left and admitted that not only the trade unions but also the *Confindustria* were to blame for the Italian crisis.[37]

When Agnelli succeeded Valletta, he began to gradually disengage Fiat from the DC. Agnelli attempted to build up a special relationship with the PSI and to support its unification with the Social Democratic Party (PSDI). The Fiat-owned Turin daily *La Stampa* became somewhat pro-socialist. The DC too, however, was developing its own independence in economic matters. Until the early 1960s the DC had delegated economic policy to the private sector. With the development of the public sector the DC began to occupy an increasingly important economic role which led it to adopt policies which diverged from those advocated by Fiat, for example, some 'anti-car' laws were passed and petrol prices increased.[38]

For Fiat the centre-left experiment had been a failure. The coalition had not modernized the Italian economy in the way it had hoped. All that had happened was a massive extension of the state sector. Furthermore, the workers' struggles of 1969 had challenged the entire assembly-line system of large firms with the engineering workers (the bulk of Fiat's workforce) in the forefront of that militancy.[39] Agnelli continued to challenge the DC from the left and, in alliance with Pirelli, began to develop in the early 1970s a new, more progressive, political strategy. This was based on a formula which became known as 'the alliance of profits and wages against rent'. The meaning of this was that the 'productive classes', i.e. entrepreneurs and workers, should enter into an agreement against the backward features of the Italian economy exemplified in the 'parasitical' rent sector, the 'abnormal' profits deriving from speculation, commercial and real estate activities.[40] The economic implications of this formula have always been vague, particularly as the distinction between 'rent' and 'profit' is, in practical terms, fairly arbitrary. As in many other countries the industrial bourgeoisie is not purely industrial because its own interests are deeply intertwined with land and the entire banking and financial sector.[41] Politically the strategy was clearer: the 'rent' sector to be attacked was none other than the clientele system of the DC which had colonized the economy through the operation of the state sector. Because the Italian public sector had been created by Catholic politicians (and, before them, by the fascists) and not by 'enlightened' social democrats it had always been possible to take a stand against it from a left-of-centre position (as the PDS-led progressive did in the 1990s).

A good example of reformist capitalism was the 1970 Pirelli report to the *Confindustria* which advocated a form of planning which, instead of delegating everything to the state, should be entrusted to a wider 'democratic' consultation between the private sector and the trade unions.[42] This policy was further developed by Gianni Agnelli in 1974 when he became president of the *Confindustria*. In his inaugural speech he called for a 'new pact' which, 'thirty years after the defeat of fascism would determine the national aim of the Italian people for the 1980s and 1990s'.[43] In tune with the times, Agnelli, while attacking state interference in the private sector, had made definite overtures to the trade union movement and beyond that to the communist opposition, when he had declared as early as 1972 that 'The reconstruction of a competitive and efficient industrial system and social reforms are not contradictory aims, on the contrary they complement one another.'[44]

In the early 1970s the clash between Fiat and the DC, or at least that section of the DC which was regrouped around the party leader Amintore Fanfani, took the form of a struggle within the *Confindustria* between the chemical giant Montedison and the Fiat-Pirelli group. The Montedison group had been formed in 1966 as a result of the merger between the chemical group Montecatini and Edison, a former electricity oligopoly (the electricity industry had been nationalized and the huge compensation paid enabled the Edison shareholders to use the vast liquid resources thus acquired for the merger). Montedison was a private firm even though the government had acquired enough stock to control it.[45] In 1970 Eugenio Cefis, former boss of ENI, the state oil company, became President of Montedison which by then had managed to accumulate amazing losses and was in debt to the banks (in turn controlled by the state, i.e. the DC). Cefis further expanded the company and diversified its holdings into fibres and textiles, finance companies and newspapers (at a certain stage it acquired the *Corriere della Sera*, Italy's most prestigious newspaper).[46] Cefis could expand Montedison because he enjoyed the support of Fanfani and hence of the vast financial resources of the State. The aim was to place the chemical industry at the centre of the entire industrial system. The plan, which eventually failed,[47] was a direct challenge to the dominant role of Fiat and Pirelli. The clash took the form of a dispute within the *Confindustria* about its organization. Cefis was able to impose his version of the reform, but the main issue soon became the election of the president of the *Confindustria* who would have had the key task of implementing the reform.[48] Cefis was able to assemble a broad coalition of interests: the chemical and oil refining industries, the financial system, small Catholic entrepreneurs grouped around Fanfani and the bulk of the DC, but, given the power still in the hands of Agnelli, a compromise was reached whereby Agnelli became president of the *Confindustria* with four vice-presidents including Cefis and Pirelli.

The fortunes of Cefis took a turn for the worse when the 1974 divorce referendum resulted in a dismal defeat for the Fanfani line of strong anti-communist opposition. Now the initiative was in the hands of Agnelli who put forward his strategy of a 'social contract' negotiated with the left, i.e. both the PCI and the trade unions. The basis of this contract (which coincides with the spread of 'neo-corporatist' negotiations between employers and trade unions in many European countries) was:[49]

1   The reciprocal acceptance that economic efficiency should be the main principle guiding the operation of firms.
2   The principle that firms would not pursue a special relationship with any one political party.
3   The PCI and the trade unions would be involved in a policy of modernization, productivity and efficiency.
4   Real wages would be defended while differentials would be reduced. In fact in 1975 the *Confindustria* signed a new, more egalitarian, agreement on the indexation of wages.

Even though the PCI and the trade unions did not deny that there could be a temporary coincidence of interests between the labour movement and the private sector, the importance of Agnelli's proposal was that it represented an attempt by Italy's main private industrialist to gain a leading political role on behalf of the private sector. The period in which the private sector delegated the management of the political system to the DC in exchange for dominance in the economic field was over. If the DC was going to intervene in the economy, then big business had to do the same in politics. Agnelli's proposal was the first attempt by the big bourgeoisie in Italian history to recognize the legitimacy of some trade union demands, even when these entailed economic sacrifices by the private sector.[50]

The 1970s heralded the growth of Fiat independence from the DC. Not only did Fiat challenge the DC on the political terrain but it also attempted to reform it from within. Taking advantage of the internal divisions within the DC, Umberto Agnelli, younger brother of the Fiat chairman, was elected senator for Turin in the DC list in 1976. Unconnected to any of the main DC factions, Umberto Agnelli tried to become a rallying point among dissatisfied DC backbenchers. The experiment was a total fiasco: Umberto Agnelli was humiliated and ostracized by the leadership and abandoned active politics after only three years.[51]

The 'productivist' and modernizing line adopted by Fiat never had a chance of being implemented. It implied the assumption that economic growth was impeded by the existence of a backward sector whose chief representative was the DC (or at least some important sectors within this party). In reality 'backwardness' was functional to the kind of economic growth Italy had enjoyed and even enabled the country to survive the crises of the 1960s and 1970s. There would have been no cheap labour for Fiat without the existence of a depressed South. There would have been no cheap energy and steel without the role of the state. There would have been no southern market without the existence of southern clienteles based on the DC control over the public purse. The only modernizing line which could exist as an alternative to the DC was an alternative to the system of power of the DC. Such an alternative would have entailed a leading role for the main opposition, the PCI, but this was not acceptable to Fiat. Later in the 1970s Italian large private enterprises – like those of other countries – suffered a major profit squeeze leading to a further decrease in their possibility of self-financing, an increase in their indebtedness and in their recourse to state help.[52] This was far from being an Italian peculiarity due to its unique blend of 'backwardness' and 'modern industry'. The automobile sector from Detroit (Chrysler) to the UK (British Leyland) was hit by the crisis. The only strategy open to big Italian firms was either to expand on a multinational level or to decentralize through a network of small firms. Fiat chose the first path (together with Pirelli, which had merged with Dunlop, and Montedison) becoming a large financial holding in which the car division accounted for no more than half of total turnover.

What was and is particular to Italy is the traditional weakness of large private enterprise and the fact that there are very few large firms, though their numbers have been growing in the last fifteen years. In 1980 there were only eleven Italian firms in *Fortune*'s list of the top non-USA 500 companies, the same as Spain and the Netherlands (a much smaller country), and less than Switzerland (13), Sweden (26), Canada (31), France (42), West Germany (62), the UK (88) and Japan (121).[53]

The 1994 *Financial Times* list of Europe's top 500 companies by market capitalization reveals that there are 25 Italian firms but not one among the 25 most profitable. Of these top Italian firms fourteen are banks, insurance, financial services and investment holdings, one is in retail, two are telephone companies, one is the gas utility and one is in communication. Only the remaining six are concerned with actual manufacturing: Fiat, Pirelli, Montedison, food (Parmalat and SME), Olivetti. Silvio Berlusconi's Fininvest was not yet a public company, its accounts were not published and, consequently, did not figure on any of the listings of top firms. Before the privatization programme launched in 1992 over one-third of industrial activity and two-thirds of the banking and financial sector were controlled directly or indirectly by the state.[54]

One of the reasons why there are so few large private firms in Italy is that it is difficult to raise capital on the Italian stock exchange. Small and medium-sized firms, usually dominated by the founder and his heirs, are reluctant to become listed on stock exchange. When there are in difficulties they are usually 'saved' by a larger firm – often a public sector company.[55]

The great weight of the public sector made it difficult for private industry to emerge as a political protagonist. This partly explains the eventual defeat of the Agnelli line. The end of the old DC-Fiat alliance of the 1950s and 1960s was one of the factors which had weakened the DC, but it has also left the private sector with limited options. Agnelli's enthusiasm for the 'modernizing' line of the socialist leader, Bettino Craxi, in 1983, could not survive *Tangentopoli*.

In the late 1970s and early 1980s the *Confindustria* returned to a policy of confrontation with the trade union movement: the agreement on the wages indexation system signed in 1975 was challenged in 1982. In October 1980, Fiat achieved mass redundancies after defeating a five-week strike thanks to a demonstration by 40,000 white-collar workers, middle managers and supervisors in defence of the 'right to work' and against the trade union. This was the signal for other companies to make massive lay-offs.[56]

The Fiat counter-offensive (which could be seen as parallel to the offensive started at the same time in the UK by the management of British Leyland against its workforce – with the difference that British management was openly encouraged by the Thatcher government) further reinforced its independence from the DC and the other political parties. The *Confindustria* was more prepared than in the past to confront the unions directly without the mediation of the DC.

The attempt to introduce in Italy some of the economic concepts of the 'New Right' (propagandized in the USA and in the UK by supporters of the Reagan and Thatcher administrations), could not be successful because of the considerable weight exercised by public sector firms – reluctant as ever to challenge the unions. Those willing to embrace some Italian version of neo-liberalism were the small and medium-sized firms of the North. These, however, did not have their own independent voice. They were the closest supporters of the DC, were hostile towards the large firms and did not really have 'union problems'. When the Northern League emerged as an anti-tax and anti-Southern force, the small industrialists believed that they had finally found their representative, though many subsequently supported

Berlusconi's *Forza Italia*. In practice, Italian private entrepreneurs approached the end of the century without a coherent political strategy. The large firms hoped that the privatization programme would create an adequate private sector which will enable Italian capitalism to be more similar to its European counterparts. But all the main parties of the 'Second Republic' profess their commitment towards privatization. The small and medium-sized industrialists are split between the PPI and the other fragments which have survived the implosion of the DC, Berlusconi's *Forza Italia* (whose long-term survival cannot be taken for granted) and the unpredictable Northern League.

In the midst of this complex and uncertain position, pro-Europeanism seems a promising strategy. The assumption is that a Federal Europe will be a more reliable political regulator than the unpopular Italian state. There is no reason, however, to assume that a new European political master will be prepared to tolerate the disregard for rules, regulations and taxes which have traditionally prevailed in this sector. Italian capitalism is at an impasse, as indeed, is Italian trade unionism.

The Church

The Church emerged from the war and the fascist period considerably strengthened. With the Lateran Treaty and the Concordat it had signed with the fascist regime in 1929 it obtained sovereign status (the 'City of the Vatican'), virtual control over marriages, important financial concessions as well as a monopoly in religious education in state schools.[57] Its basic strategy of coexistence with the regime enabled it to expand its ecclesiastical structures through numerous parallel organizations among the laity (of which by far the most important was the *Azione Cattolica* (AC)). For nearly twenty years the Church was the only official alternative to fascism and provided an organizational home for political and intellectual cadres who became the leaders of the post-war DC.[58]

By the end of the war, the Italian middle classes had shed some of their traditional anti-clericalism which dated from the period of the *Risorgimento*. Unlike the political parties the Church had a powerful centralized organization and an obedient following. It had also developed a political ideology, known as the 'social doctrine' – a fairly vague set of principles which could be used for social and political activity and which was constantly reinterpreted by the Church.[59] Its central tenet was class reconciliation.

In the immediate post-war period only three forces posed a threat to the Church.[60] The first was anti-clericalism. This was not a serious threat because its main political expression, the Action Party, was electorally a small force which soon evaporated and because the PCI, having voted in favour of the inclusion of the Concordat in the new Italian Constitution, demonstrated that it had no wish to engage in a religious civil war.

The second threat was modernity. In the long run this would prove to be the most formidable, particularly as the development of the Italian economy and the growth of the consumer society, urbanization and emigration loosened the traditional ties which had been the strength of the Church. However, in the immediate post-war period, modernity was not considered by the Vatican to be as menacing as the third threat: 'atheistic Marxism'.

The post-war strategy of the Church was to compete with this threat (embodied in the PCI) by becoming more like a political party. It organized new forms of mass devotion and large processions. These had once been religious and local. They now became national and semi-political. The Church used the media through a popular radio slot known as 'God's microphone' and organized mass rallies and mass preaching.[61] *Azione Cattolica*, led by Luigi Gedda, became increasingly political. As Poggi has written: 'The impression was given that for the Head of the Universal Church himself the solution about to be offered to the problems of how to form an administration in a little town somewhere in Southern Italy was a more momentous matter than what was happening or about to happen in the Catholic communities of Africa or Asia.'[62]

Although it behaved more and more like a political party, the Church was necessarily dependent on the existence of one or more political parties which would seek to guarantee its power in Italian society. Some Church exponents believed that the Church would have had more influence if it did not tie its own fortunes too closely to a single party.[63]

The emergence of a single Catholic party and the principle of the 'political unity' of Catholics had to be fought for by the DC leader, Alcide De Gasperi. He tried to prevent the reconstruction of a Catholic movement opposed to liberal culture and at the same time the emergence of a left-wing Catholic party. The strength of the DC, the international recognition they received from the USA and their success in obtaining from the Church the suppression of the tiny *Partito della Sinistra Cristiana* (Party of the Christian Left) meant that by 1947–48 the Vatican had no other political option apart from the DC.[64]

It has often been suggested that the DC was no more than the long arm of the Church, at least in the immediate post-war period. It is true that the DC used the influence of the Church and its organizations in order to gain electoral popularity in Italy and that, to some extent, it became its political guarantor, but it was always able to maintain an effective autonomy. The relation between the party and the Church was thus a relatively complex one, even in the early years and just as the DC sought to maintain some independence, the Church never officially accepted the doctrine of a single party for the Catholics and the Pope never explicitly told the faithful to vote for the DC: thus the Pope intervened in the 1948 elections instructing Catholics to vote for candidates prepared to defend God's law and Christian doctrine. The Church's political role was not directly promoted by its own hierarchy but by the large lay organization, AC.[65]

Soon, however, De Gasperi was strong enough to use the support of the Church not only to prevent the formation of an alternative Catholic party but also to win his internal battles against his rivals, particularly the leader of the left-wing faction Giuseppe Dossetti. The Church was not always happy with De Gasperi's independence and tried to use its influence within the DC by playing one faction against the other. At times, especially in the early 1950s, it also tried to use the threat of favouring the formation of a second more right-wing Catholic party in order to control the DC. In general political matters, however, the Church could do little else than to follow the lead of the DC. To illustrate this we shall take two examples: the Church attitude to the PCI and the Church attitude to the 'Southern Question'.

The anti-communism of the Church had been evident throughout its modern history. However, it had not been able to stop DC-PCI cooperation in the period 1945–47 in government, in the Constituent Assembly and in the trade union movement. The diaries of De Gasperi tell the story that on 12 November 1946 he received the visit of 'an important member of the Vatican hierarchy' who told him that any cooperation with the 'anti-clerical parties' (i.e. the communists and the socialists) could no longer be tolerated.[66] De Gasperi had to explain to the Vatican envoy that it would have been impossible to obtain the inclusion of the Concordat in the Constitution without cooperating with the PCI. Giulio Andreotti, then a close aide of De Gasperi's, later many times Prime Minister, has revealed that this 'Vatican personality' was none other than the Assistant Secretary of State (or 'Deputy Foreign Minister') of the Vatican G. B. Montini who became Pope Paul VI in 1963.[67]

It was only after the expulsion of the PCI from the government (at a time of De Gasperi's choosing) and after the victory of the DC in the 1948 elections that Pope Pius XII made his most important statement on communism. On 13 July 1949 a papal decree was published which prohibited Catholics from joining the PCI, from writing or reading or publishing or distributing any communist literature. Those infringing any of these prohibitions would be *ipso facto* excommunicated and would not receive any of the sacraments. Two weeks later the Holy See explained that excommunication would apply not only to those who joined or supported the PCI but also to any of its associated organizations or allies including the trade union CGIL and the PSI.[68]

From a political point of view this move was a mistake as it did not stop the growth of communist electoral support over the next thirty years nor did it stop the rapprochement between the DC and the PSI in the 1960s. Furthermore, it seriously weakened the Church's freedom of action as it tied its fortunes to the most intransigent anti-communist factions of the DC which were precisely those factions which, in the long run, would prove to be the weaker.

If we examine Church policy towards the peasantry and the South and we compare it to government policy (see Part One) we can detect a similarly 'tailist' attitude by the Vatican. When peasant struggles for the land began in 1944 the initial attitude of the Church was to depict them as instances of criminal behaviour, mindless violence and class hatred. The peasantry was seen as an ignorant mass easily manipulated by communist agitators.[69] The expression 'Southern Question' was never mentioned in Vatican documents and there was no admission that the *latifundia* had to be eliminated. As the DC began to establish deep roots in the South by formulating a series of proposals for an agrarian reform the attitude of the Church began to change. This is, of course, not entirely due to the influence of the DC. The Holy See had been made more aware of the misery of the South by its own clergy as well as by those active in the charitable programmes for the South instituted by the Vatican. In November 1946 the Pope described small peasant property as a genuine rural civilization which he set against the city, the 'expression of the domination of big capital not only over economic life but over man himself.[70] The association of small peasants, the Coldiretti, was considered a representative of the Church in the countryside as well as being a vote-gatherer for the DC. By 1948 the Church had joined the DC in supporting the principle of the agrarian reform.[71]

The populist defence of small peasant property with its anti-modernist undertones was modified in the late 1950s when the Church began to move from exclusive support for smallholdings to accepting the need for greater efficiency in modern farming and for larger capitalist farms – just as the DC had done. In the encyclical letter *Mater et Magistra* (1961) Pope John XXIII, elected in 1958, implied that small peasant holdings were no longer the best form of economic life in the countryside. Christians had to consider developing the whole infrastructure of transport, water, the health system, etc.[72]

The *Mater et Magistra* showed that the Church and particularly the new Pope, John XXIII, intended to move with the times. The encyclical no longer harked back to medieval corporatism but looked favourably on scientific and technical advances. It coincided not only with the debate on the modernization of the Italian economy but also with the debate on the constitution of a centre-left government of the DC in alliance with the PSI. The PSI – usually more hostile to the Church than the PCI – welcomed the *Mater et Magistra* which it interpreted as a papal blessing for the centre-left government.[73] With this encyclical the Pope was trying to force through a new course for the Church because most of the ecclesiastical hierarchy was clearly opposed to political as well as religious modernization.

The debate on the centre-left had begun in the late 1950s and seriously divided both DC and PSI. The Church hierarchy had intervened on the side of the opponents of the centre-left. In April 1959 the Holy See reminded Catholics that it was forbidden to vote for Marxist parties and asserted that it was similarly forbidden even to vote for parties which might call themselves Christian, but in fact helped the communists or cooperated with them. The Jesuit journal *Civiltà Cattolica* suggested that Christians should not support those who still cooperated with the PCI (i.e. the PSI) or those who called themselves Marxist (as the PSI still did). The problem was that even the pro-American and anti-communist Social Democratic Party still called itself Marxist and yet it had been a close ally of the DC since it had split from the PSI in 1947. Taken literally the *Civiltà Cattolica* article was a clear sign of support for a centre-right coalition.[74] This was in fact the policy of the right wing of the DC.

Again in May 1960 the Church hierarchy attempted to establish its supremacy in Italian affairs. A leading article in the *Osservatore Romano*, the official Vatican daily, enunciated the following 'basic points':[75]

1   The Church must guide the faithful in both ideas and practice.
2   The Church cannot be politically neutral.
3   The Church must be the judge of whether political cooperation between the faithful and non-believers was permissible.
4   The Church cannot allow believers to cooperate with Marxists.

A few days later, however, Montini, the future Pope Paul VI, by then Cardinal of Milan, specifically declared that the 'opening to the left' (as the centre-left operation was called) was not permissible 'in the manner and form now being contemplated'. This could be read as meaning that there was no objection in principle: it was just the 'manner and form' which was wrong.[76]

The divisions within the Church enabled the DC to circumvent any opposition from the Vatican. At the Eighth Congress of the DC, on 27 January 1962, Aldo Moro formally proposed support for a centre-left coalition declaring: 'Our independence means that we must take risks on our own and this is our way of being of service to the Church.'[77] This meant that the strategy of the DC would be determined by political not religious considerations. Although the DC remained a Christian party, it had to be the judge of how it could continue to prevail as the sole political representative of the Catholics.

It was in the course of the 1960s that the Church began to follow its own political path and to develop, at one and the same time, its political independence from the DC and a new international outlook.

The first steps along this road were taken by Pope John XXIII. At first he distanced himself from Italian political affairs which he delegated to the Italian bishops.[78] The immediate results were that in fact the Italian Church, that is the Italian bishops as distinct from the Vatican, intervened more rather than less in national politics, particularly, as we have seen, in the hope of preventing the centre-left government. Pope John's political strategy was to revise Church relations in three directions: (1) towards Eastern Europe; (2) towards capitalism; (3) towards non-Catholics including Marxists.

The process of *détente* with Eastern Europe was initiated through a series of symbolic acts, the most important of which was the welcome the Pope gave to the Polish Cardinal Wyszinski, who had been considered by Pius XII as a collaborator of the communists, and the private audience he granted to Nikita Khrushchev's son-in-law Alexei Adzubei, editor of the Soviet newspaper *Izvestia*.

The 1961 encyclical *Mater et Magistra* began to question the support given by the Church to capitalism.

The important 1963 encyclical *Pacem in terris* opened up the possibility for a dialogue with communism. It made a distinction between 'false ideologies' (e.g. communism and Marxism) and the political movements they inspired (e.g. the actual communist movement). It argued that political and social movements, unlike doctrines and ideologies, are never static, they change with history and may produce just and worthy demands. The repercussions in Italy of *Pacem in terris* were very far reaching. In practice the Pope had given his effective blessing to the new coalition.

The changes in the Church were also underlined by the papal decision to convene an ecumenical council (the twenty-first in the history of the Church and the first since 1870). The Council, known as Vatican II, was to modernize the Church as an organization, develop better relations with other religions and face the problems of modern society.[79] Vatican II lasted from October 1962 to December 1965 under Pope Paul VI (John XXIII died in 1963). It did not modernize the Church, but produced sufficient material for the reformists within the Church to build on.

The position of the bishops was considerably strengthened by instituting the synods of bishops to be elected by the national Churches. The distinctive contribution that the laity could make to the Church was recognized and encouraged: the Church was no longer to be the exclusive prerogative of the clergy. An important aspect of the tradition established by St Thomas Aquinas was thus abandoned together with its rigid conceptual framework in favour of a return to more flexible biblical concepts. The abolition of Latin for most rituals permitted more freedom of interpretation: translations allowed for a multiplicity of views.[80]

Relations with the other Christian churches, particularly the Eastern Orthodox Church were improved; clerical anti-Semitism came under attack as Jews were 'acquitted' of the ancient accusation of deicide (the murder of Christ).

The new Pope, Paul VI, had at first to contain the zeal of the reformists in order to avoid a split in the Church. He continued the policy of *détente* with the East and pursued vigorously a policy of dialogue with the Third World. As the Vatican became a more international body, it also became less of a 'Christian Democrat' supporting system. The important encyclical *Populorum progressio* (26 March 1967) declared as incompatible with Christian principles a system which puts at the centre of everything the pursuit of private profit and competition and the absolute right to private property. The encyclical even asserted that there were exceptional circumstances – such as the struggle against a permanent and cruel form of despotism – in which revolution was permissible.[81] In the *Octogesima adveniens* (14 May 1971) Paul VI asserted in the strongest terms his belief that no single social system could be derived from the 'social doctrine' of the Church. If there was no 'Christian political thought' then it followed that there could be no 'Christian political party'.[82] The same man who, when working in the Vatican Secretariat had accepted the principle of the political unity of the Catholics in the DC now suggested that Catholics could be active in various political parties.[83]

Octogesima adveniens marked a decisive turning-point in the history of the modern Church and constituted the parting of the ways between the Vatican – seen as an international organization based in Italy – and the DC.

The DC, while it had been able to establish its independence from clerical influence was not prepared to allow the Church to have an autonomous role. Church autonomy might endanger its monopoly of Catholic support and contract its electoral and social basis. Already organizations such as the Association of Italian Christian Workers (ACLI), and even AC had rescinded all official links with the DC, and in the case of ACLI even those with the Church hierarchy. The DC still needed the help of the Church particularly as it had suffered a major defeat when in 1970 the parties of the centre and the left had legalized divorce.

The Church strategy was to seek a modification of the law and had expected that the DC would act as a mediating force with the pro-divorce parties. But the DC, by taking a more intransigent anti-divorce stand than the Church, obliged it to tail once again behind the DC. The Vatican was unhappy about the DC leader Fanfani's strategy to use a popular referendum to abolish the divorce law; it was worried that a referendum would cause a major religious split in Italian society. Fanfani was more worried that a compromise over divorce would cause a split within the DC.[84]

The Vatican attitude was in keeping with the new tendencies within the Church, and in particular with the strengthening of the power of the national bishops which had been sanctioned by Vatican II: the entire conduct of the anti-divorce campaign was delegated to the Italian bishops with little backing from the Vatican hierarchy. The attitude of the Vatican could not but encourage Catholic dissent in Italy. The youth branches of ACLI came out in favour of divorce, ACLI itself refused to take a position and so did a number of leading bishops and cardinals. Many leading Catholic intellectuals fought openly on the side of the divorce parties and during the course of this campaign loosened their ties with the DC and forged new links with the parties of the left, particularly the PCI. In 1976, two years after the divorce referendum, many of these Catholic intellectuals were elected to parliament on the PCI lists.

The referendum was to be held on 12 May 1974. On 5 May, speaking in St Peter's the Pope did not condemn divorce, preferring instead to invoke religious peace. Two days later even the Italian bishops in their final meeting before the poll did not condemn the growing pro-divorce Catholic lobby.[85] The opponents of divorce were able to muster only 41 per cent of the vote. Clearly a large number of Catholic voters supported the lay position. It has been estimated that 16 per cent of DC supporters voted in favour of divorce. Fanfani, defeated, did not hesitate to blame divisions within the Church for the setback, and in particular the more 'progressive' interpretations of Vatican II.[86]

The Vatican disengagement from Italian politics led to the decline in the political involvement of its main lay organization, AC. In 1962 AC was still by far the largest association in Italy with 3.6 million members. In 1964 Paul VI named Vittorio Bachelet as head of the association. Under Bachelet, AC was considerably democratized, became more autonomous from the clergy and stressed its religious nature as opposed to political involvement. It ceased in fact to be a 'transmission belt' for DC politics at the cost of a massive decrease in membership (down to 800,000 in 1973). Under the leadership of Livio Labor in 1961 ACLI too began to cut its ties with the DC. By 1975–76 the DC feared that it had lost its monopoly over Catholic representation. The 1970s were in fact traumatic for the Catholic world in Italy and elsewhere.

As a result of the turmoil of the 1960s, the end of the 'economic miracle', the growth of political dissent, the student movement, the workers' unrest, the birth of feminism as well as the changes within the Church itself, young Catholics became interested in and attracted to new forms of internationalism and particularly by the 'new theology' emanating from Latin America as well as by new anti-authoritarian forms of organizations. The development of an anti-institutional Catholic culture meant not only that many young Catholics voted in favour of divorce or against the DC, but that they began to construct for themselves new organizations outside the control of the Church and the established political parties.[87]

The new Catholic groupings now constitute one of the main elements of the Catholic world in Italy. It has been estimated that there are some 8,000 communities involving several hundred thousand people. It has been estimated that the total membership of all Catholic or Catholic-dominated associations (including sport clubs and the scouts) is approximately four million.[88] Some are deeply religious groups committed to a mystical and ascetic personal religiosity; others are community-based and active in organizing marginal groups in society, like the, handicapped or drug addicts; others still are deeply committed to a Third World form of politics or to the anti-nuclear and peace movement.[89] But these groups are only one element, albeit the most modern, of the Catholic world. One should not discount the traditional lay organizations such as ACLI and AC as well as lay organizations such as *Comunione e Liberazione*. This is a 70,000-strong movement of young people based in the North and the Centre against modern capitalism and technical progress.[90] It seemed to signal a return to the anti-modernist tradition of the Church. Yet *Comunione e Liberazione* is organized like a modern political lobby and soon became yet another vehicle for ambitious politicians. Through its *de facto* political arm, the *Movimento Popolare*, it used to sponsor DC candidates and sought to condition DC politics without giving up its freedom of action. After the collapse of the DC it maintained its apparatus relatively intact, one of its leaders, Rocco Buttiglione, was briefly at the head of the *Partito Popolare* (one of the post-1992 successors to the DC), another, Roberto Formigoni, became President of Lombardy, Italy's most important region. It would be wrong, however, to treat all Catholics as if they belonged to a monolithic faith (regardless of the intention of some of their leaders). Among modern Italian Catholics there is no longer (assuming there ever was) a coherence between their definition of themselves as belonging to the Church and observing its teachings. For instance the Veneto is the most Catholic region in Italy, yet its low birth rate indicates that the use of contraceptives is as prevalent there as elsewhere. It is not the case that Italians divorce less than British or American people because they are Catholic though it may be true that a generic Catholic culture has created a more solid foundation for family life and that this, in turn, is the reason behind the lower divorce rate. In fact, 'good' Italian Catholics are now conscious that they are a minority, even though 90 per cent of the population calls itself Catholic. For some of these 'good' Catholics, religion is still the principal reference point of their life. When they participate in civic life, when they vote, when they join an organization, they do so as Catholics (some may even join the parties of the left *because* they are Catholic). For others, religion constitutes a space where old rituals can be performed as a way of standing back from modernity.[91]

Whatever the practice or the intention of the Vatican and of the Pope, political Catholicism can continue to rely, however indirectly, on the still formidable apparatus of the Catholic Church in Italy, with over 25,800 parishes (28,000 in the 1970s) performing every Sunday religious services which are attended by 30 per cent of the population (1990 data). Its cultural machine is responsible for the production of hundred of books a year by a string of publishing houses and over 50 weeklies. One of these, *Famiglia Cristiana* is the largest circulation weekly in Italy with over 1 million copies sold. The monthly *Il Messaggero di S. Antonio* distributes more than 900,000 copies. There are also hundreds of parish weeklies which sell a total of 1.2 million copies of Catholic magazines every week.[92] The religious personnel is larger than the personnel of all Italian political parties put together: nearly 200,000 people including 61,000 priests and 134,000 nuns.[93] Of course, in Italy, as elsewhere, there has been a crisis of religious vocation. It is increasingly difficult to recruit men to the priesthood. This decline is a long-term trend. In 1881 there were 2.89 parish priests per 1,000 inhabitants, in 1951 this had dropped to 0.99, in 1970 to 0.80, in 1980 to 0.72 and in 1989 to 0.65. The number of ordained priests had decreased but not constantly. In 1969, 740 priests were ordained, only 347 in 1981, though the numbers went up in 1988 to 526 and down again in 1989 to 431.[94]

There has also been a transformation in the real functions of the Church in Italian society.[95] Its social functions, i.e. its hospitals, charities and educational establishments, have contracted remarkably as the growth of the welfare state has enabled the state and local authorities to intervene in areas which had been for centuries the prerogative of the Church. Its spiritual functions, i.e. its ritualized intervention in some of the fundamental moments in people's lives such as birth, marriage and death have also contracted, although not as much as it is commonly suggested. The lay state cannot provide any appropriate substitute for these functions which are still demanded even by people whose commitment to religion is very limited. Thus 97.9 per cent of the population had been baptized in 1988, virtually the same as in 1970. Religious marriages have decreased but they still constitute by far the prevailing form of marriage: 83.6 per cent in 1988, though 97.7 per cent in 1970.[96] Italians, on the whole, appear more committed to a religious view of things, at least when asked by pollsters, than the average European: more of them believe in God, the afterlife, the soul, the devil, hell and heaven and resurrection.[97] The Church still provides a focus for social life through the local parish and various Church-based associations though the trend towards the secularization of leisure time is unstoppable. It is now almost unthinkable that a religious radio or television channel would be listened to or watched by more than a small percentage of the population. Church attendance since the war has decreased steadily, though it is likely that the 30 per cent presently attending regularly are a more committed group than the 80 per cent of women and the 57 per cent of men which used to go to church every Sunday in 1956 because there was little else to do.[98]

In the immediate post-war period the Italian Catholic world was still enclosed in a traditional Church. By the 1980s it was faced by a bewildering pluralism of great complexity. The processes which had begun to develop in the early 1960s had come to fruition. All attempts by the DC to 'colonize' the Church and vice versa had come to naught. The most significant development has undoubtedly been the gradual transformation of the Church from a Eurocentric body for whom Italy was the leading country, to an international body whose centre of interests has spread to the Third World, particularly Latin America.

When Pius XII died in October 1958 the College of Cardinals had 55 members of whom 36 were European (18 Italian). Europe had the highest number of baptized Catholics. When John Paul II was elected twenty years later in October 1978 the College of Cardinals had doubled in number with 56 non-European cardinals, 44 of whom came from the Third World, and Latin America had the highest number of Catholics (40 per cent).[99] The Pope was no longer an Italian but a Pole, a citizen of what was then a non-capitalist country. John Paul II had no need of a specific power basis in Italy and no wish to grant leading Christian Democrats privileged access or special support. The difference with his predecessor but one, Paul VI, is striking. Paul VI had been a powerful member of the Vatican Secretariat and then Cardinal of Milan, and in these roles had followed all the vicissitudes of DC politics from the very beginning and was in close contact with its leaders.

When Karol Wojtyla became Pope he was heading a Church which had become more self-confident. Having detached itself from the politics of the West, the Church could project itself far more than ever before as a non-aligned force working against the hegemony of the two superpowers and the nuclear balance of terror. In his first encyclical *Redemptor hominis* (4 March 1979) the Pope announced that the post-Vatican II period was now over and so was the period of intense self-criticism.[100] Now freed from any commitment towards any given economic system, capitalist or otherwise, the Church would try to give religious and not political answers to the problems of modern society.

The charismatic figure of the Polish Pope and his overt use of the media, exemplified in his constant travels, all suggest that the Church felt that it could re-establish a direct relation with the masses without the help of political parties.

In the Italian context this meant not only that the DC could no longer rely on the Church, but that not even those Catholic groups which had emerged in Italy in the later 1960s and throughout the 1970s would look to the DC as the 'party of the Catholics' or the 'party of the Church', only as an instrument which is more or less likely than others to implement their wishes and aspirations.

When, on 27 March 1995, the President of the CEI (the Conference of Italian Bishops), Cardinal Camillo Ruini, accepted officially the end of the political unity of Catholics, he simply recognized that there was no possibility of reconstructing a single Catholic party in Italy. The DC had not been replaced by one party but by several fragments aspiring to that role. Yet, well before the collapse of the DC, the political unity of Catholics was more an object to be reconstructed than a reality.[101] Catholics have rarely been united in political matters. All the DC had achieved was to ensure that there would be as little conflict as possible between the development of the modern Italian state and the basic rules of the Church.[102] The DC may have been the party of Catholics, but only 50 per cent of its electorate went to Church regularly. The PCI may have been the 'anti-Christ' for some but 40 per cent of its electorate believed in God and 10 per cent went to Church regularly. It could thus legitimately claim to be the second Catholic party in Italy.[103]

After the collapse of the First Republic, political Catholic personalities emerged in various parties and the Catholic electorate became deeply divided, voting less than ever before along strictly religious lines (though religion mattered more than in Britain or France, but less than in Bavaria, Belgium or Holland). In 1994, of those who went to Church every week (30 per cent of the total population), 30 per cent voted for Berlusconi's *Forza Italia* (a right-of-centre secular party), 17.5 per cent for the *Partito Pòpolare* (the main successor to the DC), 11.5 for *Alleanza Nazionale* (the successor to the right-wing MSI), 11 per cent for the PDS (the successor of the PCI) and 7.5 for the *Lega Nord*.[104] Obviously, the Catholic vote weighs more in the smaller parties (such as the *Lega* or AN not to speak of the PPI). A different way of reading the same data is to say that 70 per cent of PPI electors are practising

Catholics, and so are 32 per cent of *Forza Italia*, 23 per cent of the Greens, 21 per cent of the *Lega Nord*, 19 per cent of AN and 13–14 of both the PDS and *Rifondazione Comunista*. One of the most prominent Catholic politicians is Irene Pivetti, former President of the Chamber of Deputies and member of the *Lega Nord*, who is a follower of the most intransigent traditional wing of the Roman Catholic Church (that founded by Bishop Marcel Lefebvre excommunicated in 1988). She declared, in her opening address as President that as a Catholic she invoked 'the help of God to Whom belong the destiny of all nations and of History', a declaration that no Christian Democrat previously elected to a similar high office had ever made. A Catholic political scientist and admirer of the reactionary Catholic thinker Joseph De Maistre, Domenico Fisichella, joined AN and was briefly Minister of Culture. In 1994 Romano Prodi – a Catholic technocrat, once President of IRI, became the leader of the PDS-dominated left-of-centre 'progressive' coalition and, after the elections of 1996, the Prime Minister of Italy's first left-wing coalition – though there was a decrease in the total vote of left-of-centre Catholic parties. In other words, Catholicism is still a force but it is no longer organized as a single political party.

When, in 1991, the Pope condemned the Gulf War as the wrong way of resolving disputes, the Church became a rallying point for many of those who took a pacifist position.[105] Later it became the focus for those campaigning for a fairer treatment towards the immigrant. Sicilian cardinals and bishops have preached against the mafia and the most successful, if short-lived, anti-mafia party in Sicily was the largely Catholic *La Rete*. Clearly the future of the Church in Italy is far more likely to be in the direction of becoming a campaigning organization. One might even be tempted to call it one of the 'new political subjects' were it not for the fact that it is the oldest of them all.

The areas of concern of this 'political subject' are a cautious mixture of tradition and modernity. The Pope has been intransigent in repressing dissent within the actual apparatus of the Church, but relatively tolerant *vis-à-vis* the laity. He has upheld traditionalist positions on matters of contraception, celibacy for the clergy, ordination of women, abortion and divorce. But he has steadfastly refused to join the chorus of neo-liberal celebration on the collapse of communism. In his 1991 encyclical on the end of communism, *Centesimus annus*, (on the centenary of the famous *Rerum Novarum* and dated, significantly, 1 May), though he did not, obviously, shed tears over the crisis of Marxism, he defended the labour movement as an expression of the movement towards human emancipation, asserted that the free market – though the best instrument for the distribution of resources – cannot fulfil most fundamental human needs, and denounced the burden of debt on the Third World.[106] Catholics should have a positive attitude towards capitalism, he wrote, but only if capitalism is regulated and disciplined by law and morality, if it is the servant of human freedom. The fact that communism had been eliminated, he added, did not mean that the problems it denounced have disappeared.[107]

As the 1995 UN Conference on Woman, to be held in Peking, approached, the Pope also addressed a Letter to Women in which he offered a Catholic 'feminist' re-interpretation of the teachings of the Church, apologized for the 'objective responsibilities' the Church may have had in the past for the conditions of inferiority in which women have been kept. Without in any way altering the Church's fundamental position on the ordination of priests, abortion and divorce, the Pope used a language which was unmistakably influenced by feminism.[108]

In the Italian situation – not, clearly, the Pope's own principal context – this could be interpreted in legitimizing the repositioning of the clergy towards the centre-left. This explains, at least in part, how Italy's post-communists could have selected in 1994, as leader of the centre-left coalition, an observant, if uncharismatic, Catholic technocrat like Romano Prodi.

Mass media

The mass media form part of an information system which involves messages sent to receivers, an entire electronic industry, a telecommunications system, education, marketing, etc. The main surveys which have investigated this question all stress the need for a global approach.[109] The growth of data banks, television satellites, computers, information technology, teletext, video-recorders, etc. give support to the view that we are in the midst of a transition from an industrial society based on the factory system to an information society based on microprocessors.

While actual changes may not occur with the rapidity some of the commentators suggest, there is little doubt that mass communication is one of the central terrains of a radical restructuring of the world economy. This restructuring has two essential characteristics: a very pronounced centralization of production in the hands of a few – mainly American – multinational companies and a widespread decentralization of distribution.[110] This process is particularly evident in the most important of the mass media, television.

That production is increasingly centralized is not in question: the Japanese and the other east Asian manufacturing countries have a virtual monopoly in the manufacturing of television and video-related equipment, while the Americans have control over the manufacture of television programmes (80 per cent of TV films for instance, are made in the USA) and their relay via satellite.[111]

The centralization of the world market has caused difficulties for national governments. The general rule in Europe was that television broadcasting systems were publicly owned and closely regulated. By the 1990s ownership has become far more diversified. Though the national states have retained some form of public ownership, there is no longer, in most European countries, a state monopoly. The rapid development of satellite communication, the spread of the Internet, the adoption of fibre optic systems able to carry hundreds of programmes means that the possibility of regulating the electronic media is briskly receding.

In Italy the monopoly of public broadcasting was decisively broken by a decision of the Constitutional Court in July 1976. The Court upheld the monopoly of RAI (the public network), for national broadcasting, but decided to permit private broadcasting as long as it was not on a national scale. This led to the formidable growth of local private radio and television stations whose output has been totally unregulated – the only case in Europe, perhaps in the world (even in the USA a licence is required). It was estimated that in 1983 there were more than 700 private televi-sion stations in Italy.[112] Of course, most of these transmitted very little and were created by local or national groups purely in order to occupy a transmission band. What is perhaps more significant is that the RAI audience crumbled to 50 per cent by the end of 1983 when more people were employed by private television and radio stations – directly or indirectly – than by the public sector (20,000 against 13,500). As a direct consequence the RAI's total share of advertising revenue went down from 25 per cent in 1977 to 20 per cent in 1981.

Private television stations soon became vertically integrated with advertising agen-cies and – at first – the main publishing groups. In the absence of regulation three television groups emerged which eventually controlled the entire private sector. They came under the control of a single company, Fininvest whose owner, Silvio Berlusconi soon became Italy's best-known entrepreneur. Though these networks were Italian, most of the fiction programmes they transmitted – films, TV films and cartoons – had been purchased from abroad mainly from the USA and Japan.

The international structure of the information system and the subordinate role Italy plays within it were mirrored within Italy itself in the unevenness between North and South. If we look at 'traditional' or written information we will notice a persistent gap: in 1975 the South – with one-third of the total population – published only 400 out of 12,000 book titles a year, printed only 16 out of 87 daily papers (all with a distribution inferior to 100,000 copies), bought only 10 per cent of daily papers and 17 per cent of periodicals.[113] In 1994 the gap was still there. Southerners published fewer books, read fewer newspapers, and had borrowed only 39,000 books from public libraries against 226,000 in the North.[114] Southern culture has no outlet. The role of the South in this domain is, even more than that of the rest of Italy, its traditional one: a market for goods made elsewhere. In the domain of television, however, there is virtually no 'consumption' gap between North and South: near-saturation had been reached throughout the country by the early 1980s. There is, however, a production gap. Nearly all new 'fiction' programmes have been imported. Italy is a passive recipient of mini-series, serials, soap operas. Most originate from the USA, but some also come from Britain, Germany and Latin America (the *telenovellas*). The country of Dante, Verdi and Italo Calvino or, more relevantly, of Federico Fellini, Michelangelo Antonioni and Roberto Rossellini appears to be unable to produce its own TV fiction material. By 1996 the supply of television appeared to be confined to three categories: imported soaps (serials and mini-series) old films and chat shows of varying degree of vulgarity and im-becility. This sorry state of affairs has been largely the result of the uncontrolled spread of private television stations.

This growth was facilitated by the political parties ruling Italy in the 1980s. They never seriously attempted to regulate broadcast television while the considerable state aid to the newspaper industry freed resources for investment in the far more profitable television sector.[115]

There had always been a close link between the DC political elite and the leading publishing groups. Until the mid-1970s radio and television was a state monopoly (the RAI). As parliamentary control over public broadcasting increased the DC had to share some of its influence in the RAI with its main allies in government, that is with the PSI. This made it all the more urgent for the DC to be able to influence the private sector.

Before explaining the growth of private broadcasting, we shall examine state involvement in the newspaper industry which dates back to fascism. Italian journalists belong to a 'registered' profession with restricted entry and high salaries; the price of newsprint is regulated by a state commission on paper; the price of newspapers – controlled until 1988 – is part of the basket of goods which is used to calculate the cost-of-living index which in turn affects the indexation of wages (it is thus in the government's interest to keep the price of newspapers down); there are various forms of direct aid and subsidies and newspapers are virtually exempt from most taxes.

Newspapers as such turned out to be an increasingly unprofitable industry, but integrated with radio, television and advertising they represented a state-subsidized loss-making sector which indirectly contributed to the profitability of the rest of the industry: radio and television, the newsprint industry, advertising, etc. State support for newspapers provided an outlet for advertising, a demand for newsprint and an information network for radio and television. The main newspapers are owned by banks (these are under DC influence), or by big firms such as Fiat (owners of *La Stampa*), or by state companies such as ENI (owners of *Il Giorno*) or by the *Confindustria* (owners of the leading financial paper *Il Sole-24 Ore*).

Italy is also the only European country with a large circulation political party daily paper: *L'Unità*, the organ of the PCI and now of the PDS which sells 143,000 copies a day (1994). However, there is no mass circulation popular daily press as in West Germany or the UK. Italy's most prestigious newspaper, the *Corriere della Sera*, has the highest circulation, but this is only of 691,000 (1994 figures). It is followed by the Monday edition of the *Gazetta dello Sport*, one of the three dailies entirely dedicated to sport. Italy has a daily newspaper readership of 116 per 1,000 inhabitants against 580 per 1,000 in Japan (1991), 556 in Finland, 535 in Sweden, 269 in the UK, 176 in France and 132 in Greece.

Italy's readership exceeds, in Western Europe, only that of Spain, Portugal and Turkey. Furthermore, the number of readers has been around 5 million (excluding sport dailies) for nearly fifty years. The most obvious explanation for this low level of readership is that Italy is a latecomer in the field of mass literacy and mass education. When this was achieved, the age of television had already come. This may substantiate the view that the newspaper is becoming an obsolete means of distributing information destined to survive only for the benefit of political, cultural and economic elites (as is the case in Italy) or by becoming an entertainment sheet (as is the *Sun* in the UK) where there is an already existing mass habit of buying newspapers. Against this one may point out that in the last twenty years several newspapers have been created in Italy; two of these, *Il Giornale Nuovo* (1974) and *La Repubblica* (1976) set themselves out to appeal respectively to a right-wing and a left-wing elite. Attempts to create popular dailies – as was the case with *L'Occhio* – failed. The only mass press readership is in the field of weekly magazines. While the daily press hovered around the 5 million mark the weekly glossy magazines sold, on average, 14,291,000 copies per week (1993).[116] The overall standard of cultural consumption of the average Italian is remarkably low. According to a survey conducted in 1993, 26 per cent of those classified as 'teachers and intellectuals' do not read even a book a year; students fare worse: 33 per cent are non-readers of books as are 66 per cent of pensioners and 91 per cent of rural workers.[117] More generally, only 51 per cent of Italians read books against 74 per cent of British. This is almost certainly a consequence of the fact that half of the population has left school at the age of 14, 72 per cent have left immediately after the school leaving age against 46 per cent of French, 35 per cent of British and 22 per cent of Germans. This cultural crisis, however, cannot be the result of a lack of graduates because the ratio of graduates to the active labour force is 6 per cent (better than Austria and Portugal). Nor can it be the result of the lack of teachers as Italy has one of the highest ratios of teachers per head and an excellent ratio of teachers to students: 12.8 per cent in primary school and less than 10 per cent in secondary school (1988 data).[118] The context for this is a country characterized by the near-total absence of a national popular or mass culture. There is no tradition of popular literature. Best-selling novels, like much television, originate abroad. Stephen King and Ken Follett dominate the bookshops: they have no Italian rivals. The same can be said for children's books. This was not always the case: the grandparents and great-grandparents of today's young Italians read the adventure stories of Emilio Salgari, Collodi's *Pinocchio* (the best-known Italian fictional character in the world) or De Amicis' *Cuore*. On the other hand, young Italians have an unusually high degree of access to television. A study on a sample of 300 Roman children found out that 45 per cent have their own TV (in their room), but 53 per cent of them cannot play in the open air as they have no private garden or internal courtyard and there are no public parks in the vicinity.[119]

There are, in fact, two Italies. A relatively tiny elite reads voraciously a high quality press as well as the books on display in the well-stocked bookshops which are a common features of urban centres. This elite, however, is not easily influenced by newspapers. Consequently, controlling the press is of little significance in terms of mass electoral politics, though, of course, they tend to set the agenda for television news and TV and radio news programme give enormous prominence to the printed press: many of the morning news bulletins dedicate a significant proportion of time to reading the headlines of newspapers – thus driving the boredom index to new heights.

In spite of the connections between the press and the governing party, DC, much of the daily Italian press, particularly since the mid-1960s was not pro-DC but tended to favour the smaller parties of the centre and the socialists. Ideologically, the leading dailies have tended to espouse various aspects of the liberal tradition whether in its radical (*La Repubblica*) or centrist form (*Corriere della Sera*). The collapse of the DC further strengthened the centre-left position of the leading papers, most of whom resolutely opposed the centre-right coalition led by Silvio Berlusconi. In so doing, they reflected also the wishes of their owners – powerful industrialists whose antipathy for Berlusconi may be due to a mixture of personal animosity and the understanding that, in the long term, it may be preferable for capitalists to have a governing class which is not beholden to the interest of only one of them.

The absence of mass circulation dailies means that the Italian press, even more than in other countries, has been unable to shape electoral opinion. Before 1992, the DC and the PCI were able to obtain nearly 70 per cent of the popular vote even though most of the press was against them. The success of the Northern League (and its previous incarnation as the Lombard and Venetian Leagues) in 1990–94 owes nothing at all to a positive press or TV coverage which was uniformly hostile. The attitude of the media was to ridicule the League which was in turn ostracized by the entire political establishment because they appeared racist, or dangerous, or stupid or against the unity of Italy. This may have played into the hands of the League whose success relied on being able to appear anti-establishment while espousing themes which the media itself had made familiar: corruption, inefficiency and the dominance of old parties.[120] The same could be said for the rise of the former neo-fascist *Alleanza Nazionale*: in its preceding incarnation as the MSI it encountered far more media hostility than the communists. Yet the fact of being excluded from the media turned out to be of advantage to the MSI-AN once the old parties crumbled.

Television has been of far greater import for the formation of public opinion than the press, which is why the DC, as the dominant government party until 1992, concentrated its efforts in controlling broadcasting. Yet even this influence should not be over-estimated. Until the early 1970s the DC had a virtual monopoly of television, yet it was in constant electoral decline.

In the 1950s and early 1960s DC monopoly consisted in controlling the news in a blatantly propagandistic manner. The voice of the opposition, particularly that of the communist opposition was virtually ignored. The rest of broadcasting was in the hands of cautious producers who were left fairly free provided their output did not offend Catholic values (which caused problems with variety shows).[121] In the 1960s this changed because of: (1) the development of a second channel which introduced an element of competition among broadcasters (2) an increased ferment among the intellectual elites (in turn a reflection of the student and labour struggles of the period); (3) the growth of the whole information system. Thanks to the increased availability of and the demand for US programmes, Italian television had acquired the production structure of the modern media.[122]

Media messages must be produced following particular techniques and these determine their form of presentation. This rule is valid not only for 'sit-coms' or soap operas or variety shows but also for news and current affairs. Increasingly, politicians must be prepared to accept that the information they want to broadcast be processed through the media whose structure is that of a market. What they say must be properly packaged and properly presented; political discourse must change and politicians must at least in part, adapt themselves to media techniques.[123] Political discourse must become more like a 'show', a spectacle. It becomes more uniform because all politicians are subjected to the same rule. Politics becomes more 'Americanized'. This creates difficulties not only for the governing party but also for the communist opposition whose entire outlook on communication was based on the development of 'alternative' information such as their own newspapers, magazines, live entertainments, rallies, etc. – all increasingly obsolete forms of communication.[124]

The 'Americanization' of politics in terms of media presentation is only one aspect of the 'Americanization' of the rest of Italian society.

By the 1960s the model of social behaviour and the consumption habits described in American situation comedies was something which was no longer seen as the image of a distant society characterized by great wealth, but as one which could be attained by many Italians through the expansion of the market. Furthermore, the very class structures of Italian society became 'Americanized', as traditional industry entered a period of continuous decline, as the tertiary sector expanded and an increased part of production was directed towards the communication system.[125]

The 'Americanization' of the media signalled a growing autonomy on the part of the information system as a whole from politicians. These had to accept the 'form' of the media, but sought to retain control over its contents in the mistaken belief that the 'message' could be isolated from the apparatus which produces it.

In opposition to the DC the other political parties also sought to intervene at the level of the 'message'. By the mid-1970s a greatly weakened DC was no longer able to aspire to the exclusive monopoly over the RAI and had to compromise with those who wanted reforms. This compromise was embodied in Law 103 which was enacted in April 1975. With this law, control over the RAI shifted from the government to parliament, which established a parliamentary committee of forty members in proportion to the strength of the political parties in parliament. The committee's task was to ensure that the RAI was a pluralistic organization which represented all shades of opinion. The committee, however, necessarily had a majority corresponding to the governing majority. The law also required that the ruling body of the RAI, the *Consiglio d'amministrazione* or Board of Governors be composed of sixteen governors, ten nominated by the committee (i.e. the political parties) and six nominated by the RAI's shareholders (these are in fact IRI, the state holding company). In other words the board, too, had a majority which reflected the governing majority. Control of the RAI had passed to an oligopoly of political parties. In 1985 party political control was further strengthened: all sixteen members of the Board were to be appointed by the parliamentary commission on broadcasting (twelve for the majority parties and four for the opposition). The PSI had a right to three seats while the PCI, with nearly three times the electoral weight, had four. In practice the Board and the parliamentary committee do not intervene on resources (except on the level of advertising permitted) or on planning or on the licence fee (which was under the control of the Minister of Posts and Telecommunications). However, the board is responsible for all senior and middle-level appointments.

The personnel thus was made up almost entirely by people politically trusted by the ruling majority. These people, however, also possessed the technical skills with which to run a modern media. This knowledge enabled them to play a significant role in the elaboration of a media policy.[126] Thus, even though the Board of Governors was on paper an all-powerful body, in practice it tried to obtain 'correct' political messages by appointing the 'right' personnel. Party political control was thus limited by the fact that the apparatus of the RAI, like all apparatuses, has a life of its own. There was also another important limitation: mass behaviour was not much influenced by the degree of bias in news programmes, otherwise one would be unable to understand how the PCI managed to obtain up to one-third of the vote when having only a minute percentage of 'favourable' television time. Mass behaviour, however, may well be influenced by the whole range of television messages, by what these messages define as being 'normal' and 'acceptable' or 'reasonable'. Political control cannot be established over the totality of television output because this depends on the entire cultural industry, that is, on the cinema, on the theatre, on the press, on the educational system and on all producers of information within and without the nation-state. Thus the colonization of the RAI by the governing political parties could not prevent the growing autonomy of the media while increasingly subordinating it to the world (i.e. American) communications and culture industry.

The blatant nature of this colonization was formalized by an agreement made by the DC and the PSI soon after Law 103 was passed. This stated that the DC would be the dominant voice in Channel 1 (television) and Radio 2, while the PSI would get Channel 2. A parallel agreement was made for radio channels.[127] This agreement also at first completely excluded the PCI from any representation on the Board of Governors of the RAI (after 1977 four PCI representatives took their seats on the board). The significance of this carve-up lay in the control established over the news programmes of the two channels because the evening news had the highest rating on Italian television. The DC-dominated evening news programme (TG1) was organized in direct competition with the PSI-run TG2 in a successful attempt to maximize the audience. The news programmes partly overlap, but TG1 achieved a far greater rating than its socialist rival. Journalists could choose which channel they wanted to work for. The results show not only the political colour of the two news and current affairs sections but also that political affiliation is virtually universal among journalists: of the 95 journalists opting for TG1 four were communists, one socialist (most of the other socialists having opted for TG2), two social democrats, one republican, two Liberal Party members, five 'independent' of left-wing orientation and the remaining 80 were all DC or DC-leaning. As for the senior executive positions such as head of channel or departmental heads there were eight DC, four PSI, two PSDI, one PRI and one left-wing independent.[128]

Control over the message generally took the form of giving far more time to the ruling parties than to the opposition (in the late 1970s and early 1980s the news programme of Radio 2 was unashamedly the mouthpiece of one of the factions of the DC). According to the Radical Party, from 1 March 1981 to 31 January 1982 the leaders of the five government parties were interviewed for a total of over ten hours, while all opposition leaders together were interviewed for two hours.[129]

Again it should be stressed that there is no evidence that the media were able to influence electoral results significantly. However, there may be some influence over a small percentage of the population which thus contributes to the small electoral swings. With a system of proportional representation these small swings, while not affecting the overall result, have great symbolic value and affected the composition of the ruling majorities.[130]

The carving up the RAI apparatus revealed the growing crisis of legitimacy of the political parties. The ability to control the output of television news was necessarily very limited, first of all because – as previously stated – political messages must be transformed by the media and this means that the political parties are less and less an independent source of information; they tend to become mere items in an information system dominated by television. Secondly, overall mass behaviour is affected by the entire information system and not just by television. This information system, being transnational, goes against the very logic of the nation-state and of national politics. Finally, the carve-up of the RAI assumed that the state would be able to maintain its monopoly over broadcasting. This assumption turned out to be unwarranted. In 1976 Italy's Constitutional Court decided that state monopoly was valid only for national broadcasting. It saw no reason why regional broadcasting should not be in the hands of private entrepreneurs. This opened the way for the unrestricted expansion of hundreds of private radio and television stations. By 1978 there were 434 private TV stations in the country.[131] This development was greeted by near-universal approval. The prestige of the RAI was low, especially after the political carve-up. Far-left groups, radicals and libertarians naively thought that there was a golden opportunity for the diffusion of community programmes with a high political content. As the initial capital required for this was quite modest, they hoped to start a whole network of 'alternative' broadcasting. These hopes were soon dashed. Those who benefited were the press barons and other entrepreneurs who threw their energies into the enterprise. By the early 1980s three leading television private TV channels emerged: *Canale 5* owned by Silvio Berlusconi Fininvest, *Rete 4* owned by Italy's largest publishing group Mondadori and *Italia Uno* owned by another publishing group (Rusconi). By 1984 Berlusconi had become the master of all three. In no other West European or North American country could this have occurred. The Fininvest empire was born and the RAI-Berlusconi duopoly had been established. By 1995, the hundreds of TV stations outside this duopoly have only 2 per cent of the audience. *Telemontecarlo*, the largest of them has only 1.13 per cent.

How did this state of affairs come about? After the Constitutional Court decision, it was expected that the government would legislate to regulate radio and television broadcast. This was not done. Anyone could set up a station and broadcast anything they liked, provided it did not breach existing laws on pornography or libel. Though the matter is still far from clear, it seems that the decision of the succeeding governments not to regulate broadcasting stemmed from two considerations. In the first place, the parties in power preferred to have to deal with one owner than with a multiplicity of channels with different and competing political tendencies. Pluralism in the printed media had not produced a docile press. Why risk a replica of this situation in the far more politically sensitive field of broadcast TV? Better wait until the development of a private monopoly emerged and deal with the victor. Secondly, the close political friendship between Bettino Craxi, the PSI leader who was Prime Minister throughout these events, and Berlusconi was undoubtedly one of several factors working to the latter's advantage.[132] In 1985 the legislation which formally made official the party political carving up of the RAI Board also accepted the legal existence of private networks broadcasting throughout the national territory while still refraining from regulating them.

Finally, on 6 August 1990 the long-awaited regulation became law: Law 223 also known as the Legge Mammì (after the Republican Party minister). This law specified how many networks a single company could have, tried to limit cross-ownership of printed and broadcast media, established a Regulator. The effect of this law was to sanction and preserve the market shares gained by Fininvest and the RAI. It accepted the high degree of concentration in the advertising market – 24.5 per cent of which is controlled by Berlusconi's Publitalia – it did not regulate pay TV, cable TV and satellite broadcasting.[133]

The printed media lost heavily (which may explain their intense dislike for Berlusconi) because the state network was allowed to increase its share of advertising revenue, thus restricting the amount of money available to the printed media. Thus by 1993 the RAI (who had always been able to raise advertisement revenue) was funded two-thirds by state and one-third by advertisement. The law prohibiting the owner of three networks to own a national paper was easily circumvented by putting Berlusconi's brother in charge of the conservative daily *Il Giornale*. When its editor and founder the respected veteran journalist Indro Montanelli tried to assert his freedom to criticize his owners, he was fired. In fact, after the Mammì Law was passed, Berlusconi was also able to buy Mondadori, the largest publishing house in the country which, in turn also owned many important weeklies magazine such as *Panorama* (529,000 copies sold), *Epoca* (206,000), *Donna Moderna* (634,000), *Grazia*, *Marie Claire* and the TV listing magazine *TV Sorrisi e canzoni* (2,246,000). To this empire we should also add Standa, Italy's most important retail chain as well as the Milan football club.

The number of local independent TV stations decreased, though in the early 1990s there were still nearly 1,000 of them, more than those existing in the whole of the USA.[134] The cost of obtaining a concession to broadcast remained small: 100 million lires (c. £40,000) for national network. Far from re-invigorating local communities and promoting alternative life-styles, private radios broadcast a constant stream of pop music interrupted by painfully amateurish news reporting. The standards set by the RAI were already low. Private radio and television succeeded in setting lower ones. As ratings in the private sector improved, the RAI was forced to follow. It produced even fewer high quality documentaries, virtually stopped producing its own fiction (its few celebrated products, such as *Marco Polo* and *La Piovra* loom as exceptions). By 1981 Italian television companies (RAI and the private system) imported 2,369 films plus 2,043 made-for-TV films and episodes of television serials – a total of 4,412 units of which 18 per cent were bought by the RAI.

Politicians remain more convinced than ever that TV brings votes. Berlusconi's subsequent political rise appears to confirm this. Further selected evidence may be deployed to substantiate this view. Yet one should not forget that the near-absolute control exercised by the old political parties over the public system and the support they enjoyed of the monopolistic owner of the private sector did not prevent them from being electorally wiped out after the corruption scandals of 1992–93.

Once Berlusconi's main protectors, Craxi's PSI and the DC, had vacated the scene, Berlusconi entered the political scene, ostensibly to fill the vacuum of power and to prevent the 'communists' (by then the PDS) from taking power. Whatever his intention, the effect was to make the introduction of anti-trust legislation even less likely. Once Berlusconi had entered politics such legislation would not be introduced with him in power while – if he was out of power – it could not be introduced without it appearing as an attempt by his opponents to punish him. The centre-left opposition tried to use a referendum to force parliament to legislate, but this backfired. In June 1995 a clear majority of Italians expressed the wish to see the preservation of the Fininvest monopoly in the private sector. They may have feared to be deprived of some of the existing channels and hence of choice. They need not have been so perturbed. No anti-trust legislation would repair the enormous cultural damage done over the years by the RAI and Fininvest, by the constant necessity to increase ratings at the expense of quality, by the politicization of the personnel, by the appallingly low technical standards of presentation of programmes, by the vulgarity of its chat-shows and the astonishing provincialism of its most popular figures. Television had offered Italians the golden opportunity to popularize and diffuse what was best in Italian culture, particularly its cinema – one of the finest in the world. This opportunity was wasted. In the coming era of multichannel digital broadcast it will not re-appear. The cultural elites may be able to carve for themselves a space for refined and arty programmes. The rest of the population will be left with low-level entertainment.

Endnotes

1 Apter and Eckstein 1963, p. 327.
2 Romagnoli and Treu 1977, pp. 11–12.
3 Salvati (Beccalli) 1972, pp. 1967.
4 Pizzorno 1980, p. 103.
5 Triola 1971, pp. 617–87.
6 Pizzorno 1980, p. 105.
7 Ibid., p. 106.
8 Ibid., pp. 106–7.
9 Lama 1976, pp. 33–4.
10 Romagnoli and Treu 1977, p. 24.
11 Ibid., pp. 28–9.
12 Ibid., pp. 569.
13 Farneti 1978a, p. 417.
14 Romagnoli and Treu 1977, pp. 62–3.
15 Ibid., p. 76.
16 Ibid., pp. 83–4.
17 Farneti 1978a, p. 430.
18 Pizzorno 1980, p. 141.
19 Lama 1976, p. 53.
20 Romagnoli and Treu 1977, p. 87.
21 Turone 1976, p. 86.
22 Ibid., p. 93.
23 Rieser 1981, pp. 62–3.
24 Amendola 1979.
25 For a critique of the factory council system see Trentin 1982. Trentin was one of the principal architects of the factory council system; see also Trentin 1977 and Trentin 1980.
26 Pennacchi 1982.
27 Accornero 1991.
28 Ibid., p. 299.
29 Accornero 1992, p. 120.
30 Carli 1977, p. 75.
31 Castronovo 1981, p. 1261.
32 Ibid., pp. 1278–80.
33 Comito 1982, pp. 133–7.
34 Cassano 1979, p. 71.
35 Comito 1982, p. 142.
36 Castronovo 1981, p. 1282.

37 Turone 1974, pp. 349–50.
38 Comito 1982, pp. 137–9.
39 Castronovo 1981, p. 1290.
40 Sylos Labini 1974, p. 149.
41 Ibid., pp. 85–6.
42 See text in Villari 1975, vol. 11, pp. 692–3. A pro-planning attitude was becoming diffuse among Italian entrepreneurs. Even Olivetti, the most intransigent defender of the freedom of enterprise lamented the fact that there was 'no national plan for electronics', see Forcellini 1978, p. 117.
43 See text in Villari 1975, pp. 717–23.
44 Cited in Comito 1982, p. 139.
45 Libertini 1976, p. 30.
46 Castronovo 1980, pp. 322–3.
47 Addario 1982, p. 106.
48 Ibid., pp. 107–9.
49 Ibid.
50 Ibid., pp. 108–10.
51 Comito 1982, pp. 141–7.
52 Garavini 1977, p. 30.
53 See the issues of *Fortune* of 13 Aug. 1979 and 10 Aug. 1981, also cited in Comito 1982, pp. 14–15.
54 All 1994 data in *Financial Times*, FT500 survey in issue of 20 January 1994.
55 Forte 1974, pp. 350–1.
56 Revelli 1982.
57 Poggi 1972, pp. 136–7.
58 Carlo Cardia in Baget-Bozzo 1979, p. 83.
59 Poggi 1972, pp. 144–5.
60 Ibid., pp. 140–1.
61 Ibid., p. 147.
62 Ibid., p. 153.
63 Magister 1979, p. 49.
64 Ibid., pp. 41–7.
65 Baget-Bozzo 1974, pp. 220–3.
66 See extract from the diaries in Scoppola 1977, p. 293.
67 Andreotti 1977, p. 73.
68 Magister 1979, pp. 132–3.
69 Casmiri 1980, p. 208.
70 Cited in Casmiri 1980, p. 219.
71 Ibid., p. 235.
72 Ibid., p. 289.
73 Pierini 1965, pp. 309–10.
74 Baget-Bozzo 1977, pp. 190–2.
75 Ibid., p. 270.
76 Ibid., p. 272.
77 Moro 1979, pp. 64–5.
78 Magister 1979, pp. 237–8.

79 Jerkov 1966, pp. 57–61.
80 Baget-Bozzo 1979, pp. 128–9.
81 See the contributions by Lucio Lombardo Radice and Luigi Pestalozza to the debate on the *Populorum progressio* in Lombardo Radice 1967 and Pestalozza 1967.
82 Baget-Bozzo 1977, pp. 41–3.
83 Chiarante 1979a, p. 48.
84 Magister 1979, pp. 416–22.
85 Ibid., p. 432.
86 Ibid., pp. 447–9.
87 Note the birth in 1973 of *Cristiani per il Socialismo*, a political group which accepted Marxism as a methodology while criticising the Church, the DC as well as the PCI for being too institutionalized. See Milanesi 1976.
88 Riccardi 1994, p. 346 and Garelli 1991, p. 152.
89 Cardia 1979, pp. 48–50.
90 On the ideology of this movement see Accatoli 1989.
91 Garelli 1991: pp. 154–5.
92 Riccardi 1994, p. 343 and Cardia 1979, pp. 51–2.
93 Garelli 1991, p. 159.
94 Brunetta 1993, p. 536.
95 Garelli 1977, pp. 165–7.
96 Data in Riccardi 1994, p. 341.
97 1991 Data in Pace 1995, p. 139.
98 Data for 1956 in Weber 1981, p. 190.
99 Chiarante 1979a, pp. 43–4.
100 John Paul II, *Redemptor Hominis*, 4 March 1979.
101 This thesis is developed in Pace 1995.
102 Pace 1995, p. 58.
103 Garelli 1995, p. 253.
104 Ibid., pp. 254–5.
105 Berselli 1991, p. 872.
106 Paul John II 1991, paragraphs 26, 34, 35.
107 Ibid., par. 42.
108 Paul John II 1995, pp. 5ff.
109 See in particular *Les activités d'information de l électronique et des technologies des téle communications sur l'emploi, la croissance et le commerce*, OECD and the Unesco report of the International Commission for the Study of Communication Problems chaired by Sean McBride, Unesco 1980.
110 On multinational companies and the communications industry see Mattelard 1979.

111 On US dominance in the information system see Tunstall 1977.

112 Data obtained from the RAI's *Centro di Documentazione e Studi*. For an examination of the development of Italy's private television broadcasting system and its effects on the public sector see Sassoon 1985, pp. 119–57.

113 Data in Vacca 1984, pp. 25–30.

114 ISTAT 1994, p. 165.

115 Vacca 1984, p. 72.

116 CENSIS 1994, p. 596.

117 Paci 1993, p. 211.

118 Missiroli 1995, pp. 6–7.

119 Survey cited in Guadagni 1995, p. 11.

120 Ruzza and Schmidtke 1993, pp. 4–6.

121 Cesareo 1981, pp. 22–3.

122 Ibid., pp. 24–5.

123 Ibid., pp. 28–9.

124 Cesareo 1981, p. 29. Pinto 1977 points out that in the 1950s the PCI leadership in trying to uphold the principle of freedom of information concentrated its attention exclusively on news programmes while communist intellectuals had a distinct old-fashioned disregard for the whole phenomenon of mass communications. This situation changed only in the 1980s.

125 Vacca 1982, p. 5.

126 Gentiloni 1980, p. 149.

127 Ibid., p. 149.

128 Fracassi 1982, p. 17.

129 Ibid.

130 Rositi 1981, p. 88.

131 Fiori 1995, p. 90.

132 On the links between Craxi and Berlusconi see Fiori 1995, esp. pp. 105–30.

133 Silva 1993, p. 131.

134 Ibid., p. 132.

Part three

Politics

Chapter 9

Elections

In June 1946 the Italian people elected a Constituent Assembly and, at the same time, decided, by referendum, that Italy should become a republic. The majority – 54.3 per cent – was decisive but not overwhelming. The referendum results also revealed how divided the country was on this question. In northern and central Italy the pro-republican vote was, respectively, 64.8 and 63.3 per cent, while in the southern mainland it was 32.6 per cent, in Sicily 35.1 per cent and in Sardinia 39.1 per cent. Most of the pro-monarchist votes came from the ranks of the Christian Democratic Party (DC) and reflected more a general conservative attitude rather than an outright commitment to the monarchy. In fact the Monarchist Party in post-war Italy was never a strong force, obtained only 2.7 per cent of the votes in the elections for the Constituent Assembly and disappeared completely after 1968, its few remaining followers merging with the neo-fascists of the MSI.

The Constituent Assembly was elected by universal suffrage and with a system of proportional representation (PR). The adoption of this system for all future elections was debated in the Constituent Assembly. It was, however, decided that it should not be incorporated in the Constitution. Article 56 says only that the Chamber of Deputies should be elected by universal suffrage. In deference to the wishes of the Italian Communist Party (PCI) that some mention should be made of PR, a motion was passed by members of the Assembly in favour of PR.[1] There are, of course, different types of PR and we shall briefly examine the one which was adopted in Italy. It should be pointed out, however, that even though there is no necessary link between an electoral system and the numbers of political parties represented in parliament, it is clear that the more an electoral system is proportional the greater the likelihood for all political forces to be represented. In June 1946, 56 political parties fought the election, eleven of which presented national lists which collected 96.5 per cent of the votes. Of the national parties represented in the 1987 Parliament six belonged to this original group of eleven (although some parties changed their names). The total percentage of votes of the original six in 1946 was 91.32, by 1987 it was still 84 per cent. Thus from the very beginning a wide but highly stable array of political forces had established itself: it dominated Italian politics throughout what has come to be known as the First Republic, that is until 1992–93.

Before the fascist dictatorship, Italy had experienced various types of electoral systems. In the period to 1882 MPs were elected in single constituencies on a first-past-the-post basis after a second round of elections (unless a candidate obtained an absolute majority in the first round – as is the case now in France). Between 1882 and 1891 there were multi-member constituencies and electors had as many votes as candidates. Between 1891 and 1919 Italy reverted to the pre-1882 procedure. In 1919 the country adopted PR – to the acclaim of the anti-corruption Sicilian historian and polemicist Gaetano Salvemini who felt that a first-past-the-post system put MPs at the mercy of wealthy and unscrupulous notables. After Mussolini was appointed Prime Minister he introduced the Acerbo Law (1923) which gave a 'majority premium' of two-thirds of the parliamentary seats to the winning electoral list as long as it obtained at least 25 per cent of the vote.

If we examine Italian electoral history in the period to 1992 we can make the following observations concerning the degree of stability of the Italian political system until 1987 and its subsequent crisis (refer to Table 9.1):

1   The DC remained the largest party and never had to face a significant split. Between 1948 and 1979 it was always around or just below the 40 per cent level. It then declined and in 1992 it plummeted to just under 30 per cent.

2   The PCI increased its vote regularly until the 1979 elections. Decline then set in.[2] By 1992 it had changed its name into the *Partito Democratico della Sinistra* (PDS) and was reduced to 16.1 per cent.

3   The Italian left (i.e. PCI, PSI and other smaller left-wing parties) had in 1946 nearly 40 per cent of the vote. In the three subsequent elections (1948, 1953 and 1958) it obtained respectively 31.03, 35.35 and 36.99 per cent. Since 1963 the PCI and PSI were no longer allied but their joint vote, if added to that of the smaller left-wing parties, went beyond the 40 per cent level. In 1976 (if we include the Radical Party but exclude the social democrats of the PSDI) the total vote of the left reached its highest level: 46.70 per cent. By 1987 the left (as for 1976 plus the Greens) was still at 46 per cent. In 1992 the total 'left' vote (including the PSI, *Rifondazione Comunista* and the Greens but excluding the Radicals and the PSDI) was down to 38.1.

4   The centrist vote (PSDI + PRI + PLI) oscillated more radically, reaching a peak of 14.47 per cent in 1963 and its lowest point (7.8 per cent) in 1976.

5   The right-wing vote (neo-fascist plus monarchist) also followed an oscillating course, obtaining the following percentages in the twelve elections we are examining (i.e. 1946–92): 8.4; 4.8; 12.7; 9.7; 6.9; 5.8; 8.7; 6.1; 5.3; 6.8; 5.9; 5.4.

6   The combined vote of the two largest parties (DC and PCI) hovered just below the two-thirds mark throughout the 1950s and 1960s. In 1976 the joint vote reached 73.20 per cent, then went down to 68.7 per cent in

Table 9.1 Election results of national parties, 1946–92 (1946: Constituent Assembly, 1948–87 Chamber of Deputies); percentages and seats (figure in brackets)

	1946	1948	1953	1958	1963	1968
PCI	19.0 (104)		22.6 (143)	22.7 (140)	25.3 (166)	27.0 (177)
PSIUP				4.5 (23)		
PSI	20.7 (115)		12.7 (75)	14.3 (84)	13.8 (87)	
PCI+PSI		31.0 (183)				
PSU						14.5 (91)
PSDI		7.1 (33)	4.5 (19)	4.6 (22)	6.1 (33)	
PRI	4.4 (23)	2.5 (9)	1.6 (5)	1.4 (6)	1.4 (6)	2.0 (9)
DC	35.2 (207)	48.5 (304)	40.0 (262)	42.3 (273)	38.3 (260)	39.1 (265)
PLI	6.8 (41)	3.8 (19)	3.0 (13)	3.6 (17)	7.0 (39)	5.8 (31)
Monarchists	3.1 (16)	2.8 (14)	6.9 (40)	4.9 (25)	1.8 (8)	1.3 (6)
MSI	5.3 (30)	2.0 (6)	5.8 (29)	4.8 (24)	5.1 (27)	4.5 (24)
Others	5.5 (20)	2.3 (5)	2.9 (4)	1.4 (5)	1.2 (4)	1.3 (4)
Total seats	556	574	590	596	630	630

	1972	1976	1979	1983	1987	1992
PCI/PDS	27.2 (179)	34.4 (227)	30.4 (201)	29.9 (198)	26.6 (177)	16.1 (107)
PSIUP	1.9 (0)					
Far Left/RC	1.3 (0)	1.5 (6)	2.2 (6)	1.5 (7)	1.7 (8)	5.6 (35)
PSI	9.6 (61)	9.7 (57)	9.8 (62)	11.4 (73)	14.3 (94)	13.6 (92)
Radical		1.1 (4)	3.4 (18)	2.2 (11)	2.6 (13)	1.2 (7)
Green					2.5 (13)	2.8 (16)
PSDI	5.1 (29)	3.4 (15)	3.8 (20)	4.1 (23)	3.0 (17)	2.7 (16)
PRI	2.9 (15)	3.1 (14)	3.0 (16)	5.1 (29)	3.7 (21)	4.4 (27)
DC	38.7 (266)	38.8 (263)	38.3 (262)	32.9 (225)	34.3 (234)	29.7 (206)
PLI	3.9 (20)	1.3 (5)	1.9 (09)	2.9 (16)	2.1 (11)	2.8 (17)
Lega Nord						8.7 (55)
MSI	8.7 (56)	6.1 (35)	5.3 (30)	6.8 (42)	5.9 (35)	5.4 (34)
Others	0.7 (4)	0.6 (4)	1.9 (6)	3.2 (6)	3.3 (7)	5.1 (6)
Total seats	630	630	630	630	630	630

Notes: Constituent Assembly Election. In 1948 socialists and communists (PCI) had a joint list. In 1968 the socialists and the social democrats joined in a single party called the PSU (United Socialist Party), dissident socialists fought under the banner of the PSIUP (Socialist Party of Proletarian Unity). In 1991 the PCI changed its name into *Partito Democratico della Sinistra* (PDS), a dissenting minority split and fought the 1992 elections under the name of *Rifondazione Comunista*. *La Rete* (The Network) is a Sicilian anti-mafia party led by former Christian Democrats

1979 to 62.8 per cent in 1983 and 60.9 in 1987. In 1992 this total was down to 45.8. This data alone indicates the depth of the crisis reached by the Italian political system.

7 The combined vote of the three largest parties (DC + PCI + PSI) has usually been well over 75 per cent, reaching a peak of 82.9 per cent in

1976 and falling to 74.2 per cent in 1983 and 75.2 in 1987. In 1992 this combined vote was down to 59.4 per cent.

Thus until the 1987 election the Italian electorate had behaved with remarkable stability giving three-quarters of the vote or more to its three leading parties. However, if we consider all elections from 1948 to 1987 we note that the electorate has eliminated one political party (the Monarchist Party) created two small left-wing parties, added 10 per cent to the PCI vote and reduced considerably the electoral strength of the PLI. This would suggest that the DC maintained its total vote by decreasing the strength of the parties to its right (Liberals, neo-fascists and monarchists) while losing some votes to the left.

It is more difficult to ascertain party political support in terms of sex, occupation and educational level because this has to depend on surveys. This is more difficult to establish in Italy because of the multiplicity of political parties and because too many people decline to answer. A survey conducted in 1980 by Demoscopea, one of the leading polling agencies, provided some indications.

1 *Women.* According to the survey the DC was by far the favoured party of Italian women.[3] Fifteen years later women still appeared to favour, disproportionately, the Catholic parties which had emerged out of the meltdown of the DC, that is the CCD and the *Partito Popolare Italiano* as well as Berlusconi's *Forza Italia*.[4] The Northern League as well as the PDS, the right-wing *Alleanza Nazionale* and their predecessors always attracted fewer women than men.

2 *Education.* In the period 1948–92 small parties such as those of the liberals and the far left had a disproportionately highly educated electorate. The lowest education level was that of DC voters followed by the PCI. By 1995 the Catholic parties seemed to have lost their poorly educated electorate to *Forza Italia* while graduates were over-represented in the PDS.[5]

3 *Occupation.* Traditionally nearly one-quarter of DC voters were old-age pensioners, 15.8 per cent were blue-collar workers, 29.2 per cent were housewives, 4.2 per cent were in agriculture (1980 data). In 1980 over one-third of communist voters were blue-collar workers as were 23.4 per cent of the PSI voters, and 19 per cent of the MSI). By 1995 it appeared as if old communist voters had decided to support the hard-line *Rifondazione Comunista* rather than the PDS. The *Lega Nord* was overrepresented among the self-employed, as was the PPI. *Forza Italia* was overrepresented among housewives and old-age pensioners. The PDS was slightly overrepresented among workers but, otherwise, reflected surprisingly accurately the occupational spread within the population at large.

The electoral system adopted by Italy after 1946 was one of the most proportional in Europe. Basically it was a list system, that is, voters chose a party, then they could also indicate three or four candidates of the party for which they have voted by using what is called the preference vote. In the elections for the Senate a modified system operates in which each party presents only one candidate per constituency.[6]

The Chamber of Deputies was made up of 630 members on the basis of 32 constituencies or electoral districts, each of which returned more than one deputy (except the Val D'Aosta region). To win a seat it was necessary to achieve a quota of votes. This was calculated by dividing the total number of votes cast by the sum of the seats allocated to that particular constituency plus two. The addition of two to the denominator lowered the quota thus making it easier for a small party to gain representation in the Chamber of Deputies. A party which obtained twice the quota gained two deputies and so on. For example, if the quota was 50,000 votes and a party obtained 325,000 votes it would return six deputies and the 'surplus' 25,000 votes would be added to a national pool where all the 'rests' were added on. Usually, about one in ten seats ended up being allocated through the national pool. To obtain seats through the national pool a party had to obtain at least one quota of the votes in one constituency and 300,000 votes in the whole country. In 1976 the Radical Party exceeded the quota in the Rome constituency by only 351 votes and, having polled 392,419 votes nationwide, qualified for the national pool and obtained another three deputies (in addition to the one elected outright in Rome). Thus, thanks to 351 voters, the Radical Party was able to send four deputies to the Chamber. In 1972 none of the smaller leftist parties obtained a quota in a constituency and, as a result, nearly 1 million votes were 'wasted'.

Having calculated the number of seats each party has won, the preference votes were then counted to ascertain which candidates from the list have been elected. Many voters simply voted for a party and did not bother to indicate a preference, but some did. These personal votes were counted and the candidates of each party ranked accordingly. If a party won, for instance, six seats in a particular constituency these would be given to the six candidates with the most preference votes. Candidates could stand for election in more than one constituency (and many leaders did) and decide after the election for which constituency to opt. In this case the first of the non-elected candidate could obtain the seat thus left vacant. The first of the non-elected could succeed a deceased deputy or one who retires in the life of a parliament. There was thus no need for supplementary elections.

Let us use as an example the 1979 elections in the largest constituency for the Chamber: the Rome-Viterbo-Latina-Frosinone constituency to which 53 seats were allocated. The total number of votes cast was 3,173,556. To find the quota this number must be divided by 53+2 which gives 57,701. Thus in order to win a seat outright a party had to poll at least this amount. All national parties except the PDUP (a leftist party) obtained at least one quota. The DC polled 1,163,820. By dividing this by the quota we get 20 (the number of seats allocated to the DC), the surplus of 9,800 votes went to the DC national pool. To find out those elected among the 53 DC candidates it is necessary to examine the preference vote. As was to be expected the most prestigious candidate topped the preference vote: Giulio Andreotti, then Prime Minister for the fifth time (he was later accused of murder and associating with the mafia and tried). Andreotti had obtained over 300,000 preference votes which means that nearly one DC voter in four had voted for him. The runner-up had over 100,000 votes and the twentieth had just over 38,000.

In practical terms the system meant that in order to be elected a candidate had to ensure that his/her party obtained as many votes as possible and also that his/her party's supporters would 'prefer' him or her. In most parties, particularly in the DC, this led to highly personal electoral campaigns. The PCI, however, could count on such a degree of discipline from its supporters that it could ensure that all or most of those the leadership wished to see elected were successful without requiring a personal campaign. It was common practice for active supporters of the PCI to obtain from the local party branch a list of preferred candidates.

Prior to the polling day, each party would have presented its list of candidates, usually naming as many candidates as there are seats in the constituency. The effect of the system was to give a remarkable importance to political parties. In the first place the electoral system as a whole facilitated a multi-party system (as opposed to the two-party system as it exists in the UK and the USA); it then put before the electorate a range of parties rather than personalities by subordinating the casting of the preference vote to the all-important choice of a particular party; unlike the single transferable vote system it was not possible to vote across parties (i.e. the voter could not write in the names of candidates from different parties); it made it quite impossible to be elected to the Chamber without the support of a party, i.e. without being on a party list. However, once the parties had chosen their candidates they had no formal control over who among them would actually be elected. The PCI relied on a discipline based on ideology and not on possible sanctions while the expensive struggle for the preference vote remained an important aspect of internal factional strife within the DC and the PSI. In fact the preference vote was used much more by the electors of the DC and of the PSI than by those of the PCI, and was used more frequently in the South than in the North and Centre.[7]

Prior to 1994, the elections to the Italian Senate (which had exactly the same powers as the Chamber of Deputies but only 315 seats) proceeded on the basis of the so-called D'Hondt Highest Average Formula (while the one used for the Chamber is a modification of the *Imperiali* system). Each region was divided into various senatorial districts according to population size (except the Val d'Aosta which has only one district). Each party nominated one candidate per district. Any candidate with more than 65 per cent of the votes in a district was elected outright (this hardly ever happened). All party votes were added up in each region. The number of seats to be allocated to each party in a given region was determined by calculating the 'average' of each party. This was obtained by dividing the party's total regional vote by the number of seats won outright in that region. If no party had yet gained a seat because none of its candidates had obtained 65 per cent in a district then the first seat was allocated to the party with the highest regional vote. Then that party's average was recalculated by dividing its regional vote by two (i.e. the number of seats it had gained so far plus one). If its average was still higher than anyone else's total vote, it would also get the second seat (which would lead to the recalculation of the average total vote divided now by three, and so on). An example may clarify.

Let us take the Abruzzi region and the senatorial elections of 1979. Seven seats were to be allocated and none of the candidates got 65 per cent in any of the

Table 9.2 Results of the senatorial elections for the Abruzzi region, 1979

DC	311,872
PCI	213,556
PSI	56,553
MSI	39,756
PSDI	15,649
PRI	13,558
PR	11,181
PLI	6,571

Table 9.3 Proportion of votes to seats in the Chamber of Deputies and Senate, 1979

	Chamber of Deputies (1979)		Senate (1979)	
	% votes	% seats	% votes	% seats
DC	38.5	41.6	38.4	44.1
PCI	30.5	31.9	31.5	34.6
PSI	9.8	9.9	10.4	10.2
MSI	5.3	4.8	5.7	4.1

districts. The results are as given in Table 9.2. The DC had the highest number of votes and hence got the first seat. Its average had now fallen to 311,872/2 = 155,936. The highest 'average' was now that of the PCI (213,556) who obtained the second seat. This lowered the PCI's own average to 106,778 (i.e. its total vote divided by two) and gave the third seat to the DC. The DC's new average was now 103,957 (total vote divided by three) which was lower than the PCI's last average, hence the PCI got the fourth seat. Now the PCI's average had fallen to 71,185 (total vote divided by three). This meant that the fifth seat was gained by the DC. The DC's new average is 77,968 and, as this was still higher than the PCI's last, the DC got the sixth seat as well. Now the DC's average was down to 62,374 and the seventh and last seat goes to the PCI. The PCI had won three seats and the DC four. None of the other parties had a total vote higher than the last average of the DC or PCI and, consequently, they were not able to obtain any seats. Had the PSI obtained an extra 15,000 votes or so it would have gained one seat at the expense of the PCI.

This procedure determined the number of Senate seats which went to each *party* in every region. All regional candidates were then ranked according to the proportion of votes each party had collected in each district and the seats distributed to the party's candidates beginning with the one which tops the ranking. In our example the PCI candidates for the seven seats would be ranked accordingly and only the top three would gain a Senate seat.

The method used for the Senate elections was less proportionate than the one used for the Chamber elections and was more favourable to the two largest parties. This is shown in Table 9.3.

The number of political parties represented in a parliament is not directly related to a particular electoral system. The British first-past-the-post system does
not make a two-party system inevitable even though it undoubtedly penalizes any
small party whose votes are fairly well distributed throughout the country. Until
1992 Italian political parties were, on the whole, well represented throughout the
country. The PCI was strongest in the Centre and weakest in the North-east, while
the DC was strongest in the North-east and weakest in the Centre. However, both
parties were always the top parties in all Italian regions (except in the Trentino
where the largest party was the South Tyrol People's Party, STVP). In all regions
(again excluding the Trentino) the PSI was third and the MSI fourth. The electoral
system contributed very little to the difficulties in forming stable coalitions. Generally speaking, the centrist coalitions which dominated Italian politics from 1947
to 1963 and those of the centre-left which were the rule between 1963 and 1992
had relatively comfortable majorities – at least by the European standards. These
majorities succeeded each other with monotonous continuity. What really protected
them – and encouraged dissident parties to bring down governments – was the
knowledge that they could not be penalized at the polls. The exclusion of the PCI
and of the MSI from coalitions 'forced' the other parties to be permanently in
government.

From the end of the war until 1993 there was only one serious attempt to modify
the electoral system, allegedly in order to ensure more stable majorities. The law
of 15 March 1953 established that if a party or an alliance of parties succeeded
in obtaining 50 per cent plus 1 per cent of the national vote that party or that alliance of parties would obtain 64 per cent of the seats. There was an outcry against
this legislation not only by the PCI (which promptly dubbed it the Legge Truffa –
the fraudulent law) and the PSI but also by dissidents in the centrist parties. As
it turned out the alliance of DC-PLI-PRI-PSDI obtained (with the STVP and the
Sardinian Action Party) only 49.8 per cent of the votes, while in the previous elections (1948) they had obtained 62.61 per cent.[8] Thus by slightly more than 50,000
votes the PR system was maintained. Later the law was repealed.

The objections which have been levelled in Italy against the existing PR system
is that it produces too many political parties, makes decision-making more difficult
and does not offer the electorate a clear-cut alternative between potential governments. *De facto*, the Italian electorate does not vote for a future government but
to strengthen a particular party's parliamentary representation. At most the Italian
electorate is able to rule out a possible coalition government. For example, the
centrist coalitions which dominated Italy after 1948 were no longer possible after
1976 because they no longer had a majority, while governments of national unity
(i.e. including both PCI and DC) and centre-left governments (i.e. including both
PSI and DC) have always been possible.

In the 1980s a debate was started on electoral reform. At the time there was very
little evidence that the population was dissatisfied with the electoral system, though,
according to opinion polls, they were dissatisfied with the existing parties. The percentage of abstention was extremely low, with a 12 per cent peak in 1983. The
proportion of voters was much higher than in the UK and most other European

countries. There was a high level of electoral participation even in local elections, European elections and referendums. Voting, though not compulsory, was generally regarded as a 'civic duty'.

In the closing years of the First Republic the electoral system based on PR came under repeated attacks. Indeed, one could argue that the 1993 electoral law, which effectively abolished the old system, was the final nail in the coffin of the First Republic. Well before then, however, a wide consensus had emerged which attributed Italy's problems, whether economic or political, to its electoral system. It was said that there were too many parties resulting in a highly fragmented party system. This, it was alleged, led to paralysis as a small party with only a few seats could blackmail the executive. It was also claimed that, in fact, the electorate was never in a position of choosing a government because this was always the result of deal made behind doors by potential coalition partners. Until the 1980s the advocate of electoral reforms were few and far between, usually mavericks like Marco Pannella, the leader of the small Radical Party or political commentators seeking to align Italy to an idealized Westminster-type model. The reformers claimed that a new electoral system would offer the electorate a clear-cut alternative between a left- and a right-wing bloc, ending so-called *consociativismo* (the alleged informal entente between DC and PCI). A new system, it was also claimed, would lead to fewer parties, end corruption, enable voters to choose their own candidates rather than political parties and bring about stable government. There were disputes over which electoral system would bring about such alluring state of affairs. One thing is almost certain, though. Had Italy adopted the British electoral system in 1946, the most likely consequence would have an uninterrupted and lengthy period of Christian Democratic rule. It is clear, in fact, that the DC has always been the first party in all Italian regions (and in all areas) except in a minority of areas in which the PCI was first. In other words, the most likely alternative scenario would have been a strong and hegemonic DC able to rule firmly without needing to resort to constant negotiations with unreliable allies facing an unlectable left dominated by the PCI.

It is largely for these reasons that the PCI had been the main defender of the PR system. It believed that, as it was systematically excluded from power, it could at least enjoy a parliamentary representation commensurate to its strength in the country. To some extent, such defence implied accepting its subordinate and opposition role. This is why, in the 1980s, communist supporters began to examine alternative electoral systems.[9] The electoral victory of the French socialist-communist alliance appeared to suggest that the adoption of the second round system with one-member constituencies would force the PSI into an acceptance of an electoral pact with the PCI and offer the electorate a clear cut choice in the second round between a candidate of the left and one of the 'right' – i.e. the Christian Democratic Party.[10] This system, it was believed, would also compel the small secular parties of the centre (the social democrats, the Republicans and the liberals) to decide whether they preferred to make a deal with the DC or whether they preferred to join a progressive alliance. Finally, this system would at last eliminate the MSI from the political arena because, in the circumstances prevailing in the 1980s, it was still considered politically unacceptable for any democratic party to join forces with the neo-fascists.

Until the late 1980s these views were still those of a small minority. The two main parties defended the old system. The DC because it had served it well, the PCI because it still believed that a left bloc in which it would be, unlike in France, the most influential party would be unacceptable to the powerful Italian middle classes and their even more powerful international allies. Besides it was reluctant to offend the PSI and the smaller parties of the centre who, understandably enough, were unwilling to change the system which had granted them an influence out of all proportion to their actual electoral importance. Nevertheless the defence of the status quo became increasingly eroded, so much so that, by the time the crisis of *Tangentopoli* erupted, the debate on electoral reform had advanced so much that the consensus had shifted towards change in the comforting belief that all problems could be resolved by the simple mechanism of changing the electoral system.

All debates on electoral reform are conducted as if the intention is to promote a fairer system. Perhaps inevitably, all proponents tend to opt for a system which they believe will favour their parties. It was only after the sensational defeat of 1983 (a drop of over 5 per cent) that some leading members of the DC began to suggest changing key aspects of the system. It was becoming clear to them that PR had led to a situation in which the DC was eminently blackmailable by its allies. Strengthening the executive seemed an increasingly sensible prospect. Thus, in 1984, after the DC electoral defeat of 1983, its then leader, Ciriaco De Mita suggested that allied parties should make a pre-electoral coalition pact, the so-called *patto di legislatura*. The electorate would still vote for parties but the coalition elected would stay in power for the length of parliament. Should it fall because of internal dissent there would have to be new elections. In practice this would mean that the DC would lock its allies into an agreement which would last for an entire parliament.[11] This proposal was turned down by all and sundry but resurfaced in 1991, as the debate intensified. Now De Mita – at odds with the leaders of the DC and with Craxi – added to his previous plan the suggestion that the prime minister should be elected by parliament (as in Germany rather than appointed by the President). De Mita's objectives had not changed: to compel the DC's coalition partners to renounce the constant political blackmail to which they had become accustomed.[12]

Eventually even the PCI joined the debate on electoral reform but only after its leader Occhetto had proposed, in November 1989, its dissolution and the formation of a new 'post-communist' party. Various plans were put forward, though never officially. Its preferred option was close to the German system: 300 seats on the basis of first-past-the-post, 270 seats allocated on the basis of a regionally based form of PR and the remaining 60 seats on national PR. The party wanted electoral reform to be part of a wider institutional change: a smaller National Assembly, a Regional Chamber, the direct election of city mayors and regional presidents and the parliamentary election of the PM.[13]

The debate on electoral reform was part of a wider debate on the country's institution. Among opinion-makers, it became commonplace to argue that many of Italy's problems could be solved more easily if parliament was made weaker and the executive stronger.[14] Some argued that the direct election of the President of the

Republic (hitherto elected by parliament) would achieve the desired result. Others thought that what was required was the direct election of the prime minister for a full five-year term. These particular proposals originated from the right of the political spectrum and were, at first, condemned by the left as designed to lead to a semi-presidential system which, given Italy's past, might degenerate into a semi-authoritarian regime. With the passing of time, these qualms became less manifest. Francesco Cossiga, President of the Republic between 1985 and 1992, became an advocate of presidentialism, as did Bettino Craxi – when he was no longer prime minister – presumably on the assumption that he stood a good chance of becoming president himself though he refrained from suggesting that PR should be abandoned – not surprising as with PR the PSI would remain an essential element of any eventual coalition, whether of the centre-left or of the left.

As the crisis of the political system developed and after the electoral reform of 1993, the desire for 'locking-in' the executive for at least a full parliamentary term became manifest even among progressive public opinion.

As it turned out the first reform of the electoral system consisted in abolishing the electors' option to vote for up to four candidates of the party of their choice, the so-called 'preference vote'. The choice was now to be narrowed to a single preference. The leading proponent of the June 1991 referendum which led to this was Mario Segni, a senior Christian Democrat acting on his own initiative. He was soon joined by others, including the PDS, but not by his party's leadership or the PSI whose leader, Craxi, invited voters to boycott the polls. The apparent reason behind the referendum was to the assumption that the preference system had led to a veritable market in votes where candidates were, in effect, making definite specific promises to key sections of their party's electorate, in other words, trading votes for public expenditure commitments or jobs. Left with one preference vote, voters would cast their ballots for the best known politicians, the factions leaders who would thus become like 'generals with no armies to command'.[15] The claims made on behalf of this shift from four preferences to one may appear overstated.[16]

It is doubtful whether the change would really do much to decrease corruption or the inner party competition for preference votes. It certainly would have decreased the options facing the electors. Be that as it may, the fact remain that the electorate itself backed Segni's referendum massively: though only 62.5 per cent turned out, 95.6 per cent of voters endorsed the change.[17]

In the long run, the 1991 reform may appear a puny one indeed. In 1992 the Tangentopoli crisis erupted. The death-knell for the coalition parties had sounded. In 1993 a new referendum buried the old electoral system once and for all. Nevertheless, the massive support behind the one-preference vote should be seen as a further sign of the electorate's discontent with the party system as a whole and as an indication that it was becoming converted to the proposition that it was possible to solve the crisis of confidence in the Italian political system by changing the electoral system.

The 1992 elections (see Table 9.4) demonstrated that voters' discontent with the political parties had reached a point of no return. As the new post-communist PDS

Table 9.4 Share of the vote, Chamber of Deputies, 1987–96

	1987	1992	1994	1996
PCI/PDS	26.6	16.1	20.4	21.1
Rifondazione Comunista	—	5.6	6.0	8.6
Socialists	14.3	13.6	2.0	—
Radicals	2.6	1.2	3.5	1.9
Green	2.5	2.8	2.9	2.5
La Rete	—	1.9	1.8	—
Alleanza Democratica	—	—	1.4	—
PSDI	3.0	2.7	—	—
Republicans	3.7	4.4		
DC	34.3	29.7	—	—
PPI	—	—	11.1	—
Prodi List	—	—	—	6.8
Segni List	—	—	4.6	—
Dini List	—	—	—	4.3
Lega Nord	—	8.7	8.4	10.1
Forza Italia	—	—	21.0	20.6
CCD	—	—	—	5.8
MSI/AN	5.9	5.4	13.5	15.7
Others				

Notes: In 1994 the CCD, right-of-centre Catholics were included in the list of *Forza Italia*. In 1996 the PPI (left-of-centre Catholics) were included in the Prodi list. The *Dini* List is a centrist list which includes Catholics, Liberals and former PSI supporters. *Alleanza Democratica* was a disparate alliance of former communists, left Catholics and various opinion makers – all cooperating with the PDS

was in disarray, deeply divided and now facing a rival on its left, *Rifondazione Comunista*, the ruling four-party coalition (i.e. DC, PSI, PSDI and PLI) should have had an easy ride. The PDS obtained only 16.1 of the vote, 10 per cent less than the already poor results obtained in 1987. *Rifondazione* obtained 5.6 per cent. The combined vote of the two offshoots of the old PCI, 21.7 per cent, was inferior to the share of the vote gained by the PCI in all post-1948 elections. This unquestionable defeat for the communist left produced no benefits to the ruling coalition. Craxi's PSI, which had tried to ignore the significance of both *Tangentopoli* and the dissolution of the PCI, had re-affirmed its commitment to continuing its alliance with the DC, instead of benefitting from the losses of the PDS, stood still (actually losing 0.7 per cent). The real loser was the DC which lost a considerable segment of its northern electorate to the newly formed Northern League – an amalgamation of the various 'leagues' (*Lega Veneta*, *Lega Lombarda* and so on) which had been formed in the course of the 1980s. In 1992 the Northern League gained 25.5 per cent of the vote in the Veneto, 23.6 per cent in Lombardy, 16.3 per cent in Piedmont and 14.3 per cent in Liguria.[18] Much of this vote appeared to come from the DC which, for the first time in the post-war period obtained less than 30 per cent of the national vote (see Table 9.4).

The ruling coalition (now a four-party coalition because the PRI had left it) had not achieved a majority of the vote in any of the northern regions. Indeed, it no longer had a majority in parliament. The DC and the PSI had become, increasingly, the repository of the southern vote. This was all the more disturbing for Bettino Craxi who had cultivated an image of modernity.

The pressures towards electoral reform could no longer be deflected particularly as Mario Segni's call for a new referendum was now being supported even by the PDS. Strictly speaking a referendum could only delete existing legislation. It was decided that voters should be asked to delete the 65 per cent threshold for winning three-quarters of the senatorial districts. In practice this would have meant that 75 per cent of senatorial seats would be contested under a British-type system with the remaining seats being allocated according to a PR system.

Having attempted to slow down the pace of reform the political parties now tried, a little late, to jump on the bandwagon. With the exception of the small parties such as the anti-mafia southern party *La Rete*, the Greens, *Rifondazione Comunista* and the MSI, they all now supported change. On 18 April 1993 82.8 per cent of Italians (on a turnout of 75 per cent) voted in favour of abolishing the old electoral law for the Senate, making it inevitable that parliament would have to change the entire electoral system. There can be little doubt that the electorate was expressing its profound dissatisfaction with the old political parties and the old system. By an even greater majority (90.3 per cent) it abolished state funding of political parties – a measure which was, somewhat hypocritically, supported by all political parties – and with varying degree of support voters even supported the proposal to abolish three government ministries, such as that of agriculture, long considered as important instrument of the DC's clientelist practice. The fact that the country may have required a ministry of agriculture was disregarded by voters eager to punish, with whatever means at their disposals, the former rulers.

The 1992 parliament had become, in effect, delegitimated, particularly as an ever-increasing number of MPs were under investigation for corruption. There was little doubt that parliament would have to accept that the electorate wished to change the electoral law, particularly as there was now a major asymmetry between elections to the Senate and election to the Chamber. The resulting electoral laws, approved on 4 August 1993, appeared to be a compromise between those who wanted to maintain a PR system, such as the far-right MSI and the far-left *Rifondazione Comunista* (who could not yet hope to do well under any system which compelled parties to seek allies) and the first-past-the-post.[19] The PDS was isolated in its support for the double ballot French-style system. The Northern League favoured a first-past-the-post because it believed that it could achieved the objective of becoming the only party representing the North or, at least, the North East.

The new laws (Laws 276 and 277) confirmed the changes brought about by the referendum for electing Senators and radically transformed the method of election for the Chamber of Deputies. In other words, 237 Senators would be elected on the first past the post system, making it virtually impossible for small parties to win a seat unless highly concentrated locally. The remaining 78 senatorial seats (25 per cent of the total) would be allocated on the basis of PR using the D'Hondt Highest

Average Formula (described above) as in the past. This would, in practice, still constitute a significant obstacle – a *de facto* threshold of 10 per cent – to the representation of small parties, unless they presented a joint list.

As for the Chamber of Deputies, the new law established 475 single-seat electoral colleges distributed across 26 larger constituencies (the Val d'Aosta would have a single-seat college constituency). To win in any one of these colleges the candidate is required to obtain a simple plurality of the votes – as in Britain or the USA. The law also established 155 Chamber of Deputies seats – 25 per cent of the total – to be allocated according to the proportional system. Voters have two ballot papers, one for the single-member constituency and another for the party list presented in the proportional section. The precise and complex mechanism by which these seats are allocated to parties in the PR section and which candidates win seats need not detain us here.[20] It is sufficient here to point out that only parties which obtain at least 4 per cent of the national vote can participate in the allocation in the PR list and that parties with a winning candidate in a constituency have the votes necessary for that candidate's win deducted from the total for the proportional section. Suppose, for instance, that a constituency includes electoral colleges A, B, C and D. Suppose that the PDS has one candidate elected in college A with 25,000 votes and that that candidate would have won even with only 20,001 (because the next in line had 20,000). The procedure – or *scorporo* – is to deduct 4,999 votes from the PDS vote in that constituency. Thus reduced, the PDS votes are nationally summed up and seats are allocated to its national candidates in the rank order of presentation established by the party by calculating how many quotients each party gets.

In practice the PR section restores a kind of proportionality to parliamentary elections thus reducing the immense distortion that a British style electoral system would bring about to a country which has had ten or more parties for 50 years. In spite of the rhetoric which accompanied the reform, one thing must be made clear: under the new system Italian electors lost all the powers they had to select a particular candidate within a party list. Before 1992 they could choose up to four candidates. In 1992 they could choose only one, but still had a choice. After 1993 they would be faced in the constituency by a candidate pre-selected by a party or a coalition of parties while in the PR section they would be able to vote only for a party symbol. The assertion that the elector remains free to decide for whom to cast his/her vote in the single-member college is disingenuous: the vast majority of voters – at least in Europe – cast their ballots in terms of broad political families. In practice the electors decide for which party or party list they wish to cast their vote. This decision may be based on the values, or policies, or tradition, or image, or the leading personalities of the party or party list. They are hardly ever based on the personality of the actual candidate except perhaps where the local candidate has made specific commitments regarding local jobs or local expenditure, in other words where what is involved is precisely the kind of 'vote-trading' or 'pork-barrel politics' which all electoral reforms wished to avoid.

The 1994 and 1996 elections confirmed all this. To maximize their support parties presented common lists or common candidates. In 1994, in the North, Berlusconi's

Forza Italia and Bossi's *Lega Nord* agreed on candidates for single-member colleges while in the South *Forza Italia* made a pact with the former neo-fascists of *Alleanza Nazionale*. Southern conservatives who disliked *Alleanza Nazionale* and liked Berlusconi found themselves forced to vote for former neo-fascists in order to keep the left out. The same constraints were imposed on left-wing voters in most regions where the PDS had formed lists with candidates whose local following was negligible in overall terms, but sufficiently significant to deprive the left coalition of victory in certain key electoral colleges.

The illusion that a system similar to the British or American one would result in a two-party system was an astonishing piece of naivety. While it is true that the first past the post protects better than others the two main British or American parties, it cannot create two parties where many exist. Italian political parties played the new system well in order to maximize their votes. It forced them into coalitions as the previous system had done, though in a dissimilar way. Whether it will lead to government stability is another question. The omens of the first two elections under the new system do not point in this direction.

The results of the 1994 and 1996 elections also confirmed that the sought-after reduction in the number of political parties had not been achieved. Before 1992 the Italian political system consisted of two large parties, the DC and the PCI, an intermediate force, the PSI, three small centrist parties (PRI, PSDI and PLI) and a far right party, the MSI; in all, seven parties. To these one could add some tiny formation such as the Radical Party, the Greens, etc. After the electoral reform of 1993 and following the 1996 elections the party system is made up of two large parties: the PDS and *Forza Italia*, three medium-sized ones: *Alleanza Nazionale*, *Lega Nord* and *Rifondazione Comunista*, to these must be added at least three further groupings: the Catholic right (CCD), the Catholic left (*Partito Popolare*) and the list headed by Lamberto Dini; in all, eight parties. It is true that, with the exception of the *Lega Nord*, these have organized themselves into two counterposed blocs, but then the First Republic also could be seen in terms of blocs.

Furthermore, the idea that the electorate would be revitalized by the adoption of the new system turned out to be false: the rate of abstention – a rough approximation to an index of alienation or disenchantment – continued to increase.[21] In 1994 over 14 per cent did not vote and, of those who voted, a further 7–8 per cent spoilt their ballot papers (whether intentionally or not is not always clear) or refrained from filling it.[22] In other words, nearly a quarter of the votes of the electorate remained unused.

What next? It is clear that as long as the problem is seen to be the formation of coalition governments and as long as the solution is always seen to be nothing more than electoral reform, then the next step will be to tinker further with the electoral system perhaps adopting a French-style system which would contribute more decisively to the creation of two rival blocs. Others – mainly on the right – seek to weaken parliament further by turning the direct election of the president or of the prime minister. Some on the left may be tempted to move in that direction, comforted by the knowledge that the French presidential system enabled the socialist leader François Mitterrand to rule for fourteen years. It is doubtful that such foreign imports can be fruitful. In the United States the directly elected president is, in reality, a relatively weak figure who must engage in constant battle with a strong Congress and a federal system which grants 50 states considerable powers – a situation which is the result of a constitution and not an electoral system.

In Italy, a directly elected president would create the pre-conditions for an unparalleled concentration of powers if this president were to be supported by a sturdy parliamentary majority – as De Gaulle was. But if this president were to be faced by a recalcitrant parliament then Italy would have all the problems of 'governability' of the past.

Endnotes

1 See Falzone et al. 1976, p. 181.
2 The best analysis of the decrease in PCI votes in 1979 is in Mannheimer 1979, pp. 694–714.
3 The results were published in *Panorama*, no. 740, 23 June 1980, shortly after the regional elections. Similar results also emerged from a survey undertaken by Renato Mannheimer and Roberto Biorcio on behalf of the PCI, see 'Autoritratto dell'elettore comunista', *Rinascita*, no. 10, 23 March 1985.
4 Data of September 1995 provided by the *Osservatorio Socio-Politico* ISPO/ *Corriere della Sera* /Nielsen.
5 Data of September 1995 provided by the *Osservatorio Socio-Politico* ISPO/ *Corriere della Sera* /Nielsen.
6 A good explanation of the voting system for both Chamber of Deputies and Senate can also be found in Wertman 1977, pp. 44–5. This volume contains interesting analyses of various aspects of the 1976 elections.
7 Pasquino 1991, p. 335.
8 Ghini 1975, p. 113.
9 See Cotturri 1983 and Pasquino 1980.
10 The French electoral system is based on the single-member preferential method with a double ballot. People vote for one particular candidate in a single-member constituency (as in the UK and the USA). If no candidate wins more than half the votes a second ballot is held a week later. Some of the candidates may withdraw and any candidate with less than 12.5 per cent of the total electorate (not of the votes cast) must withdraw. In the second

ballot the candidate who has a plurality of the votes wins the seat. In practice the outcome of the elections will be heavily determined by the agreements entered into by the candidates' parties.
11 Messina 1992, pp. 33ff.
12 Ibid., pp. 42–3.
13 Ibid., pp. 80–6.
14 Early advocates of this were conservative political scientists such as Sartori 1973, and Fisichella 1975. They were eventually joined by socialists such as Giulio Amato, see Amato 1980, pp. 173–95.
15 Parker 1996, p. 41.
16 For a staunch and enthusiastic defence of the one-preference system see Pasquino 1993.
17 For an analysis of the referendum see McCarthy 1992, pp. 11–28.
18 Data in Diamanti 1996, p. 115.
19 That the resulting system is not a 'compromise' but a variant of systems in operation elsewhere is made clear in Gambetta and Warner 1996, p. 361.
20 Useful descriptions can be found in Hine 1993, pp. 27–34 and Lo Verso and McLean 1995. The best commentary is Gambetta and Warner 1996. The best polemic against the system adopted is Sartori 1995, a collection of articles originally written for the *Corriere della Sera*.
21 The rate of abstention may also be due to an increase in the proportion of elderly voters (see Mannheimer and Sani 1988, ch. 2), but the fact remain that there is a correlation between the increase in abstentionism in the 1980s and the increase in

the vote towards 'new parties', see Mannheimer 1991, p. 16.

22 A compendium of the insulting remarks
written on spoilt papers appeared later in
1994 under the title of *Cazzi vostri io
domani vado in Svizzera* edited by Gian
Marco Chiavari (with an interview with
Renato Mannheimer) (see Chiavari 1994).
The title (taken from one of the remarks)
could be roughly translated as 'Up yours,
I'm off to Switzerland tomorrow.'

Chapter 10

Governments

Between June 1945 and June 1996 Italy has had 55 governments. This is an average of just over eleven months each. Only three governments lasted more than two years.[1] This constitutes one of the highest rates of government instability in Western Europe, higher than Belgium, or France under the Fourth Republic. Of course the same politician can be prime minister several times, for instance Alcide De Gasperi was PM eight times and Andreotti seven. This brings the total number of Italian prime ministers between 1945 and 1996 down to 24. Until June 1992 they were all Christian Democrats except for Ferruccio Parri (Action Party) in 1945, Giovanni Spadolini (Republican Party) twice in 1981–82 for a total of eighteen months and the PSI leader Bettino Craxi twice between 1983 and 1987 – nearly five continuous years in office (the second longest span after Alcide De Gasperi).

Changes in governments have been due to any one of the following factors:

1 Internal dissent within the leading Christian Democratic Party (DC) facilitated by the secret ballot system which allowed DC parliamentarians to vote against their own party or abstain without being detected and disciplined.
2 Internal dissent within the coalition parties.
3 The dissolution of parliament and new elections.
4 The decision of the prime minister to resign because of his inability to hold his coalition together.
5 The decision to establish a different coalition system as when, in 1962–63, it was decided to 'open to the left', bringing the Italian Socialist Party (PSI) into the coalition.
6 The establishment and subsequent resignation of a 'temporary' government (often called a 'summer' government) which had been put into office with the sole purpose of filling the gap between major coalition realignments.

Between each government there is a period of intense negotiations known as a 'government crisis'. The President of the Republic proceeds to a series of consultative rounds with a whole range of politicians. There is a ritualized element: first he consults former Presidents of the Republic, then former prime ministers, then party leaders and other politicians. He can then designate a potential prime minister either because he has reasons to believe that a relatively stable coalition can be formed, or because he hopes that the very fact of designating someone will lead to a resolution of the crisis. In most cases the designation of the prime minister occurs because party leaders have agreed on a particular coalition. In practice, the powers of the president (constitutionally empowered to designate the prime minister) are limited by the decision of party leaders. Thus political parties have a decisive role not only in bringing about the collapse of a government, but also in creating a new one. The new electoral system, far from empowering the president, as some had hoped, is likely to make him (or her, should a woman ever be elected) even less decisive, particularly if two counterpoised left and right blocs face each other – a possible but by no means inevitable result of the new electoral system. Should this scenario be the outcome of the crisis of recent years, then the president would be reduced to the role of a mere figurehead, not dissimilar to that of the British monarch.

In theory, once appointed, it is the prime minister who decides on the make-up of the government, distributing ministerial positions. In practice, the actual composition of the government – that is, not only which parties will be in the coalition but who will get which job – is decided by the leaders of political parties. Party leaders themselves hardly ever sit in the government, but as they make and unmake governments, decide who is to be prime minister and who is to be a minister and as their period of tenure is considerably longer than that of the average prime minister, their power is considerable. Again, this practice is unlikely to change.

The length of a government crisis is very often determined by the length of the negotiations to distribute ministerial jobs and seldom by controversies surrounding the government programme.

There are different formulae for forming a government, as follows:

1   A government can be made up of a coalition of parties all of whom vote for it in parliament and all of whom obtain some cabinet posts. This is the most common type of government.

2   A government can be made up of only one party with the support or abstention of other parties not holding cabinet posts. This is called a *governo monocolore*: there have been fifteen of these between 1945 and 1996.

3   There can be a coalition of parties within the government relying on the support or abstention of other parties in parliament. This is the case with the Prodi government installed in office in 1996. The ministers are drawn from the Olive Tree alliance (the PDS plus the Prodi and Dini lists) but they rely on the abstention or support of *Rifondazione comunista* in the Chamber of Deputies where the alliance does not have a majority.

4   A government of experts and technocrats (those led by Carlo Azeglio Ciampi and Dini in the 1990s) supported a coalition of parties.

In the entire history of the Italian Republic there has never been a case of a government made up of a single party relying exclusively on its own votes in parliament. In 1948 the DC obtained a clear majority in the Chamber of Deputies (though not in the Senate). However, it chose to govern in coalition with other parties because it was aware how impermanent its success was likely to be and realized that it had to avoid being isolated from other potential allies.

The rapid succession of prime ministers has obviously contributed to the erosion of their powers of government-making. The process of ministerial appointments has become a rather precise art in which the electronic calculator eventually played a role. Massimiliano Cencelli, the private secretary of a DC notable, Adolfo Sarti, became famous in the 1970s for having perfected a mathematical system for the distribution of ministerial jobs according to the relative strength of coalition partners and the relative strength of the DC factions (as established at the preceding DC party congress).[2] Within the DC, power depended not so much on the size of the faction, but rather on the preference votes obtained by faction leaders in general elections. There was thus a constant link between elections, governments and ministerial appointments. The proportional system was, in a sense, applied to the distribution of government positions and these in turn depended to a large extent on the preference system. As the preference vote was the main avenue for political promotion, it is not surprising that it constantly increased over the years as DC notables devoted a considerable part of their energies to preserving and increasing their personal vote. Given the clientelist nature of the system, the size of the preference vote depended in turn on the power of patronage wielded by DC notables. This introduced an element of stability: a good preference vote opened the door to a ministerial position which in turn enabled the holder to exercise patronage leading to a further increase in the size of his personal vote. Two Italian political scientists, Mauro Calise and Renato Mannheimer, were able to quantify this process and isolate the variables which enabled a junior minister to become a minister.[3]

The preference vote, when sufficiently high, opened the door to the continuous holding of ministerial power. This, and the fact that the Italian electorate, like most West European electorates, was fairly stable, resulted in great stability and continuity in Italian governments. We are thus faced with a paradox: the Italian political system, if measured in terms of numbers of governments, was the most unstable in Europe; but if the yardstick was the continuity of government personnel it was the most stable.

The most remarkable element of stability derived from the dominance of the DC throughout the post-war period: it was the keystone around which over 50 coalitions were formed for nearly 50 years. No political party in any democratic country in Western Europe and North America has been able to control the chief political position without interruption for such a long time. Continuity of government and political stability can also be calculated in terms of the continuity of government personnel. Calise and Mannheimer examined the percentages of government ministers who were also present in the previous government and discovered that the average rate of stability/continuity between 1946 and 1978 has been 58.6 per cent. This means that, on average, well over half of the ministers of each government were ministers again in the next government.[4]

Government stability under DC hegemony led a number of political scientists to characterize the specificity of the 'Italian case' as one of 'limited democracy' (*democrazia bloccata*), i.e. one in which an alternative government cannot emerge. The communist opposition was excluded from government after 1948 by its lack of international and national legitimacy. Non-communist Italian political parties repeatedly asserted either that the presence of communists in the government would be a threat to Italian democracy or that it would not be acceptable to Italy's international allies (i.e. the USA) or that it would destabilize the political system because powerful political and economic interests would sabotage any coalition which includes the communists. Thus the DC, according to this view, was virtually forced to rule and the only 'alternative' to a DC-led coalition government was another DC-led coalition government. In these circumstances the range of possible coalitions was fairly limited. The following were those which were technically possible:

1   A *coalition of 'national unity'*. This includes the DC, the Italian
    Communist Party (PCI) and the PSI (and, but not necessarily, the other
    smaller parties of the Centre).
2   A *'centrist' coalition*. This is made up of the DC and the other smaller
    parties of the Centre: the Italian Social Democratic Party (PSDI), the
    Italian Republican Party (PRI) and the Italian Liberal Party (PLI).
3   A *centre-left coalition*. This is made up of the DC and the PSI. It will also
    include the PSDI and the PRI and, at times, the PLI (e.g. after 1979).
4   A *centre-right coalition*. This is any DC-led coalition which relies on the
    support of the neo-fascists (MSI).

Of these four coalitions only that of national unity and of the centre-left have always had sufficient parliamentary backing throughout the 1945–94 period. Centrist and centre-right coalitions had a technical majority only until 1976. The elections of that year were an authentic electoral turning-point because they narrowed the options facing the DC to two: national unity and the centre-left.

A left-wing alternative defined as a coalition of communists and socialists in alliance with the Radical Party and the far left group has never been possible. A wider left and centre alternative which would also include the PRI and the PSDI was possible after 1976. The chances of this sort of coalition were always, however, fairly remote.

Until the fall of the First Republic the only coalitions which were both technically (in terms of seats) and politically feasible were those of the centre-left and of national unity. Thus the choice was fairly stark: either the PCI and the DC were in coalition together (thus 'squeezing out' the PSI) or the DC and the PSI were to join forces to exclude the PCI.

The range of possibilities and the actual governments are illustrated in Table 10.1.

As can be seen, between 1945 and 1994, there have been only two periods of coalition governments in which the votes of the neo-fascists have been required: 1957–58 and 1960. These represented an attempt of the right wing of the DC to block the advance towards the formation of a centre-left coalition. The attempt failed. The 1960 Tambroni government which was supported by the neo-fascists had to

Table 10.1 Possible coalition and actual coalition governments, 1946–92

Legislature	Possible coalitions	Actual coalitions
1946–1948 (Constituent Assembly)	NU, CL, C, CR, LA	NU (1947–48)
1948/1953	NU, CL, C, CR	C
1953/1958	NU, CL, C, CR	C, CR (1957–58)
1958/1963	NU, CL, C, CR	C, CR (1960), CL (1960–62)
1963/1968	NU, CL, C, CR	C (1963), CL (1963–68)
1968/1972	NU, CL, C, CR	C (1968 and 1972), CL
1972/1976	NU, CL, C, CR	C, CL
1976/1979	NU, CL, (LA+ small centre parties)	NU, CL (1979)
1979/1983	NU, CL, (LA+ small centre parties)	CL
1983/1992	NU, CL, (LA+ small centre parties)	CL

Notes: NU – National Unity; CL – centre-left; C – centrist; CR – centre-right; LA – left alternative

resign because of a wave of popular discontent it had sparked in a number of Italian cities. After 1976 it could not have a majority in Parliament. The centre-left governments of 1960–62 did not include the PSI. We have called them 'centre-left' in Table 10.1 because they enjoyed the abstention of the PSI and were governments which were meant to pave the way to what was called the 'organic' centre-left, i.e. governments with socialist ministers. Disregarding these specific variables we can therefore describe the succession of Italian coalitions in these terms:

1 *1944–47*: governments of national unity.
2 *1947–62*: centrist governments.
3 *1963–68*: 'organic' centre-left governments.
4 *1968–76*: crisis governments: succession of centrist and centre-left coalitions.
5 *1976–79*: governments of national unity (in reality three years of *monocolore* DC backed by the abstention and then the supporting votes of all other parties including the PCI and excluding the neo-fascists).
6 *1979–92*: centre-left governments (but, unlike those of 1963–68, these have no coherent programmes of reform, they exist simply because, given the difficulty of having a coalition with the PCI, they are the only way in which Italy can have a government).
7 *1992–96*: Crisis of the First Republic. The governments of this period exhibited considerable diversity. If coalition stability was the norm during the preceding 47 years, now the system because unstable. The governments of the period include:
   – a centre-left coalition (the Amato government of July 1992 to June 1993) semi-independent from a largely delegitimized parliament and formed largely by experts untouched by the corruption scandal.

- a technocratic government headed by the former governor of the Bank of Italy, Carlo Azeglio Ciampi, from May 1993 to the April 1994 election and supported by the old ruling parties with the abstention of the PDS and *Lega Nord.*
- a right-of-centre government (May 1994 to December 1994) led by Silvio Berlusconi, the media magnate, who had entered politics a few months before the elections, formed by two relatively new parties (the *Lega Nord* and *Forza Italia*) in coalition with a recycled neo-fascist party, now labelled *Alleanza Nazionale.*
- a second technocratic government (January 1994 to February 1996) led by Lamberto Dini, a former senior Bank of Italy official who had been Minister of Finance in the preceding Berlusconi government. This government was supported by the PDS, the ex-DC *Partito Popolare* and the *Lega Nord* and enjoyed the less consistent and grudging support of *Forza Italia, Alleanza Nazionale* and *Rifondazione Comunista*. It remained in charge until the April 1996 elections.
- a centre-left coalition, also known as the Olive Tree Coalition. This government started life in May 1996 and was led by a Catholic technocrat, Romano Prodi, in alliance with the former communists of the PDS and other smaller groups with the outside support of *Rifondazione Comunista.*

The profound contrast between the first six types of governments (and the three types of coalition – centrist, centre-left and National Unity – experimented) and the seventh highlights the rupture represented by the period 1992–96. Until then, in fact, in spite of the multiplicity of governments and the hegemony of the DC, the vicissitude of Italian coalition formation was not as dissimilar from that of the rest of Western Europe where some form of alternation of parties in government did exist.[5] For example, the governments of national unity of 1944–47 correspond to the various governments with communist participation which ruled France, Belgium and many other countries in the immediate aftermath of the war as well as the Labour government which ruled the UK between 1945 and 1951. From the late 1940s to the early 1960s Italy was ruled by centrist governments which corresponded to the conservative governments of the UK and West Germany in a similar period. The birth of the centre-left coalition (1962–63) corresponds to the victory of the Labour Party in Britain after thirteen years of Conservative rule (1964) and the German grand coalition of the Christian Democratic Union (CDU) and the Social Democrats (SPD) of 1966. The programme of modernization adopted by the centre-left corre- sponds to the modernization plans of the Wilson government of 1964–70, of the SPD in West Germany and De Gaulle in France. The 1970s represent a period of reassessment and crises for most European states characterized, in Italy, as else- where with a shift to the left, irrespective of actual governments, where governments seek the agreements of trade unions on economic policies. In Britain there was a rapid succession of policies: Edward Heath's Conservative attempt to cut down on state intervention (1970–72) followed by incomes policies and confrontation with the trade unions (1972–74), followed by a Labour government committed to a 'social contract' with the trade unions (1974–76), followed by a drastic Labour deflation paving the way for a Conservative victory (1979). In both France and West Germany we have a long period of rule by the same coalition; a social demo-cratic one in West Germany and a conservative one in France, but in both cases by the end of the decade these governments were in difficulty and had to surrender power in the course of the early 1980s. During the 1980s the dominance in gov-ernment of Bettino Craxi (five years prime minister) coincides with the revival of socialist fortunes in much of southern Europe (Felipe González in Spain, Andreas Papandreou in Greece and François Mitterrand in France).

In practice these political cycles correspond to specific economic cycles: the period of immediate post-war reconstruction, the long period of economic growth (to the mid-1960s) leading to attempted modernization, further interventionism and development of welfare policies in the 1960s and the 1970s, neo-corporate policies in the 1970s, onslaught of neo-liberal economic policies in the 1980s.

How each country coped with the transition from one cycle to the next has obviously been determined by a complex interaction of traditions, institutions and external constraints. Changes in policies are always necessary to cope with changed circumstances, but changes in policies do not always require changes in govern-ments. Given the *de facto* exclusion of the PCI from political power, Italy had to resort to changes in the type of coalition government, changes which, in turn, were subjected to the constraint of DC dominance. The changes in governments within each coalition phase corresponded very often to no more than government re-shuffles. The establishment of political parameters which assigned to the PCI the role of permanent opposition and to the DC the role of permanent ruling party were a far more significant and important phenomenon than the succession of 50-odd governments. Seen in this light the main special feature of the Italian government system until 1992 was its extraordinary stability.

The volatility exhibited since then is unlikely to bring about a volatility in pol-icies. By the 1990s the West European economies have become so interdependent and the process of political and economic integration has accelerated so much (the formation of the Single Market and the Maastricht Treaty) that Italian governments of the centre-left or of the centre-right are unlikely to differ substantially. Italians may have obtained the effective pleasure of being able to vote out of office a set of politicians and replace them by another, but they have not achieved a genuine choice between radically different political platforms. This situation would be quite familiar to the electorate of most other West European states.

Endnotes

1 I have generously included in the length of governments the period in office of a prime minister while a successor is being found. See also Battegazzore 1987 who, less gen-erously discounts the 'in-between-crisis', which in many instances lasted over one month.

2 Venditti 1981.
3 Calise and Mannheimer 1982.
4 Calise and Mannheimer 1979, p. 60.
5 The idea of a comparison of 'political cycles' in Europe has been suggested by Somaini 1979, pp. 174–7.

Chapter 11

Parliament

In parliamentary democracies based on the two-party system it is often the case that the powers of parliament are seriously limited by the ability of the government of the day to use its majority to set the agenda of debates and to enact legislation. In a multi-party system – such as the Italian one – there is no pre-given majority. A majority must be constructed by negotiations between the parties. The new electoral system does not necessarily bring about this state of affairs. It would be perfectly possible for an alliance of parties to enter into an electoral agreement without also agreeing to form a coalition. This is what happened in 1994 when *Forza Italia* entered into an agreement in the South with *Alleanza Nazionale* and in the North with the Northern League. It was not inevitable that a coalition between these three parties would emerge. Indeed, it took over a month of negotiations to bring this into being and it did not last long. The situation had altered in 1996 when both the right-wing bloc (*Forza Italia* and *Alleanza Nazionale*) and the centre-left one (the Olive Tree coalition) presented a programme of government. For the first time the electorate was formally offered a choice between two distinct programmes. Nevertheless, because the winning side, the Olive Tree, did not have a majority in the Chamber of Deputies, some negotiations with *Rifondazione Comunista* (which had an electoral pact with the Olive Tree but not a coalition agreement) was inevitable.

In the United Kingdom a majority is 'constructed', i.e. is determined by the workings of a particular electoral system, the existence of particular cleavages in the electorate, the geographical distribution of these cleavages and the internal cohesion of the parliamentary groups. In most British elections since the inter-war period the electoral system has produced a governmental majority. In Italy the effect of pre-1994 elections was to produce not a majority but rather a particular distribution of forces within parliament. The construction of a majority occurred after an election. This is not a necessary effect of the electoral system, just as the creation of a pre-given majority is not a necessary effect of the British system. In the Italian case – even under the old system – it would have been perfectly possible to imagine a coalition of parties entering into a pre-electoral agreement around a given programme. This, however, has never happened, and one of the consequences of this has been the succession of governments described in Chapter 10. It does not follow, however, that Italian electors never knew what sort of coalition would emerge. In 1963 and 1968 the electorate was perfectly aware that a centre-left coalition led by the DC and the PSI would be formed. The same was true in 1979, 1983, 1987 and 1992.

The existence of weak and unstable governments might suggest that the real powers of parliament was much greater in Italy than in the UK (at least under the informal rules of the First Republic) and that deputies and senators were able to exercise considerable power as governments attempted to mediate and aggregate interests on the floor of the two assemblies. In fact this work of mediation and interest aggregation was not conducted in this way. The real protagonists of the construction of majorities were the political parties, particularly those which were 'legitimized' to form a coalition government. The legitimation of parties was only in part due to the electorate. This had given the Italian Communist Party (PCI) up to one-third of the vote in parliamentary elections and has never given the Italian Social Democratic Party (PSDI) more than 7.2 per cent of the vote. Yet the PCI never held government seats after 1947, while the PSDI was part of the ruling coalition virtually uninterruptedly throughout its existence. The main source of legitimation therefore was not the electorate as such, but rather the ruling Christian Democratic Party (DC). It is this party which, until the early 1960s, had defined the centrist parties as being the sole legitimate parties, exclusive tenants – with the DC – of the so-called 'democratic area'. The 'opening to the left' and the creation of the centre-left government was defined by the DC as the 'enlargement of the democratic area', so as to include the Italian Socialist Party (PSI) in the coalition. After the 1976 elections the DC was forced to ask the PCI to abstain in parliament. This was the result of the PCI's electoral gain, and the PSI's refusal to support the DC government should the PCI oppose it. The DC, however, was still able to define the limits of PCI involvement in policy-making: there could be no question of the PCI becoming a member of the government. The PCI accepted this, i.e. accepted that it was not yet legitimized to enter the government.

If we were to put in a nutshell the essential differences between the British and the Italian systems in so far as parliamentary decision-making powers are concerned, we would say that while in the UK the powers of parliament have been taken over by the Cabinet (and perhaps by the prime minister), in Italy these powers are firmly in the hands of the leadership of the 'legitimized' political parties. This position has not been changed by the new system. Formally, of course, the British parliament is completely sovereign as it is not even hampered by a written Constitution. At the formal level, however, the Italian parliament, too, has considerable powers. Unlike the USA the government cannot veto bills. Unlike the UK the government does not decide on the parliamentary agenda. The government cannot impose a 'guillotine' motion to curtail obstructionism. Members of the Italian assemblies can use a secret ballot and thus can escape party discipline; they can also initiate any legislation except budgetary laws. Government bills do not have priority (as in the UK). Unlike the American president, the prime minister or the President of the Republic are not directly elected by the people. The government depends on a majority in both assemblies. The President of the Republic is elected by both houses in joint sessions. Both houses also elect one-third of the members of the Constitutional Court.

All these are, however, formal powers. In practice – as in many other countries – there are numerous important centres of political power: political parties, the civil service, the trade unions and the private and public sectors of the economy and various pressure groups. Parliament has then served as the place where the political parties establish their ideological differences.[1] Legislation often tended to concentrate on the protection of relatively small corporate interests through so-called 'mini-laws' or *leggine*, i.e. laws devised specifically for the protection of small groups.

Before 1971 the presidents of the two assemblies had considerable powers. They could determine the agenda of their respective chambers, they could assign bills to the standing committees and decide whether a bill could be enacted by a committee or whether final approval should be referred to the assemblies. In turn the presidents of the standing committees also had considerable powers and could even decide whether a bill could be 'killed' in committee thus preventing legislation. Up to 1968 most presidents of the Chamber and of the Senate were members of the DC. The DC had also the lion's share of the presidencies of the standing committees. These, however, had limited powers. They could not, for example, subpoena officials of the state bureaucracy or employees of state agencies.[2] These limitations were not very important as long as the DC controlled the standing committees as well as the civil service and the state agencies.

In 1971, as a direct consequence of the weakness of the governing coalition after the crisis of the centre-left coalition, the rules were changed. The powers of the presidents of the assemblies to set the agenda were transferred to the 'standing conference of the leaders of the parliamentary groups' (including the leader of the PCI group). These *capigruppo* would meet and decide unanimously the agenda for the subsequent three months. Furthermore, it was decided that parliament could set up its own investigative committee and could subpoena state officials.[3] The decrease in the powers of the presidents of the Senate and of the Chamber of Deputies made it easier for the PCI to obtain the presidency of the Chamber in 1976–79 (after the biggest pro-communist swing in post-war elections) and again after the 1979 and 1983 elections. Furthermore, during the 1976–79 legislature when the PCI was in the parliamentary majority (though not in the government), the communists were able to obtain the presidencies of many important standing committees.

The 1971 changes in parliamentary procedure did not signal a transfer of power from the DC to parliament, but rather a fairer distribution of power among the political parties, with the lion's share still firmly in the hands of the DC, a practice which was later criticized as *consocialismo* but which is common to the rest of Europe. This confirms that it is in fact unusual for parliament to have much power in a modern 'parliamentary' democracy. In the first place, there are other major centres of power. In the second place, parliamentary power depends on the weakness of political parties and on that of the executive branch of government. Most European countries have very strong executives (e.g. the UK and France) that can discipline their parliamentary groups *and* strong political parties. It is virtually impossible to achieve political success without being associated with a political party. The USA which has a very loose party discipline in Congress has a strong executive: the president. Italy has a weak executive but very entrenched political parties. Thus what is peculiar about the Italian system is not the lack of effective parliamentary power, but the fact that this power is concentrated in political parties and, until 1992 in one party – the DC, which has always been able to maintain its hegemony. The changes in parliamentary procedure of 1971 were an expression of the weakening of this hegemony and at the same time of the inability of the Italian political system as it was then constituted to express an alternative to this hegemony.

At the beginning of this chapter we suggested that the construction of a parliamentary majority is a task which is entrusted to the potential partners of a coalition government and that the central role was in the hands of the DC. The DC, however, was never a monolithic bloc. Taken as a whole it was undoubtedly a strong political party, but in order to be 'taken as a whole' it had first to become a 'whole'. Its own unity had to be achieved and maintained at the same time as it established alliances. Its leadership was itself the product of intense negotiations and had to accept as more or less 'given' its own internal distribution of power. This was determined, in the final analysis, by the electorate through the preference vote. The basis of the power of the DC was democracy itself. It follows that if anyone at all was to be blamed for the hegemony of the DC it was the Italian voter, or, rather, a majority of them which achieved this feat by voting for the DC and its allies. They too have to be blamed for the kind of politicians sent to parliament for the DC was not the final arbiter in deciding who will be elected.

In the PCI, parliamentary work was simply a task given to leading party members or activists. This was so – at least partly – because the communist electorate could be relied to use its preference vote according to the wishes of the local and national leadership. Maurizio Cotta's research on Italian members of parliament for the period 1946–72 provides evidence for the different approaches of the PCI and the DC to the selection of the parliamentary élites.[4]

The first feature of the post-war Italian parliament which emerged is that it had little continuity with its predecessor, the last pre-fascist parliament. Only 15 per cent of those elected in the Constituent Assembly in 1946 had previously been MPs.[5] This percentage drops to 3 per cent for the parliament elected in 1948. Thus an entirely new generation of politicians emerged after the war. Comparing the turnover of parliamentarians in subsequent Italian Parliaments with the turnover in the British House of Commons, the US House of Representatives, the German Bundestag and the Austrian Nationalrat, Cotta was able to establish that Italian turnover was consistently higher: each new parliament between 1946 and 1972 consisted of at least one-third newly elected members. This figure was mainly due to the extremely high turnover of PCI deputies and senators, because the percentage of newly elected DC parliamentarians was similar to that of other countries.[6] The chief reason for this was that DC parliamentarians left parliamentary life either because of electoral defeat or because they retired or died, while communist parliamentarians were not re-elected simply because they were not reselected by their own party.[7] This was programmed by the PCI leadership. In general only the party leaders and some of the experts were regularly reselected. Other parties' deputies and senators usually last for no more than the life of two parliaments.

To become a senator or a deputy was for many communist cadres no more than one of the many aspects of party work; for some it was the prelude to retirement. A long period of parliamentary activity was not, for a communist, the necessary prerequisite for a political career. The leader of the PCI, Enrico Berlinguer, became a member of the Central Committee in 1945, a member of the Executive Committee in 1948, leader of the PCI youth organization in 1949, member of the PCI Secretariat in 1958, in charge of party organization in 1960 but entered parliament for the first time only in 1968. A year later he was elected deputy leader of the party and in 1972 became party leader until his untimely death in 1984. Thus his advancement in the party did not depend on a long parliamentary career, and when he became party leader he had but a limited parliamentary experience. For the communist MP the party remained the main focus of his/her loyalty, whereas Christian Democrats had the parliamentary group, the government, the party, the faction they belong to, a particular leader, local and/or national interest groups.[8] Research has shown that communist MPs gave far more importance to party cohesiveness than did DC MPs, that they were far less likely to introduce bills without party approval and that they tended to use information which came from their own party to a greater extent than did Christian Democratic MPs.[9] In other words, they behaved more like British MPs than did Christian Democrats. As the PCI jettisoned more and more features of its Leninist past, the communist parliamentary group acquired greater independence from the party. Once the PCI turned itself into the PDS, the principles of democratic centralism were abandoned altogether.

What did communist MPs do in parliament? As the PCI had been forced into the role of permanent opposition it could be expected that its sphere of action would be rather limited and that it would use the parliamentary platform essentially to express its ideological differences with the DC. On the whole this had never been the case. In a parliamentary system in which the opposition could always hope to become government (as in the UK) it followed the principle that 'the duty of the opposition is to oppose' in order to demarcate itself in the sharpest possible manner from the government and offer the electorate a clearcut choice (even though its actual behaviour in government may not be so dramatically different from that of its opponents). In Italy, however, the communist opposition needed to gain legitimacy and be able to modify and amend legislation to establish that a vote for the PCI is not wasted. The important role standing committees played also enabled the PCI to use the floor of the Houses of Parliament to make the more general ideological and political points while in standing committees it participated fully in legislative decision-making. A sample survey of 326 laws (out of a total of 7,781) passed between 1948 and 1968 shows that a very large proportion of laws (over 80 per cent) were passed in committees and not by the whole House.[10] Hence three-quarters of all legislation in the twenty years after 1948 was passed with the approval of the PCI.[11] In the period 1968–72 when the centre-left coalition was in shreds the PCI was able to contribute decisively to major pieces of legislation.

These were the reform of the penal and civil codes, the law instituting divorce, the so-called Workers' Charter on trade union and individual workers' rights, a new family law, the establishment of the regional system, reforms of the education, health and fiscal systems, as well as the 1971 parliamentary code.[12]

Thus even though the distance between the political traditions of the DC and the PCI may appear to be vast, the actual functioning of the Italian parliament was far less conflict-orientated than that of the British House of Commons. Even though one party has always had a relative majority, it has had to negotiate not only with its potential partners but also with the opposition while maintaining its unity.

The crucial question which was (and still is) at the centre of many political debates in Italy throughout the 1970s was whether the weakness of the executive was due largely to the strength of parliament or, rather, of the parties in parliament. The PSI, in particular, insisted that the most important reason why it was so difficult to govern Italy was that the executive was too weak. The government was faced with massive problems: it had to attempt to resolve some of the basic economic contradictions of Italian development while facing the constant pressures that interest groups were able to advance. Political parties used parliament to satisfy the corporate, localistic and selfish interests of these groups. Politics became a market where votes were swopped for pieces of legislation. In these circumstances no government could offer a coherent programme. The PSI saw parliament as an arena where interest groups could find satisfaction for their demands. Demands, however, increased at a much faster rate than political and economic resources. Thus the Italian political system suffered from an excess of demands: it was 'overloaded'. Only a strong executive with greater legitimacy – the PSI believed – could tackle the situation. Throughout the 1980s the PSI made suggestions on ways to strengthen the executive, for example, by abolishing secrecy in parliamentary votes of no confidence to force the rather undisciplined MPs of the DC either to bring down a government openly or suffer the political consequences for their action, or to support it even when legislation threatens some of their favoured interest groups. When Craxi became prime minister he became a convert to the idea of directly electing the the President of the Republic or the prime minister.[13] The only significant reform was a fast track system which enabled some government legislation to obtain priority (something quite normal in the UK but unusual in Italy). Craxi and his successors also used government decrees with increasing vigour and secrecy in parliamentary voting was also abolished in most cases.[14]

The DC, too, as explained in Chapter 9, sought to strengthen the executive and accepts the PSI's view that Italy's chief problem is one of 'governability'.

Both the DC and PSI seem to want to insulate the executive from parliament as much as possible, the DC by giving the executive more electoral legitimacy, the PSI by giving it more decision-making powers. In both cases, however, the powers of party leaders increase at the expense of individual MPs. The reforms advocated by the DC and the PSI seem to be aimed essentially at resolving their internal problems of discipline.

The PCI had few problems of discipline. Its MPs accepted the decisions of their groups and voted in a fairly united fashion as MPs did in the British parliament (where, however, there is no secret ballot) and the lack of discipline of other parties worked to its advantage. It is therefore little wonder that it promoted the idea of parliamentary power. This is connected to the fact that, as long as it kept the label of communist, it was unlikely to achieve government power. In the 1990s, after it had become the far more acceptable PDS, it too sought to increase the power of the executive though it always balked at the idea of directly electing the president or the prime minister. By 1995–96 the PDS was prepared to discuss the issue. It is quite possible that, in a situation in which alternation is possible, the last principled objections will be dropped. When it was excluded from power the PCI did not accept that the country's basic problems could be reduced to the apparently technical question of 'governability'. In any case governability is not a technical problem. Governments and parliaments find it increasingly difficult to rule in virtually all other countries in Western Europe – irrespective of their differing constitutional arrangements. They are subjected to the constraints of an increased dependence on the international economy, are faced by the ever-growing complexity of their societies and the rise of new cleavages and by the growth of bureaucracy and pressure groups. Furthermore, new technologies in surveillance and social control and the increase in political violence have increased the powers of the military and police establishment, powers which are seldom subjected to public scrutiny and accountability and which, in some cases, cannot be made public precisely because they depend on secrecy for their efficacy. The PCI, however, pointed out that the question of institutional reforms could not be reduced to a question of the relations between parliament and government, but that it was fundamentally a question of political power. It maintained that the reason why decision-making was more difficult in Italy than in other West European countries was that only in Italy the opposition could not become government. The permanent majority party, its factions and its allies have colonized the bureaucracy, the media and the public sector of the economy.[15]

The PCI accused the other political parties of having usurped the functions of parliament by carving up among each other control over the apparatuses of the state. Far from having too much power, parliament had virtually no control over who really made economic policy, who controlled the military and police establishment and the information system. Thus, in the past, all communist institutional proposals were aimed at strengthening the powers of parliament by cutting down on the number of government decrees, increasing parliamentary control and the coordination between parliament and the regions.[16] The PCI did not deny that the executive had to be strengthened, but sought to achieve this by enabling the prime minister to form his/her own cabinet (as the Constitution requires) rather than allowing the task of Cabinet formation to be monopolized by the leadership of the coalition parties.

The PCI as well as many socialists also wanted to abolish the Senate. Giuliano Amato, when he was an academic and not a politician, pointed out that the Italian two-chamber system is virtually unique in the world because both chambers have identical powers and have the same kind of representation.[17] A communist political scientist, Giuseppe Cotturri, pointed out that greater efficiency could not be the only reason for abolishing the Senate: the incessant negotiations which occurred between the Chamber and the Senate over every piece of legislation worked to the advantage of the DC. The time it took for a bill to go from one chamber to the other enabled the DC to make deals between its various factions and lobbies. He pointed out that the number of DC amendments to DC legislation always tended to be much higher than that of the PCI. Legislation was thus a process which occurred 'within' the DC, enabling it to achieve and maintain its unity.[18]

In the post-1994 situation, the reform of parliament appears to be used as a smokescreen to hide other, more important, non-institutional reforms. The most important of these would be the creation of greater clarity in the party system and, above all, the establishment of clear-cut alternatives. This cannot be achieved by purely institutional means but by the parties themselves. Parties which obtain representation in parliament only because they are able to enter into electoral pacts with others will always, inevitably, complicate the legislative process. Parties which depend on the personalities or charisma of those who lead them are, equally inevitably, a source of chronic instability.

Yet parties are universally regarded as the chief culprits as are professional politicians. Disregard for parliament and for professional politicians has led to the selection of a new personnel on the basis of their achievements in other spheres of life. It is now commonplace to select candidates (especially in local elections) on this basis and not on their probable competence as politicians. The local doctor has a much greater chance of being elected mayor than the local party leader. The five prime ministers of the 1992–96 period came to politics rather late in life: Giuliano Amato was a university professor, Carlo Azeglio Ciampi was a banker as was Lamberto Dini, Silvio Berlusconi a media tycoon and Romano Prodi a professor of economics and chairman of the IRI, the state public company.

In the 1970s the referendum was a procedure where the population was consulted on major questions such as divorce and abortion. By 1995 it had been transformed into an instrument where the population is consulted not just on electoral reform, but even on relatively minor matters such as whether shopkeepers could trade on Sundays or whether films broadcast on TV could be interrupted by advertising.

To some extent the delegitimation of parliament was a phenomenon which was taking place before the *Tangentopoli* scandal. The scandal appeared to validate the popular view of politicians as corrupt and unreliable. That many were corrupt and unreliable has been established in Italian courts but the lack of parliamentary legitimacy and the growth of an 'extra-parliamentary' mentality is even more dangerous for a democratic system. This mentality is far more evident on the right than on the left of the political spectrum and is manifested in the belief that a 'majoritarian' electoral system means not just that the winner 'takes all' in the single constituencies but that the winner takes all everywhere. Thus when Berlusconi became prime minister he used his majority to grant members of the ruling coalition the presidency of all the parliamentary commissions, the chairmanship of both chambers and appointed both of Italy's commissioners to the European Community (in this instance the practice pre-dated Berlusconi).

The Prodi government did not follow this procedure, conscious, presumably, that the preservation of the rights of the minority is, in the long term, in the interest of all.

Endnotes

1 Cazzola 1972, p. 80.
2 Leonardi et al. 1978, p. 165.
3 Ibid., pp. 167–9.
4 Cotta 1976. Cotta uses his data for other purposes, namely to demonstrate that the PCI has not accepted the basic principles of parliamentary practice, i.e. principles arbitrarily constructed by Cotta himself.
5 Ibid., p. 80.
6 Ibid., p. 82.
7 Ibid., pp. 84–94.
8 Leonardi et al. 1978, p. 177.
9 Ibid., pp. 174–6.
10 Cazzola 1972, p. 80.
11 Ibid., pp. 84–5.
12 Di Palma 1979, vol. 2, p. 404.
13 A view proposed by his erstwhile supporter Giuliano Amato, see Amato 1980, pp. 186ff.
14 Calise 1994, pp. 86–7.
15 Centro per la Riforma dello Stato 1983, pp. 170–1.
16 Ibid., pp. 173–5.
17 Amato 1980, pp. 182–3.
18 Cotturri 1982a, pp. 11–12.

Chapter 12

The Constitution

The Constituent Assembly which drafted the Italian Constitution was elected on
2 June 1946. On the same day a national referendum was held to decide whether
Italy was to be a monarchy or a republic. The victory of the republican cause meant
that the first words of the Constitution ('Italy is a democratic republic') had been
enshrined by means of direct democracy rather than by the decisions of a representative assembly. The Constituent Assembly designated 75 of its members to form
a committee which presented a draft at the end of January 1947 which was discussed between March and December of that year. The Constitution took effect on
1 January 1948. It was signed by the provisional President of the Republic, a liberal representative of the pre-fascist political elite, Enrico De Nicola, the Christian
Democratic (DC) leader and Prime Minister, Alcide De Gasperi, and the communist President of the Constituent Assembly (who had spent most of the inter-war
years as a political prisoner) Umberto Terracini. The three signatories symbolized
the compromise between liberalism, socialism and political Catholicism which the
Constitution embodied.

By the standards of Italian parliamentary proceedings, or indeed by any standards,
the drafting and approval of the Constitution was a speedy affair. Yet the works of
the Constituent Assembly took place in a rapidly changing political climate. When
it first met, in June 1946, the Cold War had not yet begun and the Italian Communist Party (PCI) was still in the government. By the time the Constitution was
approved the left had been expelled from the government and Europe was divided
into two spheres of influence. Inevitably, the political situation had an influence on
the proceedings, but the government did not try to prejudice the debates directly
and did not use ongoing political controversies as a bargaining tool in the Constituent Assembly.[1]

The Constitution was approved by 453 votes against 62. The three main parties,
the DC, the PCI and the Italian Socialist Party (PSI) (including the social democrats
which by then had split away from the PSI) voted in favour. Only the extreme right
voted against. The fact that the Italian communists had taken an active part in the
proceedings, had initiated or approved most of the main articles and had had one
of their most distinguished leaders as president of the Constituent Assembly gave

them considerable constitutional legitimacy. Henceforth it would be difficult to maintain – though many have done so – that the PCI was a straightforward 'anti-system' party since it helped to create and systematically defended the charter which gave institutional form to the Italian state. In the years that followed the PCI was, in words and deeds, an upholder of the Italian Constitution. It will not be difficult to understand why, once we have examined the fundamental features of this document.

The role of the working class

The first article of the Constitution gave a particular role to the working class: 'Italy is a democratic republic founded on labour. Sovereignty belongs to the people, who exercise it within the forms and limits of the Constitution.' Lelio Basso (PSI) and Giorgio Amendola (PCI) had wanted the wording 'Italy is a workers' republic', but the majority felt that this would appear to give a position of superiority to a particular class (even though Basso and Amendola denied that this was their intention). It was, however, accepted that it was important to give recognition to human labour as a fundamental value of the Italian state. The 'workers' republic' option was rejected by only twelve votes and Fanfani's wording prevailed: 'a democratic republic founded on labour'.[2]

Non-Marxist constitutional lawyers, such as Massimo Severo Giannini and Costantino Mortati (the latter a member of the Constituent Assembly), have maintained that the insertion of this article signalled the acceptance within the Constitution of the Marxist principle of the emancipation of the proletariat.[3] On the other hand, leftist critics of the Constitution such as Antonio Negri postulated that the first paragraph sought to protect productive labour, i.e. exploited labour thus subsuming all values to those of production and capitalist organization.[4]

A special recognition of the working class appears elsewhere. Article 4 enshrines a 'right to work' in the Constitution, which at the time was widely considered to entail a demand for full employment.[5] It is an example of the way the Constitution dealt not only with an existing state of affairs but also with a desirable one, a future society which was still to come. In 1965 the Constitutional Court decided that Article 4 meant that it was the duty of the state to increase jobs and that no one could interfere in the people's choice of work or how they went about performing it. This gave rise to interpretations asserting the rights of strike-breakers.[6] The right to strike is enshrined in Article 40 even though the same article specifies that it must be exercised 'within the sphere of laws which regulate it'. The DC had argued that civil servants should not have the right to strike while the PCI trade-union leader Di Vittorio insisted that there should be no legal restriction. The compromise reached established a right, but refused to make it an absolute one.[7]

Article 46, which has been read by some as establishing a right for industrial democracy and workers' control,[8] and by others as establishing the principle of class collaboration, is another instance of ambiguous compromise. It states: 'With a view to the economic and social advancement of labour and in harmony with the needs of production, the Republic recognizes the right of workers to collaborate, in ways and within limits established by law, in the management of enterprises.' This article was in part inspired by the experience of the workers' councils which had taken over the management of many Italian factories immediately after the war. The legal owners, many of whom had collaborated with the fascist regime, gradually returned to exercise control, but in 1946 the situation was still fluid. A communist proposal stated simply that the article should read: 'The workers have the right to participate in the management of the enterprise.' The DC was split because its left wing (especially Fanfani) agreed with the PCI. The drafting committee accepted a wording which retained the expression 'participation' (October 1946), but on 12 May 1947 the tripartite coalition government fell and the left was expelled from the government. The following day the Constituent Assembly had to vote on the article. To save its substance the left wing of the DC accepted the word 'collaboration' instead of 'participation'. The communist trade union leader Di Vittorio accepted, while explaining that for him 'collaboration' means 'active participation.[9]

Clearly the Constitution, like any other, offered ample scope for conflicting interpretations. The clauses discussed here show that this is a document which, though ambiguous, was open to a 'pro-working class interpretation' particularly when one looks, as it is legitimate to do in Italian legal practice, to the 'intentions of the legislators'.

The radical nature of the Italian Constitution was particularly enhanced by Article 3, one of the most controversial. This article had two sections. The first paragraph was a declaration of formal equality for all: 'All citizens have equal social dignity and are equal before the law, without distinction of sex, of race, of language, of religion, of political opinion, of personal and social condition.' The second paragraph read: 'It is the task of the Republic to remove the obstacles of an economic and social nature which, limiting in fact the liberty and equality of citizens, prevent the full development of the human personality and the effective participation by all workers in the political, economic and social organization of the country.'

The first paragraph represented the classical 'liberal' position: everyone is equal before the law, no one must be discriminated against. The second aspect enlarges and, according to some, even negates the first: people are not in fact equal; there are obstacles to their being equal; these obstacles are of a social and economic nature; the new republican state is not indifferent to this; it neither accepts that these inequalities are inevitable or natural nor does it assume that they will wither away on their own; it must actively intervene to eliminate these social and economic obstacles. Umberto Romagnoli has gone as far as saying that the intention of Article 3, paragraph 2, was to reject the existing social order and the model of formal equality in favour of 'real' equality.[10] Others warn that the wording and intentions of Article 3, paragraph 2, were also open to a reformist interpretation: the second paragraph does not say that a new social order should be created, it merely says that there are still some inequalities and that these should be removed. An enlightened upholder of capitalism would readily agree that capitalism has an 'unacceptable face' which can and should be eliminated.[11]

There is strong evidence that the 'intentions of the legislators' were radical. Piero Calamandrei, a noted jurist and veteran anti-fascist who was neither a socialist nor a revolutionary, had no doubt as to the revolutionary nature of Article 3 when he declared in the Constituent Assembly on 4 March 1947, that this was 'the prelude, the introduction, the announcement of a revolution, in the juridical and legal sense, which has yet to come'. The author of the second paragraph was Lelio Basso, a socialist leader who represented the most radical wing of the non-communist socialist tradition in Italy. Basso wrote: 'The reason why I was keen to insert this article is precisely that it negates all the statements in the Constitution which assume as existing that which is yet to come (democracy, equality, etc.)'.[12]

Article 3 constitutes one of the most visible instances of the departure from a strict observance of the principles of classical liberalism. It is by no means the only one. Liberal principles are modified or 'enriched' even in Article 2 which was, at first sight, an orthodox declaration of human rights because it began with the words: 'The Republic recognizes and guarantees the inviolable rights of man', but it then continues 'whether as an individual *or in associations* through which his personality develops' (my emphasis). The Republic is not a mere conglomeration of individual citizens whose political participation is embodied in individual acts such as the vote. The individual has rights not only as an individual but also as a member of an association. Here there was a clear convergence between the PCI and the DC, even though their ideological starting point was quite different. The PCI was worried that a mere declaration of individual rights could be used to block social and economic reforms. The DC wanted to limit the powers of the state by enhancing not only individual rights but also those of voluntary associations.[13] The attempt to give constitutional force to collective rights as well as individual rights is another illustration of the ideological strength of the non-liberal and anti-individualist traditions in the Constituent Assembly, 75 per cent of which was made up of Catholics and Marxists.

Private property

To counterbalance the collective rights for independent working-class action there were guarantees for property-owners. The nature of the constitutional compromise which protected private property was explained by the communist leader, Togliatti, when the communists abstained on a socialist proposal to give constitutional protection only to some forms of private property, namely cooperatives and small firms. Togliatti argued that the Italian Constitution should not be a socialist one, that it should lead to a state in which different forms of property would coexist and that the struggle ahead should not be directed against private property in general but only against monopolies and vast concentrations of wealth and power. The protection of private property was eventually upheld by Articles 41 and 42. Article 41 establishes that 'private economic initiative is free', with the limiting clause that it should not develop 'in conflict with social utility or in such a manner as to damage security, liberty and human dignity'. The article went on to specify that legislation could try to coordinate the public and private sectors of the economy towards social ends, thus giving constitutional legitimacy to economic planning. Article 42 recognized private property as well as state property or other forms of collective property such as cooperatives. It also gave constitutional validity to nationalization by asserting that 'private property may be expropriated with compensation for reasons of general interest'.

Therefore the property rights and the principles of free enterprise were not absolute and 'inviolable', as were human rights in Article 2, and were not even enshrined in the 'Fundamental principles' of the Constitution.[14]

Democracy

The election of representatives to a national assembly was only one of the forms in which popular sovereignty is exercised.

Article 75 specified a non-representative form, or direct form, in which popular sovereignty could be exercised: a referendum. This could be held if 500,000 citizens (or five regional councils) signed a petition. However, a referendum could not legislate. It could only repeal, partially or totally, a piece of legislation (except international treaties, taxation or budgetary laws and laws dealing with amnesty). In practice such instrument was not used until 1974 (the referendum on divorce). As we have seen in the preceding chapters, it was used increasingly not only for major reforms (abortion, electoral systems) but even for relatively secondary issues, such as shopping hours or whether films shown on TV could be interrupted by advertising. The final section of Article 75 required Parliament to determine the procedures for a referendum, but this was not done until a law was finally passed in 1970.

The other main form in which sovereignty is exercised is through political parties as established in Article 49: 'All citizens have the right to associate freely in political parties in order to compete by democratic methods to determine national policy.' The Constitution thus designated political parties as legal entities (a similar clause was rejected by the French Constituent Assembly in the same period), even though it refrained from establishing any form of legal control over them. This was done successively, for instance with laws on the funding of political parties.

Popular sovereignty was not unlimited. In the first place it could only be exercised according to the 'democratic method' meaning 'without recourse to violence or the threat of violence' (i.e. the interpretation of the Constitutional Court, July 1967).[15] Secondly, Article 139 stated: 'The republican form is not subject to constitutional amendment.' Thus there is no constitutional way in which the people or its elected representatives could abolish the republic. Thirdly, Article XII of the section on transitional and final arrangements states: 'The reorganization under any form whatsoever of the dissolved Fascist Party is prohibited.' This article symbolized both the anti-fascist unity which prevailed in the Constituent Assembly and the desire to give the Constitution a clearly anti-fascist character. Its value was more symbolic than practical. There was never a clear-cut way of banning a fascist or quasi-fascist party as long as it avoided an overt use of fascist symbols or ideology as the Italian Social Movement (MSI), the obvious candidate for the title of 'reconstructed fascist party', was always careful to do.

Finally, the Constitution attempted to establish alongside parliament other forms of representative democracy in order to devolve political power.

Article 5 required the widest administrative decentralization in the services which depend on the state. Having established this general principle the Constitution offered a detailed series of rules on local government: Article 114–33. Article 5 and the rules on local government were important because they sought to break the centralist tradition of the Italian state, a tradition which had been established after the *Risorgimento* and which had been most stringently enforced by Italian governments at the end of the nineteenth century and by the fascist regime. The most explicit exponents of the principle of decentralization were the Christian Democrats. In the first place they did not identify with the principles of the *Risorgimento*. In their view this had been led by anti-clerical forces who had forced the unity of Italy on the Roman Catholic Church and had disregarded the religious feelings of the population. Secondly, the main preoccupation of the DC in the Constituent Assembly was to promote the development of as many as possible intermediate layers between the state and the individual.[16] They did not seek simply to protect the individual against the state but to promote collective organizations within civil society and to protect these against the state. This aim coincided in part with that of the PCI, who sought the maximum guarantees for organizations such as political parties and trade unions. Finally, the promotion of local government had a long history in the Catholic movement. In the 'Catholic-rural' conception of Luigi Sturzo, founder of the *Partito Popolare* (the first fully-fledged Catholic party in Italy, established in 1919 and suppressed in the 1920s), local government would promote local rights particularly in the countryside.[17]

This regionalist and decentralizing tradition was foreign to Italian communism as it emerged from the war. The communists had sought to present themselves as the authentic heirs of the *Risorgimento* whose principles they alleged, had been 'betrayed' by the bourgeoisie. The socialists adopted the same standpoint. Both PCI and PSI were thus reluctant to follow the DC in the direction of decentralization. The DC wanted to give the regions legislative powers in matters defined by the Constitution. The PCI and the PSI wanted to give them only regulatory powers defined by ordinary legislation (i.e. without a constitutional entrenchment). Eventually the PCI accepted the position of the DC and the principle of devolution of power to the regions, but fought tooth and nail against any attempts to transform Italy into a federal state. Consequently it voted in favour of the regions, leaving only the traditional right to oppose them.

One of the paradoxes of post-war Italian history is that the DC, a pro-regionalist party but in full control of the state after 1948, did not implement the articles of the Constitution which dealt with the regions until the late 1960s. Until 1970 only five regions had been formed: namely those which the Constitution had given a special status, i.e. by giving them more powers than the remaining fifteen 'ordinary status regions'. These five regions had all special characteristics: either a deep-rooted tradition of autonomy and resistance to excessive centralization as in the case of Sardinia and Sicily, or the presence of linguistic minorities, the Slovenes in the Friuli-Venezia-Giulia region, the French in the Val d'Aosta and the Germans in the Trentino-Alto Adige region (South Tyrol). The fifteen 'ordinary' regions did not receive the appropriate legislation until the 1970s. As for the PCI, widely regarded as the obvious 'Jacobin' party, it soon became the most vociferous exponent of decentralization and devolution of powers at all levels including the regional level. This change occurred as it gradually abandoned the centralist tradition which had been part of the communism of the Third International and as it sought to use its power in the three regions of central Italy to experiment with new forms of local democracy.

It is this which made the PCI's successor party, the PDS, a credible proponent of federalism once the rise of the Northern League had put this issue on the agenda. In the immediate post-war period the only real federalists were some southern (mainly Sicilian) politicians.

As has been seen so far the relation between the DC and the PCI dominated the workings of the Constituent Assembly. From the very beginning the PCI, recognizing that the DC, as the 'party of the Catholics', would have a dominant role in the Italian political system for the foreseeable future, was prepared to downgrade its alliance with the PSI in order to be recognized as legitimate by the DC. This attitude did not change even after the left was expelled from the government.

The Church

One of the more delicate issues which the Constituent Assembly had to decide upon was the constitutional position of the Roman Catholic Church. The PCI did not want to reopen the 'cold war' which had existed between the Italian state and the Roman Catholic Church before 1929 when the issue had been resolved by the Concordat and the Lateran Treaties signed by the Vatican and the fascist regime.

The PCI expected and hoped that the DC would fulfil two fundamental historical tasks: to convince the Catholic and peasant masses of Italy to accept the new democratic republic and to convince them that the PCI was entitled to play a major role in it. Eventually the DC was able to achieve the first of these 'missions' but had no advantage in promoting the second. At the time, however, the PCI leader, Palmiro Togliatti, had proposed a compromise: the Lateran Treaties would not be enshrined in the Constitution but the Italian state would promise not to revise the Concordat unilaterally. The original communist text was thus formulated: 'The State recognizes the sovereignty of the Catholic Church within the juridical order of the Church itself. The relations between State and Church are determined by both (*in termini concordatari*).'

This did not satisfy the DC who wanted the Lateran Pacts to be specifically mentioned. The secular parties, including the PCI, were uneasy: if the treaties were incorporated in the Constitution then each and every article of the Constitution itself would have to avoid contradicting each and every article of the Lateran Pacts.

They were, of course, right to worry. Article 1 of the treaty stated that 'Roman Catholicism is the sole religion of the State'. Article 1 of the Concordat (the Lateran Pacts were made up of a treaty and a 'Concordat') asserted the 'sacred' character of Rome, defined as the 'Eternal City'. Other articles maintained that ordained priests were exempt from military service and jury service, that marriage was the foundation of the family, that it was indissoluble and could only be annulled by an ecclesiastical tribunal and that Italy considered the Catholic doctrine as the foundation of public education.

The DC tried to assuage these fears by proposing the following text – eventually Article 7 of the Constitution: 'The State and the Catholic Church are, each in its own order, independent and sovereign. Their relationships are regulated by the Lateran Pacts. Modifications of the pacts, which have been accepted by the two sides, do not require a constitutional amendment.' Giuseppe Dossetti, who was the DC drafter and proponent of Article 7, explained that it was not his intention that this should be read as an attempt to incorporate into the Constitution every single article of the treaties. Those who opposed him did so on the grounds that they thought that the article did precisely that. Thus the intentions of all the legislators, both the proponents and the opponents, was that it was undesirable that each article of the treaties would have constitutional validity.[18] The more intransigent defenders of the secular state, mostly the socialists, were not satisfied. The article – adopted by 350 votes to 207 – was supported by the DC, the extreme Right, the Italian Liberal Party (PLI) and, significantly, by the PCI voted for it. Had the PCI voted against, the DC would have been defeated. Article 7 was seen for years to come as the most vivid instance of communist subservience to Catholic ideology. This widely held view has very little substance.

The constitutionalist Francesco Finocchiaro has written that Article 7 represents no more than a declaration of 'religious peace'. It could not stop a future government from passing legislation against the wishes of the Church.[19] Thus, in spite of marriage being declared 'indissoluble' by the treaties the Italian Parliament was able to legalize divorce in 1970. In fact none of the religiously controversial legislation later passed by the Italian Parliament – such as the legalization of abortion – was declared unconstitutional. The assumption that Article 7 had somewhat subjected Italy to the Roman Catholic Church is one of the main red herrings of postwar Italian history.

This does not mean that at the time the communist leadership had not been prepared to compromise even on the question of the indissolubility of marriage. The original text of Article 29 stated that the state recognized 'the rights of the family as a natural society based on the indissoluble marriage'. Togliatti as well as two leading communist women members of the Constituent Assembly (Nilde Jotti and Maria Maddalena Rossi) declared that they did not think the word 'indissoluble' should be inserted, but they refrained from trying to delete it, fearing to offend the DC. It was a humble socialist backbencher, Umberto Grilli, who put forward an amendment deleting the offending word. The PSI and the PCI felt obliged to support the Grilli amendment which passed by only three votes, but only because 170 members (including a large number of Christian Democrats) were absent.[20] The revised Article 29 now also included not only the definition of the family as a 'natural society' but also the assertion that marriage is based on the 'moral and legal equality of the [two] parties'.

Notwithstanding this declaration of equality the Constituent Assembly's view of women was distinctly traditional. Thus even though a monarchist amendment which specified that only men could serve in the armed forces was not passed, the commission in charge of the draft suggested that the armed forces should themselves examine which tasks of a 'caring nature' would be particularly suited to the 'disposition and gentle nature of women'.[21] Nor was it just the Catholic contingent of that overwhelmingly male Constituent Assembly which sustained a traditional view of women's role. Pietro Calamandrei, a representative of Italian radical culture and a veteran anti-fascist, objected to sex equality (Article 3) on the grounds that in civil law the husband was defined as the 'head of the household'. It was a communist woman, Maria Maddalena Rossi, who answered that, if so, 'Women will change civil law!'[22]

However, changes in legislation were not achieved easily. The Constitutional Court defended, in November 1961, Article 559 of the penal code which said that the adultery of the woman could be punished with a prison sentence, whereas that of the man was not a criminal offence – a position which had been established by the Pisanelli statutes soon after unification.[23] The court maintained that this did not contravene the sex equality article of the Constitution because a woman's adultery is an act of 'different and greater entity' than that of a man. The court changed its mind only in December 1968.[24] Many of the discriminatory features of Italian laws were finally abolished in the 1970s.

A new Concordat between the state and the Church was arrived at only in 1984. Roman Catholicism was no longer the sole religion of the state, there were no references to the 'sacred' character of Rome, the jurisdiction of religious courts in divorce cases was eliminated as well as many educational and economic privileges hitherto enjoyed by the Church. This new Concordat, like the old one was achieved after negotiations between the two parties. Italy as well as the Church had moved on.

The constitutional compromise

As we have repeatedly pointed out, the Constitution bears the mark of the compromise between Italian communism and Christian Democracy which was a feature of the Resistance and of the first post-war governments. Both the PCI and the DC wanted to establish certain principles which could be accepted by the other side while allowing for an interpretation which would favour, or at least not contradict, their own political line. The PSI was decisive in putting forward a number of propositions, such as the 'revolutionary' Article 3, paragraph 2 discussed above, but it could never impose its will on a matter of major importance against the other two main parties. It was the PCI which systematically sought to be the compromiser, siding with the DC on certain matters, such as Article 7, against the other secular parties and joining them when it felt that it had to oppose the DC.

On some questions the DC-PCI convergence was due to tactical considerations. The PCI wanted a strong parliament and a weak executive because they had realized that their electoral weight would guarantee them a major role in parliament, but that the gathering Cold War would preclude them access to government. The DC, at that stage, was still suspicious of the state and sought to keep executive powers at the minimum. It was concerned to maximize the guarantees to be given to all intermediate groups in civil society. Only the Liberal Party (PLI) was in favour of a strong executive. But the old PLI was now no more than a rump. Its real strength did not lay in votes, but in the influence of its economic ideas and political tradition. It could be argued that this tradition was so strong that it produced a 'liberal' Constitution in spite of the numerical strength in the Constituent Assembly of two political ideologies hostile to this tradition: Marxism and Catholicism. A socialist constitutionalist like Giuseppe Mancini could thus write that while it is true that left-wing ideas contributed important innovations such as Article 3 and the principle of the self-organization of the working class (Articles 39 and 40), it did not alter the fact that the Constitution was a 'neo-capitalist' document.[25] This could be interpreted to mean that the Constitution reflected positions which were then those of enlightened and progressive capitalism, one no longer committed to laissez-faire but to a 'technocratic' and 'modern' market economy, one which recognized the role of the State to redress injustices, create equality, and control private industry not to destroy it but to make it 'useful'.

The Italian liberals were all opponents of this interventionist state. There was, it is true, a 'Catholic neo-Keynesian' interventionist position, but it was still relatively dormant in the commodious entrails of Italian Catholicism. It could not yet worry the old liberals because – as Romagnoli has wryly written – the members of the Constituent Assembly could spend all day long saying to each other that the Liberal State was dead and buried, yet the Bank of Italy and the Treasury were in the hands of great liberal economists such as Luigi Einaudi.[26] It was there that the liberals, with great success, fought their battle in defence of what they called the comparative advantages of the Italian capitalism, progressive or otherwise: a reserve army of two million unemployed and the consequent low wages. As for the Catholic interventionists, their chief representative in economic matters was Amintore Fanfani who sought to introduce the principles of Catholic corporatism into the Constitution. At that stage Fanfani and his followers were still orthodox Catholic corporatist and not Keynesian. They did not seek state intervention in the economy but other forms of collective controls. They were inspired by the Church teachings on the social question as originally defined by Leo XIII in the encyclical *Rerum Novarum* (1891) and further refined by Pius XI in *Quadragesimo Anno* (1931). The latter, in particular, not only reaffirmed the necessity of class collaboration as an instrument against socialism but also a denunciation of monopolies and 'economic imperialism' responsible, it said, for an economic system which is 'horribly harsh, inexorable and cruel'.[27]

As originally envisaged by Fanfani, Catholic corporatism entailed the control of economic activity not by the state and even less so by the 'invisible hand' but by economic councils made up of the representatives of professional associations, trade unions, employers. He accepted that political society would be organized around the state, parliament, political parties, etc., but not the economy which belonged to the sphere of civil society and non-political organs based on the people's role in the production process. These propositions had also inspired fascism which had promoted corporatism as the answer to the twin evils of capitalism and socialism, and Fanfani, in his younger days, had been an upholder of fascist economic policies. Now freed from the embarrassment of a compromise with fascism the Catholic corporatists continued their battle against the Liberal State. Their attempt to establish a leading role for their particular ideology in the Constitution failed and the architects of this defeat were the communists. Against the Fanfani proposals the PCI proposed a formula which would be incorporated, after some modifications, in Article 41: the principle governing the economy would be that of democratic control over production not that of instituting economic councils made up of representatives of professional and occupational categories.[28] The only 'corporatist' principle which was introduced in the Constitution was in Article 99: 'The National Council of Economy and Labour is composed . . . of experts and of representatives of the productive categories.' This is, however, a purely consultative organ which remains to this day subordinated to parliament and to the political parties. It was not even used when there developed – in Italy as in most Western countries – a tripartite system of consultations between government, employers and trade unions.

Conclusion

A constitution gives us the formal ground rules within which political activity takes place. Formal rules are not unimportant because they establish a consensus within which differing political forces can pursue their objectives. The Constitution thus engenders a terrain of struggle and political debate, but that is not the only terrain. Alongside the formal Constitution another one appears which is made up of less formal but very real ground rules which define not only how the Constitution itself must be interpreted but also what is politically permissible and what is not. The triumph of the DC in the elections of 1948, the Cold War and the spread of anti-communism changed the political climate and created new 'real' ground rules different from those of the immediate post-war period. Many of the governing principles of the Constitution, precisely because they were vague or generic or simply because they were principles and not legally definable precepts, remained dormant. In the final analysis a society does not become more equal simply because the Constitution says so. To say that the economy should be subject to 'democratic control' does not get one very far unless the forms and powers of such control are clearly established. Nevertheless, the founding fathers (there were few mothers) of the Italian Constitution wanted to delineate what the general values of the new Italy would have to be and this they did.

Although the end of the tripartite coalition of 1947 had the effect of making the constitutional debates much harsher, there was no drastic rupture. Yet the effects

of such rupture were long-ranging: the exclusion of the left from the government gave birth to a political principle which characterized the 'real' Constitution.
This principle, described by the Catholic jurist Leopoldo Elia as a *conventio ad
excludendum* (an agreement to exclude), sanctioned the non-legitimacy of the PCI
as a government party and defined the arena of 'legitimate politics' in political and
not in constitutional terms.[29] In the 1950s and 1960s the political parties which
were supposed to administer and implement the Constitution corresponded to only
a part of those who actually wrote it.

Soon after the promulgation of the Constitution, the *Corte di Cassazione* (the
highest court then, as there was as yet no Constitutional Court) made a distinction
between 'prescriptive' and 'programmatic' constitutional norms, giving legal status
only to the former. Prescriptive norms were those which established practical norms
of political behaviour as well as organizational rules, for example that there are two
chambers, that there must be elections, that everyone over a certain age has the
right to vote, etc. Programmatic norms were all those which talked of the transformation of society, which pointed to a desirable future to be eventually achieved,
for example the removal of inequalities. This distinction, made within a month
of the promulgation of the Constitution, was overturned by the very first decision
of the Constitutional Court (the equivalent of the US Supreme Court) when it was
finally established in 1956.[30] Article 137 of the Constitution made parliament responsible for passing the legislation essential for the creation of such a court. As
a result many fascist laws were left on the statute books – at first because there was
no Court to establish whether they were constitutional, later because the Court was
unwilling or unable to strike down large sections of the penal code. It was only in
the few years following 1968 that much fascist legislation was repealed and labour
rights were upheld.[31] By then, of course, the political climate had changed considerably. While the principle of excluding the communists from government office
was maintained, it was no longer possible to resort to the anti-communism of the
1950s, the centre-left governments had put back on the agenda the principles of social
reforms and the trade union organizations were stronger than they had ever been.

With the creation of the Supreme Council of the Magistrature, the self-governing
organ of the judiciary, judges became more independent of the state. This formal
independence, however, disguises the fact that the chief organizational principle
of the Italian State, namely rule by political parties, applies also to this Supreme
Council. Italian magistrates organize themselves into factions and pressure groups,
each with its own electoral list and each faction is closely connected to one or more
political parties. Even the Constitutional Court follows a practice which makes it at
least partially dependent on political parties. This court is made up of fifteen members
who serve nine years each. Five are chosen by the President of the Republic, five
by parliament in joint session and five by the highest ordinary and administrative
courts. The five judges elected by parliament require a three-fifths majority. Thus
an agreement between the three main parties is needed to elect these judges.

The Constitutional Court has achieved a remarkable modernization of Italian
legislation and has had a progressive role in Italian politics. What it has not been
able to do is to remove the structural defects of the Italian legal system. This is a

political task which should have been done by the governing parties. Our examination of the Constitution has highlighted some of the more progressive aspects. This should not disguise the fact, for example, that despite existing legislation the state can keep people in prison awaiting trial for a very long period of time. In 1983 there were 20,000 criminal cases still pending. The average delay between the opening of a case and its conclusion in front of a judge takes two years.

Blame, however, can only be attached to those who are politically responsible for this state of affairs. Constitutions can only provide the formal ground rules. The Italian one lays down the general conditions which make Italy a governable country. It can do no more. The crisis of the First Republic was not due to the Constitution, but to the corrupt behaviour of its leading politicians. Nevertheless, a change in the Constitution is on the agenda.

Changing the Constitution is not a simple affair. A referendum must also be held to decide on any amendments to the Constitution unless the same amendment has been passed by both chambers with a two-thirds majority. A major change, amounting to a re-writing of the sections dealing with the political system: i.e. elections, the powers of the President, the Prime Minister, parliament, devolution of powers, etc., should take place through a new constituent assembly elected under proportional representation or, at the very least a parliamentary commission so that all the political forces of the country could hammer out a new compromise. The objective would be to redefine the rules of the game with the consent of all the new political parties which emerged since 1992. Whether such a redefinition would produce stable governments and a regular alternation of left and right is something that a revised constitution can only facilitate, no guarantee.

Endnotes

1 Terracini 1978, p. 31.
2 Mortati 1975, p. 11.
3 Ibid., p. 13.
4 Negri 1977, pp. 38ff.
5 Mancini 1975, p. 199.
6 Ibid., p. 203.
7 Baget-Bozzo, 1974, p. 208.
8 Ghezzi, 1980.
9 Ibid., pp. 119–25.
10 Romagnoli 1975, p. 162.
11 This was the way the article was widely interpreted by practitioners, according to Romagnoli 1975, p. 166.
12 Quoted in Romagnoli 1975, p. 166.
13 Barbera 1975, p. 51. See also Baget-Bozzo 1974, pp. 198–9.
14 Antonio Baldassare, 'Le trasformazioni dell'impresa di fronte alla Costituzione', in *Democrazia e diritto*, 1977, p. 27, quoted in Galgano 1978, p. 24.
15 See Galgano 1978, p. 44 and Mortati 1975, p. 8.
16 Galgano 1978, p. 55.
17 Baget-Bozzo 1974, pp. 192–3.
18 Finocchiaro 1975, p. 343; Rotelli 1967, pp. 328ff.
19 Finocchiaro 1975, p. 347.
20 Terracini 1978, pp. 56–8, note, however, mistakenly refers to Grilli as a 'communist comrade'.
21 Ibid., p. 89.
22 Rodotà 1983, pp. 16–17.
23 Kelikian 1996, p. 378.
24 Romagnoli 1975, p. 187.
25 Mancini 1975, pp. 216–7.
26 Romagnoli and Treu 1977, p. 32.
27 Candeloro 1982, p. 515.
28 Galgano 1978, p. 40.
29 Elia 1970, p. 657.
30 Romagnoli 1975, p. 167.
31 Vercellone 1972, pp. 127–8.

Chapter 13

Local government

Italian local government is based on a hierarchy. At the bottom we have the *comune* (the municipality), then the province and finally the region. The *comuni* are very different in size: they range from major cities such as Rome or Milan to small communities of a few thousand citizens. There are well over 8,000 *comuni*. The province is constituted by a main town or city and its surrounding *comuni*. Thus Milan is a *comune*, but it is also a province which includes the smaller *comuni* around it. The powers of the provinces and their functions are very limited. Thus the *comune* of Milan has over 30,000 employees, but the province of Milan has only 4,000.

The Constitution envisaged that the regions should have real powers (see the preceding chapter) and should become independent centres of decision-making. According to the Constitution, the state should have established the main frame of reference within which the regions could regulate themselves and should have passed legislation to enable them to be financially autonomous.[1] However, past governments have always been reluctant to give even a modicum of financial autonomy to local authorities. These have the right to raise revenue from local taxes which, however, provide only a fraction of what is required, so that they are forced to turn to the central government or to borrow from financial institutions. All this adds to their dependence on central government.[2]

From the very beginning there was an extensive conflict between local authorities (of whatever political persuasion) and the central government. Due to the delay in passing legislation, there were no regional elections until 1970 (except in the five regions whose special status allowed for greater autonomy) and, even then, there was no clear legislative framework defining the powers of the regions.

Between 1970 and 1976, 25 per cent of regional laws were delayed or vetoed by the central government. After 1976 the need to obtain Italian Communist Party (PCI) support in parliament level forced the government to concede greater funding and greater powers to the regions and to extend the devolution of power through the creation of neighbourhood committees in the *comune*.[3]

Neighbourhood committees were also established because of two other distinct sets of pressures: in the first place it was getting increasingly difficult for large towns to govern themselves and there was an objective need for some form of decentralization at the micro level. In the second place, after 1968 there arose in Italy, as in many other Western countries, a plethora of issue-orientated movements asking, among other things, for more and better housing, child-care facilities, transport, etc. These movements were increasingly critical of political parties accused of being insensitive to local needs. Moreover, the PCI had pursued similar aims in the cities they controlled, such as Bologna where they had established a highly effective system of neighbourhood committees.[4] Challenged by this the governing parties, and in particular the Christian Democrats (DC), moved towards meeting these demands so as to recoup some of the political support they seemed to be losing.

The 'explosion' of 1968 and 1969 had shown that the level of political tension in Italy was very high. The regions were, at least in part, a response to this in so far as it was an attempt to diffuse tension instead of concentrating it.[5] The bulk of the intelligentsia was at that time moving in favour of the greater political decentralization. The governing parties, however, were not prepared to concede more than administrative decentralization. In particular, they wanted the regions to be a set of institutions which would be able to provide those social services – including health – which the governments of the centre-left coalition had not been able to provide adequately. The state would still be able to control the regions through public spending and subsidies, but once it was no longer in direct charge of the services it would not have to assume any of the responsibilities.[6] Furthermore, the regions were also seen as an instrument which would enable the governing coalition, and in particular the DC, to involve the PCI in decision-making without granting it any greater say at the centre. Besides, as the PCI's involvement at the local level increased it was likely that its own relations with the various social movements and pressure groups would become more tense.

The DC coalition was in favour of the regions as instruments of social control, but never gave them sufficient resources with which to satisfy local demands. The final word was left in the hands of central government.[7] It would be a mistake, however, to see the setting up of the regions purely in terms of an attempt to diffuse tension. Behind the regional system there was also a wide coalition which saw the regions as offering a way out of the crisis of the Italian political system. The regionalist movement was very diversified. We can isolate the following tendencies:

1 *The 'planners'*. These insisted that the regions should be seen essentially as planning mechanisms. The new regions should be given wide planning powers so that they could make the system of public administration more efficient, ensure an adequate level of local participation in planning and allow a more diffuse and locally responsible system of state intervention. Not having been able to obtain an adequate planning system at the central level during the 1960s under successive centre-left administrations, the planners tried to respond by devising a regionally decentralized system of planning. This would go a long way towards responding in a positive manner to the new trade union demands which had shifted away from purely wages issues towards social demands (e.g. social services, health, transport, etc.).[8]

2   *The 'participationists'*. These saw the local community as the principal
    basis for the political organization of the state. This position had captured
    some of the emerging anti-statist concerns and a good deal of the
    ideology of the late 1960s and 1970s: 'small is beautiful', ecology,
    control over one's environment, etc.
3   *The 'state reformers'*. These saw the regions as an instrument with which
    to increase the democratic basis of the state. The regions would provide
    the link between the smallest locally elected assembly and parliament.[9]

None of these positions were identified with a single political party. Nevertheless, it is clear that the bulk of the planners were in the DC, the Socialist Party (PSI)
and the Republican Party (PRI), in other words the political parties which had
constituted the backbone of the centre-left coalition. The 'participationists' were in
the more libertarian tendencies of the PSI and the PCI, but also in the new Radical
Party which had become a vociferous exponent of the 'small is beautiful' movement and which was advocating a strategy they called 'the anti-institutional use
of the institutions'. The second main component of this position was made up of
Catholics who were the inheritors of the localism of the Italian tradition of political
Catholicism. These envisaged the local community as an instrument of families,
local associations, charities, etc.

All parties were agreed that the central aims of the new regions would have to be:

1   Urban planning. This was felt to be vital because of the anarchic growth
    of cities which had occurred during the internal migration of the period
    of the 'economic miracle'.
2   Social services, particularly health, housing, education, child care, care of
    the elderly, leisure and transport, in order to balance the growth of the
    private sector in these fields.
3   Efficiency in public administration.
4   Meeting demands for more popular participation.
5   Breaking the power deadlock at the centre and opening up to new
    political forces such as the PCI.[10]

The regional experience was successful only in parts. In the first place it was
able, albeit in a very limited way, to narrow the gap between the countryside and
the town; to help small and medium-sized firms; to begin a debate over the future
of agriculture; to slow down the destruction of the environment; to enhance public health. Furthermore, the regions created a space where various interests could
negotiate. In agriculture, for example, farmers, though they would still deal directly
with the state through their pressure groups, could now also turn to the regions.[11]
There is now less secrecy in decision-making and functions which were fragmented
were now better coordinated.

On balance, however, the regional reform was a failure. In the first place, the
central administration always refused to give the regions unimpeded control over
any single function, in other words it has always tried, usually successfully, to retain
some instruments which would give it overall control. The regions themselves have
always been reluctant to stress their autonomy and have preferred the simpler way

of trying to cooperate with the central government even when this 'cooperation' disguised the fact of ultimate central control. Often the regions have themselves been over-centralist and have preferred to control and direct rather than guide.

The continuing strength of the clientele system meant that the periphery-centre link ran not only from the town to the region to the central government but also from the local notable to the politicians in Rome. The relationships and the activities that enable the Italian mayor to gain some resources from the state are not dependent on institutional arrangements such as the regional system. Sidney Tarrow, who examined this issue in depth, established that the main network open to local politicians was a partisan network through their own political party. Tarrow quoted a mayor as saying: 'I prefer to go to the politicians first with something important, and then, possibly, I would turn to the prefect for minor questions.' Thus the use of partisan mechanisms for resource allocation, which in other countries may be the exception, in Italy is the rule.[12]

Had the reform been more radical it would have clarified the powers of both the centre and the periphery. Had that been done, however, the clientele system would have been seriously challenged. A radical reform would not have necessarily destroyed it but, rather, modified its main features, for example by strengthening local ties and giving rise to various forms of separatism. What stopped the central government from promulgating a more radical reform, however, was not the fear of separatism – which, in those pre-*Lega Nord* days, was not significant- but the fear that this would weaken the clientele system. Thus the central government still directly financed projects which could be funded through the regions. Various state institutions, such as the *Cassa per il Mezzogiorno* (Fund for the Development of the South) coexisted with the regions in such a way that there was considerable overlap. Because there was no clear demarcation between regions and central government, political bargaining was a constant activity, in the course of which the stronger and more efficient regions obtained more resources.[13]

Let us take, for instance, the question of southern development. The regional experience has fragmented the 'Southern Question'. The South was no longer a major item on the political agenda. Instead there were a number of competing regions. The best performing were those of the centre and the north. They exhibited sustained economic development and were more integrated with the rest of Europe while the southern regions were more and more marginalized and dependent on state funds. Instead of developing their autonomy, they cultivated their dependency on the centre because they felt that this was the only way of obtaining resources.[14]

Thus the relations among the regions and between the regions and the central government were not determined by institutional rules but by a process of political bargaining.

In the bargaining process, what weighs heavily are not only the economic resources which each region possesses, but also informal resources such as technical competence, public opinion and party influence. Robert Putnam has measured the actual performance of the various regions in terms of the extent to which they have been able to meet the aims of regional autonomy, administrative efficiency and regional economic development.[15] The twelve indicators measured included – among others – the stability of regional governments, the speed at which the budget was approved (virtually no region has ever been able to approve its final budget by 1 January, as required by law), whether they spent all the funds they received (in 1977 Emilia Romagna spent 59 per cent of a special government fund for employment whilst Latium did not spend any), regional planning, etc.

The result of this research showed that in the 1970s and 1980s the most 'efficient' regions were the 'red' regions and the northern regions. Emilia Romagna, Umbria and Tuscany, all central regions, have been run by the PCI since the first regional elections of 1970 and continue to be a stronghold of the PDS. The Veneto, a northern region, was under virtual Christian Democrat control throughout the period of in which Putnam conducted his research as was Lombardy. Putnam and his co-researchers found a very high degree of correlation between efficiency and a high level of socio-economic development, a strong civic culture and a low level of demographic change (i.e. no excessive emigration or immigration). The highest degree of correlation, however, was obtained between efficiency and a strong socialist (later, communist) tradition: those regions where there was a strong socialist movement before fascism were also scoring high on the efficiency table. The importance of civic culture may well have been over-stated, given that the concept is rather vague, nevertheless there is little doubt that the idea of efficiency in communist regions, especially in Emilia, is expressed not only in its public administration but even more in the development of its medium and small industry.[16]

The fact that the regional framework has not achieved any significant redistributive effect except in favour of regions already well endowed with resources characterizes the main failure of regionalism. But it was not only the hopes of the pro-southern development forces which were dashed. None of the regionalist forces could feel satisfied with what had happened. Those who had thought that the regions would be able to plan had not foreseen that the inflationary spiral of the 1970s would have involved the government in anti-inflationary policies tending to centralize spending so that the regions became mere tools for the distribution of resources rather than instruments for their expansion. Those who had hoped that the regions would provide a closer arena for political participation were disappointed too because the 1970s witnessed an increased reluctance on the part of ordinary people to become involved in political activity. Furthermore, when there was local participation this tended to be used more to increase support for ongoing politics rather than as a genuine form of control from below. Finally, the new issues, such as ecology, feminism, consumer protection, etc., tended on the whole to transcend local politics. Those who had seen the regions as the stepping-stone towards a decentralization of the state and the creation of various levels of elected assemblies were never able to see their aims realized because the new structures had to coexist with the old ones: alongside the regional councils there was the state-appointed prefect, alongside the southern regions there was the *Cassa per il Mezzogiorno*, alongside the new school councils, democratically elected by parents and school staff, there was the old school superintendent appointed from Rome.[17]

What effects did regional reform have on Italian political parties? It had been assumed by some that the transformation of Italy into a regional state would have led to substantial changes in the Italian political system. The party system, in particular, would have had to adapt: at the very least political parties would have had to reorganize themselves at the regional level. On the whole this has not happened. Political parties did little more than strengthen their regional committees.[18] They have all remained centralist organizations and this has led to the politics of the centre being reproduced at the local level: the political conflict going on in Rome at the parliamentary and government levels was faithfully reproduced at the regional level and throughout all local elected assemblies down to the local neighbourhood committee. The regionalists had believed in the regions because they thought they would bring about a novel conception of political power. The party struggle, however, continued in the same old way.[19]

What the regions did do was to offer the existing political parties a further terrain of struggle, confrontation and cooperation. It appeared that, once again, the DC had scored a remarkable political success: regional reform had not changed significantly the face of Italian politics. In the regions they controlled, new powerful instruments of political patronage had been created while the PCI, as a pro-regionalist party, was forced to defend the regional experiment in spite of its bureaucratic distortion. In 1975 the PCI obtained a significant victory in the regional elections. This confirmed its supremacy in the traditional 'red' regions of Tuscany, Emilia Romagna and Umbria and enabled the PCI to form regional governments with the PSI in Piedmont, Liguria and the Marche. During the period of the government of national unity (1976–79) the PCI was also involved in one form or other in the government of other regions. In these – as a writer on regional affairs has stated – nothing could be done without PCI approval.[20]

The main party beneficiary of the new regional system, however, had been the PSI. The system of proportional representation for local elections meant that it was extremely difficult for a single party to form a regional or local government on its own. Even when this was possible the leading party still tried to have other coalition partners because it needed their help elsewhere. Thus the PSI – at the regional level as well as the national one – benefited from its unique position as the 'central' party between the PCI and the DC. It could choose with whom to ally and could dictate its own terms thus obtaining political control out of all proportion to its real electoral strength which averaged between 10 and 15 per cent. In order to examine the disproportion between electoral success and political power, we turn to the results for the regional elections of 1970–85 (Table 13.1) bearing in mind that we are looking only at the fifteen 'ordinary status' regions and that the results for the elections of the municipality (the *comune*) and the province do not differ significantly from the regional results. After each election and the subsequent formation of the regional governments the share of posts in all regional governments for each of the main parties is given in Table 13.2.

While the DC always obtained a greater percentage of posts than of votes and the PCI always a smaller percentage, the real winner or 'vote maximizers' was always the PSI who, in 1981, was able to obtain twice as many posts as it had votes. Further research showed that the PSI obtained more power positions in coalition with the PCI than in coalition with the DC. This was in part due to the fact that left coalitions were usually between two parties only (PCI and PSI) while coalition

Table 13.1 Election results: regional elections, 1970–85 (fifteen ordinary status regions) (% and numbers of seats won)

	1970	1975	1980	1985
PCI	27.9 (200)	33.4 (247)	31.5 (233)	30.2 (225)
Leftist	3.2 (16)	1.6 (8)	2.1 (100)	1.5 (9)
Green				1.7 (9)
PSI	10.4 (67)	11.9 (82)	12.7 (86)	13.3 (94)
PSDI	7.0 (41)	5.6 (36)	5.0 (31)	3.6 (23)
PRI	2.9 (18)	3.2 (19)	3.0 (18)	4.0 (25)
DC	37.9 (287)	35.1 (277)	36.8 (290)	35.0 (276)
PLI	4.7 (27)	4.7 (27)	2.7 (15)	2.2 (13)
MSI	5.2 (32)	6.3 (40)	5.9 (37)	6.5 (41)

Table 13.2 Percentage of members of regional government per party; percentage of posts in regional governments

Party	1971	1976	1981
DC	57.8	45.4	44.0
PCI	11.5	17.4	16.4
PSI	14.2	20.2	23.6

Source: Cazzola (1982a)

Table 13.3 Percentage of PSI seats in regional councils and PSI posts in regional governments, 1971–81

	Coalitions with the PCI		Coalitions with the DC	
	Posts	**Seats**	**Posts**	**Seats**
1971	22	7.5	18.4	10.7
1976	31.5	10.9	21.2	11.9
1981	38.3	12.3	26.8	12.3

Source: Cazzola (1982a)

with the DC nearly always also included the smaller parties of the centre. The PCI was not under the same kind of pressure as the DC: it did not need to satisfy powerful groups of local notables and therefore could grant more posts to its allies. The data demonstrating the political gains made by the PSI, respectively, in PCI-led and DC-led coalitions are given in Table 13.3. As can be seen, when the PSI was in coalition with the PCI it was able to obtain three times its share of posts, while in coalition with the DC it obtained 'only' twice its proper' share.

The PSI's success rate in playing the PCI against the DC was further highlighted by examining the most important local government post in 92 main municipalities

Table 13.4 Number of mayors per party, 1971–81

	DC	PCI	PSI	Others
1971	67	12	12	1
1976	50	21	16	5
1981	51	21	15	5

Source: Cazzola (1982a)

between 1971 and 1981 (see Table 13.3). In 1971 the PSI and the PCI had the same number of mayors. The elections of 1975 signalled a significant advance of the PCI and a far smaller increment for the PSI, yet the PSI increased its share of mayors more or less in the same proportion as the PCI (see Table 13.4). In 1971 the PSI had twelve mayors of whom eight were at the head of a left-wing coalition and 4 at the head of a centre-left coalition. In 1976 the PSI sixteen mayors, fifteen of whom were leading a left-wing coalition. In 1981 the PCI losses led to the PSI losing four mayors in left-run cities, but gaining three in centre-left cities.[21]

Political bargaining has not been limited to the local level. Negotiations for the formation of a government have often spilled over to the periphery. When the first centre-left coalition was in the making, in the early 1960s, the DC had tried to obtain from the PSI the undertaking that whenever possible it would try to form a centre-left coalition at the local level. This was often difficult because local social-ists tended to be reluctant to switch from the PCI to the DC in the knowledge that such deals were not acceptable to their electorate. As the PSI became more and more involved in the political system and as it acquired its own clienteles it became less reluctant to play the DC card, particularly as governing with the DC at the local level sharply increased their uninhibited use of political patronage. Furthermore, because the DC was in difficulty it was less reluctant to part with posts and power in order to consolidate its alliances. The PSI did gain from its local alliances with the PCI, but it had lost power at the centre in 1976–79 when it was being squeezed by the DC and the PCI in the government of national unity. The only real threat to the balancing act of the PSI was the historic compromise between the PCI and the DC. An agreement between the two not only limited the political resources left for the PSI, but the PSI would no longer be able to play one party against the other.

In 1983, following elections which signalled a massive loss for the DC, the PSI was able to obtain the most coveted prize: the post of prime minister. The price to pay was an undertaking that he would endeavour to facilitate the formation of centre-left governments at the local level. This political development illustrated clearly the failure of the regionalist dream. Local politics remained subsumed to national politics.

In the field of electoral politics and reform, however, local politics led the way. The surge of the PCI in 1976 – which led to the formation of a government of national solidarity – had been preceded by communist victories in the regional elec-tions of 1975. The victories of the left in the mayoral election of important cities such as Turin, Naples, Rome, Palermo, Venice and Genoa in 1993 – and the concomitant collapse of the Christian Democrats – convinced Berlusconi that he should start his own party in alliance with *Alleanza Nazionale* to stop the advance of the left at national level – a goal he achieved in 1994. The victory of the left in the regional elections of 1995 signalled the revival of its fortunes and helped pave the way for the victory of the Prodi coalition in 1996. Since 1993 a new law for local government elections had been operational. Under the First Republic there was that of a uniform electoral system for both local and national elections (except in the *comuni* with less than 5,000 inhabitants). Since March 1993 local elections have been held under a system which approximated the 'presidentialist' proposals made by many for national elections (and discussed in Chapter 9). Mayors and presidents of provinces were to be directly elected after a second ballot if no candidates had obtained an absolute majority in the first. The list supporting the winning candidate would have a majority premium, and the mayor would chose his/her own local government executive. In regional elections a proportional representation system has been operating for the election of 80 per cent of regional counsellors, the remaining 20 per cent of the seats would be allocated to the list (composed by a single party or a coalition of parties) which obtained the largest number of votes. The leader of the list would become the president of the region. All this, inevitably, strengthened the tendency towards a greater degree of bipolarity in Italian politics as parties were drawn to side for a candidate of the left or of the right.

By the time Italy was struck by the corruption scandals, regionalist politics had been transformed by the advent of the Northern League. Though the causes for its rise are complex – we shall examine them later – the limited autonomy enjoyed by the regions contributed to the successes of the League. A much wider autonomy was advocated, especially after 1987 when the Lombard League displaced that of the Veneto as the principal focus of regionalist sentiment. Real autonomy, claimed its followers, entails the possibility of doing one's military service in Lombardy, giving Lombards priority in (local) public employment, taxes and pensions controlled by Lombards themselves.[22] The growth of the *Lega Nord* under its charismatic leader Umberto Bossi forced all parties to reconsider their position on regionalism. The new word was 'federalism', signifying a far more thorough devolution of power. It is not clear where the balance could be struck. The degree of autonomy which would satisfy the Northern League and its electorate might be too pronounced to enable the Italian state to reduce the North-South gap. Nevertheless, the whole direction of economic policy in the 1990s was aimed at the reduction of the public sector deficit. The consequent sacrifices would weigh disproportionately on the South.

The paradox is that the regionalism of the League was based on the assumption that the existing system of distribution of public resources was strongly biased against the North. To back this case a vast array of statistics has been deployed. Some prove a somewhat tautological proposition: the richer parts of the country pay more in taxes than the poorer ones. This occurs, inevitably, in any country in which most taxes are based on earning (direct taxation) or expenditure (Value Added Tax). If we look at the amount of state expenditure directed to the comune we find a rather mixed picture as Table 13.5 shows.

Leaving aside the special case of the most 'favoured' region, the Val d'Aosta, a small mountain region on the border with France whose inhabitants – mostly

Table 13.5 State transfer to local government

Region	Funds transferred from the state to the *comuni* in 1993, per capita	Ranking (1 = top receiver)
Piedmont	1,719.65	10
Val d'Aosta	2,273.29	1
Lombardy	1,732.41	9
Veneto	1,890.72	3
Friuli	1,845.40	6
Liguria	1,416.98	18
Emilia Romagna	1,536.76	14
Tuscany	1,479.44	16
Umbria	1,591.83	13
Marche	1,648.45	11
Latium	1,445.55	17
Abruzzi	1,784.36	7
Molise	1,848.60	5
Campania	1,437.03	19
Apulia	1,889.36	4
Basilicata	1,507.48	15
Calabria	1,608.55	12
Sicily	1,769.29	8
Sardinia	1,894.54	2
Italy	1,775.20	

Note: My calculation on the basis of ISTAT 1995 and CENSIS 1994. I have excluded the Trentino Alto Adige whose special status makes its data not comparable in this instance

Protestant – speak a language close to French, it appears that the Veneto does as well as Sardinia and Apulia while Lombardy and Piedmont are just below the average. The regions which might feel hard done by the distribution of state resources to the *comuni* include the southern regions of Campania, Basilicata and Calabria as well as 'red' regions of the centre such as Tuscany and Emilia. There are, of course, many other ways of calculating the size of funds obtained from the state. All we sought to demonstrate here is that the question of state funds to the regions is a small part of the controversies surrounding regionalism in contemporary Italy.

If the regional problem is looked at simply from a point of view of the disproportion of resources existing between South and North then the answers are not novel: one way would be to allow the North to keep most of its wealth and let the South remain impoverished. Those who believe in market solutions will say that, as southern wages become significantly lower than northern ones, northern (and foreign) entrepreneurs will invest in the South enabling it to catch up. The pessimists say that this would give a green light to the Mafia to run the South as a major centre of drug production. The fact of the matter is that one-third of the electorate lives in the South, that Italian elections are won by a fistful of votes, that both left and right derive considerable support from southern voters, and that the South has consistently gained less from Italian economic growth and lost more when this growth has faltered. Reports indicate that since the mid-1980s the gap between the North and the South has accelerated, that the southern economy has grown by only 1.5 per cent against 6 per cent in the North in 1992–96. The result is that the gap, in 1996, had moved back to the levels of the 1950s.[23] It is, therefore unlikely that any Italian government would promote a regional reform which would seriously harm the South.

Endnotes

1 Modica 1983, p. 13.
2 Allum 1973b, pp. 217–20.
3 Putnam et al. 1980, p. 220.
4 For an account of the organization of the neighbourhood committees in Bologna see Jaggi et al. 1977.
5 Farneti 1976, pp. 99–100.
6 Rotelli 1979, pp. 424–5.
7 Ibid., pp. 425–7.
8 Barbera 1981.
9 Ibid.
10 Barbera 1979, p. 729. Barbera writes that party agreement existed only for the first three points. It seems to us that there was considerable agreement even on the last point as there were many in both the PSI and the DC who wanted to involve the PCI in government at the local level in order to unburden some responsibility on to the opposition.
11 Ibid., pp. 727–8.
12 Tarrow 1974, pp. 18–29; see also his book on the same general topic, Tarrow 1977.
13 Fichera 1982, p. 98.
14 Cotturri 1982b. The same point is made by Compagna and Muscara 1980.
15 The research summarized here can be found in Putnam 1993.
16 Of the many studies I would single out Sapelli 1995a.
17 Barbera 1981, pp. 3–9.
18 Amato 1980, p. 105.
19 Rotelli 1979, pp. 428–35.
20 Ibid., p. 429.
21 Cazzola 1982b, p. 62.
22 Diamanti 1993, p. 60.
23 Robert Graham, Long and bitter division, in *Financial Times, Survey on Italy*, 4 July 1996, p. iii.

Chapter 14

The political parties

The old party system

It must be obvious from the preceding chapters that parties played a major role in the Italian political system for the following reasons:

1 The electoral system of proportional representation facilitated the proliferation of political parties. This made it virtually impossible for any one party to achieve an absolute majority in parliament, forcing the leading party (i.e. the DC until 1992) to negotiate with others to form a government. This gave small parties considerable power; they were able to use political resources (jobs, public spending and so on) and to establish a relatively stable relationship with their particular electorate.

2 The institutional system and in particular the Constitution had brought about the formation of a strong parliament and a weak executive. Thus political parties in parliament were able to control the executive to a much greater extent than in France, West Germany, the USA or the UK.

3 The fact that state economic institutions were directly or indirectly controlled by political parties through patronage and clientelism enabled them to strengthen themselves as the state expanded.

None of these conditions were modified by the demise of the First Republic in 1992–94 and the collapse of its main parties. As I write (1996) no single party has captured or is likely to capture an overall majority of seats in the legislature, the executive is still weak, small parties can blackmail big ones and still have considerable power. Only the third feature has been somewhat modified: privatization has reduced the influence of parties in the economy while (after *Tangentopoli*) some caution may be exercised in using public spending for political ends. Above all, in its first few years of life, the 'new' republic has already achieved what had never occurred before: the alternation of parties in power, from the Berlusconi-led centre-right government of 1994 to the Prodi-led centre-left coalition government elected in 1996. However, one of the main new parties, *Forza Italia*, is virtually 'owned' by the wealthiest man in Italy who controls half of the broadcasting system. The connection between political and economic power is still very strong.

There are sound historical reason behind the strength of Italian political parties. Some can be traced back to the formation of the Italian state through the process known as the *Risorgimento*. The dominant forces which led the process of Italian unification were not strong enough to eliminate or subjugate the various local interest groups tied to the agrarian system, but were forced to negotiate with them and to make alliances.[1] One of the consequences was that the Italian dominant classes were deeply divided. They could be united only by a constant process of bargaining and negotiating in parliament – a feature which included the cooption of opposition MPs in exchange for favours (the so-called *trasformismo*). Excluded from this process were the peasant masses and the developing working class. The former had no vote and being deeply Catholic followed the papal decision not to take any part in the political life of the new Italian state whose birth had been achieved against the wishes and at the expense of the Roman Catholic Church. The working classes were in part disenfranchised and were, by and large, organized by the Italian Socialist Party (PSI), a party which stood, at least ideologically, against most of the fundamental tenets of the Italian Liberal State.

Thus, even before fascism, the Italian ruling classes had not been able to produce a strong bourgeois party. Fascism, of course, destroyed all existing political parties and proceeded to organize society from above. It established centrally controlled organizations dealing with many aspects of social life, from leisure time to culture, trade unions, etc. Italian political parties revived during the Resistance which they organized as a joint endeavour with the agreed aim of restoring a political system based on a pluralism of parties. Thus the Italian Resistance was never under the command of a single charismatic figure – as were the French under de Gaulle. After the end of the war, Italian political parties were the only organizations which had sufficient prestige to organize 'civil society' and to create or re-create its main institutions.

The multiplicity and importance of political parties was only one of the features of the Italian party system. This is not what constituted its specificity. What distinguished Italy from other Western European democratic countries was the fact that – throughout the period 1945 to 1994 – there was never an alternating government and opposition. The Italian Christian Democratic Party (DC) was always the leading party of government and the Italian Communist Party (PCI) – apart from short periods in which it supported governments of 'national unity' – was always in opposition.

The governing parties had systematically 'colonized' most of the public sector even though they lost ground in terms of public support. By the 1980s they controlled wider sections of public life than they did in 1945, while being able to deliver less. Until the late 1960s the political parties were able to aggregate interests fairly successfully.[2] If a social group had a specific demand to make, the preferred instrument would always be a political party. Since the late 1960s, however, there has been the growth of new social movements and pressure groups.

Political parties were faced with intermediary organizations better able than they were to channel popular demands. This was not their only difficulty. It had now become more difficult to perform another task which had been the preserve of political parties: the allocation of resources in what had become an increasingly complex society with an increasingly inefficient machine of public administration: resources had not been growing in proportion to the social demands expressed. The crisis of the welfare state, which affected virtually all Western countries, had in Italy the effect of weakening those institutions that depended on controlling the distribution of resources for political support: political parties and, in particular, the leading party, the DC.

Finally, political parties were no longer able to articulate an ideology or to initiate major political debates: they no longer monopolized the political agenda. The three main political parties of the First Republic, the DC, the PCI and PSI, had to modify their ideological image. By the 1970s and 1980s, the DC could no longer use religious ideology as it could in the 1940s and 1950s and could no longer resort to the crude anti-communism of that period. The PCI found it increasingly difficult to use the traditional Marxist language of class solidarity: class was no longer the principal focus of loyalty or of self-identification while the PSI attempted to become a centrist party committed to modernization.

The press, more independent from political parties, played a greater role in initiating debates; young magistrates were in the vanguard of the ecology movement; small organizations (as well as the Radical Party, until it degenerated as the personal creature of its charismatic leader Marco Pannella) took the lead in the initial stages of the fight for civil liberties. Most of the debates on issues such as peace, women's rights and crime were increasingly dominated by the peace movement, feminist groups, religious organizations (including the Church which no longer took the DC as its main political reference point), relatives of victims of criminal or terrorist acts, public personalities, etc.

It has always been difficult to measure the extent to which the political parties faced a crisis of credibility. We can, however, offer an illustration. There was only one institutional framework which allowed popular feelings to be expressed outside of political parties: the referendum system. A referendum can only abolish or amend a law voted by parliament; it could not be used as a legislative tool. Until 1987 in all referendums (not including the 1946 referendum on the monarchy) the electorate supported laws approved by parliament; in other words, those who sponsored the referendum by organizing the collection of the petition always lost. Thus, on the face of it, parliamentary legislation had direct popular support though it was not always the case that voters always followed the advice of the parties for whom they usually voted. In the referendum on divorce (12 May 1974) only two parties instructed their supporters to vote in favour of abolishing the law on divorce: the DC and the (neo-fascist) Italian Social Movement (MSI). In the 1972 election these two parties obtained together 47.64 per cent of the vote. Yet only 40.74 per cent voted against the law legalizing divorce. Clearly the DC had not been able to mobilize all of its supporters.

On 11 June 1978 there were two other referendums. The first intended to abolish the new law establishing a system of public funding of political parties while the second was aimed against the new anti-terrorist legislation. All the main parties advised their supporters to approve both laws. The referendum on state funding of parties was seen as a test for political parties in general. Only 23.3 per cent voted against the anti-terrorism legislation (a high percentage when we consider that virtually all parties recommended a vote in favour). When it came to the results on the funding of political parties, only 56.3 per cent voted in favour. Furthermore, there was a very high rate of abstention, 18.6 per cent. A majority of the population in the South voted against state funding. A study of the electoral results area by area revealed that the communist electorate was relatively more disciplined than the DC electorate. Thus this referendum, like the one on divorce, suggests that the main victim of the crisis of political parties was the DC. This was confirmed by the results of the referendum of 17 May 1981 on abortion. Here the DC maintained a low profile throughout the campaign because it realized that there would be a majority in favour of abortion. In the previous general election the anti-abortion parties (the DC and the neo-fascists) had had a total of 43.6 per cent, but the anti-abortion vote was only 32.1 per cent.

In the 1985 referendum on the indexation of wages, Italians upheld the modification introduced by the ruling coalition, but the minority (45.7 per cent) which voted against it was wider than that normally supporting the PCI – the party which had initiated the referendum. This was the last time a referendum upheld legislation already voted in parliament. By 1987 (fifth referendum series) Italian were called upon to vote on far more technical questions than previously. The referendums of 1987

- stopped the further construction of nuclear power stations;
- abolished the *commissione parlamentare inquirente*, a parliamentary commission which investigated the grounds for pressing criminal charges against ministers or the President of the Republic.
- made magistrates financially liable for the consequence of negligent action.[3]

Turnout was low by Italian standards (i.e. 65 per cent) but the referendums were carried by large majorities usually around the 80 per cent mark. Most of the political parties supported the results but, this time, it was far more a question of the political parties following the lead of public opinion rather than the other way round. Before 1987 the majority in a referendum always voted 'No', thus indicating that it did not wish a piece of legislation to be abolished. After 1987 the majority voted 'Yes', thus removing from the statute books legislation approved by parliament. The 1991 abolition of the four preference votes (see Chapter 9) was seen as an indication that hostility against political parties had reached massive proportion.

All this shows that the growing independence of the electorate from political parties began to occur well before the *Tangentopoli* investigation which led to the downfall of the coalition which had ruled Italy for decades.

We can now turn to a closer examination of the main parties.

The Christian Democratic Party and its successors

It is impossible to give a simple and straightforward definition of the DC. Like its main rival, the PCI, it was a unique party by European standards. The DC has been defined in a variety of ways: as the party of monopoly capital, as the party of the 'public sector or state bourgeoisie', as the 'party of Catholics', as a conservative party, as a social democratic party, as a conservative-democratic party with a popular mass base and so on.

The 'orthodox' Marxist position (never wholeheartedly adopted by the PCI) had defined the DC as the party of monopoly capital. According to this view the DC represented the interests of the Italian bourgeoisie or at least those of its dominant faction, that is, giant firms such as Fiat and Pirelli. The evidence adduced to sustain this thesis pointed to their growth and development during the period of DC rule and how government economic policies favoured them.

Even in the 1950s the Italian communists had not held this position. The PCI leader, Palmiro Togliatti, pointed out that after the war, private capitalism was not able to develop its own mass party (something akin to the British Conservative Party) and was forced to give its support to the only mass party which could be an effective challenge to the PCI. Thus the relationship between the DC and private capitalism has always been more conflictual and less straightforward than it would appear to the exponents of the 'orthodox' view.

A second position saw the DC as representing the interests of those who controlled public spending and benefitted from it: the so-called state bourgeoisie. Evidence for this position can be found in the abnormal expansion of the state sector and the extent to which the Italian state intervened in the economy. The DC realized that in order to maintain and reproduce its power it was necessary to expand the state sector.[4]

Franco Cassano has argued against both these interpretations.[5] His starting-point was that, for historical reasons, the DC emerged from the fascist period and from the Resistance as the leading party of the Italian political system. The peculiarity of this situation was that the only party alternative to it, the PCI was an 'anti-system party' in the sense that it was anti-capitalist. Thus a 'normal' alternation between government and opposition (as in the UK) was not possible. The DC considered itself as being 'condemned' to be always the party of government.[6] Aldo Moro wrote in 1974 that 'Realism forces us to accept those particularities which make less credible an alternation of political forces . . . Italian democracy is a . . . difficult democracy'.[7] In order to ensure the reproduction of the existing (capitalist) system the DC had to reconcile two positions: on the one hand, it had to ensure the conditions for private capitalist accumulation; on the other, it had to obtain and guarantee social peace and social legitimacy. Being the only party which could ensure the first condition (the bourgeoisie had no other party it could rely on) the DC always had great bargaining power with respect to private capital. In order to contain the communist threat, the DC was compelled to adopt some of the communist demands: reforming agriculture, state intervention in the economy, the urgency of structural reforms, and the necessity to limit private capital accumulation. Thus the gradual extension of DC control over the state machine and the public sector was not a result of a particular ideological position but rather the consequence of the chief peculiarity of the Italian political system: the presence of a strong opposition which could not be allowed to become government. This is why the DC cannot be classified purely as a conservative party.

The thesis advanced by Franco Cassano has the advantage of not reducing the DC to its social base or to the 'interests' it is supposed to represent. It is clear that the DC was the party chosen by the most powerful economic groups in Italian society to be their 'party of government'. It is equally clear that these groups did not, traditionally, have strong mass support. In 1945 Italy was still a relatively backward nation, the PCI was very strong. The DC could not establish its own rule without obtaining mass support: it had to organize the masses in competition with the PCI. Given the role of the Church in Italy the DC also had to have a special relationship with it. Given Italian backwardness, the DC also had to do something about economic development.

As Gianni Baget Bozzo has written: 'The Christian Democrats know well that, if the PCI had not existed, they would have had to invent it.'[8] The existence of a party historically committed to international solidarity with the Soviet Union gave Italian voters from left of centre to the conservative right a strong motivation to maintain the DC in power irrespective of its actual policies or performance. As the Italian communists distanced themselves from Moscow, it became increasingly difficult for DC leaders to describe the PCI as an anti-Western party. The crisis of the DC in the 1980s was, at least in part, due to the difficulties it had in depicting the PCI as a pro-Soviet party.

Baget Bozzo illustrates another contradiction which affects the DC, stressing the fact that this is a dynamic party which has changed its role over the years. The DC, having emerged from the war as the Catholic party, saw its main task as one of mediation between the newly enfranchised Catholic masses and a capitalist state.[9] As it acquired control over this state it had to develop not only the economy, but also some of the values appropriate to this economic system. The DC became, increasingly, a liberal-capitalist party committed to a 'Western' conception of individualism. It became an 'American' party, not only in the sense that it was pro-American, but also in the sense that it oversaw the evolution of Italy into an American-type society – secularized, materialist and consumerist.[10]

The DC was able to be for so long the party of government in Italy because it had considerable and unique advantages.[11]

1 It had, thanks to the Church, an important social base, particularly in the Catholic regions of the North-east and in the South.
2 Its Catholic ideology could appeal to both middle classes and lower classes.
3 It had always given great importance to local associations and local movements as well as to a variety of voluntary organizations. It was thus well implanted in Italian society.
4 Ideologically, it was not committed to any particular form of state or the dominance of private forms of ownership. It could thus attract support from different sources.
5 It could be anti-communist without being totally committed to a capitalist-liberal system.
6 During the fascist period the political personnel of the Liberal State had either been coopted by the regime or had been repressed by it. Left-wing

political cadres had had to act clandestinely. The Church, however, had been allowed a relative degree of autonomy. Thus the only political organization which emerged from fascism with competent political personnel was the DC.[12]

The DC obtained not only the support of the dominant classes but also the decisive support of the USA. In exchange, the DC could guarantee the USA that Italy would be a loyal and devoted ally of the West and that it would never seek an independent role in foreign policy. Some DC leaders, such as Amintore Fanfani, aspired to develop a 'Gaullist' Italian foreign policy towards the late 1950s and early 1960s, but such attempts came to naught.

Any interpretation of the DC must also take into account the fact that this was a party which constantly evolved and changed positions. After the war it faced several ideological and strategic options: the one which emerged victorious was that of its first leader, Alcide De Gasperi. He defeated the attempt to transform the DC into a clerical party which would be subject to the dictates of the Church and at the same time prevent the success of the Dossetti group which sought to develop an original Catholic-populist line with unmistakable anti-capitalist traits.[13] At the same time De Gasperi had to ensure that no overtly pro-capitalist liberal party could gain popular support. The risk that this would happen was felt to be very real because of the relative prestige that some pre-fascist liberal figures, such as the philosopher Benedetto Croce and the economist Luigi Einaudi, had in Italy at the end of the war.[14]

De Gasperi's strategy had to operate at several levels. The task of the DC was to insert, for the first time in Italian history, the Catholic masses into the Liberal Democratic State. Excluded and self-excluded by the *Risorgimento* and the state which arose out of it, oppressed and dominated by the Fascist State, devout Italian Catholics never felt 'at home' in Italy. The DC would thus complete the task left unfinished by the Risorgimento.

The DC was also aware that it would have to tackle the problem of economic development by controlling politically the free enterprise system. It was also necessary to promote social reforms, not only to preserve social peace but also in order to make sure that the creation of a larger working class which would result from economic growth would not strengthen the left. At first the DC toyed with the Utopian idea of the 'non-proletarianization' of society, but it eventually aimed at creating a complex stratification in Italy by political and economic means to prevent the formation of a large politically united factory proletariat.[15]

Clearly, the strategy of the DC developed in symbiosis with that of the PCI. Preventing the PCI from dominating the Italian political system became the fundamental task of the DC. It could achieve this objective because it was able to combine what may appear to be a 'backward' ideology (traditional Catholicism) with a practical concern for the modernization of Italy. Thus the anti-communism of the DC was not simply the reflection of traditional Catholic values, it was also an instrument used to create a demarcation line between those who could participate in the DC system of political mediation and those who could not.

When, after De Gasperi's death, Amintore Fanfani became the leading strategist of the DC, he sought to develop the Italian economy by acquiring direct control over the public sector and expanding it. This was done by combining Catholic ideology and political realism: a 'Christian' view of the role of the state entailed that the economy and private enterprise had to be subordinated to an ethical view of society.[16] At the same time it was necessary to control the activities of the dominant economic groups to stop them obtaining resources at the expense of less privileged groups, thus narrowing the consensus needed by the DC to maintain the existing social order. Furthermore, Italian capitalism has always been structurally weak, always subordinate to the international economic system, and devoid of two indispensable resources: energy and technological know-how.[17]

To pursue this strategy Fanfani attempted to multiply power centres by expanding public sector institutions, seeking the support of the leading banks (state-controlled) thus by-passing parliament. To defend himself from the more traditionalist and conservative factions of the DC, he centralized power in his own hands, managing, in 1959, the unique feat of being at the same time party leader, prime minister and foreign minister. Even Bettino Craxi, another great centralizer of power, had to concede the foreign ministry to Giulio Andreotti when he was both prime minister and leader of the PSI.[18] Fanfani was eventually ousted because it became impossible to manage in a centralized manner a power bloc where power itself had been diffused in so many directions. Nevertheless, his long-term project of alliance with the PSI was achieved soon after.

As power centres multiplied so did the factionalism of the DC. It became a formalized affair in which the relative strength of the various factions was calculated on a percentage basis and positions and jobs (including cabinet posts) were distributed according to inter-factional agreements and relative strength. The centre-left coalition was established only after Aldo Moro had managed to convince the other DC leaders that the 'opening to the left' (i.e. the alliance with the PSI) was the best option for maintaining the centrality of the DC in the system. In the 1960s, with the centre-left well under way, ideology played a decreasing role in the DC, a process parallel to what was taking place in the PCI and the PSI.

After the failure of the centre-left governments of the 1960s the DC became even more ideologically fragmented and was no longer able to elaborate a general strategy. Its purpose was reduced to maintaining the existing system and, in particular, its dominant role in Italian society. Power had become an end in itself.

There is one aspect of the De Gasperi project which the DC never abandoned: the attempt to influence social stratification. Through the system of clientele and patronage the DC built cleavages which cut across the social structure so as to form obstacles to the development of class solidarity.[19] The clientele system has often been considered a clear instance of the backwardness of Italy, both political and economic. This is a one-sided view which is based on the assumption that clienteles and modernization cannot go together. Yet the classical locus of a clientele system is that of American politics, a system which also exhibits the phenomenon, almost unique in advanced capitalist countries, of not having a strong working-class party. It is true that the clientele system was organized, at first, by local party bosses, but soon, as Allum has demonstrated in his study of Naples, this system gave way to a more modern one based on a party-centred political machine rather than personalities, and direct state intervention in investment projects rather than purely the procurement of favours from the centre.[20] This modified class relations in a massive way. The agrarian reform and the creation of the *Cassa per il Mezzogiorno* restricted the numbers of absentee landlords, created a large class of small land-owning peasants and united them in a political bloc which stopped communist advance in the South.[21] Through the development of the state sector a large class of white-collar workers, of managers and entrepreneurs was created. This class owed its existence to the DC and did not – as in other countries – appear to be the 'natural' consequence of economic development.

The DC did not just contribute to the creation of various social strata. It also organized them. This was done at times by the DC as a political party, at times through its control of state institutions, but more often than not through the creation and development of a large number of organizations known as 'parallel organizations': the ACLI, an organization of Catholic workers; the CISL, the Catholic trade union; *Azione Cattolica*, a lay organization which appealed to all Catholics; the UCID, the Catholic organization of entrepreneurs and managers; the UCIIM, the Catholic organization of secondary school teachers, the AIMIC, that of primary school teachers; the UGC that of Catholic lawyers; to these must be added youth groups, women's organizations, etc.[22]

Of course, the mere fact of creating social groups and associations does not ensure that they will continue to support the party which has generated them. Urban strata in particular, gradually deserted the DC who, after 1975, lost control of major cities. Furthermore, the creation of a large state sector was not a mere act of will on the part of the DC. It was also a logical requirement of the economic system given the incapacity of Italian capitalism to look after itself. Finally, the creation and extension of public sector institutions generated interests which assumed, at times, a force of their own. Problems were 'resolved' by the DC by creating further institutions to deal with them which, in turn, created 'problems' and developed their own autonomy.[23] This generated new 'solutions', greater spending and a more complex bargaining system. What kept the entire mechanism ticking over was the constant expansion of public spending made possible by the expansion of the national and international economy.

The extension of the state sector multiplied the numbers and size of social groups which owed something to the state: their jobs, their positions, their power, their status. This practice of government was the object of constant criticism in the Italian press by journalists and leading political scientists well before the corruption scandals of 1992–94 broke out.[24] One of the main critics of the clientelist system was Giuliano Amato, a socialist political scientist, who eventually became an adviser to the PSI leader Bettino Craxi – later indicted for multiple corruption – and who followed him in government in 1983, and was prime minister in 1992–93. In his *Economia, politica e istituzioni in Italia* (1976) Amato characterized the DC system as a 'spoils' system (*governo spartitorio*).[25] This assumed that all divergent interests in society could somehow be reconciled. Whenever there were conflicts, be they due to old unresolved problems of economic and social development or to novel contradictions, the state, instead of seeking clear-cut solutions which might increase the numbers of its enemies, tried to distribute benefits to all and sundry. The net effect of this was, of course, a constant expansion of public expenditure.

In a spirited defence of the DC, Giovanni Bognetti pointed out:[26]

1   If Amato's analysis is correct, it did not follow that only the DC was responsible. It had always governed with allies which explicitly accepted the rules of the game and tried to use them to obtain political and electoral advantage.[27]

2   The opposition party, the PCI, never sought to stop the distribution of benefits. On the contrary, it set itself at the head of a large movement (workers, students, women, etc.) in order to wrest from the state even more benefits, concessions, etc. Thus all political parties in Italy have been in favour of more public spending.

3   To compromise among competing interests is a reasonable and defensible line. Modern 'social-democratic' states do not seek the elimination of specific interests but their conciliation. The DC – argued Bognetti – may have gone too far and failed to take into account the limited resources of the country, but – if this is so – it is not a question of principles but, rather, of whether the country could afford it.[28]

4   There remains the chief accusation: the DC nourished and developed the state sector to such an extent that it created a middle class which served no economic or productive purpose at all, living off the state and draining precious resources which could have been better used in industry. Here too, writes Bognetti, the DC may be guilty, but it is not guilty on its own. It simply bought some social peace for itself by meeting without any resistance all the demands that the trade union movement and the PCI were advancing.[29] This is why it accepted, after 1969, a constant increase in wages, particularly in the state sector and never tried to contain the ever-growing demands of public employees over pay, conditions, pensions, leave, etc.

This 'defence' of the DC makes an important point: the system which is being described is virtually the same as the 'social-democratic consensus' which prevailed in the UK and a number of European countries from the end of the 1940s to the mid-1970s. This was accepted by all political parties which regarded the construction of a welfare state and the political use of public spending as highly desirable. The need to ensure a social consensus, to reconcile interests and constantly to increase living standards was a common feature of West European politics in the golden age of capitalism (1945–75). The difference between the Italian experience and that of other European countries is that in Italy the distribution of benefits was not undertaken by a state which appeared to be above political parties alternating in power. Until 1992 the Italian state coincided largely with one specific political party: the DC. Thus the 'DC-state' had all the hallmarks of a regime. Herein lies the specificity of the Italian political system.

After the oil crisis of the 1970s and the end of the full employment system, there were fewer opportunities for brokerage and for an increase in public expenditure, and the DC began to face enormous difficulties. In the early 1980s, under the leadership of Ciriaco De Mita, the DC attempted to present itself as a modernizing force ready to relaunch itself as a party with a neo-liberal ideology, and able to obtain the trust and support of the main entrepreneurial groups in order to restructure the Italian economy. In so doing it tried to challenge directly the PSI which was adopting a similar vision.[30] The results of the 1983 election showed that this new strategy was encountering massive difficulties: the DC lost six percentage points. In the 1984 election to the European Parliament the DC lost its position of leading Italian party by 125,000 votes: the PCI obtained 33.3 per cent while the DC had 33.0 per cent. In the 1980s it had to relinquish the post of prime minister to the PSI's Bettino Craxi for five years (1983–87).

One of the chief problems facing the DC is that it could not adopt a credible policy of economic austerity because this would hit those interests and economic groups it had created over the previous thirty years. Furthermore, De Mita's new strategy failed to unite the DC. Against it stood a group which included not only Fanfani, but also the traditional leaders of the central faction of the party, the Dorotei. This group, more moderate and conservative than De Mita's faction, accepted as given the crisis of the DC and its electoral losses and gave absolute priority to the strengthening of the ties with its coalition partners and particularly with the PSI. The purpose of this alliance was to enable the party to keep most of the positions of power it had accumulated, to stabilize the system and to ensure the continuing marginalization of the PCI. A third group, led by many of the followers of Aldo Moro, sought instead to build on Moro's strategy of mediation with the PCI and to maintain the popular roots and base of the DC. This group was by now in a minority. Their strategy stood little chance of survival after the PCI withdrew from the 1976–79 government of national unity and after the assassination of Aldo Moro by the terrorists of the Red Brigades group.

Moro had developed a distinctive strategy on the basis of the social strategy initiated by De Gasperi and Fanfani. As we explained in Chapters 2 and 3, in the late 1940s and 1950s the DC had tried to build up the strength of the middle classes in the South as the keystone of its power bloc. It was not the intention of this operation to establish a bulwark against the working class, but, on the contrary, to offer the southern working class a prospect of upward mobility. In making sure that the working class would not retreat into some sort of enclave dominated by the PCI, the DC, through public spending, ensured that the southern working class too would benefit from the rule of the DC as long as it adapted itself to the DC system.[31]

Moro was quick to recognize that the chief problem of the political system the DC had established was that it was still too narrow.[32] This had led to the centre-left governments of the 1960s.[33] The students' unrest of 1968 and the strikes of 1969 convinced him that the centre-left coalition could no longer provide the DC with the necessary political room for manoeuvre. A new strategic option had to be formulated: the so-called 'third phase' which would also involve the PCI, after the first phase of centrism in the 1950s and the second phase of the centre-left in the 1960s.[34] In 1969 Aldo Moro's supporters were in a minority. The main centrist DC faction, the Dorotei, led by Mariano Rumor, though conscious of the need for reforms, tried to continue the centre-left experiment while at the same time regularly consulting the PCI to obtain the support they often needed in Parliament.[35]

The basis of Moro's proposed 'third phase' was the following:[36]

1 The possibility of ensuring the continuing economic development of the country with the support of the trade union movement in exchange for including the trade unions themselves in a continuous bargaining process.
2 An attempt to reduce the rate of growth of public spending. This could be accepted by other political parties because it would decrease the political power of the DC.

The upshot of this strategy would be that while the DC would lose some of its political power, it would benefit from unloading on to others some of its own responsibilities. A policy of austerity could have 'worked' for the DC only if it were also accepted by the opposition, i.e. by the PCI. This was a lucid attempt to transform all other parties, including the PCI, into junior versions of the DC. In so doing, Moro was delineating a clearly 'hegemonic' project where hegemony not only means dominance but the ability to shape a social system so that all political forces take it as given and do not challenge it. Moro's death and the PCI's decision to withdraw its support from the government of national unity in 1979 put an end to the strategy of the 'third phase'.

The 1980s were difficult years for Christian Democracy. It faced declining electoral support. The failure of the historic compromise with the PCI meant that the DC had become increasingly dependent on the PSI. Consequently, it had to concede the prime ministership to Craxi (1983–87). Once this occurred the DC and the PSI became tied together by the virtual assurance that they could not be electorally defeated. Politics came to be reduced to a struggle between the two of them for an increasing share of power. This disregard for the electorate proved fatal.

The DC became, increasingly, a 'southern' party. Its links with the advanced sectors of Italian capitalism were constantly weakened. Large entrepreneurs came to regard the DC as a southern party, the party of 'lame duck capitalism' forever demanding kickbacks and special favours at a time when modern capitalism had to compete in global markets.

Moreover, the DC continued to suffer increased internal fragmentation. In Sicily a small anti-mafia party was formed under the leadership of a former Christian Democrats, the mayor of Palermo, Leo Luca Orlando able to attract significant sectors of Catholic voters, conquering 12 parliamentary seats in 1992. Although its great rival, the PCI, was facing massive problems and a declining electorate, the PSI, under Craxi, demanded an ever growing share of political posts and power. By the early 1990s the growth of the *Leiga Veneta* and the *Lega Lombarda* was threatening the great DC strongholds in the Veneto (the triangle Verona, Vicenza and Padova) and eastern Lombardy (Brescia and Bergamo). One of its leading members, Mario Segni, was conducting a campaign in favour of changing the electoral system, disregarding party discipline and loyalty. In March 1993, Segni split from the party and formed his own organization, the *Patto Segni*. Segni, the son of a former President, became one of the grave diggers of the First Republic, though this much over-rated politician exhibited profound inconsistencies beyond his single-minded commitment to electoral reform.[37]

Thus the crisis of the DC had been maturing prior to *Tangentopoli*. Its vote had been decreasing fairly consistently. In many areas of the Veneto (where the DC was particularly strong) the emerging working class of the small and medium-sized firms, though remaining substantially Christian Democrat, was showing signs of dealignment – itself a reflection of the different ways local political culture is related to its socio-economic substratum. Some evidence for this has come to light thanks to a comparative study which included Bassano del Grappa in the Veneto near Vicenza – a 'white' area dominated by the DC. In this area, in the early 1950s, rural workers were the largest group, but, by the 1970s there were more workers in manufacturing than in any other sector and the new small entrepreneurs were of working class or rural origin.[38] The local networks were strong and extensive: families were larger than average, relatives were nearby, self-help prevailed, local communities were supportive.[39] The passage from agriculture to industry was not accompanied by significant stress or major social problems: no slums and no disintegration of families.[40] Among the remaining rural workers of Bassano there was great continuity in religious attachment between parents and children and 90 per cent of this group were DC supporters. In other social groups there was a growing disenchantment with the DC, especially marked among workers.[41] When those who continued to vote DC were asked what it was they liked the least in their party, most said clientelism and corruption. When asked what made them chose one candidate rather than another the majority answered that they chose candidates who had demonstrated that they did something concrete for their area.[42] This is precisely what the League would later offer them: a 'clean' party entirely concerned with local problems.

This is the background to the final blow for the party which came from the investigations conducted by the Milan magistrates – the so-called Clean Hands (*Mani pulite*) team – and the successes of the Northern League. In the last general election fought by the DC, the party was reduced to just under 30 per cent – its lowest share of the vote ever. As the inquest proceeded, nearly one-third of the deputies elected in the 1992 parliament found themselves under investigation – and most of them belonged to the DC and its ally, the PSI. This led to the irreversible crisis of the DC. In the local elections of June 1992 the party could muster only 20 per cent, in the local elections of December of that year, it had plunged to 10 per cent. The party was formally dissolved on 18 January 1994 to be reborn with the name of *Partito Popolare Italiano* (PPI), the original name adopted by Christian Democrats exactly 75 years before – in January 1919.

In reality the birth of the PPI signalled the end – though how definitive it is impossible to predict – of the political unity of Catholics. The PPI, led by Mino Martinazzoli, fought the elections of 27 March 1994 on its own, without allies. It obtained 11.1 per cent. It was inevitable that it would fare so abysmally, partly because the electoral system penalized parties unable to form an alliance, partly because the corruption scandals could not fail to damage the electoral prospect of the successor party to the DC, partly because, without political power, the PPI was far less attractive to conservative voters wishing to keep the left out of power. But the real cause of the predicament of political Catholicism was that it had become deeply fragmented. The *Patto Segni* led by Mario Segni gathered 4.4 per cent. A group of left-wing Catholics, led by Ermanno Gorrieri and the trade unionist Pierre Carniti, formed a Christian social party which fought the election under the patronage of the left-led 'Progressive Alliance'. On the right, the *Centro Cristiano Democratico* (Christian Democratic Centre), led by Clemente Mastella and Pierferdinando Casini, fought the election with Berlusconi's *Forza Italia*. Orlando's anti-mafia party in Sicily, *La Rete*, mopped up more former DC votes while a small electoral alliance, *Alleanza Democratica*, attracted some left-wing Catholic intellectuals. Finally, some DC notables (Publio Fiori and Gustavo Selva) went to the far right of *Alleanza Nazionale*. While it is difficult to estimate the 1994 Catholic vote (some parties fought in the proportional representation list, but others did not), it is unlikely that the entire 'Catholic vote' could have been greater than 20 per cent. The rest, presumably, had gone to the Northern League, *Forza Italia* and the reconstructed far right *Movimento Sociale Italiano* (now called *Alleanza Nazionale*).

The *Partito Popolare* had defined itself as the party of the centre, at a time when the system was becoming more bipolar and each of the two poles had moved towards the centre. In 1948 the DC too had defined itself as a centrist party, but, at that time, being in the centre meant to be equidistant from a fascist past and the threat of a communist future. In 1994 being at the centre meant to be in favour of the past and against the new. The 'new' meant a bipolar system which Italy never had.[43]

In reality the PPI had found itself in an impossible position. To move towards the right meant to be under the hegemony of Berlusconi. To move towards the left meant to be under that of the PDS. In order to protect its identity it had to be the party of the centre even though, electorally speaking, not much more than the 10–15 per cent obtained could have been obtained.

After the defeat of 1994 Martinazzoli resigned and was succeeded by Rocco Buttiglione. In 1995 Buttiglione made a deal with Berlusconi. This led to a new fragmentation of the *Partito Popolare*. A minority followed Buttiglione while the majority threw its lot with the left and made an electoral pact with the PDS. The attempt to hold on to the centre in splendid isolation had proved illusory. There was no real alternative for the PPI but to accept an alliance with the PDS under the name of the Olive Tree and the leadership of Romani Prodi, himself an ex-Christian Democrat. Thus it was that what was left of political Catholicism returned to power in 1996 as the junior partner of a coalition led by the heir of its old communist opponents.

The Italian Communist Party and its successors

The PCI emerged from the Resistance as a mass party. Before 1943 it was illegal and had only a few thousand cadres. By 1946 it had nearly 2 million members. This quantitative jump was so massive that it radically changed its central coordinates. The immediate priority established by its leader, Palmiro Togliatti, was to hold together this great mass of workers, peasants and intellectuals and to give it a purpose and a sense of direction. Many of the former partisans and old cadres had assumed that, having defeated fascism, the communists should once more take up the 'class struggle', stop cooperating with the other 'bourgeois' parties and prepare for a socialist revolution. The leadership argued strongly against this line. It offered two basic reasons:

1   The partisan movement was fundamentally weak. At its peak it had 300,000 men and women under arms, only half of whom were communists. It was concentrated in the North and had been fighting a foreign force, the Germans, with the decisive help of a powerful international coalition. A struggle for socialism could not possibly count on this internal strength and would get no support from outside. The South, with its lack of a partisan tradition and socialist ideology, would be a strategic enclave for the regrouping of the counter-revolutionary forces.

2   The international situation was totally unfavourable to a communist takeover. There was no common boundary with the Soviet Union, American and British groups were still in Italy or could have easily returned. There would have been no support from the USSR: the international lines of division of the spheres of influence had been quite clearly drawn and Italy's position in the 'American sector' was unmistakable.

These considerations were sufficient to convince most of those who had been fighting in the Resistance that it would lead to a socialist insurrection. The fundamental reason why this could not be the aim of the PCI was that Palmiro Togliatti was elaborating a strategy for socialism which owed little to the classical Leninist one and was much closer to the central features of the ideas formulated by his predecessor, Antonio Gramsci, from the depths of his fascist prison.[44] Togliatti was developing a conception of the revolution 'as a process' quite different from the Soviet model and remote from any insurrectionist temptation.[45] The Resistance had been a stage in the 'anti-fascist' revolution. The next stage was not a socialist society but the creation of 'a new type' of republic, a 'progressive democracy' in whose organization the working class would have the 'leading' role. Instead of a momentous revolutionary rupture, there would be a gradual advance towards an 'Italian road to socialism' and would not follow the pattern of the Russian Revolution. As Togliatti declared:

> International experience teaches us that in the actual conditions of the class struggle in the whole world, the working class and the advanced masses, in order to reach socialism – that is, in order to develop democracy to its extreme limit which is precisely that of socialism – must discover new paths different, for instance, from those which had been chosen by the working class and the labouring masses of the Soviet Union.[46]

The PCI consolidated its alliances with the other government parties and particularly with the DC, accepted the enshrinement of the Lateran Pacts in the Constitution and proposed a social truce between workers and entrepreneurs. Its freedom of action was guaranteed by the short period of international coexistence between the two superpowers.

The Cold War completely modified this situation. The PCI was expelled from the government, and was excommunicated by the Church and criticized by the USSR for having been too keen on compromise politics. The PCI continued to develop the ideas behind the Italian road to socialism, but in a muted form. In foreign policy it staunchly defended the USSR, opposed Marshall aid and Italy's membership of NATO and, later, of the EEC.

By the middle of the 1950s the PCI was in a most difficult situation. Italian capitalism was on the verge of a massive economic take-off. The trade union movement was deeply divided along party lines. The PCI had lost its majority among the workers in the stronghold of Italian capitalism: the Fiat works in Turin. It was at this moment that one of the most important events in the post-war history of the international communist movement took place: the Twentieth Congress of the Communist Party of the Soviet Union of 1956. This is when the new Soviet leader, Nikita Khrushchev, revealed the extent of Stalin's purges, but the other novelty of this congress was the formal recognition on the part of the Soviet authorities of the possibilities of national roads to socialism. In Italy this was seen as the green light for the development of an 'Italian road'. In reality the light was never green. It was always conditioned by the state of play of the international context, that is, by the possibilities for peaceful coexistence. The invasion of Hungary polarized the situation once more and forced the PCI to choose the Soviet camp and to justify the intervention. Soon, however, the development of *détente* enabled the PCI to take a more independent role. Thus when the ideological conflict between the Russians and the Chinese erupted, the PCI refused to take part in any attempt to convene an international communist conference for the purpose of excommunicating the Chinese. This rejection was not motivated by any sympathies the PCI might have had with Peking's position but by objections to the very idea of international excommunications.[47] It was not merely a question of principles (Togliatti had admitted that the exclusion of the Yugoslav Communist Party in 1948 was a grave mistake), but was based on the view that the activity of individual communist parties should not be subject to the approval of the rest of the movement.

The principles around which the PCI was developing its international strategy were based on the Togliattian concept of 'polycentrism'. There were two dimensions to this. First, the international communist movement could no longer be directed from a single centre because there were different roads to socialism. Secondly, the international system itself was less and less bipolar and there could be, thanks to the process of *détente*, new possibilities for European countries to withdraw from the American sphere of influence. The Common Market expressed the potentialities for a movement towards European autonomy.[48] The PCI, by the early 1960s, had changed its hitherto hostile attitude towards the EEC. The split between China and the USSR meant that there was no longer a single unified and monolithic socialist camp, while the process of decolonization and non-alignment meant that a number of countries were rejecting the logic of bipolarism.

After Togliatti died in 1964 the PCI continued to develop an independent foreign policy. Under the leadership of Enrico Berlinguer, who became leader in 1972, the PCI became ever more committed to the development of the EEC. It gradually ceased to ask for an Italian withdrawal from NATO and, at the Fourteenth Congress of the party (March 1975) Berlinguer announced that 'we too believe that the Italian government must not propose to undertake a unilateral action which would alter the military strategic equilibrium between the Atlantic Pact and the Warsaw Pact'; in other words there was no question of an Italian withdrawal from NATO.[49] A year later Berlinguer declared to a journalist that he felt 'safer' within NATO because this meant that the PCI could choose its own road to socialism without constraints from Moscow.[50]

This revision of the established position had come a few years after it had become clear what these 'Soviet constraints' could be: the PCI energetically condemned the 1968 Soviet invasion of Czechoslovakia and would renew its condemnation every year on the anniversary of the intervention. The PCI tried to achieve international backing for its position within the West European communist movement. The period 1974–78 saw the rise of 'Eurocommunism' sanctioned in 1975 by the joint declaration of the leading European communist parties, the French, the Spanish and the Italian. It saw, too, that these parties were committed to autonomy and independence from the USSR, that they recognized the value and importance of all democratic principles including all those of the liberal-democratic tradition: freedom of the press, of religious belief, civil liberties, political pluralism, elections, etc. Again, the development of this line was premised on the continuation of the process of *détente* because the growth of Eurocommunism depended on the degree of polycentrism existing in the world. Should the battle lines between East and West be drawn sharply again, then the space for manoeuvre would be reduced. If the international situation was characterized by a clear 'either with us or against us' choice then there would be little room for the development of a third way.

As it turned out, the era of *détente* came to an abrupt end. The non-ratification of SALT II, the NATO decision to locate a new generation of nuclear weapons in Europe, the Soviet decision not to withdraw any of its new SS-20 missiles, the Soviet invasion of Afghanistan (1980), the US boycott of the Moscow Olympics (1980) and the USSR boycott of the Los Angeles Olympics (1984), and the unrelenting development of 'local wars' (often fought by proxy by the two superpowers) between China and Vietnam, between Vietnam and Cambodia, Somalia and Ethiopia, Iran and Iraq, the Israeli invasion of the Lebanon, the Turkish occupation of part of Cyprus – all these were so many obstacles to the continuation of the process of *détente* and the hopes of Eurocommunism. Soon the French Communist Party broke ranks and supported the Soviet intervention in Afghanistan while the Spanish Communist Party was reduced to a rump.

The weakness of Eurocommunism had been that it had never succeeded in going beyond the mere assertion of common principles. It was one thing to agree over pluralism and civil liberties, another to develop a joint programme of action over concrete questions such as energy, unemployment, the North–South dialogue, the EEC.

The PCI continued its relatively lonely path. The crushing of the Polish trade union, Solidarity, by the military in December 1981 caused it to break completely from Moscow. In a formal resolution it declared that the phase of socialist development which began with the Russian Revolution had exhausted its driving force, that the 'march of socialism depends, more and more on democratic and socialist ideas and achievements in the capitalist developed world and on the success of the most progressive experiences . . . in the countries of the Third World'.[51] Thus the PCI defines the new situation: the October Revolution is finally over and the state which resulted from it has nothing to offer to the socialist movement.

The domestic equivalent of an international strategy based on disengagement from the two power blocs would have to be a more concrete formulation of the 'Italian road to socialism'. During the 1960s the PCI had to face the fact that it was the only serious parliamentary opposition to the centre-left government (apart from the neo-fascists and the small Liberal Party). It also had a monopoly of Marxist culture. In the years 1968–72 this monopoly was seriously challenged and eventually shattered by the student revolt. The PCI was accused of being revisionist and reformist and, at the same time, authoritarian and bureaucratic. The dual eruption of workers and students caused a massive crisis in the Italian political system. In 1969, as already mentioned, a bomb in a Milan bank killed sixteen people. It was the beginning of ten years of terrorism.

This situation induced the PCI leader, Enrico Berlinguer, to give the party's strategy a more concrete formulation. The immediate reason for this redefinition was the 1973 *coup d'état* in Chile. There a left-wing government had attempted to rule against a strong Christian Democratic party and was crushed by the military. The essential problem was to provide the country with a radical reforming government without driving a large section of middle-class groups and other social forces into positions of overt hostility. Thus a mere electoral or mathematical majority was not sufficient: 'it would be illusory to think that, even if the left-wing parties and forces succeeded in gaining 51 per cent of the votes and seats in Parliament . . . this fact would guarantee the survival and work of a government representing this 51 per cent'.[52]

In order to achieve a political majority it was necessary to achieve an alliance with the Catholic masses and enter into some form of compromise with the DC. This was the political context which called for 'a great new historic compromise' among the political forces which represented the overwhelming majority of the Italian people.

The PCI recognized that it faced a problem of national legitimation and that it needed to offer some international guarantee that its presence in government would not signify a shift in the balance of forces between East and West to the disadvantage of the West.

The political events which followed the adoption of the strategy of the historic compromise seemed favourable. The right wing of the DC, now led by Amintore Fanfani, was defeated in the divorce referendum. The local elections of 1975 were a stunning victory for the PCI: the 1970 gap between DC and PCI of nearly 10 per cent was now reduced to 1.8 per cent. Communist local government power, hitherto enclosed within the three 'red' regions of central Italy, now spread to virtually all major cities. The 1975 results were not a freak: they were confirmed in the 1976 general election. The DC, however, was able to make good its losses at the expense of its potential junior partners in coalition: the social democrats and the liberals. A centre-left coalition was no longer possible because socialists, republicans and social democrats refused to enter into any coalition which rejected the PCI. In July 1976, for the first time since the break-up of the tripartite coalition of 1947 (the first 'historic compromise') a DC Prime Minister, Giulio Andreotti, had to appeal to the PCI to support his government in parliament. At the local level cooperation between communists and Christian Democrats was becoming commonplace and by June 1977 a wide-ranging government programme had been agreed between the DC, the PCI and the other parties. Though not in government, the PCI seemed to have become a party of government.

The Andreotti government of national unity was seen as a possible stepping-stone towards fully-fledged communist participation in government. This did not happen. In the space of three years the PCI lost some of the support and goodwill it had accumulated in the preceding five years. Communist leaders accepted some of the blame, explaining that, though they had a good programme, they were not able to implement it and that, though aware of the complexity of the situation, they were not really equipped to deal with it.[53] The PCI had not been able to defend and protect all its own interest groups and had to be content with modifying the initiatives taken by the government.[54] The policy of compromise had turned into a policy of subordination.[55]

The explosion of terrorism led the PCI to defend the state by refusing to negotiate with the Red Brigades over the Moro kidnapping and by accepting new anti-terrorist legislation. The intention was to uphold the democratic principles of the Italian republic and its Constitution, but the PCI could not avoid appearing to many as the defender of the entire edifice of the Italian state with its corruption, degeneration and bigotry. It was accused by many on the left of espousing an anti-libertarian cause purely in order to establish its long sought-after 'historic compromise' with the DC. As these events unfolded, the DC played a subtle game: it allowed the PCI to emerge as the stoutest defender of law and order and of austerity and to antagonize many of its supporters.

Both parties developed parallel strategies which misfired: the PCI assumed that it would be able to liberate the 'progressive' aspect of the DC through an alliance with it (the historic compromise), while the DC gambled on the eventual transformation of the PCI into a mildly reforming machine which would bring its supporters and the masses it inspired under the political hegemony of a new governing coalition led by the DC. It would enable the DC to escape from the blackmail of the PSI and play one left party against the other. Thus the DC's strategy was also a strategy of 'historic compromise'. The difference between the two parties was that each aimed at a different outcome.

At least on the surface, Moro's interpretation of the historic compromise seemed to prevail over Berlinguer's. But the DC's crisis was not simply electoral. It was due to a wider economic crisis which was restricting the political terrain for cooption.

Furthermore, it proved impossible to coopt the new terrorism (i.e. to control it), though it could be used to embarrass the PCI. The dramatic rupture of the 'historic compromise' occurred precisely when the Red Brigades terrorist group kidnapped Aldo Moro in a spectacular operation in the centre of Rome on 16 March 1978, killing his five bodyguards. They held Moro for 55 days before killing him too. Thus the Red Brigades destroyed the key man who could have paved the way for the entry of the PCI into the government. The target had been chosen with great accuracy. The victim was Moro but the target was the PCI and the policy of the historic compromise. Much has been written about this extraordinary event (Moro was the most senior politician to be killed by terrorists in Europe since the 1920s). It has been said that the Christian Democrats or the secret services (many of whom were in fact members of the P2 freemason secret society, which also included various politicians and entrepreneurs like Silvio Berlusconi) could have saved him but preferred to abandon him because they disagreed with his strategy or because he knew too much. Such speculation and conspiracy theories reveal a profound distrust of the entire political establishment. Needless to say, no firm evidence has ever been found.

A new leadership (an *entente* between Forlani and Andreotti) emerged in the DC, taking over from the Zaccagnini group which had supported Moro. This success-fully tried to re-establish its links with the PSI and its new leader, Bettino Craxi. Craxi, who had previously adopted a less intransigent line in dealing with the ter-rorists, sought now to use the crisis of the Italian political system to prepare the ground for an authentic refounding of his own party, breaking decisively with the socialist tradition and challenging the DC in the centre of the political spectrum.

By the end of 1978 the PCI had ceased supporting the government. By the end of 1980 it had changed its line officially. Between these two events there was the 1979 general election in which, for the first time, the communists lost votes. The losses were heavy, and in the South they were extremely serious. The PCI thus paid for its failure during the period of 'national unity' to demarcate itself from the DC.

This was the nail in the coffin of the 'historic compromise'. Berlinguer an-nounced that henceforth the PCI's policy would be to fight for a 'democratic altern-ative'. This meant, he explained, that the situation was ripe for a government without the DC. The proposal had little immediate application. The PSI was by then pursuing single-mindedly its own course to power which brought Craxi to the office of prime minister in the summer of 1983 and had no intention of cooperating with the PCI.

The aim of the strategy of the PCI was to open up the Italian political system which had been stagnating under continuous DC rule. The 1976–79 experiment of 'national unity' had not achieved this, but had not been wholly negative. The DC had accepted the possibility of communist participation in government thereby 'legitimizing' the PCI.

The parallel between the 1976–79 period in Italy and the experiment of the 'social contract' in the UK in 1974–79 under a Labour administration is impressive. In both cases the left tried to obtain moderate wage settlements, and in both cases any attempt to reflate the economy during an international recession failed.

Throughout the 1980s the PCI sought to develop its links with the West European left, especially the German social democrats. It embraced central elements of the programme of ecological groups and of feminism, but it failed in its central endeavour: to prise the PSI and the DC apart. The death of Berlinguer in 1994 (in the final stages of the campaign for elections to the European Parliament) was followed by profound emotion in the country as a whole. Over a million people turned up to the funeral while politicians of all sides (including the neo-fascists) paid their respect to a man whose political integrity was never in doubt and was all the more evident in the country of Bettino Craxi and Giulio Andreotti. The positive results obtained at the 1984 European elections – one of its best electoral results ever (33.3 per cent) when it became for the first time, the largest political party (due, presumably, to the sentiment of sympathy for the death of Berlinguer) – were not the signal for a recovery. On the contrary, the PCI, under the leadership of Alessandro Natta, continued to lose votes: it achieved only 26.6 per cent in 1987. The communists found themselves with a little more than a quarter of the electorate, the same percentage as the protest vote they used to have in the 1950s and 1960s.

The results seemed to confirm a depressing trend. Up to 1976 the PCI had always improved its vote; since then, three times in a row (1979, 1983 and 1987), the party had lost ground. Local elections results exhibited the same trend. Its opponents were doing relatively well: Craxi's PSI had been the real victor in 1987 – an improvement of 2.8 per cent on 1983 and its best results since 1958 (in 1968 the PSI had 14.5 per cent but it had fought the elections with the PSDI). The DC improved its percentage by 1.4 per cent and, in so doing, it interrupted a decline which had begun in 1968.

The PCI had lost votes everywhere but more in the prosperous and industrial North and in its strongholds of central Italy. The heaviest losses were registered in working-class districts and among the young. The PCI was now the third party in the 18 to 25 age group with only 20 per cent against 23 per cent for the PSI and 32 per cent for the DC.[56] The party was able to increase its vote slightly among women perhaps thanks to an exceptionally large number of women candidates (one-third of the total).[57] As a consequence 60 of the 91 women elected in the two chambers (out of a total of 945) were in the communist list.

This was of little consolation to Natta who resigned to make way for a younger leader, Achille Occhetto. By the time Occhetto had taken over, the PCI had become, to all intents and purposes, a mainstream social democratic party which called itself communist. The profile of its activists had changed considerably since the 1950s and 1960s. A survey of the one thousand or so delegates at its congress of March 1989 revealed that over one-third had university degrees. Women were one-third of all delegates and 70 per cent of those under the age of 30. Thirty per cent of all delegates no longer believed that the working class 'was central'. Sexual equality was regarded as the most important goal by 97.7 per cent. Only one in four believed in the desirability or possibility of a classless society and one in ten believed that it was necessary to abolish the private ownership of the means of production. Only 3 per cent still retained a belief in the inevitability of the withering away of the state.[58]

The principle of democratic centralism which had held the party together by formally banning the establishment of factions has lost its efficacy. The party was divided between a small group of *miglioristi* on the right led by Giorgio Napolitano and Luciano Lama (who was relatively close to the PSI), a pro-Soviet wing (led by Armando Cossutta), a left close to ecologists and pacifists (Pietro Ingrao), a centre divided into a left (Aldo Tortorella), a centre (Achille Occhetto) and a right (Gerardo Chiaromonte). Around Occhetto there was a generation of 40 year-olds who had come to politics in the 1960s.

By the time the Berlin Wall crumbled (November 1989), the PCI was thus weak and divided. Occhetto took the opportunity to announce to a group of Resistance veterans on 12 November 1989 (three days after the fall of the Wall) that it was necessary to open a process for a new 'formation of the left'. Because of the coded language in which such pronouncements were made, it was not immediately clear that Occhetto was proposing to change the name of the party. A new name, he felt, should not simply reflect the *de facto* social democratization of the PCI. It should signal a 'refounding' of the party and the beginning of a process of realignment of the entire Italian left.[59] Occhetto wrongly believed that there was an ample body of left-wing public reluctant to commit itself to a Communist Party and that it would vote accordingly. By changing the name he felt he had undertaken the final step towards the elimination of Italy's major post-war peculiarity: the lack of a united reformist party able to form a government of the left. This was 'a true watershed in the development of the Italian political system'.[60]

Some of the anger directed towards Occhetto in the course of 1990 derived from the realization that, by calling for a new party, Occhetto had indirectly accepted the position of the PCI's opponent: regardless of the numerous indications to the contrary the PCI was still communist and as such could not hope to rule the country. Every revision made – including the condemnation of the Soviet invasion of Czechoslovakia and the rupture with Moscow over Poland – was supposed to demonstrate that it had finally abandoned its communist past and embraced 'European' social democracy. Yet every time it emphasized the decisive nature of its last step, the PCI implicitly admitted that its critics had been right all along: namely that, until this final move, it had still been tainted by some of the sins of communism. The PCI found itself constantly on the defensive as if on trial: whenever it accepted a charge made by the prosecution and pronounced a *mea culpa*, a new indictment would spring up. The great paradox was that while the PCI was asked to prove, yet again, its commitment to Western democratic values, the two dominant Italian parties, the PSI and the DC, systematically ransacked the public purse.

After a year and a half of internecine disputes the PCI was finally dissolved in February 1991 at the Rimini Congress into a new party, the *Partito Democratico della Sinistra* (Democratic Party of the Left – PDS), with a sturdy oak as its new symbol. A coalition of traditionalists (Armando Cossutta) and supporters of the old 'New Left' within the party (Lucio Magri and Luciana Castellina) split and formed *Rifondazione Comunista* (RC). The PDS was accepted as a member of the Socialist International. West European communism had effectively lost its most prominent voice.

As the PDS was recovering from the self-inflicted pains of the process of trans-ition from the PCI, the *Tangentopoli* scandals erupted. The PDS had remained relatively quiet during the initial phase of the revelations. To some extent this is not surprising. It is true that it had always attacked the system of corruption and kickbacks, and that, with some important exceptions, it was relatively clean. But the PCI had never made anti-corruption an important platform of its propaganda. In the 1970s, Berlinguer had launched a campaign around *la questione morale*, 'the moral question' but this had received very little support even within his own party. The reason behind this timidity was twofold. In the first place, the PCI's insistence on its 'peculiarity' and 'specificity' as *the* clean party was always double-edged. Its opponents always seized on it to stress that the PCI's specificity was precisely that it was not fit to rule in a modern Western country, that somehow it did not belong to the Western political system. The second reason derives from the need to have allies without whom it was impossible for the PCI to become a party of government. Allies were required not only because no party could possibly hope to obtain an absolute majority in parliament under the old electoral system, but also because a communist party, however reformed, in power on its own in a West-ern country would have caused a national and international crisis. But where would the PCI find allies except among parties already in power? Its constant dilemma was whether to opt for an alliance with the DC (the *compromesso storico*) or with the PSI (the *alternativa di sinistra*). These were not policies which could be advocated while demanding the active criminal investigation of the leaders of parties with which an alliance was being sought. The polemic of the PCI was, con-sequently, always a general one: against the 'system of power' of the DC, against the *lottizzazione* (the spoil system) while, in practice, accepting it and occasionally taking part in it.

Thus the PDS did not capitalize at all on *Tangentopoli*. The elections of April 1992 were an utter disaster for the party. It was reduced to a mere 16.1 per cent while the rival *Rifondazione Comunista* obtained 5.6 per cent. The combined vote of the two parties was 5 per cent less than the already poor results obtained by the PCI in 1987. The future for the PDS appeared bleak. It sought to appear as a respectable left-of-centre party (not unlike what the PCI had been), eager to attract the modernizing middle classes which had supported Craxi. It also sought an inter-national legitimacy which could not any longer be denied to a party which had renounced the name of 'communist'. The consequence of this was that the PDS offered only a soft opposition to the Amato and Ciampi 'austerity' governments (1992–94) allowing *Rifondazione Comunista* the chance to establish themselves as a radical populist party of the left – which is why the designation of RC as an 'unreconstructed communist party' is mistaken. Indeed, in the European Parliament RC did form a group with the French and Portuguese communists preferring the company of the Spanish *Isquierda Unita* and the Danish Socialist People's Party. RC was able to increase its votes from 5.6 per cent in 1992 to 6.0 per cent in 1994 and 8.6 per cent in 1996. The risk for the Left as a whole was that the fate of *Rifondazione* would be similar to that of the MSI: to freeze and ghettoize 6–7 per cent of the left electorate. After 1996 this risk was minimized. Though *Rifondazione* could not have hoped to enter the left-of-centre coalition – had it wanted to – its votes were gratefully accepted to sustain the Prodi government.

The PDS emerged as the only party of the First Republic which had survived relatively unscathed. There was, in fact, no alternative to it on the left of the political spectrum except RC. In other words, all that remained of the Italian left was what had been included in the old Communist Party. The submerged 'left' which had been invoked by Occhetto never materialized. Nevertheless, the new party was not yet fully legitimized. The new electoral system, contrary to the rhetoric of its proponents, made the search for alliance more compelling than ever before. To ensure that the left coalition obtained a majority of votes in as many first-past-the-post constituencies the PDS was forced to construct an alliance system with the various small parties which had emerged: *La Rete, Alleanza Democratica*, the Green, fragments from the old PSI as well as *Rifondazione Comunista*. Each of these parties demanded and obtained a larger share of deputies than their electoral weight warranted. Altogether eight parties joined in the 'Progressive Alliance' to fight the 1994 elections. The alliance electoral cohesion had already been successfully tested in a series of local elections which took place at the end of 1993 when it captured important cities such as Rome and Turin. The programme of the alliance was similar to that of the PDS: decentralization of power (in part a response to the surge of the Northern League), limited privatization, control of the ever-expanding public debt (in continuity with the Amato and Ciampi governments).

Achille Occhetto, the PDS and the Progressive Alliance had been optimistic of a victory in 1994. From the point of view of the events of 1993 this optimism was understandable: the DC had been pulverized and nothing was left of the PSI. The Northern League could not hope, for obvious reasons, to become a national party. The former neo-fascist of *Alleanza Nazionale* appeared isolated and lacking in legitimacy. The Progressive coalition had not counted on the possibility that a new party, Berlusconi's *Forza Italia*, in coalition with Umberto Bossi's Northern League (in the North) and *Alleanza Nazionale* in the South, could dash their hopes of political power. When it had become clear that Berlusconi and his allies had a majority in the Chamber of Deputies, Occhetto conceded defeat. He assumed that the Italian political system had already become bipolar. In reality the situation was more fluid. Berlusconi was able to maintain his tripartite government in power for only seven months and the PDS, now led by Massimo D'Alema, became the most important force supporting the 'government of technicians' headed by Lamberto Dini throughout 1995. Much of the legitimation acquired by the PDS was due to this experience. The international markets perceived that Berlusconi was more an unreliable amateur than the barrier against spendthrift left-wing governments they had originally assumed him to be. D'Alema proceeded to forge a more coherent alliance – the Olive Tree – than the Progressive Coalition had been. Though the parties involved were similar, the Olive Tree had a recognized leader to set against Berlusconi: the Catholic economist, Romano Prodi.

D'Alema must probably be given much of the credit for the victory of the left at the 1996 elections. It had been, after all, a very narrow victory: it was only by keeping together a vast array of parties and groups, from the PPI and Dini's list on the right to RC on the left, that the Berlusconi's led coalition was denied victory. With Walter Veltroni as deputy prime minister, the veteran leader Giorgio Napolitano as the interior minister and a clutch of other cabinet posts, the majority party of the Italian left had finally succeeded in returning to government, 49 years after its expulsion. To achieve this objective it had to wait for the dismemberment of the Soviet system, abandon its name and its symbols and survive a political earthquake which had destroyed its old opponents and rivals. The Prodi government – discounting the support of RC which is not part of the coalition – was based on parties which, if taken together, had obtained less than 35 per cent of the vote – a little more than the Italian Communist Party had achieved at its peak twenty years previously in 1976.

The process of reconstruction of the Italian left initiated by Occhetto in 1989 has not yet been concluded. The constitution of a larger social democratic party with the definitive incorporation of the various fragments of the Italian left into it with a radical socialist party to its own left is – at the time of writing – the most likely scenario. It would make Italy homologous to countries such as France, Denmark, Norway, Spain and Greece where this division already exist.

The Italian Socialist Party

Though the PSI played a relatively minor role in the fight against fascism during the 1930s it re-emerged in 1943 as one of the fundamental forces in the Resistance. Although it did not have an organization able to match that of the PCI and could not count on the general support enjoyed by the DC through the Church, the PSI had greater electoral influence than the PCI: at the 1946 election it emerged as the second party. It soon lost this position and, after the 1953 elections, it remained the largest of the small parties, well behind the DC and the PCI until its demise in 1994.

Even when – as in 1946 – it had more votes than the PCI, it was subordinate to it: its internal organization was a replica of the PCI, but because it was not able to recruit widely it was a centralized party of cadres and militants without a mass base. It was subordinated to the PCI in other ways: first of all, most of its internal debates were directed not towards formulating a distinct political line but in establishing the degree of cooperation and of unity which it should have with the PCI. The most important feature of the National Council meeting of July 1945 was whether it should maintain its pact of unity with the PCI while keeping its own separate identity, or whether it should work for a fusion and the formation of a single large party of the working class.[61] The proponents of the first view (which obtained only 24 per cent of the votes) formed the nucleus of the anti-communist Saragat faction which eventually left the PSI and formed the Social Democratic Party (PSDI). Secondly, the PSI was, from the very beginning, connected to organizations already dominated by the PCI such as the cooperative movement, the leisure time and cultural organization ARCI and the trade union CGIL.[62] In foreign policy, the PSI followed a relatively close pro-Soviet line until 1956 (its leader Nenni had been awarded the Stalin prize).[63]

After the de-Stalinization process in the USSR and the invasion of Hungary, the PSI became more independent from the PCI and tried to close the gap with Saragat's social democrats (who had been part of the DC centrist coalition since the late 1940s). This was the process which would eventually take the PSI into government in the 1960s. When it formed a centre-left government with the DC it suffered a split which led to the formation of the left-wing Socialist Party of Proletarian Unity (PSIUP). It was prepared to pay this price because it hoped that a formal merger with the PSDI would create a powerful 'lay pole' to counterbalance the power of the DC inside the coalition government. The new party, now called the Unified Socialist Party, was defeated at the 1968 elections. The disastrous results made it impossible to maintain the unity of the new party and socialists and social democrats went their separate ways once more.

All in all, the experiment of the centre-left had been traumatic for the PSI. In the first place, it had to defend itself from the left (the PCI and the left-socialists) while having to face the DC, which was trying to sabotage the reform programme that was supposed to be the basis of the new coalition. In the second place, it became gradually transformed from a working-class party to a party of state and local government functionaries, of small entrepreneurs, of professional people and other urban groups.

When the workers' and students' movements emerged in 1968–69 the PSI tried to gain something from the PCI's obvious embarrassment at being outflanked from the left: it sought to become the institutional mediator between these social movements and the state, particularly as it had an advantage over the PCI: it actually was in government. In reality it gained nothing either politically or electorally while resenting the fact that the PCI appeared unsullied from the responsibilities of political power. When the PCI achieved its electoral success in 1976 the PSI was still stuck at around the 10 per cent mark. At that stage the socialist leadership felt it could no longer support a DC government on its own and while allowing the PCI to be the only opposition. In so doing the PSI increased the pressures on the DC to form a government of national unity with Giulio Andreotti as prime minister and with communist (and socialist) support.

The period of 'national unity' was a negative expérience for the PSI. In the previous centre-left governments the PSI was essential to the stability of the government and was the second most important force, while the 'government of national unity' was based on a DC–PCI axis. To both the PCI and the DC the PSI seemed an irrelevancy. What the socialist deputies said in parliament was hardly ever supported by the PCI who, in turn, had only one reference point: the DC. The communist attitude was further encouraged by the fact that the PSI played very little part in decision-making. Socialist deputies had a very high rate of absenteeism, and took very little interest in the policies being discussed. Out of 666 laws examined in those years the DC had expressed its official position in 94 per cent of the cases, the PCI in 90 per cent but the PSI in only 49 per cent.[64] The chief reason beyond this blatant socialist lack of interest in the policies of the government was that the PSI had an a priori negative view of the DC-PCI alliance, a view which, in the circumstances, was not unjustified.

In this period the PSI was more concerned with the problem of reconstructing its own image and establishing what its long-term role would be in Italian society. Its official line was that it should work for a 'left-wing alternative' government, i.e. a PCI-PSI government which would exclude the DC. Considering that after 1979 the PSI tried to reconstitute the centre-left coalition and was in bitter polemic with the PCI it is difficult to establish how far this policy was taken seriously. However, in the period 1976–80 the main preoccupation of the PSI was to demarcate itself from both the DC and the PCI and the policy of 'left-wing alternative' – then unacceptable to the PCI – fulfilled this criterion and was sanctioned by two party congresses (the Fortieth in 1976 and the Forty-first in 1979) even though these also sanctioned the victory of the new leader, Bettino Craxi, whose distaste for the PCI had always been evident.[65]

The demoralization of the rank and file in those years can be illustrated by reference to the results of a survey conducted in 1978 among the delegates to the party's regional conferences: 72 per cent thought that the party had been too subordinated to the DC, 79 per cent thought that the party was too corrupt, 94 per cent that its chief weakness was that it was badly organized. Only 45 per cent thought that the PSI ran the risk of being subordinated to the PCI in the case of a left-wing alliance (although among Craxi's own supporters this increased to 70 per cent).[66]

The PSI was self-critically aware that it had a bad image and that it had failed to win votes in the 1976 elections when the rest of the left had done so well. It realized that its members were increasingly concentrated in the tertiary sector and in the South while it was losing ground in the education system and among the working class and the intellectuals. By 1979 it sought to present itself as the only party which could guarantee the 'governability' of the country: the DC was described as a traditional conservative party in decline while the PCI was a traditional working-class party condemned to be either a part of the 'support system' of the DC, as it had been in 1976–79, or a sectarian opposition. Thus the PSI could seek to occupy the 'central' position that the DC could no longer hold and the PCI could never hope to conquer.[67]   .

A battle on two fronts was necessary in order to obtain better representation at the central government level with the DC and at the local level with the PCI. The slogan of 'governability' meant essentially stable coalition governments and, as all stable coalitions need a central element, the PSI developed the image of the 'reformist party of the centre'.

Not for the first time the PSI needed a new base on which to build its new image. After the hot autumn of 1969 it had hoped to expand its working-class base; during the 1974 battle for the referendum on divorce it sought to become the party of modern secular Italy, and during the peak of terrorism and anti-terrorism legislation it tried to be the party of civil liberties against the 'repressive' tendencies of traditional Catholicism and communism.[68] The problem for the PSI was that the PCI had sufficient political resources and ability to manage, every time, to recuperate lost positions and to occupy or conquer these 'political spaces'. In Italy the PSI might have become the party of the progressive middle classes – an influential sector ill at ease in the DC and unwilling to support the PCI. Here, however, the PSI had to compete not only with the DC but also with the other small parties of the centre: social democrats, republicans and liberals.

In pursuing the 'centre' the PSI could not ignore the fact that the success of other European socialist parties often coincided with their being identified not only with a new image of modernity and dynamism, but also with a radicalism of the left: the electoral successes of the socialist parties of France, Spain and Greece in the 1980s had coincided with a diffuse desire for change. In the case of the Greeks and the Spaniards the success of the socialists has also been facilitated by the fact that they rose to power shortly after the defeat of authoritarian regimes and that they were able to build their support after the collapse of the previous regime.[69] The French Socialist Party was successful in the 1981 elections because it was able to forge an alliance with the French Communist Party and was yet clearly demarcated from them (this was made particularly easy by the sectarian behaviour of the French Communist Party). The PSI's problem was that it faced a communist party unlikely to repeat the mistakes of their French counterparts. Furthermore, the 1983 election showed that the Republican Party (PRI) was able to mobilize considerable support among those urban middle classes which had been the PSI's main target: thus the PRI became the third party after the PCI and the DC in Milan and Turin.

By 1984 the PSI had been successful in obtaining more power, but not more votes. It obtained the prime ministership, but with only 11 per cent of the votes, still well below that 15 per cent which would have enabled it to reshuffle the cards of the political game.

In the 1980s the PSI sought to establish what was commonly referred to as 'decisionist' style, a 'resolute' approach to politics (a similar style was cultivated by Margaret Thatcher). The major role was played by Craxi himself, whose prominent political profile stood out in the otherwise relatively grey world of Italian politics. By 1981 he had established a unparalleled degree of personal power inside the PSI.[70] The PSI stopped offering political programmes and trying to appeal to a stable network of groups and social classes. It downgraded its activists in favour of direct media messages. In this sense it was a post-modern party held together by its leader not its programme.[71] Craxi's leadership style paved the way for Silvio Berlusconi. Indeed, once he became prime minister Craxi developed a close friendship with Berlusconi who was beginning to build up his own private media empire. This was mutually beneficial. Berlusconi, unhindered by any regulatory or antitrust legislation, established a private television monopoly which regularly supported Craxi.[72] Craxi, who defined his brand of socialism 'liberal socialism', had become obsessed with the theme of 'governability' and sought to strengthen the executive pending a thorough reform of Italian politics and its transformation into a presidential republic.[73] Nevertheless, the official documentation of the PSI, including its manifestos and programmes, tended to be couched in a generic and vague language (like that of most other Italian political parties) which refrained from making definite political commitments.[74] Consequently, the 'modernization' of the PSI remained nebulous. In Italy, as in some other southern European countries, modernity meant adopting a foreign model. In the first phase of Craxi's reconstruction of the PSI the goal had seemed that of building an Italian-style Labour Party. It soon became apparent that the majority of the working class would remain loyal to the PCI. Then Craxi turned for inspiration to Mitterrand's *Parti socialiste*, which was particularly enticing as the PS had just supplanted the PCF as the largest party of the French left. The idea was to adopt the French model of a federation of 'clubs'. What actually developed was an Italian replica of the old and discredited French socialist party (SFIO) of the years of Mollet: a set of federations controlled by local bosses usually loyal to Craxi who took all decisions.[75]

Craxi's neo-revisionism must be understood with reference to the peculiar position of the PSI as a minority partner in a coalition government (few other socialist parties have been in this position) and the exceptional position of being still the junior party of the left. As a governing party the PSI distinguished itself from the PCI by becoming a vociferously anti-Soviet party, accepting, more or less unquestioningly, the siting of Cruise missiles in Italy (against the strong opposition of the PCI and of many Catholic and pacifist groups). In so doing, it paralleled the policies of some of the other governing socialist parties such as the *Parti socialiste* in France – who supported the installation of the 'euromissiles' and the Spanish socialist party (PSOE), who led Spain into NATO. Nevertheless, no systematic project characterized the revisionism of the PSI. It had many and hence it had none. Projects, schemes, plans, manifestos, slogans, self-definitions were produced for specific purposes and then disposed, once consumed. How better to discomfit the enemy than to shift constantly? Now a Europeanist, now a nationalist, now pro-Arab, now pro-Israeli, now reformist, now moderate, now populist, now technocratic, Craxi kept his followers loyal by having no fixed rules, no certain principles and no directions.[76] Above all, as Gino Giugni remarked, Craxi's power depended essentially on maintaining the peculiarity of the First Republic, that is the impossibility of an alternative to the hegemony of the DC.[77]

The strategy of Craxi had been to occupy – at least in rhetoric – the political space no other Italian party could inhabit, that of a modernizing neo-liberal party. While both the DC and the PCI were parties committed to public spending and social protection, the PSI appeared less encumbered. It could cultivate the rising entrepreneurial middle classes of Milan and the rest of Lombardy while continuing to appeal to a (diminishing) proportion of skilled workers. By the end of 1989 its purported economic policies of fiscal rigour, public sector efficiency and privatization were virtually indistinguishable from those of neo-liberals.[78] In the South, however, the practice of the PSI was frankly clientelist and hence in direct competition with the DC which is why, in 1990, it re-affirmed its traditional belief that the public sector would be determinant in ending the backwardness of the *Mezzogiorno*.[79] There was thus a profound contradiction between an interventionist strategy in the South and a neo-liberal one in the North. In 'image' terms the neo-liberal strategy prevailed: in the 1980s the PSI sought to decrease inflation and the budget deficit, deregulate the financial and labour markets and reform the welfare system. In reality the PSI had become an alter-ego of the DC: by 1992 it had become a thoroughly clientelist party particularly strong in the South. Bribery had become a common mechanism for replenishing the coffers of the party and enriching some of its leading members. When the corruption scandals demolished Italy's First Republic (1992–94) a section of the DC survived but the PSI, which had just celebrated its centenary, was utterly destroyed. It was dissolved on 12 November 1994 – an ignominious end for Italy's oldest party. Many of its leaders were investigated or indicted for bribery. Craxi fled the country and took refuge in his Tunisian villa to avoid possible imprisonment. The champion of modernity had become the supreme example of everything that was old and corrupt in Italy.[80]

During his tenure in power, Craxi had received considerable support from opinion-makers and historians including those who realized that the man had little integrity. Thus Silvio Lanaro gives him credit for the good performance of the Italian economy in 1983–87 (forgetting the international recovery), the installation of Cruise missiles, the reform of the indexation of wages though he admits that Craxi was destroying his party, kept up unacceptable friendships, did not care about the diffuse corruption and favoured widespread patronage.[81] Craxi's downfall took many by surprise, but the real surprise was that he was caught at all, not that his record had not been unblemished.

Very little remained of the PSI after the downfall of Craxi. Various fragments tried to re-establish a socialist presence including the Laburisti Italiani led by Valdo Spini and the *Socialisti Italiani* initially led by the former trade unionist Del Turco. None of these small groups could hope, on their own, to obtain the minimum electoral quota required to win seats on the proportional list. The total social democratization of the PDS will, inevitably, make it unlikely that a socialist party independent of it could ever rise again. The ambition of many socialists was to eliminate the Italian 'anomaly': a strong communist party and a weak socialist party. In 1994, Italy had become, at least in this respect, 'normal': there was a small communist party (*Rifondazione Comunista*) and a strong socialist party (the PDS). Paradoxically, this occurred only when the old Italian PSI had gone for good.

The *Lega Nord*

It is significant that the party which contributed the most to the demise of the First Republic has not been one of the 'old' parties – such as the PCI or the far right MSI – but a new formation: the Northern League which was quite distinct from the older regionalist parties such as the *Union Valdôtaine* (in the Val d'Aosta), the *Südtiroler Volkspartei* (the German-speaking party of the Trentino-Alto-Adige) and the *Partito Sardo d'Azione* (in Sardinia).

The League is itself an associations of various local leagues of which the most important was, originally, the *Liga Veneta* (the Venetian League – the Venetian term *liga* was used in preference to the Italian *lega*). When it achieved 4.2 per cent in the Veneto (and 10 per cent in some parts of the province of Vicenza – a stronghold of the DC) there was considerable surprise, but most commentators assumed that this would be little more than a 'flash' party, a protest vote expressing voters' discontent.[82] Diamanti, the leading specialist of the *Lega*, did not join such consensus). By 1987 the *Lega* (I shall use this term as the collective noun for all the leagues of northern Italy) had lost a few votes in the Veneto (down to 3.1 per cent) but had already established itself in Lombardy (3 per cent) and Piedmont (4.3 per cent). In the regional elections of 1990 the *Lega* obtained 18.9 per cent of the votes in Lombardy. This signalled its insertion into national politics for two reasons: such a significant score cannot be ignored in a country with more than half dozen parties and Lombardy is the financial and entrepreneurial centre of the country.

The investigations into corruption which developed after February 1992 provoked an immediate outcry. As a result the *Lega*, whose popularity had been growing for some months, emerged as the major force in much of the North. Though it obtained only 8.7 per cent of the national vote (a slightly higher percentage than in 1994 when it captured 8.4 per cent), it destroyed in one fell swoop the monopoly of power achieved by the Christian Democrats and the Socialist Party in Lombardy, Venetia and some areas of Piedmont where it obtained between 30 and 40 per cent of the vote. By the end of 1993 the *Lega* had won all local elections held in Italy's richest region, Lombardy, and captured its most coveted prize, the municipality of Milan.

The central campaigning theme of the *Lega* was the same as the object of the magistrates' investigation: the misappropriation of public money by the political parties. Though the *Lega*'s overt political appeal was regionalist, at times even secessionist, it was never a classic 'nationalist' party like the Scottish National Party in Britain or the Corsican nationalists in France or the Basque in Spain. In spite of the efforts made to invent it, there is no nationalist Lombard or Venetian consciousness. Even to talk of a strong regional consciousness in Lombardy or Venetia would be an exaggeration. With the exception of Sicily and Sardinia there is little deep-seated regional awareness in Italy. There is, of course, a strong city-based consciousness: people may be proud to be Milanese or Turinese but being a Lombard or a Piemontese is less significant. The *Lega Nord* appealed to a diffuse anti-southern sentiment with strong racist overtones: northerners are 'modern', 'European', honest, frugal, work hard, are efficient, enlightened, educated; southerners are backward, practically African or Arabs, are thieves, lazy, inefficient, intolerant, beat their women, prostitute their wives and daughters and are insanely jealous. There were times in which Bossi stooped to straightforward racist tirades as when he declared to a weekly magazine that skin colour differences are detrimental to social peace: 'Imagine if your street, your piazza was full of people of colour, you would not longer feel at home.'[83] On the whole, however, the anti-southernism of the *Lega* was not really 'ethnic' though it was built on prejudices which were well rooted in the North. The anti-southernism was directed against the State, Rome, against clientelism, against public spending in the South. As Umberto Bossi put it, with characteristic bluntness, politicians are 'all thieves'.[84] As the president of the DC, Ciriaco De Mita, warned in 1991 and as Berlusconi discovered to his cost in 1995, this makes the *Lega* difficult to co-opt.[85]

The more sophisticated *leghisti* would claim that the South and the southern question (defined as a question of backwardness) has somehow perverted the Italian state, dragging it down into an unhealthy and parasitic *mafioso* capitalism sustained by public handouts and creating a culture of dependency. Like other regional-nationalist in other European countries, the *Lega* is strongly pro-European, arguing that an independent North would be able to strike for itself a better bargain in a federal Europe. Thus the *Lega* cannot be seen as a purely Italian phenomenon. It espouses the nationalism of the better-off regions, such as the Catalan and Basque nationalists in Spain and, to some extent, that of post-oil boom Scotland.

The central characteristic of the *Lega* was that it gave political form to a taxpayers' revolt against an increasingly dysfunctional welfare state. A book written by a leading *leghista*, Giulio Savelli (a former 1960s radical) called *Cosa vuole la Lega* (What the *Lega* wants) is almost completely dedicated to the question of taxes. It contains very little nationalism.[86] Fiscal revolts have been a common feature of the politics of the West for well over twenty years as the willingness of taxpayers to tolerate a high tax burden constantly decreased from Denmark – where Mogens Gilstrup's Progress Party became the second largest party in 1973 – to California – where tax-cutting referendums repeatedly gained majorities.

The typical *Lega Nord* voters were not Lombard nationalists but angry and frustrated taxpayers for whom the Italian state had become a corrupt machine whose main purpose was to syphon off their hard won resources and transfer them to southerners in exchange for votes.[87] As Bossi explained: 'The Centre and the South contribute only 36 per cent of GDP, yet it absorbs 55 per cent of public expenditure. Rome takes far more than it gives to the North: the clearest example is Lombardy which receives from the capital less than two-third of what it gives the state. An authentic legal robbery.'[88] A typical electoral poster of the *Lega* depicted a Piedmontese goose laying golden eggs in the direction of Rome and the South.

Southerners thus became the Italian equivalent of those single mothers, welfare scroungers and undesirable immigrants who, elsewhere, have become the principal targets of conservative politicians.

According to the popular northern prejudice which the *leghisti* have embraced, if Northern Italy were allowed to go its own way, it would rapidly become modern, efficient and clean. Everything would work. It would be just like Switzerland instead of being like North Africa. Its inhabitants would pay less tax and be more prosperous. There would be no corruption. The *Lega* is the Italian expression of the pro-market ideology which has swept the Western world since the end of the 1970s. The dissatisfied electorate of the DC in the North could turn to an alternative party whose identity was territorially defined (the entire North), whose message expressed a profound contempt for all established parties linked to clear anti-tax sentiments. As Bossi explained in his book, significantly entitled *La Rivoluzione*, there can be 'no taxation without representation' (in English in the Italian text): 'The Revolution led by the League is the only possible socio-economic revolution in an advanced industrial society. It signals the advent of federalist liberalism.'[89]

The anti-tax agenda of the *Lega* gained in popularity because it was directed against specific targets: the political establishment in Rome and southerners who were regarded as a drain on the national economy. It should be added that it is difficult to pinpoint the ideology of the *Lega* and that, to some extent, this lack of definition constitutes one of its strengths. In terms of media exposure, the *Lega* has achieved remarkable feats largely thanks to its leader, Umberto Bossi (few of its other leaders have obtained national recognition). Yet few political parties have been so criticized by the media. The *Lega* cannot match Berlusconi's television support and has no newspaper (with the exception of *L'Independente* which has limited circulation). In its early days, the *Lega* emphasized its anti-southern message. Later it played with the theme of secession from Italy. In 1994 it entered an electoral pact with Berlusconi and was a reluctant and highly uncooperative member of his coalition. To distance itself from the largely southern post-fascist *Alleanza Nazionale*, it emphasized anti-fascism as a component of modern northern culture. It soon brought down the Berlusconi government and, indirectly, facilitated the victory of the centre-left in 1996 by refusing to renew its alliance with the right. By then Bossi was emphasizing, once again, the theme of secession even announcing the creation, in September 1996, of the State of Padania – a publicity stunt which was not taken seriously by most Italian commentators.

At the election of 1996 the *Lega* grew in strength obtaining 10.1 per cent of the national vote. Apart from contributing to the end of the First Republic the main achievement of the *Lega* has been to implant on the Italian agenda the theme of federalism and devolution of power to which all political parties, except the far-right *Alleanza Nazionale*, have paid lip service.

It is difficult, at this stage, to predict the future of the *Lega*. Its tenure will depend on the ability of Bossi – one of the few authentically charismatic leaders to have emerged in recent years – to maintain a high enough profile to consolidate the share of the vote of the *Lega*. Its chief problem is that its regional nature – its chief asset – is also the main obstacle to its electoral growth: it is not possible for the *Lega* to become a national party. It is therefore difficult to imagine a situation in which the *Lega* could obtain more than 10–15 per cent of the national vote, that is 30–40 per cent of the northern vote.

Who are the *leghisti*? It appears that they are the most 'male' party in Italy, thus confirming Bossi's vulgar boast regarding the uncommon virility of his supporters. They attract a slightly disproportionate number of young electors with an educational level slightly lower than average. They tend to have a greater proportion of self-employed and working-class people than most other parties and they come from provincial towns rather than large centres.[90] Apart from the prevalence of the male vote, the electorate of the *Lega* does not therefore present unusual characteristics. If we wanted to attempt a generalization we could say that they represent a male section of the old DC electorate of the North: the owners of small firms and their employees. For this reason alone, the future of the PPI (the most important heir to the DC) is closely tied to the fortunes of the *Lega*: the PPI would be the most obvious beneficiary of an eventual disintegration of the *Lega*. The *Lega* has no particular religious dimension. It sees itself as constituting an 'inter-class' bloc of 'real producers' – bosses and their workers – against 'the dominant bloc of subsidized bureaucrats'.[91] Savelli, the editor of the League's newspaper, explains complainingly, with a characteristic disregard for the facts: 'Large firms can count on public contributions for their investments . . . but the small and medium-sized enterprises have no-one to defend them, are overtaxed by a greedy fiscal system, are deprived of the chance to modernize themselves, and have costs which make them uncompetitive in European markets.'[92]

They are united first of all by their regional belonging and, secondly, by a pronounced dislike of political parties and of the established political system. They are not 'extremists' in the sense that they hold a deeply held desire for a major change in the political order, though they may approve of the 'extreme' language of their leaders and may deserve the appellation of 'extremists of the centre'.[93] They do not support secession, though they may use the threat of secession to obtain more concessions from Rome. They believe in the free market but do not share the neo-liberals' deep hostility to the welfare state.[94] They are, in fact, the nearest political expression of the small and medium-sized enterprises which have been the backbone of the economic success of Italy in these last twenty years. It is for this reason, above all, that no political party will be able to ignore them. It is, in fact, remarkable that the *Lega Nord* obtained electoral successes in some of the most prosperous areas of the country where employment was relatively high, where fiscal evasion enabled small entrepreneurs to have a high rate of consumption and a high rate of savings. So the success of the *Lega* cannot be due to a deterioration in the economic situation.

While its main problem is the difficulty it has in finding allies, it has the advantage of flexibility. It can shift to the left using anti-fascist, absorb Catholics by advocating local autonomy and federalism, appeal to the centre and the right by insisting on market forces and economic efficiency.

Berlusconi's *Forza Italia*

The party created by Silvio Berlusconi is a rare, perhaps a unique, example of a commercial enterprise which becomes a political party, using largely its own personnel as 'political cadres', its own finances, its own structures to set up a network of clubs. Many of these were, in fact, the clubs supporting the Milan football team whose proprietor was Berlusconi himself. It was, of course, a rather unique enterprise as it consisted of what is generally agreed to be the most important political resource: a broadcasting system made up of three TV networks with 45 per cent share of the audience. The singularity of *Forza Italia* also consisted in the fact that it was the only significant post-First Republic party which appeared to be truly new: all the others had, in one way or other, roots in the past: *Rifondazione Comunista* and the PDS 'descended' from the PCI, the various Catholic groupings from the DC, *Alleanza Nazionale* from the MSI. Even the *Lega Nord* had started life in the 1980s though it obtained its first major successes in 1992. A further peculiarity is that this party, having been created on 26 January 1994, proceeded to win the largest share of the vote on 27 March – two months after its birth – and its leader became, albeit briefly, prime minister.

If his party was 'new', Berlusconi was a typical creature of the last stages of the old system. His rise to supreme economic power in the broadcasting media owed much to the less impressive aspects of the First Republic, namely, its dysfunctional use of public resources for private ends. The persistence of the state monopoly of television and radio had created a huge demand for diversity. The refusal of the authorities to allow the birth of a private system meant that when it finally appeared, it was largely unregulated. Without the support and the complicity of key members of the old political class, especially Bettino Craxi, it is unlikely that a single man would have been able to obtain a monopoly of the private system.

The widespread distaste which Italians manifested for established politicians meant that any non-professional aspiring politician had an advantage: the chance to appear as a 'man of the people', unsullied by political power. The fact that this 'man of the people' was the richest businessman in the country was irrelevant: Berlusconi was of humble origins, had not inherited his money but had made it himself, and had done so by developing the most popular entertainment in existence and increasing the choice available to millions of Italians. He benefitted from the strong personalization of politics – a trend which, in Italy, had been initiated by Craxi.

In a country where entrepreneurs are nearly as well known as footballers and film stars, Berlusconi was – with Gianni Agnelli – the best known. He had thus maximum visibility. None of this would have guaranteed him political success had it not been for three interrelated causes.

The most obvious was that the collapse of the First Republic gave Berlusconi both the motivation to enter politics and the electoral basis to do so. His electorate consisted overwhelming of those who had voted for the DC and the PSI. In fact in 1994 he captured nearly half the electorate of both parties and did spectacularly well in Sicily, where he obtained one-third of the vote, much more than his national average.[95] The collapse of these parties in the local elections of 1993 had given their electorates a clear indication that they needed to re-group elsewhere. Many had already proceeded to do so by switching: in the North, to the Northern League and in the South, to *Alleanza Nazionale*. There was thus an electorate looking for a party. In commercial terms – something which would not have escaped the business acumen of Berlusconi – this was a typical instance of demand waiting for the supply to materialize, as had happened in the case of private broadcasting. The strength of Berlusconi was that he was able to speak in a plain and simple language, like Umberto Bossi and unlike so many 'professional' politicians who still speak a complex language alien to that the majority of the population.

By being different Berlusconi benefited from a trend which had become apparent since the late 1970s: the constant growth in the number of people who declared that 'politicians are all the same', the regular increase in the number of abstentions and spoilt ballots and the votes for new parties (like the Green).[96] He quickly realized that the only way the success of the left could have been blocked in 1994 was to find a way of uniting the electorate of the *Lega* to that of *Alleanza Nazionale*. Though he was not able to recoup the abstentionist vote, this increased in 1994 and 1996, he appealed directly to the conservative electorate who might have been tempted to abstain by pointing out that he represented the new, that he was out to change the country in alliance with those – like the *Lega* and *Alleanza Nazionale* – who did not belong to the old establishment. The construction of an alliance with the right-wing *Alleanza Nazionale* in the South and the *Lega* in the North enabled him to 'win' the 1994 elections, though this was not enough to achieve a majority in the Senate or obtain a firm government commitment from Bossi.

The ideological appeal of Berlusconi's *Forza Italia* was based on a mixture of the appeal of Craxi: modernity, anti-communism and entrepreneurship. As a standard-bearer of neo-liberal market economics, he was far more credible than either the old PSI or the DC. Of the PDS he declared in January 1994, when he announced his candidature: 'They claim to have become liberal-democrats. But this is not true . . . They do not believe in the market, they do not believe in private enterprise, they do not believe in the profit motive, they do not believe in the individual. They have not changed. They want to transform the country in a public crowd which screams, wails, castigates, condemns.'[97]

For a while Berlusconi appeared as the embodiment of a major turning-point in Italian history. Some saw in him a man of destiny who would clean up the country and set it in motion once again, others feared him as a new charismatic leader who would revive the authoritarian tendencies of the fascist era, still others accused him of further cheapening the level of political debates by importing from the USA the technical ability to manipulate public opinion. This is the stuff of current affairs. While predicting the future in so unstable a political system is a waste of time, a more sober assessment of the Berlusconi phenomenon would have to start by pointing out that he obtained in both 1994 and 1996 around 20 per cent of the vote. This is far less than the DC had achieved throughout its 50 years of existence and even less than the PCI had obtained in all elections between 1948 and 1987. Berlusconi's room for manoeuvre is therefore rather reduced. He faces an ally, *Alleanza Nazionale*, which is more rooted as a party and whose leader, Gianfranco Fini is younger and more sure-footed than Berlusconi. The longer the leader of *Forza Italia* remains in the public view, the longer he will appear as a politician like all the others – the problem with novelty is that it never lasts long. Nevertheless, it would be wrong to assume that Berlusconi is bound to disappear, though he could, of course, decide to return to the more satisfying task of developing further his media empire. In 1996 he managed to hold on to 20.6 per cent of the vote even though, unlike in 1994, the right-wing Catholic group CCD–CDU decided to fight the election separately in the proportional list. Thus it could be argued that *Forza Italia* increased its share of the vote. Berlusconi's electorate is unlikely to desert him unless a real alternative were to appear which could be either a clearly post-fascist *Alleanza Nazionale*, or a reconstructed conservative Catholic party.

The post-fascist right

During the life of the First Republic the *Movimento Sociale Italiano* or Italian Social Movement (MSI) was Italy's fourth strongest party (around 5–6 per cent of the vote in most elections before 1994) and the most powerful 'neo-fascist party' in Western Europe.[98] It was formed on 26 December 1946 by second-level cadres of the Fascist Regime of Salò MSI with the explicit purpose of giving a voice to those who still identified themselves with fascism.[99] Its electorate, however, was largely made up of the relatively apolitical supporters of a short-lived populist party, the party of the *Uomo Qualunque* (Ordinary Man Party). The name adopted by the MSI suggested that it took its ideology from the radical anti-conservative and anti-monarchist aspects of fascism: it called itself a movement and not a party, and the word 'social' echoed the self-definition of the Northern republic created by Mussolini: the *Repubblica Sociale di Salò* – in reality a Nazi puppet state. Originally then, the MSI was fascist in everything but name: it was anti-democratic and 'revolutionary' and led by a former blackshirt, Giorgio Almirante. It was a sort of 'left-wing' fascism whose leaders reminded the Italians 'We are fascists, but we are those fascists who fought to provide the country with a social and pro-trade union legislation, we are those fascists in favour of centrally agreed wage contracts . . . in favour of trade unions as free association of workers democratically organized . . . in favour of workers participation in the running of their enterprises and in profit sharing.'[100] By 1956, however, Almirante had been ousted and the party was led by conservative figures, people who aspired to traditional values, pro-clerical principles and an authoritarian state. Throughout the 1950s the strategy of the MSI was to obtain some form of legitimacy from the Christian Democrats and to strengthen the traditionalists inside the DC. Thus, in 1952, there was an attempt to set up a municipal coalition in Rome with the DC which was defeated by the Catholic left; in 1957 the MSI supported the Zoli government, in 1959 that of Segni and, in 1960 that of Tambroni. This last was the nearest the MSI ever got to political power during the First Republic. However, following protests in Genoa against the attempt of the MSI to hold its party congress in a city with a major Resistance record, the Tambroni government was forced to resign. The MSI became a pariah party. This and the revival of left-wing extremism in 1968 led to a revival of the fortunes of the hardliner Almirante who was, once again, at the head of the party.[101]

The MSI had a strong organizational structure: many branches, tens of thousands of members, a youth section, a women's section, a students federation, veterans and even a small trade union the CISNAL. There was also a galaxy of small illegal or semi-legal organizations tied in a variety of ways to the party.[102] But this, far from transforming the MSI into a mass party (like the PCI), simply condemned to a political ghetto.

This was the fate of the MSI for much of the First Republic. It is true that, in 1970, the Christian Democrat Giovanni Leone could not have been elected president without the votes of the MSI, but, on the whole, the MSI remained a party at the margins of political life with an insignificant presence in local government: in 1984 it had only 27 mayors out of 8,000.[103] This could only be seen as a serious decline because in 1952 it had been able, in alliance with the monarchists, to control southern cities of some importance: Naples, Bari, Foggia, Lecce, Benevento and Salerno. Soon, these positions of power were lost. No other party in post-war Italian history could have felt so excluded from political power. Its leaders and supporters had virtually no access to the media and the press.

Throughout the 1960s and 1970s the MSI became an increasingly southern party (where, historically, fascism, a northern movement, was weak under Mussolini), thus strengthening a trend which originated in the 1950s and was well-established by 1972 when it merged with the Monarchist Party, in effect absorbing it. In the southern cities in which it is strong, such as Catania (Sicily) and Naples, the MSI gathered the votes of many members of the self-employed lower-middle class, the unemployed, the pensioners, and men and whenever scepticism against politicians, and anti-communist attitudes prevailed. In Rome it is particularly strong among minor civil servants and marginalized youth.[104]

Ideologically, it sought to picture itself as the defender of Western civilization against communism and the Third World. Though it adopted a pro-NATO position (having initially been against Italy joining it), a majority of its supporters had a negative view of the USA. Faithful to its origins as the party of corporatism against economic liberalism and conscious that much of its southern electorate depended on public spending, the party remained hostile – at least until the mid-1990s – to the idea of unleashing market forces. It remained statist, *dirigiste*, nationalist, an upholder of the prerogatives of the nation-state and unhappy about European integration. In foreign policy the MSI still made territorial claims on parts of disintegrating Yugoslavia and committed to a reduction of US influence in Europe.[105] Electoral considerations also dictated its support for traditional views of the family and the role of women, hence its stand against divorce and abortion. Its major theme, however, was a sustained polemic not against democracy as such but against the *partitocrazia*, the domination of parties in Italian political life and in particular, the corruption of the DC and the PSI. The corollary of this was that the main institutional reform propounded by the MSI was the direct election of the President of the Republic, a proposal which was eventually adopted by Craxi, Cossiga and Pannella before becoming adopted, after the end of the First Republic, by the entire centre-right and some sectors of the left.

During the late 1960s and 1970s the MSI had been tainted by terrorism. It was widely assumed that some of its more extremist fringes – organizations such as *Ordine Nuovo* and *Avanguardia Nazionale* created in 1955–65 – had become involved with the right-wing terrorism.[106] Partly to counter this, and partly to direct attention towards the terrorism of the left, the MSI attempted to organize a 'silent majority' against left-wing extremism. This was Almirante's dual strategy. On the one hand, it tolerated links with right-wing extremists while on the other it sought to become a respectable right-wing conservative party by declaring its acceptance of democracy. He had hoped that the merger with the monarchist party and the addition of the initials DN (*Destra Nazionale* or National Right) after the letters would help the formation of a 'greater Right'. However, this endeavour failed, though the MSI obtained its best results in the 1972 elections when it achieved 8.7 per cent.

The legitimization of the MSI began slowly: in 1982 the radical leader Marco Pannella participated at the congress of the MSI. Bettino Craxi encouraged the process further by consulting the MSI – along with all the other parties – during the process of forming his own government and Almirante was allowed to pay homage to the body of Berlinguer in 1984.[107] Until the collapse of the first republic, however, the MSI was not able to capitalize on what could have been its strongest card: the fact that its hands had remained relatively clean of corruption. It is not uncharitable to assume that this was due not so much to the honesty of its cadres than to the fact that it had been kept distant from any centre of power, be it national or local.

At the end of 1980s the MSI was still isolated but this was due as much to political reasons as to its attachment to fascism. The fact of the matter was that politics had become the prerogative of the five-party coalition whose aim was to keep the PCI out of power. The MSI was irrelevant to the system. Objectively, this isolation helped the left because its net effects was to keep frozen 5–6 per cent of the vote which might have gone to the DC or to a party with which the DC could make a deal. The insertion of the MSI (under a new name) into the mainstream of Italian politics occurred because the political framework had radically altered, not because its leaders had disowned their fascist roots. Indeed, at the January 1990 Congress of the party, Gianfranco Fini, the former leader of the youth section who succeeded Almirante in December 1987, still defined the party as the heir to fascism and condemned 'the values and life-style of the West (politically liberal-democratic, capitalist in economic matters and spiritually materialist)'.[108] This was not enough to ensure his re-election. From January 1990 to early in 1991 the MSI was led by Pino Rauti, an adherent to the revolutionary and anti-capitalist conception of the party, and close to its radical wing.[109] Fini had used his period out of office to cultivate links with the Catholics, and to develop, in the wake of the Gulf War, a distinctive pro-Western attitude. President Cossiga – by then cold-shouldered by the political establishment because of his increasingly bizarre behaviour and the revelation concerning his role in the secret anti-communist organization *Gladio* – had encouraged the young 'post-fascist' (as he should perhaps be now called) and openly demonstrated his friendship. By the time Rauti resigned following losses in local elections, Fini, now back at the helm of the party, had established a network of respectable contacts. These had not been discouraged by the fact that, in 1992, the MSI held a meeting in Piazza Venezia (from whose balcony Mussolini addressed the crowds) to celebrate the anniversary of the March on Rome. The MSI would have remained a pariah party had not the DC and the PSI collapsed after the 1992 elections. Nevertheless, there is little doubt that had the MSI remained under the control of an open admirer of fascist blackshirts such as Rauti, it would have been extremely difficult for Berlusconi to legitimize the MSI, which had changed its name to *Alleanza Nazionale*, so quickly and so effectively. By 1993–94 the party appeared transformed. While the PCI, to become acceptable, had to spend over twenty years in continuous revisionism, all the neo-fascists had to do to turn themselves into tolerable post-fascists was to accept that anti-fascism had had the merit of re-establishing democracy, and that the racism and anti-semitism of the past had been wrong. No further self-critical analysis was required. What really legitimated the party was not the pro-democratic declarations of Fini (Almirante had made similar ones previously) but the complete modification of the party system.

What are the attitudes of the party rank-and-file? Have they too accepted the rules of the democratic games? Surveys conducted at the end of the 1980s do not give an unambiguous response. Nearly a majority of activists (48.8 per cent) were keen to form part of a coalition governments with the parties of the centre including the socialists, but 28.3 per cent remained 'against the system'. Being 'against the system' led many activists to indicate that the parties they felt closest to were the far-left *Democrazia proletaria* and the Greens, and Bettino Craxi the leader they admired the most.[110] As expected a large majority (72.1 per cent) were in favour of the repatriation of illegal immigrants, 44.1 per cent, by Italian standards a high proportion.

What was less expected was that 70.8 per cent were supporters of sexual equality, 57.8 per cent against the view that 'in the family the man must take all important decisions' and 66.5 per cent in favour of income redistribution. Its supposedly anti-clerical past belied by the 54.4 per cent in favour of the compulsory teaching of Catholicism in state schools, something which had not been even attempted by Christian Democracy during its 50 years in office.[111] Later surveys conducted in the 1990s showed a persistently high level of anti-Americanism (94 per cent of the delegates to its congress think the US is an imperialist country), of anti-semitism (44 per cent say that Jews control the financial system), racism (70 per cent say that the birth rate of immigrants was a threat to national identity), and traditionalism (90 per cent view the family as the pillar of society).[112]

These surveys confirm the view that most MSI supporters (and, even more so, its voters) have a general feeling of dissatisfaction with the modern Italy and a desire for a strong and decisive leadership which will recreate a world of certainties.

One would have expected that the large influx of immigrant workers since the 1980s would have been used by the MSI as a rallying point for anti-immigration policies (as Le Pen in France). In reality the MSI refrained from becoming the anti-immigrant party. Attempts made to use the race card encountered the opposition of the hard-liners of Pino Rauti which saw immigration as a reaction to the international capitalist exploitation of the Third World.[113] Though there is little doubt that *Alleanza Nazionale* (AN) is likely to be in the forefront of an anti-immigration policies, the causes of its success cannot be traced to ethnic tension.

At the local elections held at the end of 1993 AN won the mayoralty in four cities and – in straight fights against the PDS-led coalition – nearly won that of Rome, where Fini was the candidate, and of Naples where the candidate was Alessandra Mussolini, the dictator's grandaughter. Even more important, however, was the fact that Berlusconi – who had not yet started his new party – had just declared that he supported them. AN had found a legitimation and a political role. It would constitute the southern pillar of a centre-right alliance aimed at keeping the PDS out of power.

The March 1994 elections saw the triumph of this strategy. AN which, as the MSI, had obtained only 5.4 per cent (a little less than in 1987) jumped to 13.5 per cent and obtained 109 MPs against 34 in 1992. Two-thirds of its votes were concentrated in the centre-south with 21.2 per cent in Latium, 19.8 per cent in Apulia, 14.5 per cent in Campania but less than its average national vote in Sicily, Sardenia, Calabria, Basilicata, and Molise. Its worst results were all in northern provinces. In 1996 AN did even better, obtaining 15.7 per cent. However, the strong performance of the hardliner far-right *Movimento sociale tricolore* led by Pino Rauti deprived AN of a greater success and damaged the chances of the *Forza Italia*–AN coalition to block the formation of the Prodi government. In practice, the AN inherited some of the votes of the DC and the PSI and could benefit from its record as a party untainted by massive corruption which had remained aloof (even more than the PCI) from the First Republic. What this meant, however, was that AN was stepping into the political space of the DC (and the PSI). It had become rather popular among public sector managers because it was widely considered as a statist party which would not approve of massive privatization. The section of the state sector which was protected by the DC could not turn to *Lega*, an anti-central state party, or to Berlusconi who was in favour of market forces and the private sector.

In the 1994 government of Silvio Berlusconi, AN had a limited presence. Cabinet posts were given to Domenico Fisichella (a conservative political scientist who had never been in the MSI) to Publio Fiori (a former Christian Democrat), while Fini's number two, Giuseppe Tatarella, became deputy prime minister.

The presence of AN in the Italian government caused more consternation abroad than in Italy. The assumption that it was necessary to have foreign approval for any major domestic step did not militate against the MSI. While the PCI had to make tremendous efforts to demonstrate to the USA and other European states that it was really democratic, a government with what had been until recently the 'fascist' party could be formed as European leaders manifested their disapproval, as the *New York Times* and the *Washington Post* expressed their anxiety and as the European Parliament censured the legitimation of AN.

Since the defeat of the right-wing coalition in the 1996 general elections, the AN has behaved as a 'normal' opposition party, lobbying hard for its own views of how the Italian political system should be reformed (i.e. towards presidentialism).

The legitimation of *Alleanza Nazionale* was a necessary part of the process of formation the 'second republic' – as had been that of the former PCI. This creates a situation in which all parties are formally equal and derive their strength and influence only from the votes they are able to obtain from the electorate. From the point of view of the democratic credibility of the Italian political system, such legitimation is important. The former MSI has become 'acceptable' because it has made it clear that it was committed to the basic principles of liberal democracy and not those of an authoritarian state – though, of course, it remains right-wing, centralist and authoritarian in outlook like many other parties of the conservative right. Is this commitment credible and long-lasting? It is impossible to answer this question with any certainty. Fini's party was able to join the Italian government because it had adopted a democratic discourse; Mussolini had become Prime Minister because he was ready to disregard democracy. The success of Fini's 'ancestor', Benito Mussolini, required a major parliamentary crisis preceded by acute social conflicts, an economic crisis and the unfavourable consequences of a major conflict. Should a crisis of similar proportion engulf the country once again – an unlikely prospect – it would not be just Gianfranco Fini's credibility which would be in doubt. In the absence of a crisis of democracy, it is in the political interests of all and sundry to remain democratic. History offers no guarantees.

Endnotes

1 The classic exposition of the thesis of the Risorgimento as an 'unfinished re-volution' can be found Gramsci 1971, pp. 52–120.

2 The following discussion on the crisis of political parties is in part derived from Farneti 1978b, pp. 717–19.
3 See Carocci 1988.
4 See Scalfari and Turani 1974; Galli 1978; Galli and Nannei 1976 who are the main proponents of this thesis.
5 Cassano 1979.
6 See Orfei 1976; Galli 1966.
7 Moro 1979, p. 298.
8 Baget-Bozzo 1980, p. 69.
9 Baget-Bozzo 1974.
10 Baget-Bozzo 1980, pp. 37–50.
11 Cardia 1979.
12 Chiarante 1980, p. 17; Giovagnoli 1980; Moro 1979.
13 See Chiarante 1977, pp. 27–42; Scoppola 1978; Ingrao 1977, pp. 51–83.
14 Mastropaolo 1973, pp. 316–7.
15 Cassano 1979, pp. 37–8.
16 Ibid., p. 65.
17 Ibid., p. 69.
18 In 1988 Ciriaco De Mita was party leader and Prime Minister, but not also foreign secretary.
19 Cassano 1979, p. 59.
20 Allum 1973a, ch. 9.
21 Lanza 1979, p. 181.
22 Menapace 1974, pp. 45–9.
23 Cassano 1979, p. 76. See also Baget-Bozzo 1974 and 1977.
24 For a wider analytical framework see Sapelli 1994b.
25 Amato 1976, esp. pp. 157ff.
26 Bognetti 1978.
27 Ibid., p. 88.
28 Ibid., p. 89.
29 Ibid., pp. 93–5.
30 Chiarante 1983, pp. 16–8.
31 Cassano 1979, pp. 53–4, 61–2. See also Donolo (n.d.) pp. 121–4.
32 Asor Rosa 1982, p. 6.
33 Chiarante 1980, pp. 84ff.
34 Moro 1979, pp. 195–223.
35 Mastropaolo 1973, p. 327.
36 Cassano 1979, pp. 108–10.
37 Di Virgilio 1994, p. 500.
38 Trigilia 1986, p. 220, the area Bassano is compared to is the Valdelsa, a 'red' stronghold between Siena and Florence.
39 Trigilia 1986, p. 222.
40 Ibid., pp. 249–50.
41 Ibid., pp. 280–1.
42 Ibid., pp. 292–3.

43 See the analyses in Follini 1994 and Gaiotti de Biase 1994, pp. 16–7.
44 I examined the development of the PCI's strategy in Sassoon, 1981.
45 See Palmiro Togliatti's later comments in Togliatti 1974, pp. 1073–4.
46 Togliatti 1973, p. 56.
47 The objections to any return to centralization in the communist movement were reiterated in a confidential document written by Togliatti a few days before his death in August 1964 and addressed to the Soviet leadership. Known as the 'Yalta Memorandum' it was published in the PCI weekly *Rinascita* immediately afterwards (in English in Togliatti 1979).
48 A detailed analysis of the PCI's policy towards the EEC can be found in Sassoon 1976.
49 Berlinguer 1975, p. 881.
50 Interview for the *Corriere della Sera*, 20 June 1976.
51 The resolution on Poland has been reprinted in Berlinguer 1982, see in particular pp. 16 and 17.
52 Berlinguer's article on the Chilean events and the strategy of the historic compromise was published in three parts in successive issues of *Rinascita* in September and October 1973. See the English translation in Berlinguer 1974, the passage cited can be found on p. 41.
53 See Baldassare and Di Giulio 1981, p. 6, and Napolitano 1979, pp. xvii–xviii.
54 Cazzola 1982a, pp. 199–200.
55 For the PCI's role in moderating wages see Perulli 1982.
56 Draghi 1987, p. 24.
57 Martinotti and Stefanizzi 1987, p. 25. The DC, however, remains by far women's favoured party.
58 See the supplement to *Politica e economia*, No. 6, June 1989 'Il nuovo PCI: due congressi a confronto'.
59 Occhetto 1994, pp. 181–9.
60 Bull 1996, p. 160.
61 Pedone 1968, pp. 53–5.
62 Carbone 1982, pp. 339–40.
63 The PSI was the only Western socialist party to approve the merging of communist and socialist parties in Poland, Hungary and other East European countries. See Nenni 1977, p. 90.

64 Cazzola 1982a, pp. 188–9.
65 Pasquino and Rossi 1980, p. 83.
66 Ibid., p. 80.
67 Franchi 1980, pp. 70–6.
68 Pasquino 1982, pp. 325–9.
69 Pasquino 1983, p. 37.
70 Degl'Innocenti 1993, pp. 430ff.
71 Pasquino 1992, p. 147.
72 These issues are examined in Sassoon 1985.
73 PSI 1990, pp. 113–4.
74 See, for instance, PSI 1982, pp. 107, 264.
75 See the perceptive analysis in Pasquino 1986, pp. 123–4.
76 For a wider treatment see Ruffolo 1993, pp. 120–1.
77 Giugni 1996, p. 68.
78 Rhodes 1989, p. 116.
79 PSI 1990, pp. 94–5.
80 Degl'Innocenti 1993, p. 472.
81 Lanaro 1992, p. 450.
82 Diamanti 1995, p. xix. For an English-language essay see Diamanti 1996.
83 Interview in *Epoca*, 20 May 1990 cited in Woods 1992, p. 60.
84 Bossi 1993, p. 160.
85 See De Mita's speech in DC 1992, p. 30.
86 Savelli 1992.
87 On the importance of this motivation among leghisti see Mannheimer 1994 in Mannheimer and Sani 1994.
88 Bossi 1993, p. 181.
89 Ibid., pp. 172, 179.
90 Data of September 1995 provided by the *Osservatorio Socio-Politico ISPO/Corriere della Sera*/Nielsen.
91 Bossi 1993, p. 179.
92 Savelli 1992, p. 14.
93 See Ricolfi 1993.
94 For a wider treatment see Diamanti 1995, pp. 162–6.
95 Mannheimer 1994b, pp. 48–52.
96 Ibid.
97 Cited in Segatti 1994, p. 475.
98 Ferraresi 1988, p. 71.
99 Ibid.
100 Cited in Ignazi 1994, p. 12.
101 Caciagli 1988, pp. 19–20.
102 Ignazi 1994, p. 17.
103 Caciagli 1988, p. 26.
104 Caciagli 1988, pp. 22–3; Ferraresi 1988, p. 79.
105 Segatti 1994, p. 471.
106 Ferraresi 1988, p. 80.
107 Caciagli 1988, p. 25.
108 Cited in Ignazi 1995, p. 39.
109 Ignazi 1994, p. 76.
110 Ignazi 1989, pp. 447–9.
111 Ibid., p. 453.
112 Ignazi 1994, p. 84.
113 Ibid., pp. 74–5.

Chapter 15

A tentative conclusion

Italy can be said to have been in continuous crisis since the war. The word 'crisis' itself appears regularly in the titles of articles and volumes cited in this book. The post-war crisis (1945–50) was followed by a crisis of traditional values as the Italian economy expanded in what was called the economic miracle (1958–63). This was followed by the crisis of this model of economic development (1963–68) which was followed by a generational crisis (1968) and social conflicts (1969–72). Then there was the oil crisis, terrorism and, finally, *Tangentopoli* and the final crisis of the First Republic. Throughout the period, Italians had the feeling that, somehow, the country always faced serious problems. This does not mean that everything that has happened since 1945 has been negative, but the discourse of crisis underlines the persistence of tensions which have characterized the whole post-war period. These anxieties are not particular to Italy: the British have had 'decline' and the Germans *angst*. One should never enlarge a concept so as to render it meaningless.

Far from being 'immobile' Italy has changed enormously and rapidly, and many of these changes have been for the better. Compared to 1945 the average Italian is better fed, better housed, better educated, more literate and more politically aware. The enormous gap which existed between Italians and Americans (and it is with the American model that all Italians compared their own country) has been considerably reduced. The average Italian may not be as well off as the Germans or the French, but is at least as rich as the English and has at least as many rights and civil liberties as other West European countries.

The life expectancy of the average Italian male at birth is higher than that of the average male in Great Britain, Belgium, Germany (West), France, Austria, Finland, and the USA; that of Italian women higher than Britain, Belgium, West Germany, Norway, Finland, Switzerland, Austria, and the USA.[1] Alienation from politics may be diffuse, yet a larger percentage of people exercise the right to vote than almost anywhere else. There are complaints about the state, yet social security claims are higher than in Germany, the USA, Britain, and Canada.[2]

What has happened in these 50 years is that Italy has become more similar to the rest of Europe. The same can probably be said of any other West European country. There is undoubtedly a process of continuous convergence in most socio-economic indexes. In politics alone Italy was anomalous in that it did not have different governments alternating in power. Since 1994–96 this situation has changed.

It is said that, in Italy, politics, is a national past-time. Yet there is increasing despondency. Eurobarometer surveys indicated that between 1973 and 1994 those who declared to be neither left-wing nor right-wing nor in the centre increased from 17 per cent to 30 per cent (the highest in Europe). In the same period those who called themselves left-wing decreased from 37 per cent to 28 per cent and those who called themselves centrists stayed roughly the same while those who called themselves right-wing actually dropped from 16 per cent to 11 per cent.

A survey in *Eurobarometer* (1989) showed that 40.1 per cent of Italians declared to be close to a political party. This is a far larger percentage than in France, Germany and Great Britain. Yet only 28.4 per cent of Italians were satisfied with the functioning of democracy in their country against over 50 per cent of French and around 60 per cent of Germans and British people. Italians are still, in spite of everything, committed to parties and look to them for the solution of political problems.

As we have repeatedly emphasized, Italy was the only country in Europe to have been ruled by the same political party since the war, even though this party always needed coalition partners. Italy was thus a paradox: no change in the political elites but massive changes in the social and economic fields. But, as was evident, the paradox was only apparent: in order to survive and maintain its power bloc the Italian Christian Democratic Party (DC) had to deal with the continuous crisis of the country by constantly changing strategies.

On the morrow of fascism the DC first took part in the Italian Resistance and then in post-war reconstruction in alliance with the socialist and communist forces of the Marxist left. At the outset of the Cold War, it linked its fate to that of the Western camp, to the USA and NATO, ousted the left from the government, gave free rein to private accumulation of wealth while promulgating an agrarian reform, and established some form of economic control over those sections of the economy which private capital would not have been able to develop.

Italy was thus able to ride on the wave of the longest period of economic growth enjoyed by the West in its history. When this came to an end and when the underlying tensions which this kind of economic development (anarchic, uncoordinated, unplanned) were beginning to emerge, the DC resurfaced as a party of reform and of modernization. It split the left separating the socialists from the communists in what was still the only country in Europe where this separation had not yet occurred. It systematically developed the state into the major economic force and subjected it to its own exclusive control. At the same time it loosened its ties with the Church and, in its constant consensus-seeking trajectory, colonized large segments of the private and public sectors.

It thus remained in control and in power, but did provide the new republic with a wide and stable consensus: the student unrest of 1968 and the workers' explosion of 1969 testified to that. So the DC became the party of decentralization through the new regional legislation of 1970, it acceded to students' demands by expanding the university system and to workers' demands by promulgating the Workers' Statute in 1970. This did not resolve the 'crisis', though it changed it. More groups and social subjects emerged to demand changes, and when the DC opposed these changes – as it did in 1974 when it tried via a referendum to abrogate the divorce law – it lost. Unable to cope with the economic consequences of the oil crisis of 1973, the DC was able, without any internal splits or major divisions, to turn to its only real opponent, the Italian Communist Party (PCI), and request its support in parliament in 1976. It got this support for three years and was able to re-emerge and once more form centre-left governments with the Italian Socialist Party (PSI).

The DC ruled uninterruptedly for nearly 50 years with no major change in personnel, except that which is imposed by the inexorable dance of time (no politician has ever been able to cope with death, particularly his or her own), but it did not stand still.

If the DC changed, so did everybody else. The PCI, which had been forced by its past and by the circumstances to 'choose' the USSR when everyone else in Western Europe was turning to the USA, gradually and consistently abandoned the doctrine of 'Marxism-Leninism', opened its ranks to people of varying persuasions including Catholics, de-Stalinized thoroughly, accepted with increasing enthusiasm membership of the EEC and supported European federalism, accepted Italy's membership of NATO, disassociated itself from Soviet foreign policy, and supported a DC government for nearly three years.

The PSI too changed. In the 1940s and 1950s it had been the junior partner of the PCI. Later it became the junior partner of the DC. Swinging repeatedly from left to right, perhaps unavoidably given its size and its position within the political spectrum, the PSI increasingly espoused the cause of 'modernization', rejecting its traditions of a workers' party and becoming more and more a radical party of the centre.

Everyone changed then, but everyone had to pay a price. The DC maintained its power, but only by sharing it more and more with its coalition partners. In the last elections it fought, that of 1992, it had the support of less than one-third of Italians. In 1948 it had nearly 50 per cent support. By the 1980s, however, the DC no longer knew what to do with its power except keep it. It had no perspective, no strategy, no long-term aim. Yet it needed political power; first of all to maintain its links with its clientele system and the numerous interests it aggregated through the control it exercised on the public purse and, secondly, to avoid being broken apart by its constant internal factional struggle. This was a party which had built its entire political fortune on being the sole possible governing party of Italy, the foundation of the entire political system.

As for the PSI, it had discovered long ago that it could not influence the policies of the DC – the ambition it had in the 1960s when it participated in the centre-left governments. It remained in power with the DC in order to obtain a greater share of political and economic resources, seeking to establish its own clienteles and interests against those of the DC. In so doing, it inevitably damaged the DC but became, increasingly, another party of patronage and clienteles. Yet this never paid off. In the last elections it fought in 1992, sixteen years after Bettino Craxi had become leader of the PSI with the ambition of supplanting the PCI while weakening the DC, the PSI was still stuck with less than 14 per cent of the votes.

It had long been argued that these parties could no longer cope with the increasing complexities of the Italian political system and of Italian society. Such political complexity was well evidenced by the presence of around ten political parties – all represented in parliament through what was probably the most accurate system of proportional representation in Europe. Furthermore, there were and still are not one, but three trade union federations. Even these were not able to stop the development of new non-affiliated unions in the developing sectors of the economy, adding to the old 'corporate unions' which existed among some sectors of the traditional skilled working class.

Tangentopoli parties appeared to be increasingly unable to cope with the complexities of modern Italy, but this is only part of the truth. Political parties could no longer represent everything and everyone, but the cause of this was not only greater complexity but also fewer resources. Parties not only sought to represent interests in a general way, but were also actively involved in a political market in which political resources were exchanged. Pressure groups and interest groups had to seek the support of determinate political parties. These gave economic and political resources in exchange for political support. The model we are delineating is that of the modern welfare state, i.e. a state which attempts to extend social protection to all groups or nearly all groups. In the contemporary period the welfare state is no longer able to expand; at times it has to contract and therefore is no longer able to extend social protection to all groups. Resources were distributed in an unequal manner even during periods of prosperity, but in sufficient quantity to ensure the legitimacy of all political parties who were protagonists of the market. In adverse economic conditions the choices became more difficult, some interests had to be sacrificed. According to this view the crisis of all Italian political parties was due to the fact that most of them were competing on behalf of fairly similar groups, i.e. all tried to protect popular/working-class interests.

The third and most important aspect of the crisis of Italian political parties (that can also be applied to others) was the following: the principal point of reference of political parties is the nation-state and the institutions which are connected to it, the first of which is the national parliament. In the present era, capitalist corporations are often able to escape national economic policies, international organizations tie nation-states in a thousand ways to complex international agreements, mass international communication systems penetrate deep into the national culture, transforming it into an aspect of a television-orientated world culture reducing the hallowed limits of the traditional nation-state to cosmic insignificance.

In this situation it may not be surprising that national political parties were and still are unable to offer solutions to pressing problems because many of the institutions they can use are all technically obsolete: they are all national in an era where there can be no national solution to crises.

I think there is something which is true in all these explanations: Italian society had become too complex for the existing political parties, it was no longer possible to assume constant growth and thus resources had become scarcer and, finally, the boundaries of the nation-state too narrow.

Let us take as an example the oldest national question in Italy: the 'Agrarian Question' and the South. This is no longer a question of peasants and landlords.

Now the 'Agrarian Question' must deal with an entire system of technical infra-structure, with a world market, with the advances of chemistry and biotechno-logy. It is now also the concern of technicians and experts of multinational firms. It is closely connected to the activities of the state and to the banking system. This means that the 'Agrarian Question' is no longer simply about the 'traditional' peasants but also about 'modern' social subjects: bankers and financiers, geologists and chemists, engineers and agronomists, etc. The 'Southern Question' in modern Italy is part and parcel of the mechanism of economic development and hence part of the political system because the central task of political decision-makers is to manage economic development. The concept of backwardness applied to the Italian South cannot deal with the complexities of the situation. There is, of course, 'back-wardness', but it can only survive side by side with modernity by establishing some connections with it. If it were simply a question of backwardness then two solu-tions could be tried: one is to abandon the backward sector to its fate (the laissez-faire alternative) assuming it will gradually disappear unable to withstand the impact of modernity, the other is the technocratic solution: pouring public funds into the South to modernize it directly, thus bringing it up to the level of the North. Both solutions are clearly unrealistic.

As we have seen, the problem of the South is not only an economic one, it is also political – as the rise of the Northern League further demonstrates. In fact, it is a textbook example of the impossibility of separating the two. Both the anti-interventionist liberal and the technocratic views assume that the kind of develop-ment which occurred in the North is intrinsically valid. Yet this development has been financed by the systematic drainage of the South's sole resource: human labour. In exchange the South received a constant stream of state funds which underpinned the DC regime. The money was not directed towards 'modernization' but was channelled in a thousand directions under the supervision of all sorts of interest groups including the mafia. When state funds could not be used in this 'political' way, they remained unspent. Southern banks hold enormous public funds which were supposed to be spent for child care as well as anti-natal and post-natal care. These remained idle. In 1982, 1,679 publicly funded creches were supposed to be developed; there were only 73 in the entire South.

Thus the Southern Question is not a matter of simple modernization, or of an increase in state funds. The role of the South cannot even be understood purely in terms of the Italian North, but must be thought of anew in terms of the relations between Italy and the rest of the EEC and the Mediterranean.

The key question, then, is the international role of the Italian South and therefore the international role of Italy. Here there has always been a considerable lack of ideas on the part of Italy's governing elite. Foreign policy has always taken a back seat and foreign economic policy has been virtually non-existent. The main reason why this book has not got a separate chapter on foreign policy is that there is not much to say.[3] The entry on foreign policy is one of the shortest in the most recent dictionary of Italian politics.[4] The twin pillars of Italian foreign policy have been NATO and the EEC. But membership of NATO has been interpreted as slavish adherence to whatever initiatives were undertaken by the United States. Member-ship of the European Community has been an opportunity for self-congratulation at the fact that the rest of Europe has recognized that Italy exists. As Gisèle Podbielski wrote:

> Successive governments did not have a clear and continuous view of the objectives they wanted to attain through European integration . . . There was a certain passivity in the Italian participation in the Community decision mechanisms; this was also due to the fact that greater weight was often given to the political importance of belonging to the Community than to defending the Italian point of view in negotiations on specific issues.[5]

Yet Italy and the Italians have remained enthusiastic 'Europhiles'. Where else could a government launch a new tax to meet the Maastricht criteria for a single currency by calling it a 'Tax for Europe'? Yet this is what was done in 1996 by the Prodi government, though its fate was in the hands of the least pro-Maastricht party in Italy, *Rifondazione Comunista*.

The South, as we have seen, has had the fundamental task of transferring human resources to the North. It has also transferred them to the rest of Europe. Southern Italian labour could be found working in Belgian mines, in German factories as well as in France and Switzerland. This drainage of labour came to an end at the beginning of the 1970s as the international recession ended the full employment policies which had been a feature of most European countries. The sums sent back by workers abroad began to contract and public spending in the South now became the principal available resource.

In modern societies social conflicts tend to assume the form of conflicts over the distribution of economic resources. The South is no exception. The difference is that the conflict over dwindling resources has become increasingly violent and has led to the transformation of the mafia into an independent economic and political force.[6]

Before 1945 the mafia had been the servant of the landlords. Repressed by fascism, it was reinstated in Sicily during the Second World War by the American mafia in alliance with the US armed forces. Gradually it established political links with the local DC. Until the 1970s, the mafia was at the service of politicians. It delivered votes and financed political campaigns. In exchange it obtained local contracts, was allowed to develop protection rackets, was involved in tobacco smuggling, had a virtual monopoly over the water supply for agriculture and speculated in real estate.[7]

In the 1970s, the explosion of new social conflicts could not avoid affecting the mafia. The state was less and less able to control these conflicts because it tried to resolve the problem of economic development simply by making more public funds available. These vast resources to be shared out provoked more violence. This coincided with a wave of political terrorism. Violence seemed to have become endemic. This highlighted the weakness of a political elite which seemed unable to fulfil its traditional 'law and order' obligations. It is at this stage that the mafia became an independent economic force. Until then it had prospered within the DC system of power in the South. Now it became its own master: 'the entrepreneurial mafia'. Old techniques were resurrected in order to finance modern economic activities. The shadow of state intervention was never very far from the aims of the new criminality: to cite just one example, in 1973 the kidnapping of Paul Getty Jr (whose ear had been sent back to his family to demonstrate – in time-honoured fashion – that he had really been kidnapped and that those who had done it were ready to kill) resulted in a 'profit' of 1,000 million lire (about £400,000). This was used to finance the purchase of a fleet of lorries which enabled the mafia of Gioa Tauro in Calabria to obtain the monopoly of road haulage for the construction of a modern industrial harbour financed by the government to 'help' the development of the South.[8]

The real mafia industry of the 1970s, however, was heroin traffic. Until the late 1960s heroin had been essentially an American problem in the sense that most addicts were American. By the late 1970s there were proportionately more deaths caused by heroin in West Germany and more addicts in Italy than in the USA.[9] At the centre of this international racket was the Sicilian mafia. This is an enterprise of authentic multinational dimensions: it involves importing opium from Pakistan, Afghanistan and Iran, its transformation into morphine in the Middle East and into heroin in Sicily. From there it is channelled to the USA and the other advanced industrial countries.

In most cases the initial capital outlay to finance the Sicilian operation came from the Italian state, the vast funds which successive Italian governments had earmarked for the Sicilian region.[10] Much of this remained unspent in southern banks providing liquid capital which could be injected into the circulation network of the mafia economy. Furthermore, the Italian government had for many years used private firms (controlled by a handful of mafia families) to collect local taxes, allowing them to keep 10 per cent of the moneys collected in payment. This put enormous sums at the disposal of a few leading mafia families and allowed them to enter the international heroin market. The revenues from this enterprise were in part ploughed back into the heroin business, in part invested in legal enterprises and in part sent to Swiss and Latin American banks. The Latin American connection was important because it linked the Mafia to the activities of Italian financiers such as Licio Gelli who used his financial contacts and his numerous banks to recycle mafia money in all directions. A favoured area of investment was the international traffic of arms. He was able to do so through his contacts with Latin American freemasonry and with the military in Argentina, Brazil, Peru, Paraguay, etc. He had also been invited to attend the inaugurations of Presidents Carter and Reagan.[11]

Licio Gelli was the head of the secret freemason lodge P2 which was exposed in May 1981 when a membership list containing 962 names was found. What were the functions of the P2? In the first place it sought to acquire information through its extensive political contacts. The purpose of this information was political blackmail. Secondly, it sought to create a 'party' which remained in the shadows and connected people in key political and economic positions. The people who – according to the documents found – were members of the P2 were important figures: Pietro Longo, then leader of the Social Democratic Party and Budget Minister in the Craxi government of 1983–85, socialist leaders such as Silvano Labriola and Enrico Manca, important Christian Democrats such as Gaetano Stammati and Massimo De Carolis, highly placed civil servants in the ministries of Foreign Affairs, Trade and in the

Treasury. Of the 195 members of the armed forces whose names were found on the P2 lists there were 12 generals of the Carabinieri, 22 generals of the Army, eight admirals, four Air Force generals, the head of the Navy chiefs of staff and the heads of Italy's secret services as well as judges, journalists, and the media tycoon Silvio Berlusconi.[12]

A Parliamentary Committee of Enquiry was set up in 1981 under the presidency of a Christian Democrat, Tina Anselmi, who reported in July 1984 to parliament. The report declared that all members of the P2 lodge were responsible for belonging to an organization 'whose aim was to intervene secretly in the political life of the country', and maintains that virtually all those named in the list really were members of the P2.[13]

I could go on narrating a story which seems to come straight from a best-selling novel. I have wanted to bring these facts to the reader's attention to show some of the direct connections which link state intervention, the DC, the Southern Question, the Mafia, the P2, the banking system, etc., and to show that the revelations of *Tangentopoli* were surprising only because of the exceptional magnitude of the sums – as we shall see below. I have directed my attention to the Southern Question and the mafia because these are two issues which – to many people – seem to be the hallmark of the backwardness of Italy. It is clearly not a question of backwardness: the present predicament of the Italian South has extremely modern aspects, they are features not of underdevelopment but of a modern political system. As for the mafia, it had obviously modernized itself remarkably by becoming a multinational organization. Modern *mafiosi* may use the murderous techniques they have inherited from the past, but they are at home in international financial circles.

Such modernization did not bring about a diminution in the level of criminality. Killings have not only been a mechanism whereby different mafia gangs resolve internal problems of growth and expansion – the criminal equivalent of mergers and acquisition. They have been used to eliminate politicians and judges who have tried to fight the mafia: on 25 April 1982 (the anniversary of the liberation of Italy from fascism) the Sicilian communist leader Pio La Torre – who had been in the forefront of both the peace and the anti-mafia campaigns – was killed with his driver by the Mafia. Later that year, on 3 September, the former counter-terrorism chief and then Prefect of Sicily (with special responsibilities for the fight against the Mafia) Dalla Chiesa, was killed with his wife openly in the streets of Palermo. In the summer of 1983 Rocco Chinnici, an investigative magistrate, was killed by the Mafia. In 1992, the investigative magistrates Giovanni Falcone and, later his successor Borsellino were also murdered. Yet, as the First Republic disappeared, it looked as if the state was beginning to register some success in the struggle against the mafia. The revelations of insiders allowed the arrest of leading *mafiosi*. The end of the DC meant that, for the first time, the mafia did not have a direct link with the parties in power.

Whether or not things will really change and the mafia can be brought under control (given that it is unlikely that organized crime can be completely eliminated) will depend on the shape of the emerging political system. An excessive decentralization will produce in Sicily a single bloc permanently at the helm of a much enhanced regional government. In these circumstances it would be at the mercy of the political influence of the mafia.

We began this story with Italy entering the world market after the years of fascist autarky and the war. Inevitably, it did so from a position of weakness and yet was able to carve for itself a niche in the international division of labour.

As these pages are being written Italy is making enormous efforts to meet the Maastricht criteria to be part of the first wave of participants in Europe's first common currency. Whether or not it is successful, there is little doubt that it has no alternative outside Europe and that there has been effective convergence towards the other European countries. The most important 'convergence', however, has been political, not economic.

The first edition of this text appeared in 1986. It pointed out that the most significant peculiarity of Italy was the absence of the alternation of governing coalitions. This peculiarity has now been eliminated by the obliteration of most of the parties of the First Republic. As the immediate cause of this have been the corruption scandals which rocked the Italian political system after 1992 and as these will be felt for years to come it may be appropriate to set it in context.[14]

Like many momentous events, the initial trigger was unremarkable. On 17 February 1992 Mario Chiesa, the socialist-appointed president of the municipal old people's home of Milan, was arrested. His racket was familiar to most entrepreneurs bidding for public sector contracts. To win a bid it was necessary to pay a kickback to be shared between the party and the party-appointee. He needed the money to purchase to pay for the membership dues of his branch of the PSI thus acquiring 7,000 votes to be used according to this indication received by his patrons.[15] Chiesa's demands had become increasingly immoderate and he was denounced by one of the companies involved. He was caught *in flagrante* with a few million lires in cash. Chiesa named names, and those named more names until the names everyone knew came out: Craxi, Andreotti, Forlani.

The Milan magistrates, known as the *Mani Pulite* (Clean Hands) team, uncovered a series of corrupt arrangements whereby private and public enterprises financed politicians and political parties in exchange for favours including the passage of special legislation and the awarding of public contracts. The sums collected were used to bribe more people to obtain further financial and political support or were used, quite simply, to sustain the life styles of the politicians and their cronies.[16]

Though there was evidence that all parties, including the PCI, participated in these activities, the main protagonists of this system were the two largest government parties: the DC and the PSI. More than one-third of those elected to parliament in 1992 were investigated. Two thousand people were arrested including some of the country's most powerful politicians. The five parties which dominated Italy since the war had virtually disappeared by 1994.

The most important consequence of *Tangentopoli* (*tangente* can be translated as a kickback hence 'Kickback City' referring to Milan where it all started) has thus been the end of the most stable political system in Europe.

The Italian press was prompt to baptize this change the unlamented death of the First Republic and to call the outcome *la Seconda Repubblica*. This is not surprising.

The DC was the central pivot of the system, the element of stability and continuity in what was otherwise a constantly evolving society. Many Italians have grown up not knowing a political system without Fanfani or Andreotti. Craxi, generally regarded as a 'new' politician, had actually been leader of the PSI for sixteen years when Mario Chiesa was arrested. No doubt there will be a long debate on the continuity and discontinuity between the First and Second Republic. As in all historiographical controversies, some will argue that nothing has changed, others that there has been a revolution, yet, even at this early stage it is possible to state, unequivocally, that 1992–94 constituted the most important discontinuity so far in the history of the political system of post-war Italy.

The discontinuity between the First and the Second Republic is most visible in the party system. The former governing parties have all disappeared. The former opposition parties are no longer the same. There is obviously much continuity between the PDS and the PCI but one should not over-emphasize it. *Rifondazione Comunista* – the party created by those who objected to the dissolution of the PCI – has as much claim as the PDS to be the successor to the PCI.

Of the democratic countries of Western Europe, only the French transition from the Fourth to the Gaullist Fifth Republic in 1958 can aspire to rival the discontinuity exhibited by the Italian political system in 1992–94. But in France the background to this transition was the end of empire, an unwinnable colonial war, a threatened revolt by generals – the authentic stuff of major political crises. Moreover, in France, the Fourth Republic was far weaker and more unstable than the Italian Republic. Instability in terms of coalition governments – in itself not very significant – was similar in the two countries but France lacked a hegemonic party of the centre to provide ballast.

It is true that – in France – the transition between the Fourth and Fifth Republic had a constitutional dimension so far lacking in the Italian case. The French, after all, moved from a parliamentary system to a presidential one, and drafted a new constitution. Nothing like that has yet occurred in Italy. The 'Second Republic' is far from being well-established. The main legal-political reform has been that of the electoral system which would not have occurred but for *Tangentopoli*. Electoral laws are seldom changed because those in power are usually the beneficiaries of the existing ones. As more politicians were being investigated, the popular desire for a change became focused on the electoral system with the encouragement of politicians. This explains the speed at which the signatures were collected for the referendum held in 1993 which, as we have seen, abolished existing electoral laws and forced parliament to draw up new ones.

Thus it is legitimate to claim that Italy's regime discontinuity was greater than that between the French Fourth and Fifth Republic.

A word of caution may be necessary here. As noted, the Second Republic is still far from consolidation. Will the electoral system be changed again? Will there be a new Constitution? Will the existing party system survive? Time will tell. It is possible that Berlusconi's *Forza Italia* will step into the shoes of Andreotti's Christian Democracy with Fini's *Alleanza Nazionale* playing out the role of the junior partner. The old Marxian dictum, 'the first time a tragedy, the second a farce', might be fitting were it not for the possibility that 'both times as farce' might be more appropriate. Such speculations are amusing but ultimately unproductive. We simply do not possess sufficiently precise analytical tools to engage in worthwhile predictions of this magnitude.

Sudden political discontinuities in democratic societies – that is, a transition from one democratic regime directly to another – are exceptional, not least because a democracy can seldom be called a regime. A regime can be said to have existed in Italy only because of two features: the lack of alternation of the parties in government and the systematic occupation by the governing parties of the state and civil society. Italy's main exceptional feature, the lack of alternation, was at the root of the crisis. It meant that the parties ensconced in power could proceed unchecked. Internal disputes within the establishment could be resolved by extending the spoil system. This systemic lack of alternation is what makes it difficult to study the case in comparative terms – even though corruption, kickbacks, nepotism, clientelism, the link between politics and organized crime, scandals, spoil systems, tax evasion, illegal funding of parties, etc., exist in other countries as any student of French or German or Spanish or Greek or American politics knows well. Only Japan and Mexico provide comparable instances, but the marked differences in historical traditions suggest than even a study focusing on these three instance may have limitations.

The surge of the *Lega Nord* as an anti-corruption party able to destroy the strongholds of socialists and Christian Democrats was – with *Tangentopoli* – the most important *direct* cause of the destabilization of the First Republic. The entry of Berlusconi's *Forza Italia* into the political scenario destroyed the already slim chances that a refurbished and somewhat cleaned-up Christian Democratic Party might have had. Until then, the PDS had been the only organization able to obtain electoral support throughout the national territory. The *Lega*, for obvious reasons, could not aspire to significant electoral support south of the Po Valley, while the *Alleanza Nazionale* had little support north of Rome.

The left (I mean here the PCI/PDS and *Rifondazione Comunista*) contributed very little to the end of the First Republic. It needed allies among the parties already in power. It was in disarray when the scandals broke out. For the old regime to collapse it was necessary that its own supporters had somewhere to go. Until 1992, moderate opinion was prepared to tolerate the corruption of the DC and the PSI partly because few people realized that it had reached such formidable proportions and partly because the alternative to the DC and PSI were the communists in power. Once alternatives emerged, first the *Lega* then Berlusconi and then even the eventually acceptable post-fascists, moderate and conservative public opinion discovered it had somewhere to go. Conservatives – who usually need to believe in the state – were also reassured because the attack on corruption had come not from untrustworthy communists but from magistrates, 'honest' representative of the state. Conservatives had found in the magistrates local heroes who were neither corrupt nor communist. Furthermore, they had the exceptional advantage of not being politicians. They were people who were simply doing their duty, while so many politicians were so obviously not doing theirs.

Why were the magistrates not stopped? Why was the powerful DC–PSI coalition, for so long the master of Italy, unable to obstruct the investigation? The history of contemporary Italy has been punctuated by unresolved political scandal. Seldom have corruption, scandal and the arrogance of power been less disguised than in Italy. It would be sufficient to read through old copies of weeklies like *L'Espresso* to realize how aware everyone was of the extent of this disease.

There are several hypotheses on why the magistrates were able to turn the tide, the most popular of which, appears to be the Cold War hypothesis. According to this, everything stems from the single Italian peculiarity, namely that the PCI monopolized the opposition, making the prospect of an alternation of the parties in power highly unpalatable. Had the Communist Party been elected to power there would be an international crisis of momentous proportion – or so it was widely believed. It was therefore perfectly justified to use all means, including covert action, to keep them out of power. It was necessary to strengthen the political resources of all governing parties while preparing for the worst: a communist victory. All this cost money and, the only way to fund the battle against communism was to do it covertly. Hence the unofficial legitimation of the parallel state (P2, secret services, Gladio), and the development of uncontrolled and uncontrollable parallel funding. Once the habit of illegally funding a political battle is established it is difficult to check its expansion. This creates the possibility for further corruption, private gain and, more simply, intra-party competition for these resources. The strength of the hypothesis is that it explains how the system arose. Its weakness is that it does not explain why the system came to an end. The conclusion of the Cold War, after all, cannot automatically bring to an end the political practices generated by it. It is argued that the collapse of communism enabled people not to vote for the DC and the PSI to stave off the communist threat. This argument has limited validity. After all, a majority of people did not vote for the left in 1994 and did not even vote for the PDS whose broad coalition obtained fewer votes than the PCI of Berlinguer had on its own in 1976. The largest share of the poll was obtained by the parties of the right led by Berlusconi which energetically campaigned on an anti-communist platform using a Cold War language which even Andreotti's DC had not used for years.

It is necessary to bring into play a second hypothesis, namely that the system was running out of money. For a long period it could be argued that clientelism was politically functional. It enabled the ruling coalition to fulfil tasks of redistribution which in other countries were assigned to the welfare state. Because much of this redistribution depended on an informal network and on access to political resources, the ruling parties derived a special advantage. A universalist welfare system distributes benefits to all citizens. A clientelist welfare state distributes benefits only to those who accept that a favour has been granted and must be returned. It is a contractual relationship based on exchange. In a clientelist welfare state even universal benefits may be withheld. For example, Italy provides a state pension to all citizens who have reached a certain age or worked for a specified number of years. If the state machine were efficient it would allocate a pension automatically to all those entitled to one. In reality it may take years. It may, therefore, often be necessary to by-pass normal procedures and seek the help of influential people. In this instance state inefficiency becomes functional to state clientelism.[17] It is part of the system, not a peculiarity due to national characteristics stereotypically attributed to Italians (or Spaniards or Greeks). Those who receive a pension 'as a favour' when it is in fact due to them as a right have a contradictory position. On the one hand, they have actually received the pension and paid back the favour by voting for someone in power who, it is assumed, may go on looking after them. They are part of the system. On the other hand, they have not received anything 'extra', particularly if they have paid their taxes and various contributions, so they would have an interest in ending the system. However, ending the system may bring forward unknown, perhaps unpleasant consequences. At best it may simply deliver a pension they would get anyway. Thus it would not be irrational to vote for the status quo particularly if you hold conservative or traditional values anyway and you have no faith in politicians in general.

Corruption and clientelism do not weaken the system. They reinforce it and each other. To denounce them as extensive and deplorable phenomena paradoxically strengthens them. It publicises what everyone suspects: that it is widespread, vast, enormous, that 'everyone is doing it'. The action may be illegal, strictly speaking, but, if everyone participates, it is not immoral. Those who are discovered would not be considered by their community to be amoral or asocial individuals to be treated as pariahs.

Franco Cazzola has analysed 1,000 cases of corruptions mentioned in the daily press between 1976 and 1991.[18] There were 600 cases between 1976 and 1986 and 500 between 1986 and 1991. In the first decade these illegal transactions were mainly concerned with housing – permits to build, to expand, change of use, etc. In the second period he found instances of kickbacks for funeral services – firms bribing hospital nurses to be alerted as someone died – pensions, finding a bed in a particular hospital, the license to open a shop, obtaining a council house in exchange of sexual favours, electoral fraud, avoiding military service, obtaining a driving licence and so on. Public services had been 'privatized' with market forces playing a role in their distribution.

The spread of petty corruption is its best protection. It was also the last, desperate defence, of those accused of large-scale corruption. It is the justification most frequently involved. The more corruption and clientelism were exposed in novels, films, television serials, and by investigative journalism the more they were reinforced as an omnipresent system. It creates a parallel system of social regulation which receives a double democratic legitimation: formal and informal. Informal because the majority participates in it and formal because the system is upheld electorally.[19]

A large proportion of those who used to vote for the five governing parties which constituted the political establishment had a high level of tolerance for corruption because they themselves participated in some form of clientelism, however marginally. This is not say that all communist and neo-fascist voters were untouched by it. The distinction between clientelism and corruption, analytically valid, breaks down in practice. Corruption involved entrepreneurs funding political parties in exchange for state contracts and other business-related favours. Clienteles involved political parties 'funding' citizens (jobs, privileges, undeserved benefits) in exchange for votes. Thus political parties are at the centre of this flow of transactions. The precondition which makes everything else possible is the *de facto* continuous control and possession of the state by the ruling parties. Corruption and clientelism contribute to this continuous control. Thus the system is self-perpetuating.

Tangentopoli dealt with the most exposed part of this system because the least democratically legitimized: corruption. It could not deal with the clientele system. This is what, paradoxically, protected the magistrates from the risk of a popular backlash. To move against the rich and powerful, particularly when the sums involved defy the popular imagination, is one thing, to seek out the 'little people' is another.

Who is to be included in the system of clientele? Here are some random examples:

- All those employed in the informal economy and who, by definition do not pay taxes on these earnings (though they or their spouses pay their taxes for their main 'legal' occupation if they have any).
- All those who can obtain payment for their services in cash in order to be able to avoid taxes. These include doctors, plumbers, dentists, waiters, lawyers and virtually all piece-rate home workers.
- All those who build their own home illegally or who add an extension to it in defiance of Italy's complex regulations. It is normal for an 'architect' (in reality an overqualified surveyor) to add an extra sum which will be used to make sure that there will be no inspection.
- All those who engage in a legal activity for which a permit is needed but who perform it either without the permit or who have obtained a permit through the personal intervention of a politician or a bureaucrat, for instance street vendors.
- All those who claim an invalidity pension while being perfectly healthy because they have been able to obtain a certificate from a doctor and are protected by a local political boss. Almost one in three of the 21 million pensions paid out annually goes to invalids.
- All those with two jobs, one of which is a public sector sinecure obtained thanks to networking with influential people which does not require any regular presence. Some of these jobs can even be sub-contracted to others. An example familiar to all those who have had to spend many hours consulting books in Italian libraries are the *guardiani* who sit in every room making sure that no-one defaces or damages books being used.

One could go on. The crucial point is not that this is an exclusively Italian phenomenon but that, in Italy, it is part of an established and accepted system. For instance, so-called 'welfare scroungers' undoubtedly exist in Britain but they are the regular objects of attack by politicians, especially conservative politicians, and are singled out as a group to be blamed. But in Italy no politician has ever launched a campaign against 'welfare scroungers'.

'Normal', that is legitimized taxation could not be expected to fund this peculiar Italian-style welfare state, hence the ever-increasing public debt and the escalating costs incurred by firms, especially those operating in the public sector. The signing of the Maastricht Treaty and the requirement to meet its convergence criteria accelerated the need for an austerity programme which was increasingly incompatible with the old system. Fiscal crises, which elsewhere have destabilized the so-called social-democratic model, in Italy destabilized the Christian Democratic state. A multiplicity of controls were imposed to decrease tax evasion. These singled out certain categories and forced them to establish complex accounting procedures. For instance restaurant owners and shopkeepers were forced to purchase specially sealed cash registers or adapt existing ones, be subject to controls and either submit to them or find costly ways round them. Each transaction, however modest, requires the seller to provide the customer with a special 'tax receipt' or *ricevuta fiscale* which customers, in turn, must keep until they are at a certain distance from the place of purchase and produce it to the police if requested to do so. Direct income tax is widely evaded by the self-employed but cannot be avoided by employees. The consequence is that the state has had to resort to a massive increases in indirect taxes and to multiple controls. Thus Italians found themselves increasingly controlled by an alien state in turn increasingly unable to perform its duties properly. As we know, people resent paying taxes even in 'normal' circumstances. To have to pay them knowing that a considerable proportion of the population avoids them is, understandably enough, extremely frustrating.

The left opposition could never really channel this resentment, no more than any party of the left anywhere in Europe could become the convincing leader of a taxpayers' revolt. The left, inevitably, is always seen as the party of public spending and hence of taxation. But, in Italy, unlike other countries, the ruling parties of the centre could not be the taxpayers' parties for the reasons we have suggested. For structural reasons, as well as ideology, Christian Democrats could never be Thatcherites. As we have seen only a new party, such as the *Lega*, or Berlusconi, could pick up this issue, and only as pre-electoral propaganda.

Tangentopoli had a powerful effect on public opinion because of the extent of the sums involved and the power and arrogance exhibited by those being investigated and arrested. What was involved was not so much the principle as the amounts stolen, just as big business is often attacked by populists because it is big, rather than because it is business. *Tangentopoli* did not reveal the existence of corruption. No Italian could be unaware of it. What no one had realized was the actual size of the sums involved.

Imagine an average Signor Rossi, the owner of a small bar in Milan. He keeps three or four tables and chairs on the public pavement just outside the bar – an advantage because he can legally charge his sitting customers several times what he charges those standing at the bar. However, he does not have a permit for this. It would take too long to obtain it. He does not know the right people. He might not get it. So whenever the local policeman comes around he gives him a *mazzetta*, the traditional plain brown envelope with a bit of ready cash, say fifty or one hundred thousand lires (£20–£40). Sometimes the policeman warns him of an inspection and Signor Rossi removes the tables and chairs or bribes the inspector or pays the fine. Rossi is always worried but does not complain, after all playing by the informal rules is advantageous. He will go on voting for a ruling party because he might need some help some day and, in any case, what would happen if the communists came in? Either nothing would change and, in this case, he might as well keep things as they are. Or they would launch a crusade for clean government and he might not be able to keep his tables and chairs outside or would have to pay more for his licence than he pays out in bribes. Rossi, like many Italians, does not like the government and dislikes most politicians but puts up with them just as he puts up with the rain. In these circumstances 'to lack a proper *senso dello stato*', as Italians are regularly accused by civic culture theorists, seems to me quite rational.

One morning Signor Rossi reads in the newspapers that Raoul Gardini, the much-admired boss of Montedison, the 'king' of Italian chemical industries (who has since committed suicide), had spent 150 billion lire (c. £60 million) in kickbacks, that, of these, perhaps 60 billion (c. £24 million) ended up in his own secret accounts abroad, that the rest was distributed to Craxi, Forlani, various socialists and Christian Democrats. Or he reads that, according to a memorandum written by Vincenzo Balzamo, administrator of the PSI until 1992 (when he died of a heart attack) and kept in a drawer, the party had received between 1987 and 1990 a total of 186 billion lire (c. £74 million) of which 136 billion (c. £54 million) came from private entrepreneurs, 30.2 (c. £12 million) from public sector firms, and 20.6 billion (c. £5.2 million) from various sources – on top of official state funding.

Signor Rossi is, understandably furious. These are the same people who humiliated him, forced him to resort to petty bribery, imposed on him the most absurd and bureaucratic financial controls in the whole of Europe. He is angry with the establishment. The point is that Rossi, like most Italians in his situation, does not think that he is himself involved in the corruption racket. Corruption, 'real' corruption, belongs to a minority of deviants. He feels hard done by. He worked hard and only paid out what was in fact protection money. He cannot bring himself to vote for the communists. He is, after all, the archetypal petty bourgeois and thinks he knows what his class interests are. But he will no longer support the DC or the PSI, especially since he can vote for someone else. Because our Signor Rossi is Milanese he will vote for the *Lega*. Had he been in the South he would have voted for the neo-fascists. The magistrates are now his heroes. They are not politicians. They are clean. They will humiliate the rich and powerful. When wealthy industrialists are dragged out in the middle of the night, handcuffed, surrounded by journalists and photographers, stripped of their electronic organizers and portable telephones, deprived of cronies and secretaries, with no access to their private planes and their chauffeur-driven cars, when they stand trembling before the magistrates on prime-time television, Rossi is overjoyed. It is the great revenge of the petty bourgeoisie.

The establishment, deprived of popular complicity, could not stop the investigations. It is thus not inappropriate to say that the magistrates necessarily acted like a surrogate political party with a specific programme and requiring political support. The magistrates were also helped by the fact that the *magistratura* itself enjoys considerable legal autonomy. Its independence from the executive and parliament is recognized by the Constitution (Art 104.1, 101.2, 107.1, 107.3, 110, 112). From the mid-1960s onward its personnel was recruited from less exclusive social strata and the discrimination against those who were members of sympathizers of the PCI became less marked.[20]

The independence of the magistrature was further enhanced by the strength of the PCI who, as the main opposition party permanently excluded from political power had an interest in preserving the autonomy of the judiciary. This indicates that individual magistrates – who are appointed for life – were often party supporters and that the Supreme Council of the Magistratura was usually made up of factions connected to political parties. Nevertheless the *magistratura*, as a body, has remained independent of the executive though appointed by it – just like the US Supreme Court.

This independence had to be defended. In the early 1980s Bettino Craxi and his deputy Claudio Martelli (when Minister of Justice) tried to subject investigative magistrates to the executive. These attempts failed mainly because the professional corporation – like all professional corporations in Italy – was exceptionally strong. This independence meant that, even when politicians attempted, often successfully, to block investigation, they had to respect the formal autonomy of magistrates. They could move a magistrate or an investigation to another area. What they could not do was to 'colonize' the *magistratura* and transform it into the personal possession of some party or other, as they had done with the public sector media or the banking system. To have its way the executive branch had to negotiate informally with highly placed members of the *magistratura*. For instance in March 1981 the magistrates Gherardo Colombo (now in the *Mani pulite* team), Giuliano Turone (now in the national anti-mafia squad) and Guido Viola had discovered the P2 conspiracy but were repeatedly advised by their senior colleagues to be less zealous about it. Eventually the investigation was moved from Milan to Rome where little was done. By 1983 the Swiss authorities had responded to an original request from Milan and had prepared a report on the *Conto Protezione* (Craxi's secret bank account), and was ready to send it to Rome. Similarly the investigations on the secret funds of IRI, on Roberto Calvi, on Rizzoli and many others were stopped by the simple mechanism of finding a good reason why the jurisdiction should fall elsewhere where the magistrates were more pliable.[21]

Clearly honesty, diligence and formal political independence were necessary but without wider political and popular support, without a shift in public opinion there would have been no *Tangentopoli*. This shift and this support made the magistrates feel, to use a famous expression of Chairman Mao, 'like a fish in the water' unlike the *inquisiti* (as those being investigated are called) who felt, perhaps for the first time, isolated. Used to a life of power, they discovered to be powerless. One or two weeks in jail was usually sufficient to break most of them. Without the accoutrements of power, they were weak and unprepared. When released on bail, they found themselves treated without respect, jeered at in the streets while, only a little while before, they basked in the inner satisfaction of being recognized as powerful and honourable people.

The fact that the vanguard role in this quasi-revolution has been played by magistrates and a 'social movement' turned into a party like the *Lega* appears to confirm various hypotheses on the triumph of the non-political. The non-political characteristics of politicians become important: how they look, how they speak, who they sleep with. The corruption scandals have reinforced the tendency to perceive all professional politicians as crooked. Observers have noted the intense politicization of so many aspects of Italian social life. This is not a reflection of the Italians' interest in politics but of the extent to which political parties have invaded civil society. Dislike of politics and politicization goes hand in hand. This brings about two tendencies. On the one hand there is the almost universal longing for an anti-political politician – the classic 'man' of destiny (so far no Italian woman has stepped into Margaret Thatcher's shoes). On the other hand, political parties desperately seek non-politicians as their standard bearers, partly to curry favour with the public partly because they realize that unpopular decisions have more chance of being acceptable if they are taken by those who, allegedly, have no long-term political ambitions. This is the advantage Berlusconi enjoyed at the beginning of his political itinerary – though his business success could not have occurred in the way it had without the help of political parties. This also played in the hands of Bossi and his new party, facilitated by the non-political (and rather vulgar) language he used throughout in contrast to the highly complex and in some instances virtually unintelligible jargon traditional politicians use. At every local election, political parties try to find some candidates with little or no previous political experience in the belief that some of their popularity will rub onto the party. The fall of Berlusconi himself, in December 1994, was immediately followed by a government led by Lamberto Dini, a former senior official of the Bank of Italy and, before that of the IMF, made up entirely of *tecnici*, i.e. people who are in power not because they are politicians or because they have even been elected but because they can use their technical (i.e. non-political) expertise to help the nation. This, of course, rests entirely on the unfounded belief that there is such a thing as a neutral and impartial way of resolving political problems. The PDS, which in the past had promoted the candidatures of *independenti* (mostly non-communist, left-wing intellectuals) produced its own *tecnico* to be its standard-bearer: Romano Prodi, a former president of the stateholding giant IRI and a Catholic.

In Italy the anti-political has old roots. In the immediate post-fascist period it arose, briefly, with a Poujadist party, the *Uomo Qualunque*, which anteceded Poujade by nearly ten years. The mood of disillusion with politics characteristic of those years has now, perhaps only temporarily, resurfaced. It is not unique to Italy. It is the unmistakable sign of times of rapid transition. Gramsci once wrote that during the passage from the old to the new all sorts of morbid symptoms appear. *Tangentopoli* may have contributed to opening up the transition, but it could not prevent its 'morbid' consequences.

Now that the Christian Democratic Party has been dissolved, the PCI has changed its name and has split, the PSI, the PSDI and the PLI have disappeared, the MSI has become the post-fascist *Alleanza Nazionale* and two new parties have emerged: the Northern League and *Forza Italia*, now that two distinct governing coalitions

– a centre-right and a centre-left – have succeeded each other, now, perhaps, as the leader of the PDS, Massimo D'Alema hopes, Italy will become a 'normal country'.[22] Will this 'normal' country satisfy the expectations of its people? The record of other 'normal' countries suggest this is unlikely. But what the 'second republic' is expected to achieve is to produce an impartial and reasonable justice system, an agile and efficient bureaucracy, an incorruptible political class, and a fair tax collection practice, and, last but not least, a broadcasting system which contributes to the proper development of the national culture. The omens are not favourable. I sincerely hope to be proved wrong.

Endnotes

1 ISTAT 1995, figures for c.1990.
2 OECD, *Historical Statistics*, 1989.
3 This is the theme of Sassoon 1978.
4 See Sergio Romano, 'La politica estera' in Pasquino 1995.
5 Podbielski 1978, p. 213.
6 See Arlacchi's important book: Arlacchi 1983. For a pioneering analysis of an entrepreneurial mafia see Block 1974. For stimulating and original analyses see Gambetta 1992 and Catanzaro 1991.
7 See Chinnici 1982, p. 81 and Gambetta 1994, p. 294.
8 Arlacchi 1983, p. 107.
9 Ibid., p. 215.
10 Ibid., p. 230.
11 D'Alema 1983, p. 65.
12 See reports in *La Repubblica* of 10 May 1984, and Anselmi 1984, esp. pp. 77ff.
13 Anselmi 1984, p. 53.
14 What follows is largely based on Sassoon 1995.
15 See Della Porta 1993b, p. 38.
16 See Della Porta 1993a.
17 See the lucid comments on this in Sapelli 1994b, pp. 86–7.
18 Cazzola 1992a, p. 12.
19 See Della Porta 1992, Cazzola 1988 and Cazzola 1992a; C. Sennet 1991. For another view see Marturano 1994, p. 194.
20 Neppi Modona 1993, p. 13 and Guarnieri 1991, p. 9.
21 De Luca and Giustolisi, 1993, pp. 101–17.
22 D'Alema 1995.

Bibliography of works cited

Abburrà, Luciano (1992) Tra formazione e organizzazione: percorsi dell'ascesa professionale delle donne, *Polis*, vol. 6, no. 1, April.

Accatoli, Luigi (1989) The Popular Movement: The strengths and limits of political messianism. In Robert Leonardi and Piergiorgio Corbetta (eds) *Italian Politics: A Review, vol. 3* (London: Pinter).

Accornero, Aris (1978) Il rapporto dei giovani con la società: il lavoro. In Istituto Gramsci, *La crisi della società italiana e le nuove generazioni* (Rome: Riuniti).

Accornero, Aris (1992) *La parabola del sindacato* (Bologna: Il Mulino).

Accornero, Aris (1991) Sindacato e conflitto in Italia nell'ultimo ventennio, *Il Mulino*, vol. 40, no. 334, March–April.

Accornero, Aris and Carmignani, Fabrizio (1978a) La 'giungla' delle retribuzioni. In Gabriella Pinnarò (ed.) *L'Italia Socio-economica, 1976–77* (Rome: Riuniti).

Accornero, Aris and Carmignani, Fabrizio (1978b) Classe sociale e modificazioni nella struttura sociale. In Gabriella Pinnarò (ed.) *L'Italia Socio-economica, 1976–77* (Rome: Riuniti).

Accornero, Aris and Carmignani, Fabrizio (1978c) Laureati e diplomati nell'industria italiana. In Gabriella Pinnarò (ed.) *L'Italia Socio-economica, 1976–77* (Rome: Riuniti).

Addario, Nicolò (1982) *Una crisi di sistema* (Bari: De Donato).

Ajello, Nello (1980) Il settimanale d'attualità. In Valerio Castronovo and Nicola Tranfaglia (eds) *Storia della stampa italiana* (Rome-Bari: Laterza).

Alberoni, Francesco (1970) *Classi e generazioni* (Bologna: Il Mulino).

Alberoni, Francesco (1979) Movimenti e istituzioni nell'Italia tra il 1960 e il 1971. In Luigi Graziano and Sidney Tarrow (eds) *La crisi italiana* (Turin: Einaudi).

Aldcroft, Derek H. (1978) *The European Economy 1914–1980* (London: Croom Helm).

Allum, Percy A. (1972) The South and national politics, 1945–1950. In S. J. Woolf (ed.) *The Rebirth of Italy, 1943–50* (London: Longman).

Allum, Percy A. (1973a) *Politics and Society in Post-War Naples* (Cambridge: Cambridge University Press).

Allum, Percy A. (1973b) *Italy – Republic without Government?* (London: Weidenfeld and Nicolson).

Alò, Claudio and Rosa, Giuseppe (eds) (1990) *Il Grande Gap. Infrastrutture: l'Italia ai margini dell'Europa* (Rome: Confindustria Centro Studi, Editore SIPI).

Altieri, Giovanna (1992) I redditi da lavoro delle donne: lontano dalla parità, *Polis*, vol. 6, no. 1, April.

Amato, Giuliano (1976) *Economia, politica e istituzioni in Italia* (Bologna: Il Mulino).

Amato, Giuliano (1980) *Una Repubblica da riformare* (Bologna: Il Mulino).

Amendola, Giorgio (1968) I comunisti e il movimento studentesco, necessità della lotta su due fronti, *Rinascita*, 7 June.

Amendola, Giorgio (1979) Interrogativi sul 'caso' Fiat, *Rinascita*, 9 November.

Ammassari, Paolo (1977) *Classi e ceti nella società italiana* (Turin: Edizioni della Fondazione Giovanni Agnelli).

Amoroso, Bruno and Olsen, O. J. (1978) *Lo Stato imprenditore* (Rome-Bari: Laterza).

Andreotti, Giulio (1977) *Intervista su De Gasperi* (Rome-Bari: Laterza).

Anselmi, Tina (1984) *Relazione della commissione parlamentare d'inchiesta sulla loggia massonica P2*, Camera dei Deputati e Senato della Repubblica, Doc. XXIII, no. 2, 12 July 1984, Rome (Anselmi Commission Report).

Apter, D. and Eckstein, H. (eds) *Comparative Politics* (New York: The Free Press).

Ardigò, A. (1966) La condizione giovanile nella società industriale. In AA.VV., *Questioni di sociologia II* (Brescia: La scuola).

Arlacchi, Pino (1983) *La mafia imprenditrice. L'etica mafiosa e lo spirito del capitalismo* (Bologna: Il Mulino). (English translation (1986) *Mafia Business: the Mafia ethic and the spirit of capitalism*, London: Verso.)

Asor Rosa, Alberto (1981) Il giornalista: appunti sulla fisiologia di un mestiere difficile. In Corrado Vivanti (ed.) *Storia d'Italia. Annali 4. Intellettuali e potere* (Turin: Einaudi).

Asor Rosa, Alberto (1982) La cultura politica del compromesso storico, *Laboratorio Politico*, nos. 2–3.

Baget-Bozzo, Gianni (1974) *Il Partito Cristiano al potere. La DC di De Gasperi e di Dossetti 1945–1954* (Florence: Vallecchi).

Baget-Bozzo, Gianni (1977) *Il Partito Cristiano e l'apertura a sinistra. La DC di Fanfani e di Moro 1954–1962* (Florence: Vallecchi).

Baget-Bozzo, Gianni (1979) *Questi cattolici* (Rome: Riuniti).

Baget-Bozzo, Gianni (1980) *Tesi sulla DC. Rinasce la questione nazionale* (Bologna: Cappelli).

Bagnasco, A. (1977) *Le tre Italie* (Bologna: Il Mulino).

Balbo, Laura (1976) *Stato di Famiglia* (Milan: Etas Libri).

Balbo, Laura (1978) La doppia presenza, *Inchiesta*, vol. 8, no. 32.

Baldassare, A. and Di Giullo, F. (1981) Lotta politica e riforme istituzionali, *Democrazia e Diritto*, no. 5.

Baldassari, Mario (1993) Italy's perverse enveloping growth model between economic reform and political consensus: the 1992 crisis and the opportunity of 1993, *Rivista di Politica Economica*, vol. 83, no. 8–9, August–September.

Baldassari, Mario and Modigliani, Franco (1993) Preface, special issue, *Rivista di Politica Economica*, vol. 83, no. 8–9, August–September.

Baratta, P., Izzo, L., Pedone, A., Roncaglia, A. and Sylos Labini, Paolo (1978) *Prospettive dell'economia italiana* (Rome-Bari: Laterza).

Barbagli, Marzio (1994) Le famiglie senza matrimonio. In Paul Ginsborg (ed.) *Stato dell'Italia* (Milan: Il Saggiatore/Bruno Mondadori).

Barbano, F. (1979) Mutamenti nella struttura sociale delle classi e crisi 1950–1975. In Luigi Graziano and Sidney Tarrow (eds) *La crisi italiana* (Turin: Einaudi).

Barbera, Augusto (1975) Articolo 2. In G. Branca (ed.) *Commentario della Costituzione, Principi Fondamentali* (Bologna and Rome: Zanichelli and Il Foro italiano).

Barbera, Augusto (1979) Le Regioni dieci anni dopo, *Democrazia e Diritto*, no. 6.

Barbera, Augusto (1981) Le componenti politico-culturali del movimento autonomistico negli anni '70 (appunti da sviluppare)', mimeo.

Barclays Bank (1984) *International Economic Survey*, December.

Bassi, P. and Pilati, A. (1978) *I giovani e la crisi degli anni settanta* (Rome: Riuniti).

Battaglia, Filippo (1980) *L'allergia al lavoro* (Rome: Riuniti).

Battegazzore, Francesco (1987) L'instabilità di governo in Italia, *Rivista italiana di scienza politica*, vol. xvii, no. 2, August.

Beccalli, Bianca (1994) The modern women's movement in Italy, *New Left Review*, no. 204, March–April.

Berlinguer, Enrico (1974) Reflections after the events in Chile, *Marxism Today*, February.

Berlinguer, Enrico (1975) *La Questione comunista* (Rome: Riuniti).

Berlinguer, Enrico (1982) *After Poland* (Nottingham: Spokesman Books).

Berselli, Edmondo (1991) La Chiesa e i partiti: tracce di un disegno politico, *Il Mulino*, vol. 40, no. 337, September–October.

Bianchi, Marina (1979) La condizione femminile nella crisi del 'Welfare State', *Critica Marxista*, vol. 17, no. 5.

Bianchi, Patrizio, Cassese Sabino and della Sala, Vincent (1988) Privatisation in Italy: aims and constraints, *West European Politics*, vol. 11, no. 4, October.

Bianchini, Franco (1991) The third Italy: model or myth?, *Ekistics*, no. 350/351, September/December.

Birindelli, Anna Maria (1976) The postwar Italian emigration to Europe in particular to the EEC member countries, *Census*, vol. 32, nos. 1–2.

Block, Anton (1974) *The Mafia of a Sicilian Village* (New York: Harper).

Boccia, Maria Luisa (1980) I tempi lunghi del rapporto donne-politica, *Rinascita*, vol. 22, 30 May.

Bognetti, Giovanni (1978) Stato e economia in Italia: 'Governo spartitorio' o crisi del 'modello democratico-sociale', *Il Politico*, vol. 43, no. 1.

Bonifazi, Corrado and Gesano, Giuseppe (1994) L'immigrazione straniera tra regolazione dei flussi e politiche di accoglimento. In Antonio Golini 1994a (ed.) *Tendenze demografiche e politiche per la popolazione. Terzo Rapporto Istituto Ricerche Sulla Popolazione* (Bologna: Il Mulino).

Bossi, Umberto (with Vimercati, Daniele) (1993) *La Rivoluzione* (Milan: Sperling & Kupfer).

Braghin, P., Mingione, E. and Trivellaro, P. (1974) Per un'analisi della struttura di classe dell'Italia contemporanea, *La Critica Sociologica*, no. 30, 1974.

Branca, G. (ed.) (1975) *Commentario della Costituzione, Principi Fondamentali* (Bologna and Rome: Zanichelli and Il Foro italiano).

Brunetta, Renato and Tronti, Leonello (1993) The Italian crisis of the 1990s: European convergence and structural adjustment, *Rivista di Politica economica*, vol. 83, no. 11, November.

Brunetta, Giuseppe (1993) Il clero in Italia al 1888 al 1989, *Polis*, vol. 5, no. 3, December 1993.

Bruni, Franco and Onida, Fabrizio (eds) (1992) *L'economia italiana nel mondo che cambia: 1990–91* (Bologna: Il Mulino).

Bruni, Franco and Micossi, Stefano (1992) I progetti di unione monetaria europea e l'Italia. In Franco Bruni and Fabrizio Onida (eds) (1992) *L'economia italiana nel mondo che cambia: 1990–91* (Bologna: Il Mulino).

Brusco, Sebastiano and Righi, Ezio (1989) Local government, industrial policy and social consensus: the case of Modena, *Economy and Society*, vol. 18, no. 4, November.

Bull, Martin J. (1996) The great failure? The Democratic Party of the left in Italy's transition. In Stephen Gundle and Simon Parker (eds) *The New Italian Republic, From the Fall of the Wall to Berlusconi* (London: Routledge).

Caciagli, Mario (1988) The Movimento sociale italiano-Destra nazionale and neo-fascism in Italy, *West European Politics*, vol. 11, no. 2, April.

Caldwell, Lesley (1978) Church, State and family: the women's movement in Italy. In Annette Kuhn and AnnMarie Wolpe (eds) *Feminism and Materialism* (London: Routledge and Kegan Paul).

Calise, Mauro and Mannheimer, Renato (1982) *Governanti in Italia* (Bologna: Il Mulino).

Calise, Mauro and Mannheimer, Renato (1979) I governi misurati. Il trentennio democristiano, *Critica Marxista*, no. 6.

Calvaruso, Claudio (1980) Rientro dei migranti e condizione delle collettivita italiane in Europa, *Civitas*, vol. 31, .no. 1.

Calza Bini, P. (1973) Problemi per un'analisi delle classi in Italia, *Inchiesta*, July.

Candeloro, Giorgio (1982) *Il movimento cattolico in Italia* (Rome: Riuniti).

Cantelli, Paolo (1980) *L'economia sommersa* (Rome: Riuniti).

Carbone, Giuseppe (1982) Il difficile modello di un partito secondo, *Il Mulino*, vol. 31, no. 281, May–June.

Cardia, Carlo (1979a) La Democrazia Cristiana: dalle origini cattoliche alla gestione dello Stato, *Democrazia e Diritto*, no. 2.

Cardia, Carlo (1979b) L'area cattolica dopo il 20 giugno 1976, *Critica Marxista*, vol. 17, no. 1.

Carli, Guido (1946) La disciplina degli scambi con l'estero e dei cambi nell'esperienza recente, *Critica economica*, no. 3.

Carli, Guido (1977) *Intervista sul capitalismo italiano* (Rome-Bari: Laterza).

Calise, Mauro (1994) *Dopo La Partitocrazia* (Turin: Einaudi).

Carmignani, Fabrizio (1980) Mercato del lavoro e identità giovanile, *Rinascita*, no. 45, 14 November.

Carocci, Roberto (1988) Il referendum sulla responsibilità civile dei magistrati, *Rivista italiana di scienza politica*, vol. xviii, no. 1, April.

Casmiri, Silvana (1980) Mondo cattolico, questione agraria e questione contadina. In AA.VV. *Campagne e movimento contadino nel Mezzogiorno d'Italia* (Bari: De Donato).

Cassano, Franco (1979) *Il teorema democristiano* (Bari: De Donato).

Castellino, O. (1976) *Il labirinto delle pensioni* (Bologna: Il Mulino).

Castles, Stephen and Kosack, Godula (1973) *Immigrant Workers and Class Structure in Western Europe* (Oxford: Oxford University Press).

Castronovo, Valerio (1975) *La Storia Economica Storia d'Italia*, vol. 1V, part 1 (Turin: Einaudi).

Castronovo, Valerio (1980) *L'Industria italiana dall'Ottocento a oggi* (Milan: Mondadori).

Castronovo, Valerio (1981) Cultura e sviluppo industriale. In Corrado Vivanti (ed.) *Storia d'Italia. Annali 4. Intellettuali e potere* (Turin: Einaudi).

Castronovo, Valerio (1995) *Storia economica d'Italia. dall'ottocento ai giorni nostri* (Turin: Einaudi).

Catanzaro, R. (1991) *Il delitto come impresa. Storia sociale della mafia* (Milan: Rizzoli).

Cavalli, Alessandro (1993) Senza nessuna fretta di crescere, *Il Mulino*, vol. 43, no. 345, January–February. Based on Alessandro Cavalli and Antonio de Lillo (1993) *Giovani anni 90. Terzo rapporto IARD sulla condizione giovanile in Italia*.

Cazzola, Franco (1972) Consenso e opposizione nel parlamento italiano. Il ruolo del PCI dalla I alla IV Legislature, *Rivista Italiana di Scienza politica*.

Cazzola, Franco (ed.) (1979) *Anatomia del potere DC. Enti pubblici e 'centralità democristiana'* (Bari: De Donato).

Cazzola, Franco (1982a) La solidarietà nazionale dalla parte del Parlamento, *Laboratorio Politico*, nos. 2/3.

Cazzola, Franco (1982b) Partiti e coalizioni nei governi locali. Primi risultati di una ricerca, *Democrazia e Diritto*, no. 5, September–October.

Cazzola, Franco (1988) *Della corruzione. Fisiologia e patologia di un sistema politico* (Bologna: Il Mulino).

Cazzola, Franco (1992) *L'Italia del pizzo. Fenomenologia della tangente quotidiana* (Turin: Einaudi).

Cazzola Giuliano (1992) Crisi industriale: tutte le colpe del non governo, *Il Mulino*, vol. 41, no. 339, January–February.

Ceccanti, Stefano (1993) Nessuna falcidia: I giovani, le donne, e l'elettore razionale. In Gianfranco Pasquino (ed.) *Votare un solo candidato. Le conseguenze politiche della preferenza unica* (Bologna: Il Mulino).

Cecchi, Amos (1975) Le nuove generazioni nella società italiana, *Critica Marxista*, vol. 13, no. 1.

CENSIS (1994) *28° Rapporto sulla situazione sociale del paese* (Milano: Francoangeli).

Centro per la Riforma dello Stato (1983) I termini attuali della questione istituzionale, *Democrazia e Diritto*, no. 1.

Cesareo, Giovanni (1981) Il 'politico' nell'alba del quaternario, *Problemi del Socialismo*, vol. 22, no. 22.

Chiarante, Giuseppe (1977) A proposito della questione democristiana, *Critica Marxista*, no. 3.

Chiarante, Giuseppe (1979a) Il papato di Wojtyla: Ia Chiesa del dopo-Concilio, *Critica Marxista*, vol. 17, no. 4.

Chiarante, Giuseppe (1979b) Ragioni e declino della 'centralità' democristiana, *Critica Marxista*, vol. 17, no. 5.

Chiarante, Giuseppe (1980) *La Democrazia cristiana* (Rome: Riuniti).

Chiarante, Giuseppe (1983) Tre ipotesi sulla DC di De Mita, *Critica Marxista*, vol. 21, no. 1.

Chiavari, Gian Marco (ed.) (1994) *Cazzi vostri io domani vado in Svizzera*, with an interview with Renato Mannheimer (Viterbo: Millelire Stampa alternative).

Chiesi, Antonio (1975) Alcune note sulla distribuzione dei redditi e la struttura di classe in Italia nel periodo postbellico, *Quaderni di Sociologia*, vol. 24, no. 3.

Chinnici, Rocco (1982) Magistratura e mafia, *Democrazia e Diritto*, vol. 22, no. 4, July–August.

Coda-Nunziante, G. and De Nigris, M. (1970) Projections for food and agricultural products to 1972 and 1975. In A. M. M. McFarquhar (ed.) *Europe's Future Food and Agriculture* (Amsterdam: North-Holland).

Colajanni, Napoleone (1976) *Riconversione grande impresa partecipazioni statali* (Milan: Feltrinelli).

Comito, Vincenzo (1982) *La FIAT tra crisi e ristrutturazione* (Rome: Riuniti).

Compagna, Francesco and Muscara, Calogero (1980) Regionalism and social change in Italy. In Jean Gottman (ed.) *Centre and Periphery*.

Cotta, Maurizio (1976) Classe politica e istituzionalizzazione del Parlamento: 1946–1972, *Rivista Italiana di Scienza Politica*, no. 1.

Cotturri, Giuseppe (1982a) Abolire il bicameralismo?, *Rinascita*, no. 21, 4 June.

Cotturri, Giuseppe (1982b) Quale potere per il Sud?, *Rinascita*, no. 29, 30 July.

Cotturri, Giuseppe (1983) Il sistema politico italiano dopo il voto del 26 giugno, *Democrazia e Diritto*, no. 5.

Cutrufelli, Maria Rosa (1980) Il circolo del lavoro e degli affetti, *Rinascita*, no. 29, 18 July.

D'Alema, Massimo (1995) *Un paese normale* (Milan: Mondadori).

D'Alema, Giuseppe (1983) La P2 e le connessioni economiche, finanziarie e politiche internazionali. In Marco Ramat et al. *La Resistibile ascesa della P2* (Bari: De Donato).

D'Antonio, Mariano (1973) *Sviluppo e crisi del capitalismo italiano 1951–1972* (Bari: De Donato).

D'Antonio, Mariano (1977) Questioni di politica economica: l'esperienza italiana. In AA.VV. *Lezioni di economia. Aspetti e problemi dello sviluppo economico italiano e dell'attuale crisi internazionale* (Milan: Feltrinelli).

D'Antonio, Mariano et al. (1993) Le politiche del Mezzogiorno. In Pasquale Lucio Scandizzo (ed.) *La politica economica in Italia* (Rome: Istituto per la programmazione economica/Fratelli Palombi).

Dalla Chiesa, Nando (1983) Dai bisogni alla politica. Una riflessione sui referendum del 1981, *Democrazia e Diritto*, no. 2.

Daneo, Camillo (1975) *La politica economica della Ricostruzione 1945–1949* (Turin: Einaudi).

DC (1992) Conferenza Nazionale DC, Milan 28 November to 1 December 1991, *Un Grande Partito Popolare. Storia, Presenza, Progetto* (Roma: Ed. Cinque Lune).

De Cecco, Marcello (1971) Lo sviluppo dell'economia italiana e Ia sua collocazione internazionale, *Rivista Internazionale di Scienze Economiche e Commerciali*, October.

De Cecco, Marcello (1972) Economic policy in the reconstruction period, 1945–1951. In S. J. Woolf (ed.) *The Rebirth of Italy, 1943–50* (London: Longman).

De Grand, Alexander (1976) Women under Italian fascism, *Historical Journal*, vol. 19, no. 4.

De Luca, Maurizio and Giustolisi, Franco (1993) Gli anni ottanta fra giudici e insabbiatori, *Micromega*, no. 2.

De Meo, Giuseppe (1988) Effetti economici delle migrazioni e divario Sud-Nord, *Rivista di Storia Economica*, vol. 5, no. 2, June.

De Rosa, Luigi (1992) Italian emigration in the post-unification period. In P. C. Emmer and M. Mörner (eds) *European Expansion and Migration* (Oxford: Berg).

Degl'Innocenti, Maurizio (1993) *Storia del PSI. Vol. 3. Dal Dopoguerra a Oggi* (Roma-Bari: Laterza).

Della Porta, Donatella (1992) *Lo scambio occulto. Casi di corruzione politica in Italia* (Bologna: Il Mulino).

Della Porta, Donatella (1993a) La capitale immorale: le tangenti di Milano. In S. Hellman and G. Pasquino (eds) *Politica in Italia 1993* (Bologna: Il Mulino).

Della Porta, Donatella (1993b) Corruzione, clientelismo e cattiva amministrazione: note sulle dinamiche degli scambi corrotti in Italia, *Quaderni di Sociologia*, vol. 37, no. 5, p. 38.

Department of Health and Social Security (1975) *Social Security Statistics* (London: HMSO).

Di Palma, Giuseppe (1979) Risposte parlamentari alla crisi del regime: un problema di istituzionalizzazione. In Luigi Grazioni and Sidney Tarrow (eds) *La crisi italiana* (Turin: Einaudi).

Di Virgilio, Aldo (1994) Dai partiti ai poli. La politica delle alleanze, *Rivista italiana di scienza politica*, vol. 24, no. 3, December.

Diamanti, Ilvo (1995) *La Lega. Geografia, storia e sociologia di un soggetto politico* (Rome: Donzelli).

Diamanti, Ilvo (1996) The Northern League: from regional party to party of government. In Stephen Gundle and Simon Parker (eds) *The New Italian Republic, From the Fall of the Wall to Berlusconi* (London: Routledge).

Doglio, Daniele (1981) Crisi e prospettive dei servizi pubblici radiotelevisivi. In Giuseppe Richeri (ed.) *Il video negli anni 80* (Bari: De Donato).

Donolo, Carlo (n.d.) Sviluppo ineguale e disgregrazione sociale. Note per l'analisi delle classi nel Meridione, *Quaderni Piacentini*, no. 47.

Draghi, Stefano (1987) Il modello dei flussi per capire il voto, *Politica e Economia*, September.

Elia, Leopoldo (1970) Forme di governo, *Enciclopedia del diritto*, vol. 19 (Milan: Giuffrè).

Eurostat (1992) *Iron and Steel. Yearly Statistics 1992* (Luxembourg: Eurostat).

Fabiani, Guido (1977) Agricoltura e mezzogiorno. In AA.VV. *Lezioni di economia. Aspetti e problemi dello sviluppo economico italiano e dell'attuale crisi internazionale* (Milan: Feltrinelli).

Fabiani, Guido (1980) Per quale agricoltura: un nodo della trasformazone, *Problemi della Transizione*, no. 3.

Falzone, V., Palermo, F. and Cosentino, F. (eds) (1976) *La Costituzione della Repubblica italiana* (Milan: Mondadori).

Farneti, Paolo (ed.) (1973) *Il sistema politico italiano* (Bologna: Il Mulino).

Farneti, Paolo (1976) I partiti politici e il sistema di potere. In AA.VV., *L'Italia Contemporanea* (Turin: Einaudi).

Farneti, Paolo (1978a) The troubled partnership: trade unions and working class parties in Italy, 1948–1978, *Government and Opposition*, vol. 13, no. 4.

Farneti, Paolo (1978b) Elementi per un'analisi della crisi del partito di massa, *Democrazia e diritto*, vol. 18, nos. 5/6.

Fedele, Marcello (1975) Il loro rapporto con Ia società, *Rinascita*, no. 22, 30 May.

Federmeccanica (1984) Imprese e lavoro, mimeo, 30 November.

Ferraguto, Giuseppe (1992) L'arresto dell'espansione e l'inversione del ciclo economico. In Franco Bruni and Fabrizio Onida (eds) *L'economia italiana nel mondo che cambia: 1990–91* (Bologna: Il Mulino).

Ferraresi, Franco (1988) The radical right in post-war Italy, *Politics and Society*, vol. 16, no. 1, March.

Fichera, Franco (1982) Le regioni: dalla programmazione ai 'governi parziali', *Democrazia e Diritto*, no. 1.

Filippini, Giovanna (1978) Movimenti femminili, femminismo. In Istituto Gramsci, *La crisi della società italiana e gli orientamenti delle nuove generazioni* (Rome: Riuniti).

Filosa, Renato and Visco, Ignazio (1980) Costo del lavoro, indicizzazione e perequazione delle rettribuzioni negli anni '70' in Nardozzi 1980.

Finocchiaro, Francesco (1975) Articoli 7–8. In G. Branca (ed.) *Commentario della Costituzione, Principi Fondamentali* (Bologna and Rome: Zanichelli and Il Foro italiano).

Fiori, Giuseppe (1995) *Il Venditore. Storia di Silvio Berlusconi e della Fininvest* (Milan: Garzanti).

Fisichella, Domenico (1975) The Italian experience. In S. E. Finer (ed.) *Adversary Politics and Electoral Reform* (London: Anthony Wignam).

Flora, P. (ed.) (1987) *State, Economy and Society in Western Europe 1815–1975. A data handbook*, vol. 1 (Mass.: St. James Press).

Follini, Marco (1994) *C'era una volta la DC* (Bologna: Il Mulino).

Forcellini, Paolo (1978) *Rapporto sull'industria italiana* (Rome: Riuniti).

Forte, Francesco (1966) *La congiuntura in Italia, 1961–1965* (Turin: Einaudi).

Forte, Francesco (1974) L'impresa: grande piccola, pubblica privata. In F. L. Cavazza and S. R. Graubard (eds) *Il caso italiano, vol. 2* (Milan: Garzanti).

Fracassi, Claudio (1982) Poltrona per poltrona tutto il potere lottizato alla Rai-TV, *Paese Sera*, 6 March.

Franchi, Paolo (1980) Il PSI e la sinistra, *Critica Marxista*, vol. 18, no. 6.

Frey, Luigi (1981) *Tendenze dell'occupazione*, Bulletin of CERES, January.

Fuà, Giorgio and Sylos Labini, Paolo (1963) *Idee per la programmazione economica* (Bari: Laterza).

Gaiotti de Biase, Paola (1994) *Il potere logorato. La lunga fine della DC* (Rome: Editori Associati).

Galgano, Francesco (1978) *Le istituzioni dell'economia di transizione* (Rome: Riuniti).

Galli, Giorgio (1966) *Il bipartitismo imperfetto* (Bologna: Il Mulino).

Galli, Giorgio (1978) *Storia della DC* (Rome-Bari: Laterza).

Galli, Giorgio and Nannei, A. (1976) *Il capitalismo assistenziale. Ascesa e declino del sistema economico italiano 1960–1975* (Milan: Sugarco).

Gambetta, Diego (1992) *La mafia siciliana* (Turin: Einaudi). (English translation: *The Sicilian Mafia: the business of private protection*, Cambridge, Mass.: Harvard University Press.)

Gambetta, Diego (1994) La protezione mafiosa, *Polis*, vol. 8, no. 2, August.

Gambetta, Diego and Warner, Steven (1996) The rhetoric of reform revealed (or: if you bite the ballot it may bite back), *Journal of Modern Italian Studies*, vol. 1, no. 3, Summer.

Gambino, Antonio (1975) *Storia del Dopoguerra. Dalla Liberazione al potere DC* (Rome-Bari: Laterza).

Garavini, Sergio (1974) *Crisi economica e ristrutturazione industriale* (Rome: Riuniti).

Garavini, Sergio (1977) La struttura industriale italiana e la crisi dell'impresa, *Critica Marxista*, vol. 15, no. 1.

Garelli, Franco (1977) Istituzione ecclesiale e mutamento sociale, *Quaderni di Sociologia*, vol. 26, no. 2.

Garelli, Franco (1991) La religione in Italia: verso una nuova egemonia culturale, *Il Mulino*, vol. 40, no. 333, January–February.

Garelli, Franco (1995) Destra cattolica o cattolici di destra?, *Il Mulino*, vol. 44, no. 358, March–April 1995.

Gasbarrone, Mara (1984) Le donne e il terziario, *Quaderni di Azione Sociale*, vol. 33, no. 33.

Gentiloni, Stefano (1980) L'informazione dopo la riforma. In G. Vacca (ed.) *Comunicazioni di massa e democrazia* (Roma: Riuniti).

Ghezzi, Giorgio (1980) Il sistema negoziale delle informazioni e della consultazione del sindacato nelll attuale contesto politico sociale. In Carlo Smuraglia et al. (eds) *La democrazia industriale* (Rome: Riuniti).

Ghezzi, Giorgio (1981) *Processo al sindacato* (Bari: De Donato).

Ghini, Celso (1975) *Il voto degli italiani* (Rome: Riuniti).

Ginsborg, Paul (ed.) (1994) *Stato dell'Italia* (Milan: Il Saggiatore/Bruno Mondàdori).

Giovagnoli, Agostino (1980) Sulla formazione della classe dirigente democristiana, *Il Mulino*, vol. 29, no. 267, January–February.

Giovannini, Paolo (1988) Generazione e mutamento politico in Italia, *Rivista Italiana di scienza politica*, vol. 18, no. 3, December.

Giugno, Gino (1996) *Socialismo: l'eredità difficile*, Il Mulino, Bologna.

Golini, Antonio (1994a) Le tendenze demografiche dell'Italia in un quadro europeo. In Antonio Golini (ed.) (1994b) *Tendenze demografiche e politiche per la popolazione. Terzo Rapporto Istituto Ricerche sulla Popolazione* (Bologna: Il Mulino).

Golini, Antonio (ed.) (1994b) *Tendenze demografiche e politiche per la popolazione. Terzo Rapporto Istituto Ricerche sulla Popolazione* (Bologna: Il Mulino).

Golini, Antonio and Misiti, Maura (1992) Le rivoluzioni demografiche, le migrazioni ed il mercato del lavoro in Italia. In Franco Bruni and Fabrizio Onida (eds) *L'economia italiana nel mondo che cambia: 1990–91* (Bologna: Il Mulino).

Gottman, Jean (ed.) (1980) *Centre and Periphery. Spatial Variation in Politics* (London: Sage).

Gramsci, Antonio (1971) *Selections from the Prison Notebooks*, Quintin Hoare and Geoffrey Nowell-Smith (eds. and trans.) (London: Lawrence and Wishart).

Graziani, Augusto et al. (1969) *Lo sviluppo di una economia aperta* (Naples: ESI).

Graziani, Augusto and Meloni, Franca (1980) Inflazione e fluttuazione della lira. In Giangiacomo Nardozzi (ed.) *I difficili anni '70. I problemi della politica economica italiana 1973/1979* (Milan: Etas Libri).

Graziani, Augusto (1969) *Lo sviluppo dell'economia italiana come sviluppo di un'economia aperta* (Turin: Fondazione Agnelli).

Graziani, Augusto (ed.) (1971) *L'economia italiana: 1945–1970* (Bologna: Il Mulino).

Graziano, Luigi and Tarrow, Sidney (eds) *La crisi italiana* (Turin: Einaudi).

Grussu, Silvino (1984) Ascesa e declino dell'operaio massa, *Rinascita*, no. 22, 2 June.

Guadagnini, Marila (1993) A 'partitocrazia' without women: the case of the Italian party system. In Joni Lovenduski and Pippa Norris (eds) *Gender and Party Politics* (London: Sage).

Guadagnini, Marila (1995) Qui il primato ce l'ha la cattiva maestra TV, *Reset*, March.

Guarnieri, Carlo (1991) Magistratura e politica: il caso italiano, *Rivista italiana di scienza politica*, vol. 21, no. 1, April.

Gundle, Stephen and Parker, Simon (eds) (1996) *The New Italian Republic, From the Fall of the Wall to Berlusconi* (London: Routledge).

Hellman, Stephen and Pasquino, Gianfranco (eds) (1992) *Italian Politics. A Review, vol. 7* (London: Pinter).

Hine, David (1993) The new Italian electoral system, *ASMI Newsletter*, Autumn.

Ignazi, Piero (1989) La cultura politica del Movimento sociale italiano, *Rivista italiana di scienza politica*, vol. 29, no. 3, December 1989.

Ignazi, Piero (1994) *Postfascisti? Dal Movimento sociale italiano ad Allenza nazionale* (Bologna: Il Mulino).

Ignazi, Piero (1995) Lo strano trionfo di Allenza nazionale, *Il Mulino*, vol. 46, no. 357, January–February.

ILO (1965) *Bulletin of Labour Statistics* (first quarter).

Ingrao, Pietro (1977) *Masse e potere* (Rome: Riuniti).

Ingrao, Pietro (1982) *Tradizione e progetto* (Bari: De Donato).

Isenburg, Teresa (1980) La popolazione, *Storia della Società Italiana, vol. 14: Il Blocco di potere nell'Italia unita* (Milan: Teti Editore).

Isnenghi, M. (1979) *Intellettuali militanti e intellettuali funzionari. Appunti sulla cultura fascista* (Turin: Einaudi).

ISTAT (Istituto nazionale di statistica) (1995) *Compendio statistico italiano* (Rome 1995).

Istituto Gramsci (1978) *La crisi della società italiana e le nuove generazioni* (Rome: Riuniti).

Jaggi, Max, Muller, Roger and Schmidt, Sil (1977) *Red Bologna* (London: Writers and Readers).

Jerkov, Antonio (1966) Alcune considerazioni sul concilio, *Problemi del Socialismo*, vol. 8, no. 6, January–February.

John Paul II (1979) *Redemptor Hominis*, 4 March 1979, Ed. Paoline.

John Paul II (1991) *Centesimus annus*, 1 May 1991, 6th impression, Ed. Paoline, Milan.

John Paul II (1995) *Lettera alle donne*, Ed. Paoline, Milan.

Kelikian, Alice (1996) Science, gender and moral ascendancy in liberal Italy, *Journal of Modern Italian Studies*, vol. 1, no. 3, Summer.

Kindleberger, Charles (1964) *Economic Development* (New York: McGraw-Hill).

Laconi, Renzo (1947) La regione nella nuova Costituzione italiana, *Rinascita*, no. 7, July.

Lama, Luciano (1976) *Intervista sul sindacato* (Rome-Bari: Laterza).

Lanaro, Silvio (1992) *Storia dell'Italia repubblicana* (Venezia: Marsilio).

Lanza, Orazio (1979) Gli enti del settore agricolo. In Franco Cazzola (ed.) *Anatomia del potere DC. Enti pubblici e 'centralità democristiana* (Bari: De Donato).

Leonardi, Robert and Corbetta, Piergiorgio (eds) (1989) *Italian Politics: A Review*, vol. 3 (London: Pinter).

Leonardi, Robert, Nanetta, Raffaella and Pasquino, Gianfranco (1978) Institutionalization of Parliament and parliamentarization of parties in Italy, *Legislative Studies Quarterly*, no. 1, February.

Libertini, Lucio (1976) Fascismo e antifascismo nella politica delle forze economiche, in Guido Quazza (ed.) *Fascismo e antifascismo nell'Italia repubblicana* (Turin: Stampatori).

Livolsi, M. (1976) Il fenomeno giovanile come sottosistema culturale, *Studi di Sociologia*, no. 3.

Livolsi, Marino (ed.) (1993) *L'Italia che cambia* (Florence: La Nuova Italia).

Lo Verso, Livio and McLean, Iain (1995) The Italian general election of 1994, *Electoral Studies*, vol. 14, no. 1, March.

Locke, Richard M. (1995) Una economia differenziata: politica locale e cambiamento industriale, *Stato e Mercato*, no. 43, April.

Lombardo Radice, Lucio (1967) Intervento sulla Populorum Progressio, *Problemi del Socialismo*, vol. 9, no. 18, May.

Longo, Luigi (1968) Il movimento studentesco nella lotta anti-capitalista, *Rinascita*, 3 May.

Lovenduski, Joni and Norris, Pippa (eds) (1993) *Gender and Party Politics* (London: Sage).

Maddison, Angus (1982) *Phases of Capitalist Development* (Oxford: Oxford University Press).

Mafai, Miriam (1979) *L'apprendistato della politica. Le donne italiane nel dopoguerra* (Rome: Riuniti).

Magister, Sandro (1979) *La politica Vaticana e l'Italia 1943–1978* (Rome: Riuniti).

Maitan, Livio (1975) *Dinamica delle classi sociali in Italia* (Rome: Savelli).

Mancina, Claudia (1981) *La Famiglia* (Rome: Riuniti).

Mancini, G. F. (1975) Articolo 4. In G. Branca (ed.) *Commentatio della Costituzione, Principi Fondamentali* (Bologna and Rome: Zanichelli and Il Foro italiano).

Mangoni, Luisa (1974) *L'interventismo della cultura. Intellettuali e riviste del fascismo* (Bari: Laterza).

Mannheimer, Renato and Sani, Giacomo (1988) *Il mercato elettorale* (Bologna: Il Mulino).

Mannheimer, Renato (1994) La natura composita dell'elettorato leghista. In Renato Mannheimer and Giacomo Sani (eds) *La rivoluzione elettorale. L'Italia tra la prima e la seconda repubblica*, Anabasi, Milano 1994.

Mannheimer, Renato (1979) Un'analisi territoriale del calo comunista, *Il Mulino*, no. 265, September–October.

Mannheimer, Renato (1991) La crisis del consenso dei partiti tradizionali. In Renato Mannheimer (ed.) *La Lega Lombarda* (Milan: Feltrinelli).

Mannheimer, Renato (1994) La scelta di Silvio. Dal marketing nasce il polo delle libertà, *Politica e economia*, no. 3, May–June.

Mannheimer, Renato and Biorcio, Roberto (1985) Autoritratto dell'elettore communista, *Rinascita*, no. 10, 23 March.

Mannheimer, Renato and Sebastiani, Chiara (1978) Lavoro e condizione sociale. In Gabriella Pinnarò (ed.) *L'Italia Socio-economica 1976–77* (Rome: Riuniti).

Maranini, G. (1967) *Storia del potere in Italia 1848–1947* (Florence: Vallecchi).

Martiniello, Marco (1991) Italy: Two perspectives. Racism in paradise?, *Race and Class*, vol. 32, no. 3, January–March.

Martinotti, Guido and Stefanizzi, Sonia (1987) La tentazione del centro, *Politica e Economia*, September.

Marturano, Marco (1994) *Mafia e corruzione. Un libro scritto da 150.000 italiani* (Milan: FrancoAngeli).

Mastropaolo, Alfio (1973) I partiti e la società civile. In P. Farneti (ed.) *Il sistema politico italiano* (Bologna: Il Mulino).

Mattei, Franco, Niemi, Richard G. and Bingham Powell, G. (1990) On the death and persistence of generational change. Evidence from Italy, *Comparative Political Studies*, vol. 23, no. 3, October.

Mattelard, Armand (1979) *Multinational Corporations and the Control of Culture* (Brighton: Harvester).

McCarthy, Patrick (1992) The referendum of 9 June. In Stephen Hellman and Gianfranco Pasquino (eds) *Italian Politics. A Review*, vol. 7 (London: Printer).

Melucci, Alberto (1978) Dieci ipotesi per l'analisi dei nuovi movimenti, *Quaderni Piacentini*, vol. 17, no. 65–66, February.

Menapace, Lidia (1974) *La Democrazia cristiana. Natura struttura e organizzazione* (Milan: Mazzotta).

Messina, Sebastiano (1992) La Grande Riforma. Uomini e progetti per una nuova repubblica (Roma-Bari: Laterza).

Micossi, Stefano and Pai, Laura (1994) L'inflazione italiana negli anni '80: il ruolo del settore pubblico, *Rivista di Politica Economica*, vol. 84, no. 7, July.

Milanesi, G. (1976) Religious identity and political commitment in the Christian for Socialism Movement in Italy, *Social Compass*, vol. 23, no. 2–3.

Missiroli, Antonio (1995) Ignoranza italiana: ecco le cifre dello sconforto, *Reset*, March.

Modica, Enzo (1983) Come non è stata applicata Ia Costituzione, *Regione Aperta*, vol. 13, no. 2, March.

Moro, Renato (1979) *La formazione della classe dirigente cattolica 1929–1937* (Bologna: Il Mulino).

Moro, Aldo (1979) *L'intelligenza e gli avvenimenti. Testi 1959–1978* (Milan: Garzanti).

Mortati, C. (1975) Articolo 1. In G. Branca (ed.) *Commentario della Costituzione, Principi Fondamentali* (Bologna and Rome: Zanichelli and Il Foro italiano).

Napolitano, Giorgio (1979) *In mezzo al guado* (Rome: Riuniti).

Nardozzi, Giangiacomo (ed.) (1980) *I difficili anni '70. I problemi della politica economica italiana 1973/1979* (Milan: Etas Libri).

Negri, Antonio (1976) *Proletari e stato* (Milan: Feltrinelli).

Negri, Antonio (1977) *La forma-stato* (Milan: Feltrinelli).

Nenni, Pietro (1977) *Intervista sul socialismo italiano* (Rome-Bari: Laterza).

Neppi Modona, Guido (1993) Ruolo della giustizia e crisi del potere politico, *Quaderni di Sociologia*, vol. 37, no. 5.

Occhetto, Achille (1978) *A dieci anni dal '68* (Rome: Riuniti).

Occhetto, Achille (1994) *Il sentimento e la ragione* (Milan: Rizzoli).

Occhionero, Marisa Ferrari (1976) La posizione della donna nella burocrazia ministeriale italiana, *Sociologia*, vol. 10, no. 2.

OECD (1991) *Historical Statistics 1960–1989* (Paris: OECD).

Onida, Fabrizio (1977) Il ruolo dell'Italia nella divisione internazionale del lavoro. In AA.VV. *Lezioni di economia. Aspetti e problemi dello sviluppo economico italiano e dell'attuale crisi internazionale* (Milan: Feltrinelli).

Onida, Fabrizio (1993) Does there still exist an extrenal constraint on Italian economic growth?, *Review of Economic Conditions in Italy*, Banca di Roma, no. 1, January–June.

Orfei, Ruggero (1976) *L'occupazione del potere. I democristiani 1945–1975* (Milan: Longanesi).

Pace, Enzo (1995) *L'unità dei cattolici in Italia* (Milan: Guerini).

Paci, Massimo (1973) *Mercato di lavoro e classi sociali in Italia* (Bologna: Il Mulino).

Paci, Massimo (1991) Classi sociali e società post-industriale in Italia, *Stato e mercato*, no. 32.

Paci, Massimo (ed.) (1993) *Le dimensioni della disugualianza. Rapporto della Fondazione CESPE sulla disuguaglianza sociale in Italia.* (Bologna: Il Mulino).

Paganetto, Luigi et al. (1993) La struttura industriale italiana all'inizio degli anni novanta. In Pasquale Lucio Scandizzo (ed.) *La politica economica in Italia* (Rome: Istituto per la programmazione economica/Fratelli Palombi).

Palomba, Rossella and Menniti, Adele (1994) Genitori e figli nelle politiche familiari. In Antonio Golini (ed.) *Tendenze demografiche e politiche per la popolazione. Terzo Rapporto Istituto Ricerche sulla Popolazione* (Bologna: Il Mulino).

Paoletti, Aglaia (1991) La presenza femminile nelle assemblee parlamentari, *Il Politico*, vol. 56, no. 1.

Parboni, Riccardo (1981) *The Dollar and Its Rivals* (London: Verso).

Parker, Simon (1996) Electoral reform and political change in Italy, 1991–1994. In Stephen Gundle and Simon Parker (eds) *The New Italian Republic, From the Fall of the Wall to Berlusconi* (London: Routledge).

Pasquino, Gianfranco (1980) *Crisi dei partiti e governabilità* (Bologna: Il Mulino).

Pasquino, Gianfranco (1982) Centralità non significa governabilità, *Il Mulino*, vol. 31, no. 281, May–June.

Pasquino, Gianfranco (1983) La strategia del Psi: tra vecchie e nuove forme di rappresentanza politica, *Critica Marxista*, vol. 21, no. 1.

Pasquino, Gianfranco (1986) Modernity and reforms: The PSI between political entrepreneurs and gamblers, *West European Politics*, vol. 9, no. 1, January.

Pasquino, Gianfranco (1991) Ex-voto: gli strumenti della cittadinanza politica, *Il Mulino*, vol. 40, no. 334, March–April.

Pasquino, Gianfranco (1992) Cari estinti: esistono ancora i partiti in Italia?, *Il Mulino*, vol. xli, no. 339, January–February.

Pasquino, Gianfranco (ed.) (1993) *Votare un solo candidato. Le conseguenze politiche della preferenza unica* (Bologna: Il Mulino).

Pasquino, Gianfranco (ed.) (1995) *La Politica italiana. Dizionario critico 1945–95* (Roma-Bari: Laterza).

Pasquino, Gianfranco and Rossi, Maurizio (1980) Quali compagni, quale partito, quale formula politica, *Il Mulino*, vol. 29, no. 267, January–February.

Pedone, F. (ed.) (1968) *Il Partito socialista italiano nei suoi congressi*, vol. V: 1942–55 (Milan: Edizione del Gallo).

Peggio, Eugenio (1976) *La crisi economica italiana* (Milan: Rizzoli).

Pennacchi, Laura (1982) Il sindacato non sta tutto nello 'scambio politico', *Rinascita*, no. 24, 25 June.

Penniman, Howard R. (ed.) (1977) *Italy at the Polls* (Washington, DC: American Enterprise Institute).

Perulli, Paolo (1982) Il conflitto del compromesso, *Laboratorio Politico*, nos. 2/3.

Pestalozza, Luigi (1967) Intervento sulla *Populorum progressio*, *Problemi del Socialismo*, vol. 9, no. 18, May.

Picchieri, Angelo (n.d.) Classi sociali, *Il Mondo Contemporaneo, vol. I, La Storia d'Italia* (Florence: La Nuova Italia).

Pierini, Maria Novella (1965) La Chiesa cattolica e la politica italiana, *Problemi del socialismo*, vol. 7, no. 2, May–June.

Pinnarò, Gabriella (ed.) (1978) *L'Italia Socio-economica 1976–77* (Rome: Riuniti).

Pinnelli, Antonella (1992) Modernizzazione socio-economica, condizione femmilile e nuovi comportamenti familiari e procreativi, *Stato e Mercato*, no. 36, December.

Pinto, Francesco (1977) *Intellettuali e Tv negli anni '50* (Rome: Savelli).

Pizzorno, Alessandro (1974) I ceti medi nei meccanismi del consenso. In F. L. Cavazza and S. R. Graubard (eds) *Il caso italiano* (Milan: Garzanti).

Pizzorno, Alessandro (1980) *I soggetti del pluralismo* (Bologna: Il Mulino).

Podbielski, Gisele (1974) *Italy. Development and Crisis in the Postwar Economy* (Oxford: Clarendon Press).

Podbielski, Gisele (1978) *Twenty-five Years of Special Action for the Development of Southern Italy* (Milan: Giuffrè Editore).

Poggi, Gianfranco (1972) The Church in Italian politics, 1945–50. In S. J. Woolf (ed.) *The Rebirth of Italy, 1943–50* (London: Longman).

Porter, William (1977) The mass media in the Italian elections of 1976. In Howard R. Penniman (ed.) *Italy at the Polls* (Washington, DC: American Enterprise Institute).

PSI (1990) *Un riformismo moderno. Un socialismo liberale. Tesi Programmatiche*, Conferenza di Rimini, 22–23 March.

PSI (1982) *Governare il cambiamento. Conferenza programmatica del PSI*, Rimini, 31 March–4 April.

Putnam, Robert D., Leonardi, Robert and Nanetti, Raffaella (1980) Le regioni 'misurate', *Il Mulino*, no. 286, March–April.

Putnam, Robert D. with Leonardi, Roberto and Nanetti, Raffaella (1993) *Making Democracy Work. Civic Traditions in Modern Italy* (Princeton, NJ: Princeton University Press).

Regini, Marino (1995) La varietà italiana di capitalismo. Istituzioni sociali e struttura produttiva negli anni ottanta, *Stato e Mercato*, no. 43, April.

Regonini, Gloria (1993) Il principe e il povero. Politiche istituzionali ed economiche negli anni '80, *Stato e Mercato*, no. 39, December.

Revelli, Marco (1982) Defeat at Fiat, *Capital and Class*, no. 16, Spring.

Reviglio, Franco (1977) *Spesa pubblica e stagnazione dell'economia italiana* (Bologna: Il Mulino).

Rhodes, Martin (1989) Craxi and the lay-socialist area: third force of three forces?, *Italian Politics a Review*, vol. 3, Robert Leonardi and Piergiorgio Corbetta (eds) (London and New York: Pinter).

Riccardi, Andrea (1994) La vita religiosa. In Paul Ginsborg (ed.) *Stato dell'Italia* (Milan: Il Saggiatore/Bruno: Mondadori).

Richeri, Giuseppe (ed.) (1981) *Il video negli anni 80* (Bari: De Donato).

Ricolfi, Luca (1993) Politica senza fede: l'estremismo di centro dei piccoli leghisti, *Il Mulino*, vol. xlii, no. 345, January–February.

Ricossa, Sergio (1992) 'Introduzione' to Sergio Ricossa and Ercole Tuccimei (eds) *La banca d'Italia e il risanamento post-bellico 1945–1948* (Roma-Bari: Laterza).

Ridolfi, Luca (1975) A proposito del 'saggio' di Sylos Labini. La base statistica, *Quaderni Piacentini*, no. 57, November.

Rieser, Vittorio (1981) Sindacato e compozizione del lavoro, *Laboratorio Politico*, no. 4, July–August.

Rodano, Giulia (1978) La riaggregazione delle forze giovanili cattoliche. In Istituto Gramsci, *La crisi della società italiana e le nuove generazioni* (Rome: Riuniti).

Rodotà, Stefano (1983) I diritti di libertà: valori emergenti e nuove tutele. In Centro Riforma dello Stato, *Violenza sessuale: come cambiare i processi per stupro* (Rome).

Romagnoli, Umberto (1975) Articolo 3, coma 2. In G. Branca (ed.) *Commentario della Costituzione, Principi Fondamentali* (Bologna and Rome: Zanichelli and Il Forzo italiano).

Romagnoli, Umberto and Treu, Tiziano (1977) *I sindacati in Italia: storia di una strategia 1945–1976* (Bologna: Il Mulino).

Rositi, Franco (1981) Sistema politico soggetti politici e sistema delle comunicazioni di massa, *Problemi del Socialismo*, vol. 22, no. 22.

Rossanda, Rossana (1968) *L'anno degli studenti* (Bari: De Donato).

Rossi, Rosa (1978) *Le parole delle donne* (Rome: Riuniti).

Rotelli, Ettore (1979) Le regioni dalla partecipazione al partito. In Luigi Graziano and Sidney Tarrow (eds) *La crisi italiano* (Turin: Einaudi).

Rotelli, E. (1967) *L'avvento della regione in Italia. Dalla caduta del regime fascista alla Costituzione repubblicana, 1943–1947* (Milan).

Ruffolo, Giorgio (1993) La grande inflazione craxiana, *Micromega*, no. 3, June–August.

Ruzza, Carlo E. and Schmidtke, Oliver (1993) Roots of success of the Lega Lombarda: Mobilisation Dynamics and the Media, *West European Politics*, vol. 16, no. 2, April 1993.

Salvati, Bianca (1972) The rebirth of Italian trade unionism 1943–54. In S. J. Woolf (ed.) *The Rebirth of Italy, 1943–50* (London: Longman).

Salvati, Michele (1977) Il mercato del lavoro in Italia. In AA.VV. *Lezioni di economia. Aspetti e problemi dello sviluppo economico italiano e dell'attuale crisi internazionale* (Milan: Feltrinelli).

Salvati, Michele (1975) *Il sistema economic italiano: analisi di una crisi* (Bologna: Il Mulino).

Salvati, Michele (1973) L'inflazione italiana nel contesto internazionale, *Quaderni Piacentini*, no. 50, July.

Sani, Giacomo (1976) Le elezioni degli anni '70: terremoto o evoluzione?, *Rivista Italiana di Scienza Politica*, no. 2, August.

Sani, Giacomo (1979) Ricambio elettorale, mutamento sociale e preferenze politiche, Luigi Graziano and Sidney Tarrow (eds) *La crisi italiano* (Turin: Einaudi).

Sani, Giacomo (1994) Una vigilia di incertezze, *Rivista italiana di scienza politica*, vol. xxiv no. 3, December.

Sapelli, Giulio (1994a) *Economia, tecnologia e direzione d'impresa in Italia* (Turin: Einaudi).

Sapelli, Giulio (1994b) *Cleptocrazia* (Milan: Feltrinelli).

Sapelli, Giulio et al. (1995a) *Terra di imprese. Lo sviluppo industriale di Reggio Emilia dal dopoguerra a oggi* (Parma: Pratiche Editrice).

Sapelli, Giulio (1995b) *Southern Europe Since 1945* (London: Longman).

Saraceno, Pasquale (1972) La politica di sviluppo di un'area sottosviluppata nell'esperienza italiana, Augusts Graziani, *L'economica italiana: 1945–1970* (Bologna: Il Mulino).

Saraceno, Pasquale (1977) *Intervista sulla Ricostruzione, 1943–1953* (Rome-Bari: Laterza).

Saraceno, Chiara (1979) Trent'anni di storia della famiglia italiana, *Studi Storici*, vol. 20, no. 4.

Sarpellon, G. (1992) *Secondo rapporto sulla povertà in Italia* (Milan: FrancoAngeli).

Sartori, Giovanni (1973) Proporzionalismo, frazionismo e crisi dei partiti, *Correnti, frazioni e fazioni nei partiti politici italiani*, Quaderni della Rivista Italiana di Scienza Politica (Bologna: Il Mulino).

Sartori, Giovanni (1995) *Come sbagliare le riforme* (Bologna: Il Mulino).

Sassoon, Donald (1976) The Italian Communist Party's European strategy, *Political Quarterly*, vol. 47, no. 3, July–September.

Sassoon, Donald (1978) The making of Italian foreign policy. In William Wallace and William E. Paterson (eds) *Foreign Policy Making in Western Europe* (Farnborough: Saxon House).

Sassoon, Donald (1981) *The Strategy of the Italian Communist Party. From the Resistance to the Historic Compromise* (London: Frances Pinter).

Sassoon, Donald (1985a) Political and market forces in Italian broadcasting, *West European Politics*, vol. 8, no. 2, April 1985.

Sassoon, Donald (1985b) Italy: the advent of private broadcasting. In R. Kuhn (ed.) *The Politics of Broadcasting* (London: Croom Helm).

Sassoon, Donald (1995) *Tangentopoli* or the democratization of corruption: considerations on the end of Italy's First Republic, *Journal of Modern Italian Studies*, vol. 1, no. 1, Fall 1995, pp. 124–43.

Savelli, Giulio (1992) *Che cosa vuole la Lega* (Milan: Longanesi).

Scalfari, Eugenio and Turani, Stefano (1974) *Razza padrona. Storia delle borghesia di Stato* (Milan: Feltrinelli).

Scoppola, Pietro (1978) Sulla questione democristiana (e sulla questione comunista), *Critica Marxista*, no. 2.

Scoppola, Pietro (1977) *La proposta politica di De Gasperi* (Bologna: Il Mulino).

Segatti, Paolo (1994) I programmi elettorali e il ruolo dei mass media, *Rivista italiana di scienza politica*, vol. 24, no. 3, December.

Sennet, C. (1991) *La coscienze dell'occhio* (Milan: Feltrinelli).

Sereni, Emilio (1948) *Il mezzogiorno all'opposizione* (Turin: Einaudi).

Sgritta, Giovanni B. (1993) Il mutamento demografico rivoluzione inavvertita, *Il Mulino*, vol. 42, no. 345, January–February.

Silva, Francesco (1993) Le politiche pubbliche per il settore televisivo, *Il Mulino*, vol. 42, no. 1, January–February.

Silva, Francesco and Targetti, Ferdinando (1972) La politica economica e sviluppo economico in Italia: 1945–1971, *Monthly Review* (Italian edn), January 1972 (Part 1); February 1972 (Part 2); March 1972 (Part 3).

Simone, Raffaele (1992) Studenti da cacciare studenti da salvare, *Il Mulino*, vol. 41, no. 344, 6/1992.

Smith, Anthony (1978) *The Politics of Information* (London: Macmillan).

Snyder, Paula (1992) *The European Women's Almanac* (London: Scarlet Press).

Somaini, Eugenio (1979) Crisi della sinistra e ripresa neo-conservatrice in Europa. Dinamiche distributive e mediazioni politiche, *Critica Marxista*, no. 5.

Stern, R. M. (1967) *Foreign Trade and Economic Growth in Italy* (New York: Praeger).

Sullo, Fiorentino (1972) *La repubblica probabile* (Milan: Garzanti).

Sullo, Fiorentino (1960) Il dibattito sulla programmazione economica in Italia dal 1945 al 1960. In *I piani di sviluppo in Italia dal 1945 al 1960* (Milan: Giuffrè).

Svimez (1976) *Report on the South.*

Sylos Labini, Paolo (1974) *Saggio sulle classi sociali* (Rome-Bari: Laterza).

Sylos Labini, Paolo (1975) *Oligolio e progresso tecnico* (Turin: Einaudi).

Tajoli, Lucia (1992) Il modello di specializzazione dell'Italia nel contesto europeo, *Rivista di politica economica*, vol. 82, no. 10, October.

Tarrow, Sidney (1974) Local constraints on regional reform, *Comparative Politics*, no. 1, October.

Tarrow, Sidney (1977) *Between Center and Periphery* (New Haven: Yale University Press).

Telò, Mario (1983) Mutamento sociale e blocco politico istituzionale: un'ipotesi sul 'caso italiano' 1974–1984, *Problemi del Socialismo*, nos. 27/2, May–December.

Terracini, Umberto (1978) *Come nacque la Costituzione* (Rome: Riuniti).

Therborn, Goran (1984) The prospect of Labour and the transformation of advanced capitalism, *New Left Review*, no. 145, May–June.

Togliatti, Palmiro (1973) La nostra lotta per la democrazia e il socialismo, *Il Partito* (Rome: PCI).

Togliatti, Palmiro (1974) *Opere scelte* (Rome: Riuniti).

Togliatti, Palmiro (1979) *On Gramsci and Other Writings*, ed. by Donald Sassoon (London: Lawrence and Wishart).

Trentin, Bruno (1977) *Da sfruttati a produttori* (Bari: De Donato).

Trentin, Bruno (1980) *Il sindacato dei consigli* (Rome: Riuniti).

Trentin, Bruno (1982) Dal sindacato dei consigli alla cultura del cambiamento, *Rinascita*, no. 24, 25 June.

Treu, Tiziano (1991) Il pubblico impiego: riusciremo a farlo entrare in Europa?, *Il Mulino*, vol. 40, no. 334, March–April.

Trigilia, Carlo (1976) Sviluppo, sottosviluppo e classi sociali in Italia, *Rassegna Italiana di Sociologia*, vol. 17, no. 2.

Trigilia, Carlo (1986) *Grandi partiti e piccole imprese. Comunisti e democristiani nelle regioni a economia diffusa* (Bologna: Il Mulino).

Triola, A. (1971) Contributo allo studio dei conflitti di lavoro in Italia, *Economia e Lavoro*, no. 5.

Tunstall, Jeremy (1977) *The Media are American* (London: Constable).

Turi, Gabriele (1980) *Il fascismo e il consenso degli intellettuali* (Bologna: Il Mulino).

Turnaturi, Gabriella (1991) *Associati per amore* (Milan: Feltrinelli).

Turone, Sergio (1974) *Storia del sindacato in Italia, 1943–1969* (Rome-Bari: Laterza).

Turone, Sergio (1976) *Sindacato e classi sociali* (Rome-Bari: Laterza).

UNESCO (1980) International Commission for the Study of Communication Problems (the McBride Commission), *Many Voices One World* (London: Kogan Page).

Vacca, Giuseppe (ed.) (1973) *PCI mezzogiorno e intellettuali* (Bari: De Donato).

Vacca, Giuseppe (1977) *Quale Democrazia?* (Bari: De Donato).

Vacca, Giuseppe (ed.) (1980) *Communicazioni di massa e democrazia* (Rome: Riuniti).

Vacca, Giuseppe (1982) I contenuti informativi e culturali dell'emittenza televisiva, mimeo, 24 May.

Vacca, Giuseppe (1983) Vecchio e nuovo dal mezzogiorno. In AA.VV. *La cultura: una nuova risorsa per il mezzogiorno* (Bari: De Donato).

Vacca, Giuseppe (1984) *L'Informazione negli anni ottanta* (Rome: Riuniti).

Vaciago, Giacomo (1993) Exchange Rate Stability and Market Expectations: the Crisis of the EMS, *Review of Economic Conditions in Italy*, Banca di Roma, no. 1, January–June.

Vainicher, Marco Eller (1977) La questione del terziario e la crisi italiana, *Critica Marxista*, vol. 15, no. 1.

Valiani, Leo (1973) La resistenza italiana, *Rivista Storica Italiana*, vol. 85, no. 1.

Valli, Vittorio (1979) *L'economia e la politica economica italiana, 1945–1979* (Milan: Etas Libri).

Valli, Vittorio (1980) La politica economica: una cronaca ragionata del periodo 1973–1979. In Giangiacomo Nardozzi (ed.) *I difficili anni '70. I problemi della politica economica italiana 1973/1979* (Milan: Etas Libri).

Venditti, Renato (1981) *Il manuale Cencelli* (Rome: Riuniti).

Vercellone, P. (1972) The Italian Constitution of 1947–48. In S. J. Woolf (ed.) *The Rebirth of Italy, 1943–50* (London: Longman).

Veugelers, John W. P. (1994) Recent immigration politics in Italy: a short story, *West European Politics*, vol. 17, no. 2, April.

Vicari, Serena (1993) Economia e società: le trasformazioni economiche e sociali dell'ultimo decennio. In M. Livolsi (ed.) *L'italia che cambia* (Florence: La Nuova Italia).

Villari, Lucio (ed.) (1975) *Il Capitalismo italiano del novecento*, Laterza (Rome-Bari: Laterza).

Visco, Vincenzo (1985) É inutile vantarsi se migliora l'economia, *La Repubblica*, 5 January.

Weber, Maria (1981) Italy. In Joni Lovenduski and Jill Hills (eds) *The Politics of the Second Electorate. Women and Public Participation* (London: Routledge and Kegan Paul).

Wertman, Douglas (1977) The Italian electoral process: the elections of June 1976. In Howard R. Penniman (ed.) *Italy at the Polls* (Washington, DC: American Enterprise Institute).

Williamson, J. G. (1968) Regional inequality and the process of national development: a description of the patterns. In L. Needleman (ed.) *Regional Analysis* (Harmondsworth: Penguin).

Woods, Dwayne (1992) The centre no longer holds: the rise of regional leagues in Italian politics, *West European Politics*, vol. 15, no. 2, April.

Woolf, S. J. (ed.) (1972) *The Rebirth of Italy, 1943–50* (London: Longman).

Zamagni, Vera (1993) *Dalla periferia al centro. La seconda rinascita economica dell'Italia 1861–1990* (Bologna: Il Mulino).

Zuliani, Alberto (1994) Structural factors and changes in Italian firms in the light of the 1991 census, *Review of Economic Conditions in Italy*, no. 1, January–June.

Index